STRATEGIC PLANNING IN HEALTH CARE MANAGEMENT

Editors

William A. Flexner, Dr. P.H.
Eric N. Berkowitz, Ph.D.
Montague Brown, D.P.H.

AN ASPEN PUBLICATION
Aspen Systems Corporation
Rockville, Maryland
London
1981

Library of Congress Cataloging in Publication Data
Main entry under title:

Strategic planning in health care management.

Most of the articles were originally published in
Health care management review.
Includes bibliographies and index.
1. Health facilities—Planning—Addresses,
essays, lectures. 2. Hospitals—Planning—Addresses,
essays, lectures. 3. Corporate Planning—Addresses,
essays, lectures. 4. Hospitals—Marketing—Addresses,
essays, lectures. 5. Medical care—Marketing—Addresses,
essays, lectures. 6. Health facilities—Finance—Addresses, essays,
lectures. I. Flexner, William A. II. Berkowitz, Eric N. III. Health
care management review. [DNLM: 1. Health planning—Collected works.
Hospital planning—Collected works. 3. Marketing of health services—
Collected works. WA 525   5898]
RA971.S84   362.1'1   81-2488
ISBN 0-89443-298-2   AACR2

Library of Congress Catalog Card Number: 81-2488
ISBN: 0-89443-298-2

Printed in the United States of America

1 2 3 4 5

Contents

Contributors

THOMAS A. BERGAN*
Consultant
Pugh-Roberts Associates, Inc.
Cambridge, Massachusetts

ERIC N. BERKOWITZ
Assistant Professor of Marketing
College of Business
Administration and
Research Associate
Center for Health Services Research
School of Public Health
University of Minnesota
Minneapolis, Minnesota

BEN I. BOLDT, JR.
Manager, Management Advisory
Services
Price Waterhouse & Co.
Milwaukee, Wisconsin

ROBERTA N. CLARKE
Assistant Professor of Marketing
Health Care Management Program
School of Management
Boston University
Boston, Massachusetts

WILLIAM O. CLEVERLEY*
Associate Professor
Graduate Program in Hospital and
Health Services Administration
Ohio State University
Columbus, Ohio

WILLIAM A. FLEXNER
President
Flexner & Associates
Minneapolis, Minnesota

JACOB GETSON
Assistant Vice President for
Benefits Administration
Blue Cross of Massachusetts
Boston, Massachusetts

JOHN R. GRIFFITH
Professor and Director
Program and Bureau of
Hospital Administration
School of Public Health
University of Michigan
Ann Arbor, Michigan

REGINA E. HERZLINGER
Professor of Business
Administration
Graduate School of Business
Administration
Harvard University
Boston, Massachusetts

GARY B. HIRSCH*
Director, Health and Social
Systems Areas
Pugh-Roberts Associates, Inc.
Cambridge, Massachusetts

*Position at time of original publication of article

G. DAVID HUGHES
Burlington Industries Professor
of Business Administration
School of Business
Administration
University of North Carolina
Chapel Hill, North Carolina

ANTHONY R. KOVNER
Chief Executive Officer
Newcomb Hospital
Vineland, New Jersey

DANE M. LONG
Senior Associate
Cambridge Research Institute
Cambridge, Massachusetts

HUGH W. LONG
Associate Professor of Finance
School of Business and
Associate Professor of
Health Systems Management
School of Public Health and
Tropical Medicine
Tulane University
New Orleans, Louisiana

ROBIN E. MACSTRAVIC
Associate Professor and
Associate Director
Graduate Program in Health
Services Administration
and Planning
University of Washington
Seattle, Washington

MARK D. MANDEL
Management Consultant Services
Cambridge, Massachusetts

PATRICK A. MARTINELLI
Professor of Business Administration
School of Business and Management
Loyola College
Baltimore, Maryland

CURTIS P. MCLAUGHLIN
Professor Business and Health
Administration
School of Business
Administration
and
School of Public Health
University of North Carolina
Chapel Hill, North Carolina

ROBERT A. MILCH
Professor of Management and
Director
Executive Graduate Programs in
Management
School of Business and
Management
Loyola College
Baltimore, Maryland

DUNCAN NEUHAUSER
Professor of Community Health
and Associate Director
Health Systems Management
Center
School of Medicine
Case Western Reserve University
Cleveland, Ohio

EDWARD B. ROBERTS
David Sarnoff Professor of
Management of Technology
and
Chairman, Technology and
Health Management Group
Alfred P. Sloan School
of Management
Massachusetts Institute of
Technology
Cambridge, Massachusetts

JOHN L. QUIGLEY*
Commandant
Soldiers' Home
Chelsea, Massachusetts

TERRENCE J. RYNNE
Director of Planning
Westlake Community Hospital
Melrose Park, Illinois

ALICE M. SAPIENZA
Ambulatory Care Consultant
Boston, Massachusetts

LINDA SHYAVITZ
Director of Ambulatory Care
Boston City Hospital
Boston, Massachusetts

JAMES K. SIMON
Vice President for
    Hospital Affairs
West Jersey Hospital System
Camden, New Jersey and
President
Triune Group
Cherry Hill, New Jersey

J. B. SILVERS
Treuhaft Professor
    of Management
Weatherhead School of
    Management and
Director, Health Systems
    Management Center
School of Medicine
Case Western Reserve University
Cleveland, Ohio

HELEN L. SMITS*
Director, Health Standards and
    Quality Bureau
Health Care Financing
    Administration
Department of Health and
    Human Services
Washington, D.C.

NORMAN S. STEARNS
Associate Dean of Continuing
    Education
School of Medicine
Tufts University
Medford, Massachusetts

CARL W. THIEME
President
Cambridge Research Institute
Cambridge, Massachusetts

ROBERT A. VRACIU
Vice President
Strategic Planning and Research
Center for Health Studies
Hospital Corporation of America
Nashville, Tennessee

THOMAS E. WILSON
Senior Associate
Cambridge Research Institute
Cambridge, Massachusetts

Foreword

Whether true or not, I imagine that it is necessary to have some notion of what is encompassed within and around the central focus of *Health Care Management Review* (HCMR). Management is the generic discipline (or perhaps, as some would argue, the generic set of disciplines) that we seek to portray as it can be and is applied to health care problems and issues. We like to think that there are some broad themes or strands of management thought and application that are and could be shown to be interrelated, were one to weave them together.

Of course, this task would be easier if one author undertook both the initial task of writing the units as well as the broader themes that tie various pieces together. As a review that seeks contributors of articles, not books, the issue of the overall contribution of these articles to some overarching concept of management remains in the hands of the editor and occasionally, as here, in the hands of another editor who tries to put together some coherent set of readings from the collection of articles already published.

This book pulls together articles dealing with the general area of corporate strategy and its sister areas of marketing and finance. Corporate strategists recognize the integrative nature of their work along with its foundational ties with marketing, finance, and, more generally, resource allocative processes that come under a variety of other labels.

As editor of HCMR, it is a distinct pleasure to see how well what came in as single articles contributes to the overall interest of management in the broader concept of corporate strategy. The individual and collective importance of the subjects presented here should be of interest to those who have seen or read some but not all of the articles as they were originally published. The book will also be useful to students, both those in school and those who make lifelong learning an active part of their professional and personal lives.

Just as the authors of the individual papers must have felt some joy in their accomplishment of presenting their statement on some aspect of management, we too, as editors, take pride in finding and presenting some of the themes we all share in this management business of ours.

MONTAGUE BROWN
Editor
Health Care Management Review

McLean, Virginia
1981

Preface

During the past several years, health care managers increasingly have been exposed to the subject of strategic planning. In their search for information, these managers have had to piece together references—particularly those with applications to health care problems—from numerous and diverse sources.

This book of readings is designed to bring together in one reference previously published health care articles—primarily from *Health Care Management Review*—that address the topic of strategic planning and its complementary management disciplines—marketing and finance. Our intent is to provide a synthesis, integration, and awareness of strategic planning thought and practices in the health services industry.

The articles in the book are divided into six sections. The first three sections present an overview of strategic planning, marketing, and finance, with special reference to health care issues. The last three sections present specific perspectives or applications in these same areas. Before each topical area, there is an introductory section in which the articles are briefly highlighted. An attempt is made to integrate each article with others appearing elsewhere in the book, as well as with other articles or books that deal with the same subject.

In developing the book, we had four distinct health care segments in mind as potential audiences:

1. middle- and upper-level managers in health care organizations
2. privately run educational programs on strategic planning, marketing, or finance in the health care industry (conducted by professional associations, private consulting organizations, and/or university extension services)
3. graduate programs in health and hospital administration that have or are rapidly developing courses on strategic planning
4. graduate business programs that offer courses in nontraditional business enterprises and/or have joint programs with schools of public health or hospital administration. .

For the first two groups, the book is designed to provide a broad-brush familiarity with the topical issues related to the introduction of strategic planning in the organization. For the latter two segments, the book is designed primarily to be used in conjunction with a more thorough classroom textbook on the subject of strategic planning. In this context, the book of readings should provide the specific health care examples for the more general business applications typically found in the traditional textbooks.

Section One

Strategic Planning: An Overview

The health care industry has changed dramatically in the past five to ten years. External pressures—regulations, equilibrium or oversupply of hospital beds and physicians, nursing shortages, activist consumers—have combined to force health care managers to search for new approaches in managing their organizations. One of the approaches being given serious consideration is strategic planning.

The concept of strategy has been described as a matching of organizational capabilities and resources with environmental opportunities and threats.[1] The environment of organizations, however, is constantly changing. Thus, the development of sound and effective organizational strategies requires a dynamic planning process capable of responding to changes both inside and outside the organization.

The transition to a dynamic, externally oriented planning process in health organizations will be neither easy nor assured. Yet, such a transition is essential, as Thieme, Wilson, and Long point out in the first article in this section ("Strategic Planning for Hospitals Under Regulation"). Comparing facility master planning with strategic planning, these authors note that the differences are not just window dressing. They point to four aspects of strategic planning that are fundamentally different:

1. a shift from a focus on production to one on people and population groups;
2. the definition of the organization's mission following a thorough external and internal assessment;
3. recognition of the importance of political, as well as technical, considerations; and
4. the need to integrate planning with ongoing management activities.

1

In reviewing this first article, the reader might want to consider how it relates to the four phases in the evolution of strategic planning described by Gluck, Kaufman, and Walleck in their recent article on strategic management:[2]

- Phase I. *Basic financial planning:* Emphasis on operational control with the goal of meeting the terms of the annual budget.

- Phase II. *Forecast-based planning:* Emphasis on more effective planning for growth with the goal of predicting the future.

- Phase III. *Externally oriented planning:* Emphasis on increasing response to markets and competition with the goal of thinking strategically.

- Phase IV. *Strategic management:* Emphasis on orchestrating all resources to create a competitive advantage with the goal of creating the future.

The important thing to note is that the transition through these phases will take time and careful planning because of the need to change both the structures and procedures within the organization and the values that guide the behaviors of the personnel.

At this point, some may think of strategic planning as being applicable only in large organizations. The article in this section by McLaughlin ("Strategic Planning and Control in Small Health Organizations") should dispel this notion. Arguing that managers of small health organizations need as much help as they can get, McLaughlin suggests that they begin a transition to strategic planning by linking it to the budgeting and control procedures that are typically well-developed in the organization. As McLaughlin writes, "From there one can consider embellishing and reality-testing the plan in terms of the related choice areas: mix of services, personnel, pricing policies and cost controls, funding mix, marketing plans, and organizational structure." Note the similarity between this and the transition from the first to the second and third phases suggested by Gluck and his colleagues.

As noted above, the key to effective strategy is the match between organizational resources and markets or market segments. The article by Milch ("Product-Market Differentiation: A Strategic Planning Model for Community Hospitals") focuses on one of the tools used in strategic planning to measure product-market competencies and competitive business strengths. Defining strategic business units as "product-market niches," Milch shows one way to assess a hospital's service mix in terms of the number of units sold and their unit selling price. By assessing these two variables, Milch is able to identify, in essence, the business that the hospital is actually in. He is also able to indicate the service areas that might be considered for elimination from the service portfolio.

Readers should be careful to note, however, that the resource unit in this example is the charge for the service, not the cost of producing it. Without measuring both the cost and price at the unit-of-service level (in effect, the profit/loss for the service), one cannot determine the net financial contribution of the service to the organization's total service portfolio. That most health care organizations cannot provide cost data at the unit-of-service level is a further example of the fundamental change that will have to occur within the health care organization: The financial management system will have to be restructured to reflect the shift in focus to external markets. Issues related to the requirements for sound financial management are presented in the two sections in this book dealing with the topic of finance.

Finally, one of the outcomes of the strategic planning process is the configuration of the organization's activities in relation to the opportunities and threats in the marketplace. Thieme, Wilson, and Long provide an excellent discussion of the various options that the health care manager may consider in deciding what business(es) to be in. The alternatives discussed range from nonprice competition strategies for the traditional health care services offered by the organization, through several ways to integrate vertically with supplier and provider institutions, to various horizontal diversification strategies that might take the organization into areas that have little, if anything, to do with health care.

In summary, the movement to strategic planning in health care organizations is an essential step to more effective management in the face of a rapidly changing environment. This movement will not come automatically. Fundamental changes within the organization will have to occur, both in the way the organization is structured to facilitate the planning process and in terms of the values that are given emphasis by top management. However, once the orientation of the organization shifts from internal organizational concerns to the dynamics of the marketplace, a major hurdle will have been passed and the organization will then be able to focus more carefully on the kinds of services or entire businesses that best exploit the organization's strengths.

REFERENCES

1. Charles W. Hofer and Dan Schendel, *Strategy Formulation: Analytical Concepts* (St. Paul, Minn.: West Publishing Company, 1978), p. 4.
2. Frederick W. Gluck, Stephen R. Kaufman, and A. Steven Walleck, "Strategic Management for Competitive Advantage," *Harvard Business Review*, July-August 1980, p. 157.

1. Strategic Planning for Hospitals Under Regulation

CARL W. THIEME, THOMAS E. WILSON, and DANE M. LONG

Thieme, Carl W.; Wilson, Thomas E.; and Long, Dane M. "Strategic Planning for Hospitals Under Regulation." *Health Care Management Review,* Spring 1981, forthcoming.

INTRODUCTION

From the end of World War II through the mid-1960s, rapid hospital growth was fostered by the availability of both government funds (e.g., Hill-Burton) and private philanthropy. The chief manifestation of hospital growth during this period was the expansion of physical facilities; accordingly, the focus of hospital planning tended to be facility planning and construction.

In the late 1960s, public support for continued growth began to moderate. Concern over unfettered hospital growth and the increased consumption of public monies led to numerous government initiatives to constrain growth. Most prominent of these were the Health Planning Act (P.L. 93-641) and resulting Certificate of Need laws, PSRO legislation, and various federal and state expenditure caps and rate-setting schemes. These initiatives were accompanied by a dramatic decrease in philanthropic support for hospitals.

The effects of these environmental changes on hospitals have been dramatic and, in some cases, traumatic. It has become necessary for trustees, administrators, and physicians to rethink their criteria for judging institutional success and measuring progress. Many institutions have been forced to make difficult choices about the number and types of services offered. One highly important result is that the nature of planning in hospitals has changed and continues to evolve. This planning evolution can be characterized as a change from facility planning or "master planning" to long-range strategic planning or "strategic planning." Some key characteristics of master planning and strategic planning as well as factors forcing the shift from master to strategic planning are shown in Table 1.

This article highlights the distinctive characteristics of strategic planning identified in Table 1, identifies some strategy options available to hospitals, and provides some guidelines and points to consider when organizing for strategic planning.

Table 1 Characteristics and Factors in Master and Strategic Planning

Master Facility Planning	What Has Changed	What's Needed: Key Aspects of Strategic Planning
• Expansion-oriented	• Limited opportunities for facility expansion	• Basic orientation shift from manufacturing (product) to marketing (people)
• Facility-oriented	• HSAs and CON laws have forced program planning	
• Hospital planners architecturally oriented	• Overcapacity (underutilization) has shifted focus to program development	• Strategic planning doesn't start by defining mission: institutional roles and goals emerge after careful external/internal assessment
• Planning often contracted to consultant		
• Management and physicians provided wish-lists to consultant/planners	• Competition has forced new emphasis on services to patients and physicians	• Political and negotiation skills (value changing) more important than technical (number crunching)
• Master plan was document unveiled by consultant at end of process	• Financial pressure forcing some hospitals to consider giving up services	• Planning integrated into ongoing institutional management
• Planning committees were facility building committees	• Lead time and money needed to initiate new programs have increased	
• Planning was perceived as technical process	• Government and philanthropy are limited capital sources	

CHARACTERISTICS OF STRATEGIC PLANNING

Strategic planning is not just master planning with a few additional consider-ations. It is a dramatically different approach to planning. Four important features of effective strategic planning as compared to master planning are:

1. a shift in orientation from manufacturing to marketing;
2. recognition that the mission statement is not the starting point of planning;
3. realization that planning is a political, not simply a technical, exercise; and
4. understanding that planning is an integral part of management.

These features are more fully discussed in the following section. The subsequent section describes important points to consider when organizing for strategic planning.

Basic Orientation Is to Markets not Facilities

One characteristic of strategic as distinct from master planning is that stra-tegic planning has a market orientation while master planning has a manufacturing-facility orientation. This change in orientation converts the primary question from, "What services do I want to deliver?" to "What services are needed?" and "Who will purchase them?" The starting point for the planning process is also changed. Instead of asking hospital personnel, "What services do you want to sponsor?" planning starts with inquiries to identify consumer needs that are not currently being met.

Another equally important shift in focus is implied when strategic planning is adopted. Production gives way to people and population groups as the main units of focus. While a manufacturing approach focuses on "products we want to produce," a marketing approach identifies important "people" constituencies and their needs. Hospital strategic planning addresses the multiple groups served by and related to the institution: patients, the general public, professional staff, employees, planners, and board members. Improv-ing management's ability to diagnose and be responsive to the needs of these various "market" constituencies is the main purpose of strategic planning.

Mission Development Follows External and Internal Assessments

Traditionally, hospitals (like most complex institutions) operate on a set of implicit assumptions and beliefs that define organizational identity and rela-tionships with the outside world. These contribute to the creation of an "organizational mythology" that underlies their perception of the organization's basic role and purpose—the mission of the organization. Unchallenged, this mythology can lead to planning for inappropriate roles in a context of unrealistic expectations.

Strategic planning, however, does not start with assumptions about the institutional mission. Rather, the goal/role elements of a strategic plan are derived only after external and internal assessments are completed and the associated mythologies have been fully probed and tested.

Strategic Planning Is More a Political and Negotiating Process Than a Technical Exercise

Master planning has tended to be technical and heavily quantitatively oriented. The emphasis has been on facts, numbers, and ratios. This approach has frequently been inappropriate and has often led to planning efforts that failed to be responsive to social needs or even to institutional values. In a creative strategic planning process, decisions chosen from among realistic options are more likely to reflect value judgments than quantitative assessments. As Klarman, in a recent review of "health planning: progress, prospects, and issues," observed, "value judgments—political judgments in the best sense— are central in setting priorities among problems and programs."[1]

In addition, an attempt to modify the perspectives of key publics (or power holders) is a legitimate political objective of strategic planning. Technical data will contribute, and contribute substantially, to strategic decision making, but that alone is not sufficient to ensure successful implementation. Good plans must be complemented by an emphasis on political process and negotiation.

Strategic Planning Must Be Integrated Into Ongoing Management Activities

In the past, facility or master planning was often contracted to consultants, and a final planning document was unveiled at the end of a process that occurred mainly outside the hospital. In contrast, strategic planning is fully integrated within the hospital's day-to-day management concerns. Only in this way, as Melin and Rabkin note, can choices be made that enable "the hospital to act in ways that are responsive to its external and internal environment and true to its history and goals."[2]

Integrating the planning process into the institutional management system requires broad involvement and commitment. The designation of a planner or the appointment of a marketing director does not automatically ensure that the hospital will move into an effective strategic planning mode. Similarly, unless representatives of all critical hospital constituencies are appropriately involved in resource allocation decisions, strategic planning will not become an integral dimension of management.

APPROACH TO STRATEGIC PLANNING

A conceptual approach to strategic planning, incorporating the characteristics identified above, is simply illustrated in Figure 1. Strategic planning begins with an external and internal analysis. The external and internal analyses lead to the identification and analysis of critical strategic issues. Strategic alternatives emerge from the analysis of issues. The external, internal, and issues analyses provide the background and inform the development or reshaping of an institution's mission. The development of goals and objectives set institutional strategies and link organizational activities to strategies. Each of these major components is briefly discussed below.

External Analysis

The full range of external forces affecting a particular hospital needs to be realistically identified, and the potential impact of these forces needs to be assessed. The mapping of the external environment sets the territorial boundaries for future hospital operations, defines and assesses the actual and potential markets, identifies franchise opportunities and constraints, and provides the basis for assessing how the institution "stacks up" against its neighbors and competitors (not necessarily one and the same). Without an accurate "environmental assessment," a hospital may adopt unrealistic planning goals.

This external assessment, leading toward strategy choices, involves detailed examination of many critical interfaces between the hospital and its environment. Critical components of an external analysis are discussed briefly below.

Demographic Forecasting

A key external variable is the characteristics of population groups potentially served by a health care facility. These groups are the market. Developing an understanding of the probable characteristics of the population groups to be served provides important clues as to the types and quantity of services that will be needed and demanded.

Demography is both a science and an art and is best left to demographers. For their part, hospital planners need to approach demographic projections with a healthy skepticism. By following a few simple guidelines, they can sometimes avoid significant error.

- Research and develop an understanding of the methodology used to create a projection. Projections may be based on assumptions that are appropriate when applied to a state as a whole but may not be appropriate for the local area. Adjustments may be needed.

- Search out more than one projection. Projections often have systematic biases reflecting the interests of particular agencies. For example, political units tend to overestimate populations because state and federal funds are tied to population estimates.

- Disaggregate the data. If a hospital serves a small portion of a region and there is real diversity within the region, regional data may mask important characteristics of the populations that are the hospital's markets.

Mapping the Regulatory Environment

Regulatory mapping involves the distillation of the impact of laws and regulations on an individual hospital. This usually can be accomplished by matrixing the law's key provisions against the characteristics of the health care system.

Figure 1 Elements of the Strategic Planning Process

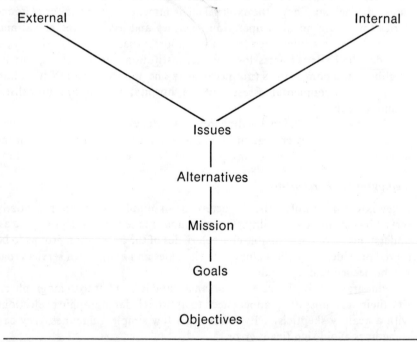

For instance, in mapping Public Law 93-641 (the National Health Planning Resources and Development Act), the left-hand rows would identify elements of the law, including the planning system, resource and development, control mechanisms, and so on. Across the top of the matrix would be the elements of the health care system or institution. The elements might include capital formation, facilities, technology, need and demand for services, access, cost, and so on. In each cell of such a matrix, a simple high, medium, or low code can be used to identify and focus attention on key high-impact areas. Such a "map" can help institutions analyze both where and how elements of the law can impact future strategic options. In addition, such mapping can assist the institution in targeting key committees and agencies on which they should concentrate their resources and focus their attention in developing working relationships to protect institutional interests. Analysis of such regulatory maps may also indicate potential threats for which the only strategic option open to the hospital is business diversification. Regulatory mapping is one of the most difficult, yet one of the most crucial elements to identify in the development of strategic options available to the institution.

Competitive Assessment

Analyzing the institution's key competitors—their strengths, weaknesses, and future plans—and identifying from this analysis opportunities and threats are perhaps the most difficult external-analysis elements for most institutions to deal with in strategic plan development. These elements involve developing information on key competitors' market positions, utilization characteristics, major changes in services and programs, medical staff patterns (age, mix, etc.), administrative management capabilities, strategic plans, financial positions and resources, building needs and conditions, and other factors. These elements of competitive analysis must be analyzed and woven together to extract important elements of competitive advantage and disadvantage. Competitive analysis also involves identification of areas in which mutual interests between institutions can be pursued.

Consumer Needs, Demands, and Preferences

As the health care industry and its institutions shift from a manufacturing to a market orientation, and as the importance of understanding consumer needs and wants becomes more important, health care institutions will have to develop additional external marketing information. Consumers may be patients, doctors, employees, or other key publics. By using market research techniques (physician surveys, consumer surveys, focus group techniques, etc.), hospitals are identifying how people access the system, what their preferences are, how they view the hospital vis-a-vis its competitors, and what they identify as critical competitive factors affecting consumer choices. Such research techniques are becoming a crucial element in the understanding of the hospital's external environment and in the development of viable strategic choices available to the hospital.

Program/Service Delivery Trends

Strategic planning requires monitoring and assessing the impact and importance of trends in the delivery of hospital care and health care services. These trends may be technologically based and thus impact a hospital's need for capital equipment, or they may reflect social or lifestyle changes that affect the need for a service or the way it is delivered. The recognition of changed attitudes and preferences has enabled many hospitals to gain a competitive advantage in maternity care by offering birthing rooms and other amenities.

The key in carrying out an external analysis is not just to accumulate data, but to assess their impact. Analysis is thus used to transform data into relevant information. For example, population projections can be transferred into bed-need estimates. A competitive assessment can identify the needs not being met. A regulatory assessment shows where an institution might be vulnerable and incur financial penalties.

Internal Analysis

To think, however, that planning deals only with externalities, is to create blind spots and to foster additional misperceptions of hospital capabilities. A comprehensive, hard-nosed internal assessment must also be undertaken. Yet this is frequently overlooked (or bypassed) because of the anxieties it produces. Such a self-analysis may indeed be painful, but it may also lead to organization development initiatives that will significantly strengthen the organization. Just as the external analysis identifies realistic horizons, an internal assessment is needed to purge organizational mythology and to develop a balanced picture of hospital limitations, strengths, and opportunities for further development.

An internal assessment requires analysis of a variety of data descriptive of an institution, including data describing

- utilization of hospital services,
- diagnoses treated,
- physician characteristics and admitting patterns,
- financial performance,

- facilities inventory, and

- organizational assessment.

The latter, the organizational assessment, is one of the components most often overlooked in an internal analysis. Essentially, this assessment is an evaluation of the organization structure and an assessment of how well it works.

Two principles are essential in an evaluation of institutional data. One is, whenever possible, compare the data to something external. Provide benchmarks that give perspective. The second is look for trends and patterns and do not worry about decimal points.

Issue Analysis

The external analysis and the internal analysis provide the basis for the identification of key issues: the critical challenges and opportunities confronting the institution. Indepth study of the critical issues results in the identification and evaluation of alternatives that provide the basis for a realistic assessment of the institution's mission.

Mission

The development of an institutional mission requires balancing the answers to four fundamental questions:

1. What (services) do we want to provide? (What businesses do we want to be in?)
2. What will we be allowed to do?
3. What do we have the resources to do?
4. What does society need?

A mission states the overall, broad purpose and role of an institution. A mission statement has to be broad enough to allow creativity and the development of a vision. Yet, by its nature it limits; it circumscribes activity and thereby provides guidance to institutional leaders.

Goals and Objectives

Goals and objectives reflect and operationalize the institutional strategy. A mission statement specifies role and purpose. Goals articulate specific strategies. Objectives specify and operationalize the strategy. Objectives should have three characteristics: (1) They should be measurable. (2) There should be a time for completion specified. (3) The person responsible should be identified.

The strength of the approach outlined in Figure 1 is that it suggests starting with an objective appraisal of the environment and of the organization and *then* reassessing the organization's mission and strategy. Starting with the identification of the mission can lead to wishful thinking not based in reality.

EMERGING STRATEGY OPTIONS

Hospitals that have undertaken planning processes like that outlined above are beginning to develop innovative strategies designed to meet the challenges posed by the environment. The increased prominence of both regulation and competition has led some hospitals to examine and develop strategies analogous to those used by firms in other regulated, yet competitive industries. Some of these strategy options are discussed in the paragraphs which follow.

Nonprice Competition

Regulation and current reimbursement schemes are leading hospitals to adopt a classic regulated industry strategy, that of nonprice competition.

Nonprice competition becomes an important strategic consideration when price competition is eliminated or restricted in importance but market conditions make competition likely. With the elimination of price as a competitive tactic, institutions turn their attention to service as the competitive variable. The history of the U.S. airline industry prior to deregulation is a case in point. The development of special clubs, in-flight movies, piano bars, and other amenities produced classic examples of nonprice competition.

Critical to this strategy is the assurance that no competitor can or will be allowed to compete on price. When price competition occurs due to loopholes in regulatory coverage or is selectively sanctioned by the regulatory agreement, those original firms who subsequently refuse to engage in price competition can lose substantial market share in a matter of months. Once lost, the cost of rebuilding market share can be a significant multiple of the cost of competitive maintenance of market share.

In hospitals, the nature of nonprice competition can take several forms:

- increased pressure for modern, beautiful facilities

- increased efforts to make services available, accessible, and acceptable to target populations

- emphasis on developing goodwill and positive institutional images in the consumer's mind.

One example of these trends is already evident in OB services. Major institutions are providing patients with a variety of obstetrical/delivery options and packages, such as 24-hour discharge plans, birthing rooms, follow-up care after discharge, guaranteed availability of desired accommodations, and candlelight dinners for new parents.

Nonprice competitive strategies occur most often around those services where consumer choice can be directly affected. Variations on the nonprice competitive strategies occur when the choices among institutions are made at the professional level, doctor to doctor.

The nonprice competitive strategy recognizes the emerging competition and, de facto, provides a transition position should pricing competition occur. Efficient volume, market penetration, and political orientation of the institution are crucial elements to have in place if some form of price competition becomes a reality.

Vertical Integration

The second major strategy pursued by firms operating within a regulated environment is vertical integration. Vertical integration may be backward or forward.

Backward vertical integration means entering into the businesses that supply the resources needed to run the main business operation. A business example would be a public utility buying a coal or oil company or a turbine manufacturer.

In many instances, the industries in which backward integration takes place are unregulated. This often creates opportunities to improve the financial performance of the parent institution. Using competitive transfer pricing, for example, institutions may be able to receive a higher return on total sales or total assets than they can currently within their own industry. Such integration may also help to produce the cash flow needed for capital formation in the regulated component.

Backward vertical integration is most beneficial when the value added is high. For instance, where high marketing costs are incurred, economies of scale are not large, and "efficient" production levels are low, backward vertical integration may be an appropriate strategy for an institution.

Hospitals already have begun to examine some of the potential opportunities in backward vertical integration. They have launched businesses in the manufacture of generic pharmaceuticals, prosthetic devices, and I.V. solutions. Traditionally, hospitals have been in the laundry business and in the group distribution and purchasing of products. The strategy concepts of backward vertical integration thus are starting to be implemented by health care institutions.

Forward vertical integration involves moving closer to the ultimate consumer or end-user of products or services. A business example would be railroads moving into the hotel or restaurant business or a telephone company moving into the manufacture of radio and television sets.

The concept has strong appeal where forward integration may offer opportunities for institutions to have some influence over the market for their mainline businesses. Such integration also has the potential for many institutions to allow packaging of a series of services at highly competitive prices. This is especially true if volume economies are created in the integrated package. Such economies may, for instance, be created by the elimination or reduction of marketing costs or by better use of management capability. Forward integration may also make feasible the provision of sophisticated capabilities that are not practical with nonintegrated units.

For health care institutions, the potential areas for forward vertical integration are numerous and exciting. They include:

- HMOs
- health related clinics (jogging, diet, smoking)
- store-front medical services
- industrial medicine programs

Moving into the above markets can, in effect, redefine the businesses of the institution. HMOs can move the institution into the organized delivery of medicine, industrial medicine into environmental health problems, and diet and smoking clinics into preventive health.

These examples of forward vertical integration raise the question, Are you in the business of acute intervention in illness, or is your business health? Your strategic choices may have a large impact on institutional perceptions of business opportunities, competitive posturing, and risk diversification.

Horizontal Integration

Another strategy coming to the fore is horizontal integration. This is the area of mergers, acquisitions, and consolidation of institutions that provide the same or complementary services. Horizontal integration may take three forms: (1) linkage of geographically dispersed institutions, (2) linkage of geographically proximate institutions, or (3) combinations of acute and nonacute inpatient services. The business objectives in employing horizontal integration may be to achieve economies of scale, concentration of management talent, increased access to capital markets, or more efficient management of capital resources.

Geographic integration has been the strategy of the for-profit chains and several large not-for-profit groups. These groups have accomplished geographic integration by acquisition, by merger, or by independently building new institutions where the need existed. A supplementary tactic in this strategy is to use management companies to gain influence over institutional direction.

The horizontal integration or expansion strategy allows centralization of management services and the ability to provide key middle-management support in an increasingly specialized and competitive environment. The specialized functions needed to implement political strategies in highly regulated environments (i.e., those of planners, lawyers, and financial experts) are affordable for these geographic systems and provide them with important competitive advantages.

The financial benefits of such integration can be substantial. The ability to generate cash flow at each institution, to centralize it, and to redistribute it to high-growth programs, services, or geographic areas is one potential advantage. The lowering of overall risk, both financial and regulatory, through geographic diversification is another. This can provide access to capital on very favorable terms.

The history of increased regulation in many industries indicates that the trend toward larger, more concentrated competitors will, for economic, management and political reasons, continue to be a viable strategy in health care.

The last form of horizontal integration in health care is to expand into a complete spectrum of acute and nonacute institutional health services. This form of horizontal integration attempts to control patient movement throughout the inpatient system. The strategy of horizontal integration of nursing homes, postacute rehabilitation facilities, hospices, and psychiatric facilities into one organization has been adopted by many providers in recent years. This particular strategy may, however, be very risky where third-party payment mechanisms are not widespread or coverage is not standardized.

POLITICAL STRATEGY: ONE KEY
TO SUCCESSFUL STRATEGY IMPLEMENTATION

A crucial element affecting the acceptability of an institutional strategy and thus its implementation is the concurrence of external constituencies. The corporate business sector has recognized the need not only for a good strategic business plan but also, especially in regulated environments, the need to develop a coordinated political strategy. Though the development of a good business plan is essential, it is not sufficient in a highly political environment. The development of a coordinated and targeted political strategy can be the means of success or failure in achieving acceptance of an institutional strategy.

The use of a political strategy alone, however, is not a unilateral option for long-term strategic success.

The corporate business sector has recognized the need to become proactive in the key external agencies and groups that comprise the external environment of the institution. The elements of such a political strategy include:

- lobbying the agencies
- public policy studies
- influencing intellectual thought
- proactive political education and constituency building
- use of public relations and the mass media

The above elements of a proactive political strategy (loosely defined) are described below along with specific examples of institutional activities related to them. The exact combination of political strategy elements used to assist in the attainment of individual institutional goals and objectives will depend on such factors as the personalities involved, the state of interinstitutional relations, and the political environment in each institution's geographic region.

Lobbying the Agencies

The development of interpersonal relationships is crucial to lobbying. This concept involves contacts and active involvement of the hospital's key personnel. It involves a multilevel interface that stresses the importance of

- developing contacts at many levels in the agencies—CEO to CEO, technical specialist to technical specialist, and so on (these relationships should be cultivated on an ongoing basis, not simply prior to institutional interaction with agency);

- initiating and participating in technical studies, planning committees, technical advisory groups, and so on;

- helping to develop criteria and understanding by agencies and the regulation of an institutional point of view prior to decisions and adoption of policies and procedures;

- loaning employees, if appropriate, to assist agencies in carrying out their responsibilities; and

- hiring former agency employees.

These are but a few of the activities that may be critical in developing a mutual trust relationship and a better understanding between the institution and outside agencies.

Public Policy Studies

Many industries recognize the importance of funding and participating in objective studies of issues that are at the interface between regulatory policy and legitimate institutional interests. Hospitals should consider the following activities:

- participation in studies that will provide objective data to help in policy formulation

- releasing internal studies that have been conducted on key issues and that may help in policy formulation (if it is in the institution's interests to do so)

- being proactive in recommending studies by regional, state, and trade associations around issues for which policy has not been formulated, so that effective association policy positions can be developed for testimony before appropriate bodies

The anticipation of issues and proactive involvement is a winning combination in highly regulated environments.

Influencing Intellectual Thought

The theories and policies followed by planning agencies and regulatory commissions usually have their roots in academic research. To the extent possible, institutions and their trade associations should encourage the development of a dialogue on key issues between leaders of intellectual thought and providers of health care. Many institutions have academicians on their boards, have hired them to conduct studies on institutional problems, or have had trade associations or other groups retain them to conduct public policy studies.

Opening up a dialogue and making the academic community aware of the operational problems and characteristics of the industry can help in the development of theories that are related to industry structure and the nature of competition and thus help to preserve legitimate institutional interests.

Proactive Political Education

One of the critical elements in strategy development and implementation is making key legislators, local officials, and agency personnel aware of institutional concerns with regard to pending or needed legislative changes. Many institutions hold legislative breakfasts and other similar events to make key external actors aware of their positions and what the impacts of policies or legislative change might be on the institution, both economically and behaviorally. Political interaction is an educational process.

Proactive Public Relations

Due to the apolitical nature of most institutions, the use of mass media and highly focused public relations activities has been neglected. In an environment that is not totally under the institution's control, consistent attention must be paid to the development of the capability to present the hospital's situation to many institutional constituencies. It is critical that institutions cultivate their own political constituency that will be willing to support the institution in a regulatory proceeding or in a situation in which special legislative relief is called for. In addition, institutions must be willing to use the media if they get in a political fight on issues affecting institutional interests.

These elements of a political strategy are critical to the successful shaping and implementation of strategy in a highly regulated environment. Lack of attention to and coordination of the above elements may block or seriously hinder the realization of the institution's long-range plans.

SUCCESSFUL STRATEGIC PLANNING PROCESSES

Successful strategic planning requires gathering together the appropriate people, providing leadership, staff support and appropriate consulting help, and developing a process that provides for meaningful involvement by key members of the organization. Following are some characteristics of a successful planning process:

- An active planning committee composed of the influence leaders among the board, administration, and medical staff. In addition to the established influence leaders, the emerging future influence leaders should be tapped.

- The planning committee is a working committee. Involvement is the key to understanding and, ultimately, to commitment.

- Leadership by a key trustee, perhaps the future chairman of the board, and by the administrator.

- Staff support to gather information and perform initial analyses. When planning fails, it is often because of the lack of staff support.

- Involvement of persons with special interests and expertise on task forces doing in-depth issue analyses. This increases the quality of the analyses and gets broader involvement.

- Third party objectivity, usually in the form of consultants, helps keep the process intellectually honest.

- A workplan and a timetable that are followed. These provide people with a sense of accomplishment and result in the formulation of strategy rather than just the accumulation of information.

CONCLUSION

Strategic planning is a management process that is being implemented by more and more hospitals. Implementing strategic planning requires a conceptual refocusing of the planning activity. It requires a shift from facility-oriented master planning to market-oriented strategic planning. Implementation of strategic planning requires bringing together the institutional leaders and engaging them in a process of candidly assessing the hospital's present situation and future options.

When they are market-oriented, institutions are more likely to develop programs that are responsive to people's needs. The development of a healthy planning process will make it more likely that the hospital will achieve a consensus and institutional commitment to implementation. When achieved, these outcomes will improve the hospital's ability to survive and thrive.

REFERENCES

1. Klarman, Herbert E. "Health Planning: Progress, Prospects, and Issues." *Milbank Memorial Fund Quarterly* (Health and Society) 56 (1978): 109.
2. Melin, Craig N., and Rabkin, Mitchell T. "Understanding the Context for Long-Range Planning in Hospitals." *Health Care Management Review* 2 (Spring 1977): 19.

SUGGESTED READINGS

Wilson, James Q. *The Politics of Regulation.* New York: Basic Books, 1980.

Kahn, Alfred. *The Economics of Regulation: Principles and Institutions.* Vols. 1 and 2. New York: John Wiley and Sons, 1970, 1974.

2. Strategic Planning and Control in Small Health Organizations

CURTIS P. McLAUGHLIN

McLaughlin, Curtis P. "Strategic Planning and Control in Small Health Organizations."
Health Care Management Review, Winter 1976.

Strategic or long-range planning is vitally important to the manager of the small health organization, but it is difficult for him to accept it as a practical process. Resources are limited, especially his time and energy as senior administrator-professional. His ability to influence the environment significantly is improbable; he has scant resources to apply to the projection and preparation for a future that is subject to rapid changes, even when it is limited to a three- to five-year horizon. The likelihood of a significant payoff often seems low. Yet every health manager knows that he is likely to end up in serious difficulties if the organization is merely swept along like a cork on a tide of external events. What is needed is a simple, relevant and low-cost planning approach. So the critical questions become "What do I need?" and "Where do I start, given my limited resources?". Where I stop expending those resources will depend on how valuable the experience ahead looks to me. Let's start with the latter question first.

ENTREE VIA BUDGET

The health manager knows that he needs all the help he can afford. Finding an efficient starting place, therefore, increases what the organization can afford; and cost can be reduced significantly by piggybacking the planning on necessary operating procedures.

Everyone has to deal with financial statements and to present budgets. At the very least these have to be developed to meet the requests of external organizations like banks, funding agencies, planning agencies, and boards of directors. While they are often based on uninteresting historical figures, they still can be the basic starting point for a planning process. The information is usually current, available, consistent and reliable.

Since many health organizations have a well-developed budgeting and control procedure, the budgeting-control area may be the least-cost place to enter into the planning process. From there one can consider embellishing and reality-testing the plan in terms of the related choice areas: mix of services, personnel, pricing policies and cost controls, funding mix, marketing plans, and organizational structure. Remember, however, that budget constraints do not set policies with respect to these related choices. The budget process is merely an entry into the iterative, cyclical process of planning. Tradeoffs are made continuously between choice areas until an acceptable strategy and plan of action emerges for the organization's future.

PLANNING AND CONTROL SYSTEMS

In 1965, R.N. Anthony offered a useful and simple way of classifying some basic processes within organizations.[1] While his work was initially applied to industry, it has since been expanded to cover nonprofit organizations.[2] He cited three processes for the internal organization: strategic planning, managerial control, and operational control. These are separate and distinct from information processing and from more externally oriented financial accounting. According to Anthony,

- **Strategic planning** is the process of deciding on objectives of the organization, on changes in those objectives, on the resources used to attain those objectives, and on the policies that are to govern the acquisition, use, and disposition of these resources.

- **Managerial control** is the process by which managers ensure that resources are obtained and used effectively and efficiently toward the organization's objectives.

- **Operational control** is the process of ensuring that specific tasks are carried out effectively and efficiently.

Table 1 lists the kinds of elements that seem necessary for the planning and control system of a health organization. All of these activities are necessary, even when the product is highly intangible and the organization is a nonprofit one. The word "marketing" may evoke concepts that conflict with your professional and personal values, but the fact remains that marketing is especially important in service organizations;[3, 4] and in public service organizations, "he who pays the piper calls the tune." This implies that there are at least three constituencies to be marketed to—pipers (professionals), payors, and dancers (clients). There may, in fact, be many more than three publics to be marketed to in the typical health program.[5]

Table 1 Elements of a Budget and Control System for a Small Health Organization

---

Strategic Planning

Long-range strategic budget
  By objective or program
  By function or item classification

Long-range funding projections
  By objective or program
  By function or item classification
  By potential sourcing
  By flexibility category or degree of discretionality

Evaluation reporting and organizational structure

Marketing strategy

Managerial Control

Cash flow projections (by month for six to twelve months)

Budget
  By objective or program
  By function or item classification
  By source or grant

Budget control—cumulative expenditures and commitments versus projected
  rates of activity
  By objective or program
  By function or item classification
  By source or grant

Activity vs. objectives comparison

Manpower budgets and training plans

Marketing plans

Operational Control

Cash and bank account control and reporting

Receivables and payable control and reporting

Trial balance, audit, preaudit and accrual activities

Property control

Grants accounting and reporting

Position control

Activity reporting

STRATEGIC PLANNING

We are all familiar with the fact that the form and quality of future revenue for health organizations is uncertain. For the nonprofit health organizations that do not provide direct care services to paying clients, it is highly uncertain. If the organization performs research or services for federal, state or local governments or is reimbursed through their agencies, it is subject to all the whims of the appropriations process. In other cases there is dependence upon uncertain demand for services in the planning period or upon an annual fund-raising campaign.

But this is no excuse for avoiding a long-range budget or long-range funding projections—which may or may not be distinct from funding objectives. Only with such figures in view can the manager identify the need for changes in strategies with respect to growth, personnel, funds acquisition, investment, mix and scope of services and activities, and marketing strategy.

Table 1 implies both a budget by program and one by function or items. There has been long and heated debate about the merits of program budgeting versus line-item budgeting. There is no doubt that the program budget is more important in long-range planning. Health organizations run programs; basically, they are to be judged by the success of those programs. Line-item budgets carry a very limited underlying assumption. They fix the factors of production that the manager is supposed to be selecting and combining to produce program results. They imply an assumption that the manager is incompetent to carry out one of a manager's most important tasks—allocating resources to make a program effective.

But sooner rather than later the manager of a health organization will translate the program budget into line items, for two reasons: Funding agencies and the program manager's supervisors will want to look at specific items, especially professional and nonprofessional personnel, travel, and supplies; and the managers of care delivery and support subunits will want to know what specifically they will have to work with and be responsible for.

This breakdown by function or item classification is especially necessary if the manager chooses to involve subunit managers in planning. Even though the head of a health organization thinks entirely in program terms, each successive level down the hierarchy that participates in the process must think less in program terms and more in terms of the specifics that he or she deals with. Regardless of how many programs are involved, the pharmacist will want to see a drug budget; the director of nursing, the funds available from all sources for paying nurses; and the motor pool manager, the transportation funds allocated there. And the manager who does not encourage subunit managers to participate in the planning process may lose both technical skills and future commitment on the part of the staff.

FOUR LONG-RANGE FUNDING PROJECTIONS

In organizations with multiple programs and multiple funding sources it is useful to prepare four funding projections. The first two of these, as shown in Table 1, correspond directly to the two strategic budgets. The third is a projection by potential sources of funds that may or may not bear a close relationship to the program budget. Preparing this projection is not time consuming, and it has the advantage of highlighting quickly the major needs or opportunities for strategic changes in program direction and for marketing the organization to funding sources.

The fourth category of breakdown is added to focus attention on the need to acquire discretionary funding rather than funding that is restricted to specific line items or program activities. It is a rare health organization that receives exactly the mix of fundings, and permissions to spend them, that meets its total needs. This is especially true of the seed money necessary for program development, staff development, travel, entertainment, reference materials, and so forth. Yet the manager must recognize that some funds for such purposes may be critical to the survival of the organization. In some cases, it is customary to acquire funding for work that already is partially completed in order to make funds available to develop the next contract. This play requires a constant feed-forward of work and money. The endowment income on general purpose donations to a local organization is often its only discretionary resource. Without the requisite amount of flexible resources, it is very difficult to have a holistic, coherent strategy and maintain the appropriate set of people and programs.

Even a relatively homogeneous, small, and profit-oriented organization like a group medical or dental practice needs to think in terms of flexible funding for staff development, equipment improvements, pet projects, and so on. If all the new income is passed through to the partners or associates, there is little motivation to make the practice more coherent and effective. If the practice is highly solvent, it is wise to build up a kitty for practice flexibility and improvement, if for no better reason than to force the partners to discuss whether or not there are group goals as well as individual goals and to provide an impetus for striving toward them.

THE PLANNING CYCLE

Having prepared a budget and funds projection, the small health organization is likely to identify gaps in funding sources, programs, or both. One relatively easy way to visualize this is in a chart like Figure 1.

Then it becomes necessary to look at the assumptions leading to these conditions, with or without a gap. This can be and usually is approached from

Figure 1 Identifying the Gap

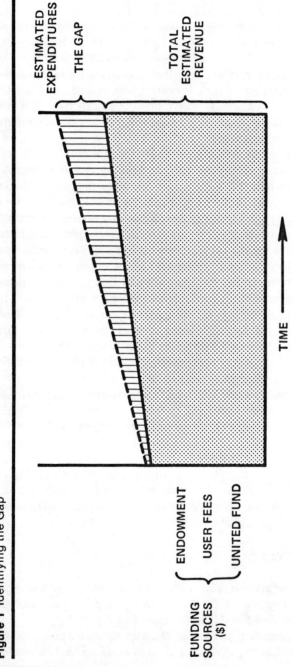

two sides. One is to examine the alternatives for solutions to observed problems in meeting the objectives. The second is to test out the sequence of assumptions used with respect to needs, costs, prices, manpower, program acceptability, social attitudes, professional attitudes, and interorganizational relationships.

Peter Drucker has outlined quite succinctly five planning steps for a service organization.[6] They are:

1. Define what is the "business" and what it should be. This should be an open consideration of alternative needs to be met and reasons for being.
2. Derive from this a clear set of goals and objectives.
3. Think through the priorities for concentrating efforts on targets, standards of performance for these targets, setting deadlines, and getting down to work.
4. Define measures of performance.
5. Provide for review (audit) of the outcomes to see which are acceptable and where effort should be directed toward change. This should include a mechanism for "sloughing off" unproductive activities. Macleod's article entitled "Program Budgeting Works in Nonprofit Institutions" is a good illustration of how a small, unsophisticated health organization was able to go through this process and even ended up sloughing off some services that its constituency was unwilling to support.[7]

The health system manager likes to think of himself or herself as a person who deals primarily with the facts. Yet the process of management really is based on a large number of assumptions. The trick is to identify those to which the management plan is most sensitive and conduct experiments with that subset that you are least sure of *and,* if proved untrue, would lead to significant changes in effectiveness. Examples of critical assumptions in health are:

- People will not accept primary care from nonphysicians.

- Medical care usage is not sensitive to prices.

- Group therapy is cheaper than individual therapy.

- HMOs are the way to cut health care costs.

- Nurse practitioners will work out well in rural settings.

- Building a new medical school at our end of the state will mean more available primary care.

- Government funding and reimbursement principles will remain consistent.

• People will accept primary care from non-physicians.

The alert manager will set up situations that probe in the direction of testing such assumptions. Controlled experiments are often out of the question, even in large organizations. The pressure of day-to-day demands and the fact that there are one-of-a-kind facilities preclude them. But it is possible to build up a set of data from natural events and from probing experiences to see whether or not a change might make sense over the long haul.

EXIT ANYWHERE

Assumption tests could affect all stages of the planning cycle as illustrated in Figure 2. The sequence around the large loop in Figure 2 is not a fixed one. Rationales can be made for numerous changes in sequencing, but the purpose of the diagram here is to lay out these activities for the manager of the small health organization, not to provide *the* sequence.

The most unusual box is labeled "coherency check" and is linked to the flexible funds projection. It is there to emphasize the necessity for the health manager to step back and see whether or not all the people and activities around his shop add up to something that makes sense, is balanced and coherent, and feels right.

On the microcosmic level, we have the same problems with task analysis for employees. We can define tasks and the skills necessary to perform specific health procedures. Yet we have no assurances that at a given time and place these tasks and skills can be combined into a meaningful job and a meaningful role. Similarly, a community mental health organization may provide the five mandated services and several others and still not make much sense as an entity. It is an important duty of the leadership to see that all the pieces (programs) fit together and that the employees understand this.

The sequence in Figure 2 is most likely to be challenged on the grounds of "which comes first, the chicken or the egg?" The order is derived from the entry point and the exit points that the manager of a small health organization might well choose. Every manager ought to be willing to go around the loop periodically, thinking in broad conceptual terms. After that, he has to make careful choices about how much time and resources should go into the detailed phases of planning, then consider whether or not to go into an even more detailed system like "management-by-objectives" with written plans, mission statements, performance targets, client satisfaction and need surveys, employee attitude surveys, and so forth.

The outcome of a very modest investment might be as simple, but as powerful, as the idea that we need to fund and add an additional nursing auxiliary in late 1976; and we need to keep an eye on how new Social Security programs affect our ability to bill for specific services and our willingness to purchase specific diagnostic equipment.

Figure 2 The Long-Range Planning Process

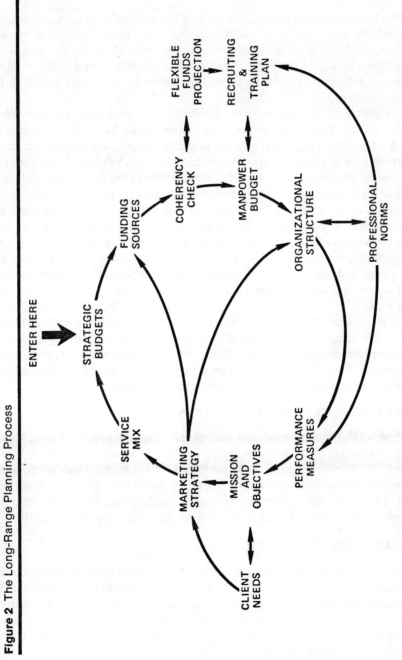

Exit anywhere when the return from continuing seems likely to be less than the effort.

WHERE DOES THE ENVIRONMENT FIT IN?

Much has been said about the details of the strategic planning process, but Anthony and Herzlinger point out that it is "largely unsystematic and informal." Decisions are made at irregular intervals, and the information required usually has to be developed specifically for the issues involved.[8] They also cite the well-known fact that this involves a continual watch on the environment.

Figure 2, therefore, does not specifically place environmental inputs into that picture. This is because a single environmental change could impinge on several boxes at once. Take, for example, the impact of unionization on the operations of a developmental disabilities center. The initial impact is likely to be upon wage rates and appear immediately in the long-range budgeting area. But bargaining on "noneconomic" issues is very likely to involve work standards and methods that in turn affect manpower budgets and recruiting and training plans, conflict with or support professional norms, change marketing strategy and service mix, and even affect accreditation aspirations. Some of these results will impact choice areas sequentially, while others will be impinged upon uniquely. The manager of the small institution must accept that the impacts of major environmental shifts can be quite varied and pervasive.

Interorganizational relationships also are a natural consideration for the health manager, but are presumably of more interest to larger organizations. Space considerations preclude dealing with this topic here, except to say that Kenneth Benson's observations on domain consensus and ideological consensus are especially relevant to health organizations.[9]

WHERE DOES EVALUATION FIT IN?

Evaluation inputs should be a part of this planning process. In the typical service program, the evaluation effort should be aimed at setting objectives and selectively allocating resources that will improve the internal operation and the outputs delivered to and impacting on the public. Evaluation efforts that are not keyed to internal information needs fall at best into the financial reporting category or are idle exercise or specialized professional skills.

MANAGERIAL CONTROL

The small health organization may be able to do strategy planning, but its efforts will be worth a great deal more in the long run if they are linked to the implementation stages of managerial control and operational control. Although I am focusing here on the strategic planning process, it seems important to deal with managerial and operational controls in conjunction with strategic planning.

Cash flow projections are critical to the survival of the organization. Even an organization making a profit can fail if it lacks the cash to meet its payroll or to satisfy the least patient of its creditors. This is also the case with a nonprofit organization. The amount of effort devoted to this activity will fluctuate depending on the variability or seasonability of cash flows. Cash flow projection is a shorter-range counterpart to funding projections.

Budgeting is something that all organizations quickly learn to live with. In order to end up without a loss, each individual must have a specific commitment to expend only a specific amount of resources and then stick to that commitment. Here, as in the case of strategic planning, it probably will prove necessary to live with three sets of budgetary breakdowns—four if the concern for flexibility of funding is carried through at this level of control.

The budget process, if carefully administered, is a major opportunity for the manager to motivate the behavior of personnel in individual subunits of the organization. If the budget is imposed from the "top down," there is often little felt obligation to establish the ends of the subunits within that constraint. Either the subunit will try to overspend to meet its goals, or it will feel justified in not meeting those goals because inadequate resources are provided. The only way to avoid this impasse is to have the subunit manager participate in a "button-up" development of the budget. This does not imply that there may not be drastic cuts from the initial requests, but these should be arrived at in conjunction with the setting of operational objectives. Only then can there be a mutual contract between the employees and the management to perform set tasks with allowed resources. A good description of this negotiation process can be found in Wildavsky's *The Politics of the Budgetary Process.*[10]

While budgets are a useful projection and negotiation device, the real day-to-day planning and control tool lies within the process of comparing the expenditures and encumbrances with the amounts that the budget planning process indicated should have been consumed at any given point in time. Table 2 gives a statement of financial condition for a crippled children's program and illustrates the utility of such a tool. It gives the total amount budgeted for the program, the amount expended, and the balance remaining by item classification. An additional column represents monies that have not been paid out but for which there already is a commitment to expend them. This, subtracted from the cash balance, indicates how much is available for future decision making. For example, the program budget period is only half complete, but the staff has already been hired and no more salary money can be committed. The item for travel is already due to be overspent. Assuming that a constant expenditure rate was planned, the program manager might question responsible subunit heads about the low rate of expenditure for foster home care, appliances, public health nurses, and health education. One might also wonder whether any plans had been made for staff training. If the

Table 2 Budget Report—As of Halfway Mark in Budget Period—Crippled Children's Program*

Budget Item	Amount Budgeted	Budget Amount Expended	Unexpended Amount	Amount Committed	Uncommitted Balance Available
Salaries of Staff	$40,000	$17,500	$22,500	$22,500	$ 0
Physicians' Fees	20,000	11,000	9,000	2,000	7,000
Clinic Physicians' Fees	10,000	3,500	6,500	1,500	5,000
Hospitalization	35,000	18,000	17,000	2,500	14,500
Convalescent and Foster Home Care	4,000	500	3,500	250	3,250
Appliances	5,000	1,000	4,000	0	4,000
Drugs and Biologicals	500	200	300	0	300
X-ray and Laboratory Work	2,500	1,000	1,500	500	1,000
Staff Training	3,000	0	3,000	0	3,000
Travel	2,500	2,500	0	300	(300)
Equipment and Supplies	1,000	800	200	100	100
Publications, etc.	500	0	500	250	250
CC Subtotal	124,000	56,000	68,000	29,900	38,100
Administrative Offices	5,000	4,500	500	500	0
Health Education	4,000	500	3,500	500	3,000
Vital Statistics	2,000	1,700	300	50	250
Local Health Offices	5,000	1,000	4,000	1,000	3,000
Public Health Nursing	10,000	1,000	9,000	0	9,000
Supporting Subtotal	26,000	8,700	17,300	2,050	15,250
Total	150,000	64,700	85,300	31,950	53,350

*Adapted from data in "How to Use Financial Data as a Basic Program Planning Tool." In *American Journal of Public Health*, Vol. 44. No. 2. February, 1954. pp. 149-157. Reprinted with permission.

rate of expenditure was not planned to be constant, then an additional column should have been added to show projected expenditures and encumbrances for the same cumulative period. Sometimes percentage columns are also provided.

It is important that the accounting system be set up on an accrual basis rather than a cash basis to give comparative information. If expenditures are compared monthly and some employees are paid weekly, portions of the pay periods that are in either the preceding or following periods should be added into the period results. Certain charges that are paid only yearly, like insurance, could also be spread out over the year, especially if such analyses are used to estimate appropriate service charges.

Also at the managerial control level there has to be an equivalent of evaluation as it was discussed at the strategic planning level. This means keeping track of objectives or service statistics of the program and comparing them with resource inputs during the period. Such comparisons are a useful indicator of whether or not the current process seems to be effective and efficient. Some analysts equate evaluation primarily with outcome or benefit measurement. But, while that is a very important type of information to the program manager, that measure in social programs comes only after considerable time has elapsed and may or may not be traceable to program activities. The manager, in the meantime, must modify program planning assumptions constantly and adjust the input and process stages in order to continue to improve operations. It is too costly to wait for the outcome evaluation before refining the process. The same holds in the manpower and marketing areas.

OPERATIONAL CONTROL

There are numerous things to keep track of in the health organization, especially when there are multiple sources of funds and many publics to be responsible to. The lack of authorization to incur openly either a profit or a loss means that controls, especially those over hiring and spending, must aim for particularly tight targets. Hiring controls are especially important since most health organizations provide intangible products and are labor intensive. Cash and bank account control and control over payables and receivables are common to any organization. Similarly, the accounting activity of accruals, audits, and trial balances is similar to that of a manufacturing organization. There is, however, especially in government organizations, the preaudit phase that requires that the expender have a budget officer review the contract to make sure that funds are still available within the constraints of budgets and to assess whether purchasing (bidding), personnel, and other requirements have been met. Since public property and government employees and money may be involved, one may have to add property control, position control, and grants accounting and reporting to the control system.

Then the management must add activity reporting as the basis for process decision and for evaluation in support of grants reporting, managerial control, and strategic planning.

NONE TOO SMALL

It is important that the manager of a small health organization become familiar with the total processes of strategic planning and control, even if he or she does not get into it in great depth or detail. This can have considerable impact on the effectiveness—even the survival—of the organization. It is not as complicated as budget analysts and program planning experts might like you to believe. It is not something to leave to accountants, agencies, or staff analysts. It is worth understanding and considering actively, regardless of your scale of operations.

REFERENCES

1. Anthony, Robert N. *Planning and Control Systems: A Framework for Analysis.* Boston, Mass.: Division of Research, Harvard University Graduate School of Business Administration, 1965.

2. Anthony, Robert N., and Herzlinger, Regina E. *Management Control in Nonprofit Organizations.* Homewood, Ill.: Richard D. Irwin, Inc., 1975.

3. Rathmell, John M. *Marketing in the Service Sector.* Cambridge, Mass.: Winthrop Publishers, Inc., 1974.

4. Shapiro, Benson P. "Marketing for Nonprofit Organizations." *Harvard Business Review,* September-October, 1973, pp. 123-132.

5. Kotler, Philip. *Marketing for Nonprofit Organizations.* Englewood Cliffs, N.J.: Prentice-Hall, Inc., 1975.

6. Drucker, Peter F. *Management.* New York: Harper and Row, 1974, chapters 12, 13, and 14.

7. Macleod, Roderick K. "Program Budgeting Works in Nonprofit Institutions." *Harvard Business Review,* September-October, 1971, pp. 59-69.

8. Anthony and Herzlinger. *Management Control in Nonprofit Organizations,* p. 28.

9. Benson, J. Kenneth. "The Interorganizational Network as a Political Economy." *Administrative Science Quarterly,* 20, June 1975, pp. 229-249.

10. Wildavsky, Aaron. *The Politics of the Budgetary Process.* Boston, Mass.: Little, Brown and Co., 1964, chapter 1.

3. Product-Market Differentiation: A Strategic Planning Model for Community Hospitals

Milch, Robert A. "Product-Market Differentiation: A Strategic Planning Model for Community Hospitals." *Health Care Management Review*, Spring 1980.

It is common knowledge, but no less true, that the American voluntary hospital industry is in serious trouble. The industry is beset by (1) runaway costs and an expanding array of regulatory controls at federal, state, and local governmental levels and (2) increasing skepticism that marginal increases in hospital expenditures result in benefits comparable to returns on similar investments in other sectors. [1-3] At the same time, it is facing mounting pressures on a number of other fronts: *social-justice pressures* for continually improved access to a demonstrably "better" quantity and quality in hospital care and services; persistent *technological-imperative pressures* for increasingly sophisticated plant, equipment, and personnel resources; and, by no means least, rising *competitive pressures* from the large publicly held hospital companies (whose earnings performance is only now attracting broad attention in the investment community) [4-6] and from labor organizations and industrial firms that have shown increasing interest in becoming directly involved in the organization and delivery of personal health care services. [7,8]

It has been demonstrated, moreover, that the market performance of the large majority of tax-exempt hospitals has not, on balance, been particularly distinguished.[9] For example, based on market-share and market-growth rate characteristics, only a few hospitals in any of the regional markets (or *portfolios*) studied to date appear to operate with the economies of scale and investment inherent in high-volume business operations. The remainder—usually including all of the nonteaching or community hospitals in a given portfolio—tend to emerge as market-followers in a remarkably clustered low-share/moderate-growth ("plodder") category.

THE DILEMMA OF NONTEACHING HOSPITALS

In part, of course, the peculiar position of the nonteaching community hospital follows from a historical but still generally accepted normative construct (reinforced by current methods of health insurance and prevailing cost-based financing mechanisms) that *assumes:* (1) that, with only a few expressly sanctioned exceptions, hospitals necessarily ought to be full-line/full-service institutions that address the common needs and wants of all people in local submarkets (undifferentiated locational marketing) rather than focusing resources on the special needs and wants of specific or differentiated buyers of hospital care (market segmentation and target marketing); and, as a corollary, (2) that purposeful specialization in selected high-volume routine services represents both "cream-skimming" and professionally unacceptable, if not overtly unethical, behavior.

The net societal effect, however, is the organization and operation of regional market structures in which individual hospitals develop plant capacity (and costs) within the constraints of certificate of need, cost sharing, utilization and rate review, and other regulatory controls to serve the product and service interests needed or demanded by all buyers in the market. But because of size and investment limitations, such hospitals are generally unable to position themselves as market leaders supplying optimally efficient care and services for any particular market segment(s).

Community hospitals thus find themselves caught up in what amounts to a self-reinforcing dilemma. Because they are social institutions that reflect the perception of needs and the product orientation of their principal physician-markets, and because they also respond to community pressures and political influence to provide "full care and high quality services" on a more or less equitable basis to their patient or client-consumer markets (Figure 1), they cannot generally gain the distinctive competencies and differential market advantages that could conceivably generate high-volume activities and higher market shares and, hence, profitability.[10, 11] Experience curve costs net of inflation, in consequence, are reduced to levels that enable a hospital to operate at near minimal marginal costs on a product-by-product or product portfolio basis. Per diem and per admission costs therefore continue to rise, in turn stimulating external regulatory control mechanisms that prevent the hospital from acquiring the resources necessary to produce and distribute economically efficient care services.

As a result, most community hospitals are content simply to defend their positions as followers in their respective geographic markets. They are satisfied, in short, to survive as well as possible—"to satisfice"—as established participants in an increasingly regulated industry—as long as the regulators and planners, however organized institutionally, in effect guarantee their

Figure 1 Hospital Strategic Marketing System

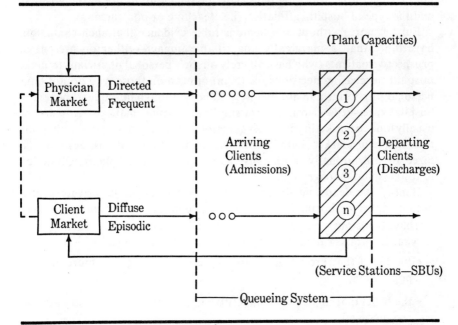

occupancy rates and exclude new-entry competitors (through planning mechanisms) and guarantee their pricing structures and equivalent return on investment (through rate-setting mechanisms). But they are satisfied only up to a point. Understandably, dissatisfaction and discontent loom large in direct relation to initiatives aimed at containing or "capping" costs (which determine revenues) and at escalating efforts directed toward the establishment of alternative, competitive health care delivery systems.

MARKETING STRATAGEMS

Perceptive hospital managements quite correctly recognize marketing as the principal—and perhaps only—affirmative means at their disposal for emerging from the community hospital dilemma. It is not surprising, however, that "marketing" has generally been limited to nonpersonal and untargeted learning-and-reinforcement or so-called persuasive communication ("public relations") campaigns. The industry is one in which (1) the use of price and most conventional promotional devices as competitive instruments has generally been considered (at least until recent actions by the Federal Trade Commission[12]) to be unethical; (2) marketing costs were not "allowable" or reimbursed by most third party payers[13]; and (3) the hospital selection decision of individuals[14] is largely determined by such factors as proximity of the hospital, prestige of the attending physician, physical appearance of the hospital, and the type of hospital affiliation (i.e., teaching or nonteaching).

Furthermore, without any demonstrable evidence that such campaigns have more than a marginally quantifiable impact—either on present or prospective patients (who basically rely on their personal physicians to make hospital purchasing decisions for them) or even on those who do not have personal physicians and are themselves active, though infrequent, buyers of hospital care—it is also not surprising that hospital managements do not usually look to marketing activities as major factors in building or maintaining their image or market share. The marketing function is almost never recognized, organizationally or otherwise, as a major policy and planning function of top hospital management.

Hence, like dead and dying "growth" industries in the private profit-optimizing sector, hospitals (and tax-exempt community hospitals in particular) have tenaciously clung to product and selling concepts of marketing[15] and to what Levitt has called the conditions of a self-deceiving cycle:[16, 17]

- the belief that growth is assured by an expanding and more affluent population;

- the belief that there is no competitive substitute for the industry's major product; and

- preoccupation with a product that lends itself to carefully controlled scientific experimentation, improvement, and manufacturing cost reduction.

With notable exceptions,[18] they have not adopted a *marketing concept,* the idea that:

> . . .business success requires being customer-oriented rather than product-oriented, that a business ought to view itself not as selling goods or services but rather as buying customers. . .(and) doing all things so that people will want to do business with you, or prefer to do it with you rather than with your competitors. Instead of talking about what to make or sell, business managers should think about what people will buy, and why. . . .Deeply implanted in all these ideas is the central notion that nothing is more important than the customer. The customer finally decides the fate of an enterprise. This does not mean that other corporate matters are less important, only that they are not more important.[19, 20]

As a practical matter, there have been (at least heretofore) very few business reasons to do so. The established system of planning, organizing, financing, and even regulating hospitals has, in essence, "bought the customers." It has done so (1) without substantially altering historical trends in the nature, scope, or product orientation of hospital operations, and (2) without requiring very much more of hospitals (except perhaps as a defensive stratagem) than detailed sequencing and control of resource allocation processes at an operational level. Strategic considerations (broad in scope and long-term in their impact), which are the focus of top management in large diversified business firms, have largely escaped the attention of hospital managers (and hospital regulators as well).[21]

STRATEGIC MARKETING/PLANNING MODEL

It seems safe to predict, however, that enlightened self-interest and increasing public and governmental pressures for change—not unlike those affecting industry during the "profitless growth" period of the late 1960s and early 1970s—will cause hospitals to abandon, at least in respect to patient care activities, such traditional indices as bed occupancy ratios and patient origin as the scalar parameters appropriate for measuring performance and will gradually force a transition toward strategic marketing concepts. On the evidence of trends since the 1920s, it seems likely that corporate strategies and planning processes in large, diversified hospital firms will come to bear a striking resemblance to corporate strategies and planning processes in large, diversified business organizations and some government agencies.

Accordingly, future organizational and operational thrusts will probably involve, at a minimum (1) identification and definition of the discrete and independent markets served and products (or services) produced—product-market niches or segments—by natural business units (strategic business units, or SBUs)[22] within each aggregated hospital firm; (2) allocation of capital and managerial resources to each such unit in more or less direct relation to its respective competitive position or business strength and its long-term product-market attractiveness; and (3) continuing reappraisal and reallocation of resources based on the short-run and long-run performance of each strategic business unit in balancing the present and anticipated future interests of the market and the hospital firm in terms of an integrated marketing system.

Assume that it is reasonable (and responsible) economic and social policy for a nonteaching hospital to seek to maximize its internal efficiency—that is to say, to produce its service and product output at minimum marginal cost, irrespective of whatever reimbursement mechanism may happen to prevail at any given time.[23] It would logically seem to follow that any such hospital should maintain capacity and incur costs, subject perhaps to definable goal-programming[24] constraints, only in those SBUs that continually demonstrate product-market competencies and competitive business strengths. All other

things being equal, SBUs that fail to demonstrate effective market performance should be terminated as quickly as possible.

The problem, obviously, is that there are neither generally accepted economic values nor noneconomic equivalents to profitability measures for
purposes of evaluating overall operating performance—much less SBU performance—in a tax-exempt community hospital. Furthermore, there are no
standards of superior or even reasonably attainable hospital performance
that are clearly defined in terms that can be consistently recognized, applied,
and measured, even by definable peer groups.

One potential model for circumventing these problems emerged from a
consulting engagement for a large, diversified hospital located in a south-
eastern rural setting. As illustrated in Figure 1, it posits a hospital as an
organizational entity that (1) actively competes with other health care organizations both for physician-clients and for patient-clients in a spatially undifferentiated geographic market characterized by an uneven distribution of
population and heterogeneous transportation and communication networks;
(2) serves physician-referred and self-referred patient-clients (customers) in
accord with classical queuing theory principles at multiple autonomous service
stations (strategic business units roughly corresponding to traditional clinical
service specialty and subspecialty designations); and (3) is compensated for
care and services rendered by each such SBU on the basis of a per-admission
charge for service.

Two aggregate measures are taken as the relevant criteria of market or
business performance of any SBU over any given time frame: (1) *units sold*
(total number of inpatient admissions or number of inpatient admissions
adjusted for the number of outpatient and emergency visits) during a stipulated
period; and (2) the *unit or average price per admission* (determined by
dividing total charges billed by each SBU by the total number of admissions
or adjusted admissions to the SBU during the same time interval).

Rank ordering of each SBU in terms of units sold and unit admission price
over any designated time horizon and identification of the median SBU in
each data set permit development of a conceptual 2 × 2 volume/price matrix.
This, in effect, reflects the relative product-market attractiveness and competitive position (business strength) of each SBU in the "portfolio" of SBUs that
constitute the functional activities of any diversified hospital firm (Figure 2).

VOLUME/PRICE MATRIX

As illustrated in Table 1, the hospital that served as the basis for the model
had 23 strategic business units, as defined above. Between July 1971 and
December 1972, the obstetrics unit recorded the largest number of admissions
(2,602), and the physical medicine and rehabilitation SBU recorded the

Figure 2 Volume/Price Matrix

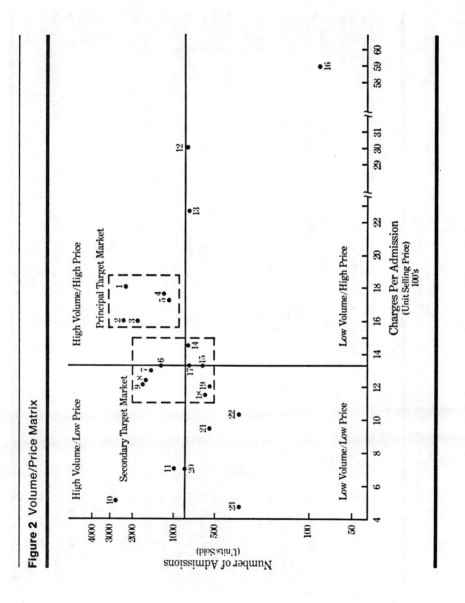

Table 1 Rank Orders of Hospital Admissions and Billed Charges Per Admission

Volume		Price	
Strategic Unit	Number of Admissions (Units Sold)	Strategic Unit	Charge per Admission (Unit Price)
Obstetrics	2,602	Physical medicine and rehabilitation	$5,905.64
Orthopedic surgery	2,394	Thoracic surgery	3,000.02
General surgery	2,298	Psychiatry	2,276.15
Cardiology	1,729	General surgery	1,801.64
Pediatric medicine	1,539	Neurological surgery	1,753.54
Gynecology	1,533	General medicine	1,725.28
Plastic surgery	1,509	Cardiology	1,576.49
Urology	1,259	Orthopedic surgery	1,574.34
Neurological surgery	1,239	Nephrology	1,436.62
General medicine	1,154	Urology	1,325.55
Otolaryngology	984	Pulmonary medicine	1,318.86
Ophthalmology (median)	891	Neurology (median)	1,318.20
Nephrology	865	Plastic surgery	1,284.21
Thoracic surgery	856	Gynecology	1,212.68
Neurology	790	Gastroenterology	1,196.30
Psychiatry	780	Pediatric medicine	1,196.11
Pulmonary medicine	656	Hematology	1,147.26
Hematology	618	Rheumatology	1,041.17
Gastroenterology	574	Endocrinology	946.13
Endocrinology	564	Otolaryngology	722.78
Dermatology	314	Ophthalmology	710.67
Rheumatology	292	Obstetrics	518.18
Physical medicine and rehabilitation	74	Dermatology	470.05

smallest number (74). The number of admissions to the ophthalmology unit (891) divided the hospital's SBU portfolio into two equal groups on the basis of total inpatient admissions. The neurology SBU was the median unit in dividing the SBU portfolio on the basis of billed charges per admission.

These (median) values for admissions and for charges per admission were used to construct the 2 × 2 volume/price matrix illustrated in Table 2 and Figure 2.

By definition, the distribution of specialty and subspecialty SBUs in each of the four cells of the resulting volume/price matrix (Table 2) raises the principal questions that govern the strategic planning process:

- What businesses are we in (or should we be in)?
- What businesses are we really not in (or should we not be in)?

Clearly, on a volume basis, the study hospital was largely in the business of supplying surgical services during the 18 months of the study period. While only 9 of the 21 SBUs included in the matrix (i.e., excluding ophthalmology and neurology) were principally surgical in nature, the surgical SBUs nevertheless accounted for 71 percent of all 23,833 hospital admissions, 71 percent of admissions in the high volume/high price cell, and 81 percent of admissions in the high volume/low price cell—but only 26 percent of admissions in the low volume/high price cell and none of the admissions in the low volume/low price cell. Only 29 percent of hospital admissions to SBUs included in the matrix were for the supply of medical and medical specialty services. Although the medical and medical specialty admissions represented only 29 percent of admissions in the high volume/high price cell and 19 percent of admissions in the high volume/low price cell, they also represented 74 percent of admissions in the low volume/high price cell and 100 percent of admissions in the low volume/low price cell (Table 2).

In short, despite the strong claims of trustees and top management personnel that the institutions furnished a "balanced program" of care services, the hospital was basically in the business of supplying (high volume) surgical services that were about evenly divided between high and low price.

The format illustrated in Table 2 may be useful for preliminary analytical purposes. Taken by itself, however, it neither yields the type of information required for satisfactorily identifying and appraising present strategies nor does it provide sufficient answers to the more relevant and important questions of strategic planning:

- What are our current product-market competencies and our competitive strengths?
- How are these likely to be affected (if at all) by environmental trends and developments over which we do (and do not) have control?

Table 2 Distribution of Strategic Business Units (Segmented on Basis of Ophthalmology and Neurology SBUs)

Strategic Unit	Number of Admissions	Charge per Adm.
High Volume/High Price:		
Orthopedic surgery	2,394	$1,574.34
General surgery	2,298	1,801.64
Cardiology	1,729	1,576.49
Urology	1,259	1,325.55
Neurological surgery	1,239	1,753.54
General medicine	1,154	1,725.28
Mean	1,679	$1,626.14
Low Volume/High Price:		
Nephrology	865	$1,436.62
Thoracic surgery	856	3,000.02
Psychiatry	780	2,276.15
Pulmonary medicine	656	1,318.86
Physical medicine and rehabilitation	74	5,905.64
Mean	646	$2,787.46

Strategic Unit	Number of Admissions	Charge per Adm.
High Volume/Low Price:		
Obstetrics	2,602	$ 518.18
Pediatric medicine	1,539	1,196.11
Gynecology	1,533	1,212.68
Plastic surgery	1,509	1,284.21
Otolaryngology	984	722.78
Mean	1,633	$ 986.79
Low Volume/Low Price:		
Hematology	618	$1,147.26
Gastroenterology	574	1,196.30
Endocrinology	564	946.13
Dermatology	314	470.05
Rheumatology	292	1,041.17
Mean	472	$ 960.18

• How can we best position ourselves to capitalize upon present product-market strengths and likely future developments so that we can maximize the internal efficiency of present and future operations?

As illustrated in Figure 2, cluster analysis (visual or mathematical) of the discrete locations of individual SBUs in the volume/price matrix can provide a framework for addressing these questions. In the study hospital, for example, it is clear that there were three distinct business strength clusters over the time interval analyzed:

1. a *principal target market* consisting exclusively of high volume/high price SBUs—general surgery (1), orthopedic surgery (2), cardiology (3), neurological surgery (4), and general medicine (5);

2. a *secondary target market* consisting of centrally positioned SBUs in all four of the matrix cells—urology (6), plastic surgery (7), gynecology (8), pediatric medicine (9), nephrology (14), pulmonary medicine (15), neurology (17), hematology (18), and gastroenterology (19); and

3. a *fringe market* consisting of peripheral and diffusely dispersed SBUs—obstetrics (10), otolaryngology (11), thoracic surgery (12), psychiatry (13), physical medicine and rehabilitation (16), ophthalmology (20), endocrinology (21), rheumatology (22), and dermatology (23).

These clusters would of course correspond to priority rankings if hospital firms were operated as competitive market structures so as to maximize return on assets and if it were assumed (and there is no reason not to do so) that (1) the business performance and internal efficiency of hospital operations—like those of production functions in manufacturing and other industries[25]—are direct functions of volume and market share and (2) experience curve effects can be realized. Presumably, the study hospital could have functioned most cost efficiently—quite apart from "quality" and other noneconomic constraints and from considerations of the way books of account might have been kept for rate-setting and cost-reimbursement purposes—if it had in fact "cream-skimmed" and limited its activities exclusively to those SBUs that constituted the "principal target market."

Given existing patient and case severity mixes and no changes—either in the levels of expertise and training of medical, nursing, support and administrative staffs or in the physical and functional characteristics of plant, equipment, support systems, and other key variables—it seems likely that *overall hospital performance* would have been significantly "better" if SBUs, at least in the "fringe market," had been eliminated. The hospital would almost certainly have been able to achieve at least some economies of scale and thus "cost savings" (whether or not returned to patients and third parties in terms of lower charges) if the low volume SBUs in the fringe market had been eliminated and the resources concentrated in the primary and secondary product-market segments.

Conversely, a deliberate decision on the part of hospital management *not* to terminate the activities of an SBU in the fringe market would represent, in terms of a strict constructionist view of business economics, a *strategic* decision (1) to incur real present (and future) opportunity costs and (2) to impose significant present (and future) external diseconomies on third parties for services that are relatively low in demand. It is, in effect, a decision to accept the costs of a thin market (so long as they are fully reimbursed) irrespective of the likely benefits to be gained and, in theory at least, to be returned to ultimate customers; and it is, in the final analysis, simply to reaffirm the community hospital dilemma.

IMPLICATIONS OF STRATEGIC DECISIONS

To the extent that hospitals in any geographic market continue to be protected from business risks and insolvency by prevailing reimbursement, rate-setting, and "common sense" planning mechanisms, and to the extent that hospitals are not obligated either (1) to adopt "optimal and desirable operating conditions for facilities and equipment"[26] or (2) to compete actively in terms of price and product and performance in a marketplace where ultimate customers (patients) can and in fact do register their preferences for higher or lower levels and prices for care services, there is probably no overwhelmingly persuasive reason why even "plodder" hospitals need to take strategic planning very seriously. There is, after all, nothing inherently "right and appropriate" or "wrong and inappropriate" about most hospital activities—whether or not they can be demonstrated to visibly benefit patients[27-29]—and, as a practical political matter, even entrenched bureaucracies can do little to alter the economic tastes and cultural preferences of most hospitals' physician-clients or patient-clients.

On the other hand, to the extent that hospital cost inflation and cost containment (if not cost control) become high national priorities—and all indications are that the hospital cost problem has finally assumed politically actionable proportions—hospitals generally, and community hospitals in particular, would seem to have every reason to identify and capitalize upon their demonstrated product-market strengths. If used properly, the product-market or SBU construct developed here, as reflected in a hospital's volume/price matrix, might do much to restore accountability and fiscal prudence in the hospital sector. It represents one means whereby privately organized and operated community hospitals can solve problems that have already badly overtaxed many public agencies.

Despite the model's limitation of dealing principally with easily measurable parameters and but one aspect of strategic planning processes (namely, decisions based on historical trends and projections of present economic activities), it does provide a framework both for rational analysis of the community hospital dilemma and for developing sensible solutions to the complex problems of accelerating hospital price-inflation—short of converting ostensibly private organizations into involuntary agents of the federal government.

REFERENCES

1. Fuchs, V.R. *Who Shall Live?* New York: Basic Books, 1974.

2. Etzioni, A. "Health as a Social Priority." In *Health Services: The Local Perspective. Proceedings of the Academy of Political Science,* edited by A. Levin, vol. 32:3, 1977, pp. 8-14.

3. Mechanic, D. "Approaches to Controlling the Costs of Medical Care: Short-Range and Long-Range Alternatives." *New England Journal of Medicine* 298 (February 2, 1978) pp. 249-254.

4. Schiff, L. "Great Expectations at the Proprietary Hospitals." *Fortune* (December 1977) pp. 57-59.

5. "Personal Products and Health Care." *Forbes* 121 (January 9, 1978) pp. 126-128.

6. Milch, R.A., and Martinelli, P.A. "Growth of Commercial Firms in the American Health and Hospitals Industry." *Business Economics* 15 (March 1980) pp. 9-13.

7. Edgahl, R.H., et al. "The Potential of Organizations of Fee-for-Service Physicians for Achieving Significant Decreases in Hospitalization." *Annals of Surgery* 186 (September 1977) pp. 388-399.

8. Herzlinger, R. "Can We Control Health Care Costs?" *Harvard Business Review* 56 (March-April 1978) pp. 102-110.

9. Milch, R.A., and Martinelli, P.A. "Community Health Markets: A Portfolio Perspective." *Health Care Management Review* 3 (Fall 1978) pp. 23-28.

10. Gale, B.T. "Market Share and Rate of Return." *Review of Economics and Statistics* 54 (November 1972) pp. 412-423.

11. Buzzel, R.D.; Gale, B.T.; and Sultan, R.G.M. "Market Share—Key to Profitability." *Harvard Business Review* 53 (January-February 1975) pp. 97-106.

12. Avellone, J.D., and Moore, F.D. "The Federal Trade Commission Enters a New Arena: Health Services." *New England Journal of Medicine* 299 (August 31, 1978) pp. 473-483.

13. Clarke, R.N. "Marketing Health Care: Problems in Implementation." *Health Care Management Review* 3 (Winter 1978) pp. 21-27.

14. Wind, Y., and Spitz, L.K. "Analytical Approach to Marketing Decisions in Health-Care Organizations." *Operations Research* 24 (September-October 1976) pp. 973-990.

15. Kotler, P. *Marketing Management,* 3d ed. Englewood Cliffs, N.J.: Prentice-Hall, 1976.

16. Levitt, T. "Marketing Myopia." *Harvard Business Review* 53 (September-October 1975) p. 26 et seq.

17. Levitt, T. "Marketing When Things Change." *Harvard Business Review* 55 (November-December 1977) pp. 107-113.

18. Berkowitz, E.N., and Flexner, W.A. "The Marketing Audit: A Tool for Health Service Organizations." *Health Care Management Review* 3 (Fall 1978) pp. 51-58.

19. Reprinted by permission of the *Harvard Business Review*. Excerpt from "Marketing Myopia" by Theodore Levitt (September-October 1975). Copyright© 1975 by the President and Fellows of Harvard College; all rights reserved.

20. Reprinted by permission of the *Harvard Business Review*. Excerpt from "Marketing When Things Change" by Theodore Levitt (November-December 1977). Copyright© 1977 by the President and Fellows of Harvard College; all rights reserved.

21. Gilmore, F.F. "Strategic Planning's Threat to Small Business." *California Management Review* 9 (Winter 1966) pp. 43-50.

22. Hall, W.K. "SBUs: Hot New Topic in Management of Diversification." *Business Horizons* 21 (February 1978) pp. 17-25.

23. Feldstein, P.J., and Goddeeris, J. "Payment for Hospital Services: Objectives and Alternatives." *Health Care Management Review* 2 (Fall 1977) pp. 7-23.

24. Wacht, R.F., and Whitford, D.T. "A Goal Programming Model for Capital Investment Analysis in Nonprofit Hospitals." *Financial Management* 5 (Summer 1976) pp. 37-47.

25. Henderson, B.D. *The Experience Curve-Reviewed. IV. The Growth Share Matrix or Product Portfolio.* Boston: Boston Consulting Group, 1973.

26. Ledley, R.S.; Thiagarajan, T.R.; and Landau, T.P. "Medical Technology and Cost Containment: Two Applications of Operations Research." *Science* 202 (December 1, 1978) pp. 979-982.

27. Brook, R., et al. "Effectiveness of Inpatient Follow-up Care." *New England Journal of Medicine* 285 (December 30, 1971) pp. 1509-1514.

28. Etzioni, E. "Health as a Social Priority." In *Health Services: The Local Perspective. Proceedings of the Academy of Political Science,* edited by A.Levin, vol 32:3, 1977, pp. 8-14.

29. Ginzberg, E. "Health Services, Power Centers and Decision-Making Mechanisms." In *Doing Better and Feeling Worse,* edited by J.H. Knowles, Daedalus, vol. 106:1, 1977, pp. 203-213.

Section Two

Marketing: An Overview

Development of a market orientation is critical to successful strategic planning. Such an orientation in health care is an essential response to environmental change, particularly as competition increases. Yet, this change in orientation from "what we want the organization to produce" to "what the organization should produce given existing market conditions" may be the most difficult for health care managers to make.

The articles in this section have been organized with two objectives in mind: first, to provide the reader with an overview of the key concepts in marketing; and second, to explain some of the tools that can aid the manager in developing sound market-oriented strategies.

As the name implies, a market orientation begins with consumers, whose aggregate behaviors help to explain market behavior. But who are the consumers? Traditionally, physicians have been identified as the consumers of health care resources, but Flexner and Berkowitz provide an example in this section ("Marketing Research in Health Services Planning: A Model") of patient-consumers who do not have a physician but who have strong feelings about their own influence on the choice of health resources to use. The presence of multiple constituencies of nonprofit organizations was first described several years ago in an article by Benson P. Shapiro: "The typical private nonprofit organization. . .has two constituencies: clients to whom it provides goods and/or services, and donors from whom it receives resources."[1] Compare this description with McLaughlin's characterization in Section 1 of the pipers, payors, and dancers and note the generic aspects of all organizations having differing consumers.

In the present section, the article by Simon ("Marketing the Community Hospital: A Tool for the Beleaguered Administrator") suggests an even broader definition by including not only the physicians and patients as consumers but also employer or labor groups, government and regulatory agencies, and even the employees. A focus on employees as consumers is reinforced in an article in Section 5 by Hughes entitled "Can Marketing Help Recruit and Retain Nurses?" Also, the need to consider government and regulatory agencies as consumers is suggested in Mandel and Getson's article in Section 4 ("Mandated Long-Range Planning for Hospitals—Where Is It Going and Why?").

Another component of a market orientation is a review of the performance of one organization vis-a-vis others in the same market area. Simon describes this as "market profiling" ("know where you are coming from—or going to") in his article in this section. Because hospitals and other health care organizations provide similar services to the same target market, it is possible to assess their strengths and weaknesses in terms of market performance. Such an assessment can provide significant input into strategic decisions for the organization.

One example of this, at the community-wide level, is provided by Milch and Martinelli ("Community Health Markets: A Portfolio Perspective"). In this article, the authors apply a widely used business approach—product portfolio analysis—to map the performance of 17 hospitals in terms of market growth rate and market share. Had the data been available, this same type of analysis could have been conducted at the level of specific services (e.g., obstetrics, emergency room, subspecialty surgery) to provide strategic information regarding the comparative market performance of each organization's service mix. Undertaking this type of analysis within the organization for the entire portfolio of services is the more common use of the approach.

In considering the outcome of a product portfolio analysis, readers should reflect on what it would mean to overall strategy to find that several services were performing as "dogs." Are you prepared to consider the possibility of eliminating specific services because of poor market performance? If not, what are the real and opportunity costs of continuing to allocate scarce resources to poor performers? Note the area of financial management entering into the picture. Readers might also want to compare product portfolio analysis with the analysis of strategic business units described in Milch's article in Section 1.

Focus on the product mix is only one of four areas that managers have available for developing marketing strategies. Simon's article in this section identifies the other three areas—price, promotion, and distribution—in his discussion of strategies that hospital administrators might consider. And the two articles by Berkowitz and Flexner in this section show that consideration of marketing mix strategies occurs only after completion of a market analysis and an assessment of the organization's strengths and weaknesses.

At this point, many readers may be concerned about how to organize and where to obtain the information necessary to assess adequately an organization's total marketing mix. The last three articles in this section provide a framework for addressing this concern.

As one begins the transition to a market orientation, a marketing audit may be an extremely useful management tool. Berkowitz and Flexner ("The Marketing Audit: A Tool for Health Service Organizations") describe the audit as an early marketing inquiry aimed at examining the entire scope of the organization's activities. Much of the information required for a full-scale audit may already be available in the organization. To complete the audit, it may be necessary, however, to go to external sources (e.g., HSAs, PSROs, governmental agencies) or to collect the information directly from primary sources.

The importance of searching for information that has already been collected is emphasized by Clarke and Shyavitz ("A Guide to Marketing Information and Market Research"—Reading 7). They point out that upon adopting a market orientation, many health care managers often hire consultants to perform health-related marketing research to identify and solve management problems. The folly in doing this, they note, is that not only might it be premature, but also the information that is really needed may already be present in the organization and simply require good detective work to locate. Other secondary sources of information external to the organization may also be found to provide the desired results. The authors also are careful to distinguish marketing information from market research, identifying the latter as requiring considerably greater sophistication to be undertaken effectively.

Regarding market research, Flexner and Berkowitz ("Marketing Research in Health Services Planning: A Model") begin where Clarke and Shyavitz end. Describing marketing research as the "organizational activity of systematically gathering, recording, and analyzing the information needed to make planning and implementation decisions," they develop a model that integrates research as a first step in the strategic planning process. Illustrating the model with field research, they identify the steps in research as, first, qualitative studies to identify the nature of the management problem, then quantitative studies to measure the extent and direction of the problem, and, finally, interpretation of the results in ways that can be incorporated into strategic planning decisions.

In summary, the market orientation required for effective strategic planning begins outside the organization with an assessment of the nature of consumer markets and their various subcomponents. From the external focus, one then turns inward to determine the organization's strengths and weaknesses and compares them with their competitors. Cutting across each stage of this process is an assessment of the variables that ultimately create the marketing mix strategies—product, price, promotion, and distribution. The glue that holds all of this together is the information-gathering activity engaged in by the organization. Without sound and thorough information responsive to management's needs, effective market-oriented strategies will be difficult, if not impossible, to achieve.

REFERENCES

1. Benson P. Shapiro, "Marketing for Nonprofit Organizations," *Harvard Business Review*, September-October 1973, p. 124.

4. Marketing the Community Hospital: A Tool for the Beleaguered Administrator

JAMES K. SIMON

Simon, James K. "Marketing the Community Hospital: A Tool for the Beleaguered Administrator." *Health Care Management Review*, Spring 1978.

Have you considered the possibility that marketing techniques may become necessary for the survival of an individual hospital? Competition has been a word very seldom, if ever, used in addressing the whole question of health care services. Yet, marketing the community hospital may well become the focus of legislation in the not-too-distant future. "We all need the health industry so very much; it's not an overstatement to say that our lives depend on a strong, vigorous, responsive health industry. . . .one possible way to control the seemingly uncontrollable health sector could be to treat it as a business and make it respond to the same marketplace influences as other American businesses and industry."[1]

The current change in attitude and perception of the health care industry is vividly underscored by the major increase in malpractice suits and the frequency with which patients seek legal courses of action against hospitals and physicians. It is suggested that these increased legal incidents are a result of change in the hospital image; the public feels negatively toward our current health care delivery system. Hospitals are not alone in this change of image; physicians too share a great part of it.

There are steps we must take to overcome this latest challenge. At the outset, it is important for us to admit candidly that we frequently use political pressure, inflation, labor unions, and so on, as crutches to explain why we are facing increasing regulation and health care costs. We have not done an adequate job in marketing our role, services, and needs to consumers.

While marketing for health services is a technique new to hospital administrators, administrators have the added challenge of marketing a negative experience: hospitalization and receipt of health services. A large group of the population feels that "services" to restore and maintain health have been oversold and are unnecessary and that the results of an individual's care will be the same with or without the introduction of hospital services. As far as the public is concerned, the checks and balances, which the health care industry states are maintained to monitor cost and quality, have not worked.

WHAT IS HOSPITAL MARKETING?

Marketing is the analysis, planning, implementation, and control of carefully formulated programs designed to bring about volunteer exchanges of values with target markets for the purpose of achieving organizational objectives. It relies heavily on designing the organization's services in terms of the target market's needs and desires and on using effective pricing, communication, and distribution to inform, motivate, and service the market.[2]

Some critical aspects for consideration in hospital marketing include the environment for the application of marketing activities, need-sensitive planning, consumer orientation, and competitive interests.

Hospital marketing is the development of an environment and organization from which effective concepts, planning, and implementation of well-coordinated and designed programs will occur. Intrinsic in this development is the understanding that such programs and activities are undertaken in response to need-sensitive studies or target populations (markets), have strong consumer orientation, and are competitive and well-publicized. Hospital marketing should provide for the development and analysis of data related to and in support of goals, objectives, and current and future roles. All marketing activities should bring about the desired exchange with the target markets. This approach to health services must be conceptual, organizational, and functional.[3]

Marketing Environment

The key to the successful use of marketing techniques is the hospital organizational environment. There are several basic considerations for modifying existing operating philosophies in the hospital that should be agreed upon before proceeding further into a marketing program. These assumptions are basic to the success of a program. They include a basic acceptance of the fact that the hospital field in general has not done everything possible to reduce health care costs. If administrators were to review objectively all practices within the hospital, they, more than anyone else, could successfully identify areas where further cost cutting is possible without affecting the quality of services.

Steps must be taken to gain the full support and commitment of the board, medical staff, administrative staff, and employees for a marketing program, because each will have an important role in its success. It is imperative that these people understand the intent, goals, objectives, and methods of marketing to be used and the rationale for such techniques. This commitment will be a keystone to marketing programs.

The practice of competing with area hospitals and health service agencies for a larger part of the marketplace must be accepted. There is no intention to propose cutthroat competition or unethical practices to achieve more patient involvement, but, unless there is open competition for this market, chances for survival or for maintaining all services that currently exist will be substantially lessened. Effective competition will control costs, keep operations more efficient, and allow for better fulfillment of community needs. Active competition must become both the style and the goal of a marketing program. Administrators must look at their patients as customers. This will not be unusual or difficult for many since, as with other industries, there is a product (service) and a reliance on others for use. Hospitals are similar to industry, and administrators need not feel uncomfortable in using proven industrial techniques to develop effectively an appropriate market for hospital services.

Staffing and Expertise

To obtain those skills necessary to launch this type of program, administrators might hire from industry a marketing specialist who has not only an excellent grasp of marketing techniques but also the imagination to provide adaptations needed for practical application in health care institutions. Such a specialist brings to the institution the planning, research, and motivational skill that, when properly channeled and modified, will provide the foundation for marketing programs.

If it is possible to secure such individuals and appropriate staff to assist them in their activities, a hospital can proceed in further development of its marketing venture. Hospitals not in the position to hire immediately a full-time staff specialist (which may well become an integral part of hospitals in the next five to ten years) may seek an alternative approach to initiating the program.

In general, the health care industry has not had the opportunity to cultivate the marketing knowledge and expertise applicable to health care. Volunteers— members of local industry with marketing expertise—have successfully functioned as key members of a marketing committee. Potentially, this approach provides administrators with an excellent introduction (without additional operating dollars) to the marketing of health services.

There are many other approaches available, but all methods should include the involvement of appropriate marketing expertise from the industrial sector.

CONSUMERS—WHO ARE THEY?

In the past, physicians were considered the primary consumers of health services. They admitted and discharged patients and wrote the orders for various tests. While this continues to be true, there are at least five distinct consumer groups identified for marketing purposes: (1) patients, (2) physicians, (3) employer or union groups, (4) government and regulatory agencies, and (5) employees.

Patients

Consumers are rapidly assuming much greater responsibility and interest in their own health care. Who is providing it? Why is it necessary? How much will it cost? Many consumers are covered by an insurance program and share no direct responsibility for the costs involved in their care. Today, however, these same patients frequently say, "The cost is too high; the charges are unreasonable for the services rendered."

Consumers, because of their improved health care "education," augmented by media coverage of various aspects of health care delivery, are now more sensitive to what happens to them when they enter a facility as a patient. Yet the consumer is still inadequately informed. Consumer education must be one of the first targets of a marketing, or competitive, health care program. Marketing requires a look beyond the user group—those with whom contact is maintained as they use health services—to include those potential users of services who will then increase the market share.

Physicians

Currently, physicians still retain a major position in managing and controlling the types of care rendered by hospitals to patients. They can control the flow of patient activities to or from a facility, private laboratory, or other health care services, thereby directly affecting the use of services within the hospital. They are also the prime source of overutilization of services and may extend the length of stay for tests or care that might be accomplished on an outpatient basis. Physicians may order a battery of laboratory tests, all of which might not be necessary or pertinent to the immediate problem facing the patient.

In the past, these particular areas of overutilization were not considered negative by the administrator but rather were considered as additional sources of revenue to assist in the constant struggle to maintain a financially viable institution and to keep pace with the requirements for new services and equipment. However, now these activities can be the source of penalties in reimbursement and in increased dealings with regulatory agencies.

Physicians are the prime sources of information (or lack of it) for the patient consumer. Physicians also play a key role in the expansion of hospital medical staff. The larger the staff, the broader the base for referrals to the hospital for both inpatient and outpatient services. Physicians as consumers are probably the most complex of the five consumer groups. They can control and maintain a hospital's position in the health care market and ensure the adequate use of existing health services and facilities. Much consideration must be given to physicians in the development of a marketing program.

Employers and Labor Unions

In the past, employers or labor unions have not necessarily been of concern to individual hospitals or administrators. Hospitals have always been recipients of reimbursement for insurance paid for by either the employer or labor union for services rendered. Now, however, these same groups are expressing concerns similar to those voiced by the public about the high cost of health, duplication of services, need for greater accessibility and less waiting time, and even more services. Growing interest in health maintenance organizations (HMOs), freestanding health centers to provide services on a more timely and less costly basis, and surgical centers now being developed to provide one-day outpatient surgery reflect the employer-labor union's growing dissatisfaction and changing requirements. Industry is not only becoming aware of its growing liability in health premiums for employees but is suggesting that perhaps they can do it better for less. Industry might assume a major role in providing health services to its own population. This group can no longer be considered just the payer of insurance premiums but must be dealt with as consumers or as potential competitors.

Governmental and Regulatory Agencies

Every hospital administrator is becoming critically aware of the increasing number of regulatory agencies influencing day-to-day life. Government influence on hospital operating activities is growing. Greater restrictions are being placed on institutional and managerial decision making. Of all the target groups, agencies have the greatest potential for bringing about major and potentially disastrous changes to the health care system.

As discussion of national health insurance, socialized medicine, and price control for health services increases, it becomes obvious that the political environment has seized health care cost as a "safe" issue to add to any campaign for gaining public support. Much time is spent seeking ways of retaliating rather than initiating ways to establish hospitals as positive and innovative marketers in this political arena.

Hospitals are not the first to be subject to the growing controls of government. The experiences, both good and bad, of other industries should be used to develop a baseline of knowledge from which a marketing program can be developed for this consumer group.

Employees

Employees are a critical part of the entire marketing program. No one wishes to lose the existing market, and maintaining it becomes a strong responsibility of the hospital staff. The attitudes and satisfaction of employees with their own jobs are important in passing on to patients warmth, interest, concern, and quality of service. It is imperative that employee relations programs not be overlooked, since they and their members compose one of the prime consumer groups. This group is the foundation, the implementor, and the primary public image to patients entering the hospital.

ELEMENTS IN HOSPITAL MARKETING

Market Profile:
Know Where You Are Coming From—or Going To

A marketing profile helps identify strengths and weaknesses in services, programs, and population draw and determines what programs should be developed or perhaps phased out. The profile identifies trends in specific areas, such as why services are not currently being used by consumers or, if being used, why these services are being obtained at other facilities and locations. This in turn is the foundation for developing marketing program goals.

Essential to any hospital administrator considering a marketing program is the recognition of the current status of the institution. Research should reveal how the hospital is perceived by competitors, the communities served, and health care regulatory agencies.

Potential Markets

Actual and potential markets must be clearly identified. One approach that might be taken in this initial endeavor is a well-designed questionnaire, geared to meet specific areas of interest. In the development of the initial market profile, West Jersey Hospital produced a number of questionnaires that were used to gather specific data about the potential marketplace.[4] Consumers, physicians, and area hospitals were surveyed with a variety of questions about health care practices, needs, and current marketing activities.

Preprofile plans can be affected by the thrust of population trends and the identification of attitudes expressed by patients, physicians, or area hospitals. Perhaps earlier planning will become invalid because of a newly developed, more comprehensive, and consumer-oriented data base.

The Changing Environment

Existing operating and planning practices will need to be modified in a changing health services environment. Specifically, this refers to the determination of when a new or expanded program should be considered as part of a health provider's role or responsibility. Frequently, motivations for new services, programs, equipment, or expansion of existing activities come from influential physicians, other political interests, or restricted donations. Motivation for new programs should be based on sound market research identifying need, potential market, and financial viability, not emotional enthusiasm. The program itself may not be a money-maker but may generate other avenues of revenue that may bring about a continued and longer-term benefit to the total institution.

Research for Effective Marketing

Occasionally, an industry will maintain a product line that is considered a "loser." The item is maintained because the ripple effect may provide substantial or offsetting revenue and it permits the industry to compete while providing an appropriate bottom line for the stockholders and board. As with industry, hospitals have programs that appear superficially to be a liability to the organization but in fact add revenue and utilization potential to other services within the total structure. The emergency room in many instances does not generate sufficient bottom-line revenues to offset its own operating expense. However, it *does,* through its emergency admissions and use of supportive diagnostic service, provide substantial revenue that influences the hospital balance sheet. An effective marketing program must be based on marketing research and the control of emotional enthusiasm for new programs.

The evaluation of marketing research is critical and must be carried out in an objective manner, eliminating to the highest degree possible the influence of those persons who have developed an "empire" and who might resist change for the purpose of retaining services that are no longer viable or properly utilized. Commitment to the program on the part of all staff, including medical, will give an additional opportunity for success.

Channels of communication with consumers are initially opened by means of questionnaires, site visits, public or private meetings, informational mailings or advertising, or mall intercept (which offers an opportunity to meet the community in a one-to-one encounter in shopping centers). Means of maintaining these open channels of communication and dialogue should be considered. These sources of data help test and update the changing requirements of the market area and evaluate the program's effectiveness in meeting consumer needs.

Strategic Planning

Most hospitals today, as in the past, plan on a brush-fire or crisis-oriented basis. In the past, planning for tomorrow today was relatively effective in dealing with the hospital's development and survival, but now it is a hazardous style of administration. Marketing endeavors undertaken in the absence of good strategic planning are ineffective.

Strategic planning provides the foundation from which a hospital might effectively pursue major elements of hospital marketing activities. Hospitals should develop a strategic planning function, patterned after the industrial approach, to establish similar planning activities. This will bring order to the development of programs and services and will permit all facets of the organization to pursue logical avenues of development in anticipation of program implementation. This type of planning should also permit a hospital to approach any planning objective fully aware of its impact, both positive and negative, on the overall objectives of the hospital. By so doing, emotional selection of planning programs or hospital objectives will be eliminated.

A strategic planning function has two primary components: planning and implementation. The planning component should become the responsibility of specified individuals, including those with marketing expertise, to work on ideas of programs to be implemented six months to one year or more ahead. It would be their responsibility to worry about the latter part of 1978, the year 1979, and beyond. They should be planning and developing those programs that are being considered for years to come, not for the immediate needs of an institution.

The implementation component should be composed of people with project expertise who work with a previously approved program preparing all facets so that the program can be properly turned over to operating staff to become an effective part of the hospital's operation. This type of strategic planning will reduce crises, increase operating effectiveness, and eliminate for the most part the "do-overs" caused by poor or nonexistent planning. When the strategic planning function has become entrenched as an integral part of the marketing foundation, the remaining elements of hospital market activities should be explored and developed.

External Planning Priorities

A look at the current and projected considerations of various state, local, and federal planning agencies and their views toward regulations and utilization should supplement the marketing profile. This may be essential in terms of both immediate and long-range planning.

In developing a program of marketing services, planning priorities established by external influences must be included, that is, political, governmental, and regulatory groups whose actions can and do influence a hospital's role and services. Preventive health care, HMOs, and new legislation to provide insurance coverage for the alcoholic patient are but a few key examples of the trends and priorities that must be considered in the development of a marketing plan.

The influence of newly emerging state and local health planning agencies (HSAs) cannot be understated. Because of their legislative planning authority, it is essential to consider, in both immediate and long-range planning, their views on planning of services, regulations, and program utilization. For example, if it is the intent of the planning agency to bring about more effective use of obstetrical services, then the agency may establish arbitrary baselines for utilization. Those facilities that fall below this baseline are pressured to phase out obstetrical services. If in a specific planning area a number of obstetrical services, all operating below effective utilization and all equally staffed, equipped, and accessible exist, then reducing the number of units (thereby increasing the use in remaining facilities) is desirable.

Trends of this nature are now a reality, and an institution should carefully evaluate the thrusts of such agencies and take steps to expand the market share. Individual services should be maintained at a level that will promote less cost, effective use, and quality of service in order to demonstrate the need for their continuing role in the marketplace.

Success in this endeavor will require sound marketing and a willingness to develop a plan based on community needs and projected service requirements. Even if the prospects for such agency activities appear to be in the future, the time to develop the market strategies is now. Identify what the targets may be for these planning groups and work toward those goals, expanding a market share. This can be easily undertaken by securing from state, local, or federal planning agencies the various studies and long-range programs they have established in order to determine how the hospital fits into their larger scheme.

MARKETING STRATEGIES

Pricing Practices

The pricing practice in hospitals is probably one of the most complex and yet most unimaginative areas of administration. It is one area that will require the hospital's concentrated focus in entering a strong marketing program. More competitive pricing can mean less cost for the same quality of services while maintaining financial viability.

At present, most hospitals, although capable of sophisticated pricing practices, rely more on a standard markup based on a rationale of unknown origin. Or their pricing practices are based on the relationship of charges or rates compared with the hospital down the street. Frequently, the basis for this practice is confirmed by a telephone call or survey to ensure similar charges for a specific treatment or service.

Pricing Structure

A pricing structure that prevents criticism of one hospital for being out of line with its peers must be developed. An objective review of charges for services, including all the direct and indirect expenses that may be related to a specific cost center, will usually demonstrate little relationship to the actual cost of providing and maintaining these services. It is not unusual to find charges marked up in excess of 100 percent on diagnostic services, such as electrocardiographs. The purported reasons are that it is necessary to profit in this service to offset a losing department or that all area hospitals charge the same. Such a situation offers an excellent opportunity to reevaluate pricing and marketing practices, to develop a means of providing the services at a lesser cost to the public, and to become more competitive in the marketplace.

The financial and management expertise of an institution should carefully evaluate the pricing structures, noting how they relate to the cost of the specific services being rendered. The impact of developing a pricing structure more closely related to the actual cost of providing a service should be evaluated.

The requirements for financial viability cannot be overlooked. However, a more imaginative approach can be developed to enhance a marketing position. Hospitals are challenged to expose their pricing activities to a marketing specialist who has expertise in this area, with the expressed charge that the hospitals must remain financially viable and that they remain in a more competitive position. An objective evaluation from an outside expert might significantly alter the pricing practices now in use.

Competitive Pricing Policy

The greatest limitation facing hospitals in developing a well-formulated competitive pricing policy may be the third party payers. Currently, reimbursement formulas serve to penalize a hospital when cost or pricing reductions are implemented. Such cost savings would not be realized in consumers' insurance premiums. A reduction in cost to the public can be negatively received if the public feels that such actions indicate a "cut-rate" pricing of services, reflecting poorer quality. Yet despite limitations encountered when revising a pricing policy, current practices must be altered. Changes must be skillfully marketed to achieve desired goals.

Richard J. Ferris, president and chief executive officer of United Airlines, said recently of price structuring:

> For setting prices, the system should move away from artificial constraints and depend more heavily on the realities of the marketplace. Market-oriented pricing would allow carriers to more closely match prices and costs. It would permit them to earn a fair return. To protect the consumer from unreasonably high fares as controls on price are relaxed, more reliance should be placed on competition. . . .[5]

Substitute "hospitals and costs" for "carriers and fares" and Ferris's words offer much wisdom for the health care industry. Progress in pricing will be necessary for future survival in the changing marketplace. It will also put hospitals in a stronger position to deal with growing external criticism of management practices.

Advertising

Despite the present controversy, advertising has been practiced by hospitals for many years under the headings of public relations, press releases, and community relations. This kind of publicity should now be expanded not only to assist in identification of services provided but also to function as an educational and motivational tool. Such a tool should awaken the public to realities facing the health care industry today while still attracting them to the available services. Some hospitals, specifically one in Las Vegas, Nevada, have aggressively advertised. Although there have been some cries of unethical practice and dollar wasting, at first indication these programs have been successful in improving utilization.[6] If properly and ethically applied, advertising will become a strong tool for the health care industry in publicizing its services to consumers.

Naturally, the goal of such advertising efforts—lower costs—may restrict an effective approach. However, the per capita cost of media advertising may compare favorably with direct mailing charges, which could prove to be prohibitive when the target audience is large. Through the use of standard media, information about new services as well as cost-saving activities can be announced. This same vehicle can identify health education activities to the public and suggest the benefits of preventive medicine.

Using appropriate advertising methods, the establishment of an identification of the hospital should be one of the marketing goals. West Jersey Hospital has advertised a unique, toll-free telephone number to bring public attention to the availability of prenatal clinics maintained for those who do not have the opportunity or the motivation to seek out their own private physician. The clinics include four outreach satellite clinics and one hospital-based clinic and have been identified with a single, easy-to-remember telephone number, although some are located 15 miles apart. Television has carried the information as a public service.

There are, of course, many ways to use advertising acceptably to create this identification. Another technique has been the publication of a directory of health services, which clearly identifies various hospitals and health agencies, the type of service they provide, room rate structures, accreditations, and all other characteristics that might provide patients a better understanding of the facility, service, or agency.[7] Hospitals need not wait for the press to pick up the story; rather, they should aggressively use marketing expertise to develop ways to introduce their own story to the press. It may be costly, but it may also be less of an expenditure and more effective than current means of providing consumer education, such as mailings.

Competition

Generally, a position of noncompetition with fellow hospitals and health agencies has been embraced; competition is unfamiliar to hospital administrators. Competition does not imply an intent to alienate area hospitals or agencies or to try to drive them out of business. However, hospitals and agencies must begin to sharpen their management styles and internal practices to withstand effectively any infringement by an outside agency.

Intelligence Network

Most hospitals probably are not aware of the potential market lost ("the leakage" of patients) from their service area to other facilities. A hospital needs a good "intelligence network" to understand what services are being used and where. This information should be developed from the marketing profile, as it will underline an important focus of future efforts in marketing. Are the programs (i.e., pickup services, convenient service hours, accessible neighborhood centers for diagnostic care) geared to the convenience of the patient? Are they similar to what patients may be receiving through other facilities?

The long- and short-range plans of other area health facilities, the types of service they plan to provide or continue to provide, and their expansion plans should be noted. It is not essential or wise to copy everything that another area health facility or provider offers, but administrators should at least know what is available so that facilities and services can be planned more effectively.

If the existence or survival of a service between several hospitals is in question, it would be in the administrator's best interest to develop procedures to provide better service at lower cost. Consumers—patients, physicians, or employers—will be attracted to such an institution. In effect, administrators will be competing to retain or establish that specific service.

It is appropriate to meet with area administrators to discuss the whole question of marketing, competition, and intentions related to this new administrative philosophy. Any future concerns or disagreements that arise out of a misunderstanding of goals may be offset by such a meeting.

Meeting the Competition

Meeting the competition requires the strengthening of strong areas of services while enhancing and developing those that are weak. Not only cost, but quality, accessibility, available resources, and existing referral patterns play a role in competition effectiveness. One of the hospital's greatest assets will be the availability and understanding of what can be offered and at what price and quality to consumers.

Hospitals must be more innovative and quicker to respond to the needs of the community to achieve service goals before other agencies have an opportunity to do so. Marketing expertise made available to hospitals can provide sound guidance in an approach toward this competitive mode. If candidly discussed with peers and professionally carried out in the best interests of consumers *and* the hospital, marketing becomes a very effective tool in upgrading the quality of services while reducing underutilized ones. This results in lower health care costs for services to the community.

Consumer Information

The complexity of health care systems and poorly informed consumers are two major roadblocks that must be overcome.

> The missing condition in the medical care industry is surely not the absence of large numbers of sellers and buyers in most markets or for most types of care. Rather, if there is a missing condition, it is the absence of consumer information.[8]
> ...of all the societies on earth today, ours would seem to be the only one that could still inject competition into the provisions of health care, allow prices to respond to consumer demand, and maintain standards of quality care that reduce or even eliminate the risk of death or disability.[9]

The health market condition lacks not only consumer information but, perhaps even more significantly, provider information about its own market.

HOW CAN MARKETING WORK FOR THE HOSPITAL ADMINISTRATOR?

Although marketing practices will vary according to each institution's needs and experience, the following ideas provide a baseline for an initial or continuing application of hospital marketing techniques.

Marketing to Patients

Marketing to patients ranks next in importance to marketing to physicians. Meeting the needs of local communities is the primary purpose of health care facilities. Programs have been implemented by hospitals to improve their marketing potential.

Promoting Positive Consumer Reactions

One approach to increase marketing potential to consumers is the "courtesy discharge" that allows patients to be discharged without stopping at the business office. Ease of entry into the health care system—by outreach clinics, family health centers, or simply reduced waiting time resulting from effective internal procedures—promotes positive consumer reactions. Consumers feel more comfortable, more wanted, and more like customers.

Admission is critical to the marketing image. Preadmission forms, including letters notifying patients of their scheduled admission and assuring them of the hospital's availability to answer any questions or provide any support prior to admission, can be very reassuring. Often, patients feel a negative reception on their first contact with hospitals. Hospitals should function in a positive manner to eliminate patients' concerns. Some hospitals have established advisory boards with a complement of members from the community to serve as a liaison in information sharing.

These same consumers influence politicians; politicians are in their current offices because the public voted them there. Identifying large voting blocks to work with in order to gain confidence and support can be a tremendously effective approach to attracting consumers and eliminating political barriers.

Coffee Klatch Approach

To further share information, auxiliary members' homes could be the sites of "coffee klatches" for which the auxiliary members extend invitations to residents of their neighborhoods for an informal discussion of health care in the hospital. Key members of the hospital staff could also attend to address informally the questions raised, to encourage greater participation in the ongoing activities of the hospital, and to seek support for the programs and ideas that will be in their best interest. Such approaches would serve to break down some of the barriers that currently exist between patient/consumer, hospitals, and health agencies.

So often singular comments in the media are taken as representative of the public's view. Political and governmental rulings purportedly reflect what is best for patients. The simple act of spending more time communicating with the direct recipient of services will produce more accurate information.

A variety of programs undertaken to determine patient/consumer reactions currently exist. Members of patient representative programs have been successful in collecting comments of patients receiving health care. Such programs also provide the opportunity to short-circuit any growing unhappiness or a patient's discontent with services, care, or personnel.

Consumer Health Education

The inpatient is a captive audience for closed-circuit television, which can be programmed for health education related to preventive health care, cost containment procedures and their effectiveness, energy conservation activities, or other information related to the impact of current regulations. To-be-admitted patients provide the hospital with an opportunity to publicize itself through preadmission handouts and flyers that fully inform patients of the services they will receive.

Outpatient services and activities can also be publicized through leaflets. The public can be made aware of ambulatory care and its availability without an inpatient stay.

Prime-Time Care Program

More should be done to generate activities that will reduce hospital charges. A program of "prime-time care" could reduce hospital charges by identifying times during the day or week when use levels are low. Patients would then be encouraged to use services during these hours at less cost than that charged during prime time. Because the hospital is underutilized at certain times, a cost benefit can accrue to the patients. Many of these services can be on an outpatient basis, so that direct out-of-pocket savings can be realized by a patient rather than by the insurance carrier. Attention should also be focused on the convenience of the hours that services are provided. Hospitals should be willing to innovate programs in the best interest of their customers, for example, earlier laboratory hours for tests to be performed before commuting to work, longer evening hours, or a larger scope of available services on weekends.

Target Markets

When marketing to patients, it is appropriate to be sensitive to "target market" individuals who, because of age, social standing, finances, or geography, may be considered underserved or excluded from the mainstream of health care. To this end, West Jersey Hospital has developed a proposal to provide a diagnostic screening program for senior citizens. The program is based on a similar service provided by a west coast hospital to offer senior citizens a battery of diagnostic tests on a prepaid arrangement. The cost to the subscriber represented only the cost of supplies (seven to ten dollars) per year. The program has been expanded to offer to this target population lunch or breakfast (depending on test schedule), along with a social setting providing health education services.

This proposal, which will be offered to a pilot group from a local community, has received enthusiastic support from the township officials. Program implementation is scheduled for early 1978 and a strong marketing campaign will alert both enrollees and the general public. Such a program offers preventive health services, responds to needed health education, and develops political support while enhancing the hospital's image.

Marketing must be a two-way street; the hospital must (1) be a good listener and (2) take responsive action where appropriate. The product must be packaged in such a way as to gain greater understanding of the public's requirements and to enhance the public's awareness of hospital goals, objectives, and problems. Efforts in this area may be difficult but not impossible. The consumer not currently requiring health services has little interest in discussing health care, whereas the hospitalized patient will show great interest. Therefore, marketing to the general public will require the best marketing skills.

By developing a warm, personal charisma and by demonstrating willingness to accept criticism while opening channels of communication, a hospital can develop its credibility and encourage the patient/consumer toward advocacy of today's services and tomorrow's programs.

Marketing to Physicians

In marketing to physicians as consumers, it is imperative to use effectively the marketing profile explained earlier and to further obtain information concerning the characteristics of each individual physician's practice. One method of achieving this goal is to establish a program of medical technology forecasting, identifying how physicians currently utilize services. It is necessary to know what patterns of care they predict will change in both their practices and hospitals in the foreseeable future as well as what type of changes are most desirable from the physician's perspective.

Categorizing Physician Needs

Records on patient activities can establish a trend of hospital use by individual physicians. Admissions can be categorized—i.e., those requiring surgery, class of admission (emergency, urgent, or elective)—and assessed at six-month intervals. The information can be graphed and used to project by month the type of utilization historically practiced by specific physicians. The same type of trends can be graphed by disease category to help develop a correlation of disease by medical specialty and by frequency to assist in projecting service and physician recruitment requirements. All questionnaire and medical forecasting data can become a component of the marketing profile, to be continuously updated through hospital records and physician input.

The directions to be taken as a result of these findings will reinforce the necessity of commitment on the part of the medical staff to this new approach to planning, particularly if such activities involve the hospital directly in medical or physician recruitment activities.

Workshops, Discussions

Workshops or retreats should be initiated or continued and should include all key members of medical staff, board, and administration. Such workshops or programs, held in a quiet location where interruptions will be limited, encourage candid discussion about projected programs, needs, and requirements as seen by physicians, the board, and management. Through this type of dialogue, one would hope to bring about a mutual understanding and willingness to support the marketing approach, particularly when it begins to identify programs that might not be totally comfortable for the medical staff. The discussions might include suggestions for prepaid activities such as the HMO, programs for executive physicians, and extension of the hospital's employee health service to provide similar programs to small industry in the area.

Another critical role that physicians play as consumers is in the recruitment of new staff. Frequently, additions to hospital staff offer limited extension into the marketplace because they are members of existing practices. Physicians who start new practices are in a better position to attract new clientele to the hospital. The medical staff heavily influences the recruitment of new physicians. This can present a critical problem if the medical staff feel that facilities and services are already overcrowded or that there is not an adequate market to support new practices and that bringing in a physician without new practice threatens to reduce their own financial capabilities. Nevertheless, in the longer run of the marketing program, one of the specific objectives should be the development of a medical staff that will use facilities effectively while supporting recruitment of additional medical expertise.

Marketing to Employers

Marketing to employers is an activity new to most hospitals. It requires identification of appropriate employers to reach into the community. Patients' origins, which can be used to identify local employers, are undoubtedly already available in many hospital records.

Here, as with the consuming public, a strong program of education and involvement in hospital activities will be appropriate and can be accomplished through industrial dinner meetings to which the key members of industry or employer groups are invited. Discussions may center on the problems of the health industry and its impact on the employer and may culminate in joint approaches to be undertaken for improvement. This same group can be an excellent focus for a marketing program providing for executive health physicals, executive spouses' physicals, and employee health services. Attractive packages can offer preventive diagnostic services on a prepaid or fee-for-service per capita basis.

These programs should try to reach those not presently covered by third party insurers. If health premiums continue to rise, some industries will seek to provide their own health care for their personnel and will do it at a lesser cost. The hospital industry should seek out a means of offering services that will be equally comprehensive but less costly to industry, thereby keeping them out of the practice of health care.

Marketing to Governmental Groups and Regulatory Agencies

Governmental groups and regulatory agencies might best be approached through their primary source of strength: the communities they serve. If, through other marketing activities, a hospital's image is changed, the hard line toward health providers today will soften. Hospitals must seize a leadership role and present to politicians and regulatory agencies a more effective program for curtailing health care cost. Such a program will have to demonstrate a strict and disciplined regimen for hospitals if it is to be accepted by these agencies. No matter how strict a program might be, if it is in the hands and leadership of the health care professionals, it will be a more effective, prudent, and successful program than if left to the governmental agencies to administer.

The hospital image to date is one of: *no*, it cannot be done; *no*, it will affect the quality of health care; and *no*, you don't understand our problems. The response has been obvious in view of the increased regulations in health services. An aggressively more positive and objective approach controlled by health facilities is more desirable than the head butting that is resulting in less effective programs with greater governmental control.

All marketing activities should be packaged in a marketing program addressed to the governmental and regulatory sector. With an improved image and the support of consumer groups, with cost stabilized or reduced through competitive activities, and with the development of sound factual planning decisions, the administrators of the health care industry can participate in the formulation of health care regulations as consultants rather than adversaries. All these actions may take hospital administrators closer to a point where they can again manage their own industry.

Marketing to Third Party Insurance Carriers

Recently, a number of third party insurance companies have been joining the bandwagon condemning hospitals and high costs. They have sought public support by obtaining a rate increase for their specific programs or by urging the public to buy their insurance to protect themselves against the overwhelmingly high cost of health care services. This may be particularly hard to accept when, on a day-to-day basis hospitals are being affected by the shortcomings of reimbursement programs. When billed, the patients themselves become aware that the policy they thought to be totally effective turns out to provide less than adequate coverage.

The third party payer market should be approached more constructively. Hospitals might seek jointly with third party payers new and innovative programs that will assist them in a reduction of their pay-out cost to the hospitals and patients while at the same time providing a broader coverage. A pilot study was successfully carried out in a Connecticut hospital with a third party insurer paying for all outpatient services over a four-month period, during which all services and activities were well controlled and monitored.[10] Savings of $150,000 were projected for the insurer under this new program. Yet today the number of insurance carriers that will pay for all outpatient services without deductibles is severely limited. In every institution, patients are occupying beds because of insurance coverage that limits benefits to inpatient care rather than out-of-hospital services.

This is only one of the critical issues to be addressed with the third party payer market. It is important to develop with insurance carriers a program of incentives. At present, cost containment programs and cost reduction efforts on the part of hospitals result, in most cases, in a reimbursement penalty. This holds true for consumers, who receive no visible benefit for prudent use of health services (i.e., greater use of preventive rather than curative services). Participation in innovative programs that will be mutually beneficial to insurance carrier, hospital, and patient alike should be the goal for all concerned.

Marketing in the Multihospital Setting

The marketing profile identifies trends in specific areas, such as why services are not currently being used by the consumer or, if being used, why these services are being obtained at other facilities and locations. This in turn is the foundation for developing marketing program goals.

The multihospital system provides a sound base for the expansion or development of new services to meet identified market needs in specific areas. The scope of services can be equally as great in any of the operating divisions of a multihospital. One multihospital system, operating three geographically separate divisions within the same county, has as its smallest component a 100-bed setting and as its largest a 300-bed setting, with the total bed complement exceeding 600. The 100-bed facility is able to provide the services and expertise of a 600-bed hospital. Facilities in three separate communities in the county permit the opportunity to provide acute and outpatient services to a much broader geographic area, creating a greater market for services.

If a hospital is to survive, it is essential that it respond to changing needs, be competitive in a variety of markets, and be identified with innovative, quality, and effective customer services. Multihospital or shared-services arrangements offer each of these elements of survival as a key product of their systems. Legislation currently exists and is being implemented by local health system agencies or planning agencies to identify as one of their goals the encouragement of multihospital and shared-system arrangements. It is urged that, in the development of a marketing profile and the establishment of the goals and objectives for a particular institution, consideration for the development of some type of multihospital or shared-service arrangement be included in both the marketing program and the long-range goals of the institution.

The multihospital system, whether proprietary or nonprofit, offers the potential for greater financial viability and growth during coming years when cost containment, regulation, and greater government control appear to be of greater consequence.

In June 1977, while addressing the American Medical Association, Joseph A. Califano, Jr., secretary of HEW, stated:

> Doctors, hospitals, pharmaceutical companies, nursing home operators, all the inhabitants of this noncompetitive, freespending, third payer world, act exactly as the incentives motivate them to act: conscious of quality, insensitive to cost.[11]

THE HOSPITAL'S ROLE IN THE MARKETPLACE

It is not a question of *if* but *when* hospitals and administrators will start to develop an effective competitive style to enhance the market for service and reestablish self-regulation. The time has come truly to consider health care as an industry, subject to many of the same influences, restraints, and consumer requirements. The public and consumers see hospitals fulfilling this role. Therefore, it would appear an appropriate time to learn how to apply new techniques to enhance hospital stability and responsiveness.

With the firm conviction of success for hospitals venturing into this new area of health services, there exists the potential for marketing to become one of the greatest assets to administrators in the development of their hospital's role in the provision of health services.

It is natural to anticipate that hospitals will not meet with success each and every time they experiment in this new area of endeavor. But the health industry needs a new image and improved credibility; marketing will help find the way.

The opportunity for change is present. Proper response can successfully influence the future of health care. Although the task is made complex by the current image and multiple consumers of services, as with other challenges faced by hospitals and health care over the years, a positive, constructive, and imaginative effort can achieve the revised goals. These goals encompass the adaptation and implementation of marketing strategies, a comprehensive information system for consumers, and a new look at competition as an alternative to total dominance through regulation.

REFERENCES

1. Pertschuk, M. "Not at Any Price." Remarks delivered at a conference on Competition in the Health Care Sector, sponsored by the FTC Bureau of Economics, Washington, D.C., June 1977.

2. Kotler, P. "The Concept of Marketing," *Marketing for Nonprofit Organizations.* Englewood Cliffs, N.J.: Prentice Hall, 1975, p. 5.

3. Ryan, W.T. "Marketing: Scope and Meaning." *Principles of Marketing, Learning Systems Company.* Homewood, Ill.: Richard D. Irwin, Inc., 1976, p. 1.

4. Simon, J.K. "A Community Hospital Looks at the Marketing Techniques for Hospital Services: A Time for Change?" Thesis prepared for the American College of Hospital Administrators, Chicago, Illinois, January 15, 1976.

5. Ferris, R. J. Paper on deregulation of the airline industry presented to the Wings Club, New York, March 16, 1977. United Airlines, Chicago, Illinois, p. 6

6. Seaver, D.J. "Hospital Revises Role, Reaches Out to Cultivate and Capture Markets." *Hospitals* 51 (Insert, June 1, 1977) p. 63.

7. "A Consumer's Guide to Connecticut Hospitals." A publication by the Connecticut Citizen Action Group and the Connecticut Citizen Research Group with the assistance of the Connecticut Hospital Association, 1973. p. 1.91.

8. Pauly, M. "Is Medical Care Different?" Paper delivered at a conference on Competition in the Health Care Sector, sponsored by the FTC Bureau of Economics, Washington, D.C., June 1977.

9. Pertschuk. "Not at Any Price."

10. Sager, T.K. "The Blue Cross Pilot Project—Danbury Hospital." Report submitted to George Washington University, School of Government and Business Administration, September 1973.

11. Califano, J.A., secretary of Health, Education and Welfare. Remarks delivered to the American Medical Association, San Francisco, June 19, 1977.

SUGGESTED READING

Rathmell, J.M. "Marketing Health Care Services." In *Marketing in the Service Sector.* Cambridge, Mass.: Winthrop Publishers, Inc., 1974, pp. 169-178.

5. Community Health Markets: A Portfolio Perspective

ROBERT AUSTIN MILCH and PATRICK A. MARTINELLI

Milch, Robert A., and Martinelli, Patrick A. "Community Health Markets: A Portfolio Perspective." *Health Care Management Review,* Fall 1978.

The decade of the 1970s has witnessed a major intensification of the emotionally charged and highly polarized public policy debate on health care that has been waged more or less constantly since Theodore Roosevelt first politicized the issue of national health insurance during his Bull Moose campaign of 1912. Rhetoric and reasoned argument have continued ever since to point to at least five areas of major concern, now escalated to "crisis" proportions: (1) cost (and efficiency); (2) quality; (3) distribution; (4) access (or equity); and (5) effectiveness (or outcome) of medical and hospital care, especially hospital care.

Unfortunately, much of the argumentation and many of the public policy solutions which have been offered have tended to be couched in ideological and normative contexts. Substantially less attention has been paid to practical ways and means that might be implemented[1] to redress areas of justifiable concern and to introduce needed changes without necessarily dismantling all that is admittedly good with the current "pluralistic nonsystem."

A failure to recognize the realities of a market system (however imperfect) in health care has itself done much to perpetuate the various problems that generally have been identified. As far as voluntary hospitals in particular are concerned, a portfolio approach, comparable to that which is finding widespread use in industry, can provide a simple and practical analytical base for rational strategic planning by both individual hospitals and regional health planners. (Beginning July 1, 1974, Maryland law authorized the Health Services Cost Review Commission [HSCRC] "to certify that total costs are reasonably related to total services offered, that aggregate rates are set in reasonable relationship to aggregate costs, and that rates are set equitably without undue discrimination.")[2] The market performance of acute care voluntary hospitals in Baltimore, Maryland, can illustrate the applicability of the portfolio concept.

VOLUNTARY HOSPITALS AS ECONOMIC INSTITUTIONS

Whatever else acute-care not-for-profit hospitals may be, they are by almost any measure large, growing, and highly competitive entrepreneurial enterprises. In short, they are businesses—competing just like any other business for land, labor, capital, and, ultimately, power and prestige in both geographic and self-defined markets. Individual hospital firms compete for professional staff, for patients, and for increasing proportions of the "health care dollar" made available through average or reasonable cost-reimbursement mechanisms (whether rate setting is retroactive or, as in Maryland, prospective) and evermore comprehensive third party insurance coverage.

Hospitals also vie for the voluntary and donative services of financially and politically influential members of their local communities. Further, except for the fact that voluntary hospitals are exempt from federal income taxation (and certain real and personal property taxes at the state level) by virtue of the scientific, educational, and charitable provisions of Section 501 (c) (3) of the Internal Revenue Code, even the accounting treatment of revenues, expenses, and funds in voluntary hospitals is in substance identical to that in ordinary business corporations.

For purposes of analysis, voluntary hospitals in any given regional or local (geographic) market can be viewed as a group or *portfolio* of organizations that share more or less common situational and behavioral characteristics (common product-market segments) but compete with one another for sales or market growth, market share, and, in the final analysis, profitability. As first conceptualized by the Boston Consulting Group,[3, 4] commercial firms (and, as will be demonstrated, voluntary hospitals) can easily be classified further into at least four segments when both market share (or cash generation capacity) and market growth rate (or cash use rate) are considered jointly. In any product-market segment, there are firms that:[5]

1. grow rapidly and are market leaders (Stars)—high market growth/high market share firms that both use and generate large amounts of cash;
2. grow rapidly but are market followers (Wildcats or Question Marks)—high growth/low share firms that have high cash needs because of their growth rates but are able to generate only low amounts of cash because their market share is low;
3. grow slowly but are market leaders (Cash Cows)—low growth/high share firms that have dominant market positions and therefore generate large amounts of cash but use little cash because of their low growth; and firms that
4. grow slowly and are market followers (Dogs)—low growth/low share firms that both generate and use little cash.

THE BALTIMORE HOSPITAL PORTFOLIO

In the preceding context, three assumptions were made in an effort to segment the portfolio of voluntary not-for-profit hospitals within the city limits of Baltimore, Maryland, on the basis of historical market performance:

1. that the gross patient service revenues of a voluntary hospital (unadjusted for discounts, contractual and administrative allowances, and uncollectible accounts) are a reasonable monetary proxy for the *aggregate market demand* for that hospital's care and services in any given year;
2. that a meaningful *real market growth rate* can be estimated by computing the rate of growth in gross patient service revenues of any hospital, expressed in terms of constant dollars, over a given time frame; and
3. that the relative percentage of total hospital patient service revenues in a given geographic market accounted for by a specific hospital in any year is a reasonable estimate of the *relative market share* of that hospital in the given year.

The study universe used to examine market characteristics consisted of all 18 of the short-stay nongovernmental voluntary hospitals within the city of Baltimore. Gross patient service revenue data were provided by the HSCRC (an independent commission functioning within the Maryland State Department of Health and Mental Hygiene) and verified for the years 1974 through 1977 by the executive director and/or controller of each institution.

Relative market share of each hospital was computed on the basis of the hospital's percentage of total gross patient service revenues, expressed in current dollars, for all 18 hospitals for the year 1976 (total portfolio revenues). *Market growth rate* was estimated by converting gross patient service revenues for 1974 to 1977 into constant (1976) dollars using the medical care components of the Consumer Price Index and then computing the compound rate of growth of constant dollar revenues for each hospital between 1974 and 1977. (The ten-month average of January through October 1977 price indexes was taken as the "annual average" for 1977. One of the hospitals in the portfolio was able to provide a trend data for 1974 to 1976 but was unable to provide 1977 data. Accordingly, market share was determined for a portfolio of 18 hospitals using 1976 data and market growth was determined for a portfolio of only 17 hospitals, excluding the hospital mentioned above.)

Relative market growth rate and market share data were then arrayed for construction of a market growth/share matrix (see Table 1). For analytical purposes, arbitrary cutoff points of 8.0 percent were used to segment high from low market share; arbitrary cutoff points of 4.5 percent and 7.5 percent,

Table 1 Relative Market Growth/Share Data, Baltimore Voluntary Hospitals, 1974-1977

Hospital and Type	Market Share (%)	Market Growth Rate (%)
High growth/high share:		
A.	22.4	6.0
Moderate growth/high share:		
B.	8.7	2.2
High growth/low share:		
C.	6.7	6.6
D.	5.2	6.8
E.	4.8	4.9
Moderate growth/low share:		
F.	4.9	4.0
G.	2.3	4.2
H.	5.3	3.1
I.	2.9	3.1
J.	0.7	2.7
K.	5.1	2.3
Moderate growth/low share:		
L.	5.1	1.7
M.	3.3	1.8
N.	0.9	1.9
Low growth/low share:		
O.	6.2	0.9
P.	7.2	(1.1)
Q.	5.3	(1.4)

respectively, were used to segment low from moderate growth rates and moderate from high growth rates (see Figure 1).

From a total portfolio perspective, the pattern displayed in Figure 1 demonstrates how one institution, hospital A, effectively dominates the voluntary hospital market of Baltimore. It is the only "star" in a voluntary hospital market that is characterized, not surprisingly, by the absence of any

FIGURE 1

MARKET GROWTH/SHARE MATRIX, BALTIMORE VOLUNTARY HOSPITALS, 1974-1977

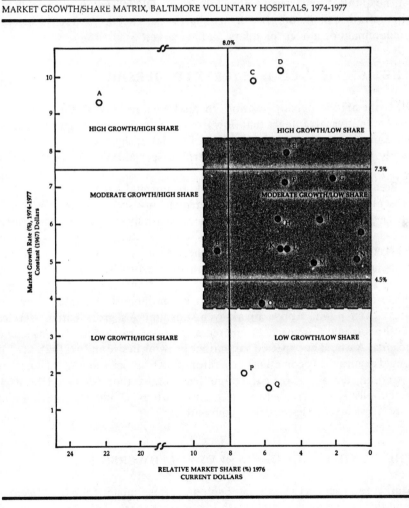

"cash cows." All other institutions, with the possible exception of hospital B, are market followers that necessarily function in a fiercely competitive low market share environment (Table 1 and Figure 1).

At either extreme of the hospitals that comprise the low share segments of the Baltimore hospital market are hospitals that are either low growth "dogs" (hospitals P and Q) or high growth "wildcats" (hospitals C and D). The majority of hospitals, however, whether considered individually or in terms of related clusters (for example, hospitals E, F and G; hospitals H, I, K, L and M; hospitals J and N; and hospitals B and O), fall within a remarkably circumscribed moderate growth/low share zone. They are, as a subgroup, the predominant or model "plodders" in the market.

THE SIGNIFICANCE OF MARKET LEADERSHIP

By virtue of its leadership position, hospital A enjoys, by defintion, a number of competitive advantages that flow from two universally observed business phenomena: effective cost-volume-profit relationships, and, more importantly, experience curve (combining learning, specialization, investment, and scale) effects.

Because of high growth and market share, hospital A is clearly in a position (absent sheer mismanagement and inadequate investment) to use and generate large amounts of cash and to become essentially self-sufficient in respect to cash flow. It can achieve economies in the production, distribution, and marketing of an increasingly comprehensive array of both inpatient and ambulatory care services, as is the case in other industries;[6-8] and, in so doing, it can reduce experience curve costs (i.e., cash flow rates divided by output rates) net of inflation to a point that it continuously operates above its break-even point. Above break-even, hospital A's gross patient service revenues would be expected to increase at a faster rate than total costs, and hospital A would be expected to continue growing in size and profitability.[9] It would eventually become a net generator of cash or "cash cow" were it not for restraining actions on the parts of governmental authorities (e.g., HSCRC), potentially strong competitors (e.g., hospitals B, C and D), and holdout consumers loyal to less efficient competitors.[10]

THE SIGNIFICANCE OF MARKET FOLLOWERSHIP

Market followers in the Baltimore voluntary hospital portfolio have in common the problems associated with low market share. They have a limited ability to generate cash, and they are denied the economies of volume operations.

Hospitals C and D, for example, operate at a substantial risk and are quite properly considered "wildcats" or "question marks." Even though they show good results in terms of market growth rate, they will certainly need large amounts of cash to sustain their current performance. But with limited market share, the opportunities for increasing volume are scarce. Thus they are caught up in what is tantamount to a Gordian knot: unless they are prepared to maintain their present growth rate and to increase market share by years of huge cash infusions, it is unlikely that they can develop a market position ("star") even roughly analogous to the market leader. If they fail to make such a cash investment, their only other option appears to be a loss of both growth and share and eventual descent into the "plodder" or "dog" categories.

Hospitals P and Q show precisely this effect. Neither currently has either market growth or share, and both are in serious operational trouble. As expected, alone among all other hospitals in the Baltimore portfolio, both demonstrate a negative growth rate for the 1974 to 1977 time frame when measured in current dollars deflated by the medical care component of the Consumer Price Index. A close examination of their performance would suggest, other things being equal, early termination of their operations.

The vast majority of hospitals in the Baltimore portfolio (hospitals E through N and possibly B and O as well) are in the moderate growth/low share category ("plodders"). On balance, they show a rather homogeneous set of operating characteristics: all are full line/full service institutions that maintain a high degree of parallel or duplicated facilities and programs; each shows remarkable stability with respect to scale of operations and health care product; and none experiences wide fluctuations in its overall funds position. Compared to the "stars," "wildcats," and "dogs" in the portfolio, they generate and use little cash. The reason is obvious: existing market conditions preclude the economies of volume operations. The institutions are simply competing among themselves for progressively smaller portions of the total market.

PUBLIC POLICY IMPLICATIONS

It seems clear from the foregoing that public policies aimed at regulating or otherwise planning and controlling the voluntary hospital industry in any geographically defined market must, at a minimum, take a total market or portfolio perspective. To do less, and to focus only on the operations of individual institutions or on the generic and theoretical aspects of hospital cost inflation, involves the serious risks of incorrect diagnoses and inappropriate therapies. All hospitals, quite obviously, do not suffer from precisely the same maladies.

For example, a hospital that has achieved optimal or near-optimal sales or market performance and is an overwhelmingly dominant firm (such as hospital A) hardly needs any incentives to improve on overall performance. It is very difficult for any firm to improve very much on high market share and high market growth.

Similarly, it is not very likely that any public or private manager, however personally gifted, can do much to improve the performance of a hospital that persistently shows both low growth rates and low market share (such as hospitals P and Q) in the presence of cost-reimbursement practices. Very few additional incentives exist.

The really difficult problems, for central authorities and private managements alike, thus arise principally when policy prescriptions must be developed for individual institutions in the "wildcat" and "plodder" segments of a portfolio. And here, of course, the relevant question is: what are the controllable marketing-mix variables that a hospital (or, for that matter, any other profit-seeking or not-for-profit organization) can use to build market share and to achieve the economies assumed to be inherent in high volume operations?

Quite clearly, there are only the traditional four: product, price, place, and promotion.

It is by no means clear, however, what the role of any of these variables is, taken either one at a time or in combinations, anywhere in the voluntary hospital industry. Empirical data are few and far between. What does seem to be the case is (1) that size alone, whether achieved by physical and/or functional or programmatic merger, does not ensure organizational or distributional economies, much less product or promotional economies;[11] and (2) that some combination of product differentiation and innovation, market segmentation and selection, and price competition *may* serve to reduce fragmentation on the demand side of hospital operations.

If this is in fact true, the purposeful establishment of specialized or limited service oligopoly positions within especially the "plodder" segments of a portfolio may provide at least one mechanism whereby central authorities and private managements can exploit their respective strengths to lower total unit costs and prices within an entire portfolio. Coupled with the adoption of aggressive purchasing policies on the part of government and other third party payers, the implementation of such competitive supply oligopolies might well have a major impact on the principal components of soaring health care costs.

REFERENCES

1. Ross, R.S. "Early Discharge after Heart Attacks and the Efficient Use of Hospitals." *New England Journal of Medicine* 298 (February 2, 1978) pp. 275-277.

2. Cohen, H.A. "State Rate Regulation." In *Controls on Health Care*. Washington, D.C.: National Academy of Sciences 1975, pp. 123-135.

3. Henderson, B.D. *The Experience Curve—Reviewed. IV. The Growth Share Matrix or Product Portfolio*. Boston: Boston Consulting Group, 1968, 1970, and 1973.

4. Day, G.S. "Diagnosing the Product Portfolio. How to Use Scarce Cash and Managerial Resources for Maximum Long-Run Gains." *Journal of Marketing* 41 (April 1977) pp. 29-38.

5. Henderson. *The Experience Curve—Reviewed. IV.*

6. Gale, B.T. "Market Share and Rate of Return." *Review of Economics & Statistics* 54 (November 1972) pp. 412-423.

7. Schoeffler, S.; Buzzel, R.D.; and Heany, D.F. "Impact of Strategic Planning on Profit Performance." *Harvard Business Review* 52 (March-April 1974) pp. 137-145.

8. Buzzel, R.D.; Gale, B.T.; and Sultan, R.G.M. "Market Share—Key to Profitability." *Harvard Business Review* 53 (January-February 1975) pp. 97-106.

9. Bloom, P.N., and Kotler, P. "Strategies for High Market-Share Companies." *Harvard Business Review* 53 (November-December 1975) pp. 63-72.

10. Ibid.

11. Treat, T.F. "The Performance of Merging Hospitals." *Medical Care* 14 (March 1976) pp. 199-209.

6. The Marketing Audit: A Tool for Health Service Organizations

ERIC N. BERKOWITZ and WILLIAM A. FLEXNER

Berkowitz, Eric N., and Flexner, William A. "The Marketing Audit: A Tool for Health Service Organizations." *Health Care Management Review,* Fall 1978.

Marketing is increasingly recognized as an effective tool in the management of health services. Some potential benefits recently cited in the literature include improved capacity to respond to the needs and wants of consumers, personnel, and the community in general; clarification in the development of long-range strategies and objectives; and more effective allocation of resources within the organization. [1-3]

Marketing of health services involves analyzing organizational interactions (transactions) with donors, patients, employees, and regulators of the organization. [4] However, before undertaking any marketing program, the factors that affect the organization's internal operations and its relations with the environment must be assessed. As Ireland notes: [5]

> Ideally, a hospital that is developing a marketing program should begin by conducting a series of research studies to gather information that will help define the characteristics, needs, and wants of its market and marketing segments, so that it can develop or revise its services and communications accordingly.

Unfortunately, assessments such as Ireland proposes are often done late in the planning process of health organizations. However, an early marketing inquiry—the marketing audit—may be more beneficial.

TWO APPROACHES TO PLANNING

Typically, the planning sequence in health organizations includes the specification of goals, translation of these into operational objectives, development of strategies to achieve the goals and objectives, implementation of the strategies, and, finally, feedback or evaluation to modify or adjust current strategies and implementation procedures.[6] Figure 1 shows this sequential process.

In this planning approach, understanding the organization's environment and particularly its marketplace usually occurs after the product and service strategies have been defined. While this information may aid in "selling" the product or services being offered, the timing is too late to determine whether the products or services being produced are those that are wanted or needed.

Marketing literature and practice provide another planning sequence (see Figure 2). In this model, the consumer of health services (whether viewed as the physician, the patient, the government, or some other purchaser) is recognized as the focal point for making the key choices that dictate the organization's success. With a marketing approach, the consumer is considered at the beginning of the planning process.[7] Consumers may be grouped into segments based on behavior or needs. Included in this initial analysis are a consideration of both the internal capabilities of the organization and the preferences and needs of the organization's current and potential consumers. This examination of the organization's internal aspects identifies the range of activities that can be performed, as well as the strong and weak points among these activities.

Once this situational or segmentation analysis is completed, the second step in the process associates various strategies with particular segments of consumers. Forecasts of the potential demand from each segment are then often attempted. Only after this step has been completed does the organization consider specific goals and objectives, and the means for implementing the chosen strategies.

As can be seen, the two approaches differ only in terms of the process flow. This difference, however, is critical in terms of structuring consumer-responsive strategies and plans. Traditionally, health service organizations have planned from the inside to the consumer. Yet regulatory, resource, and competition trends are requiring the change from a traditional to a marketing planning strategy. A marketing approach starts the process with the consumer, letting the consumer's needs and wants guide the strategy of the organization. Here the consumer is at the beginning of the planning process, around which selective strategies, objectives, and goals are constructed. For any organization changing to a marketing orientation, the process should begin with a marketing audit.

THE MARKETING AUDIT

Audits have typically been a procedure used in accounting for internal control. Because marketing can be a critical activity contributing to the efficient and

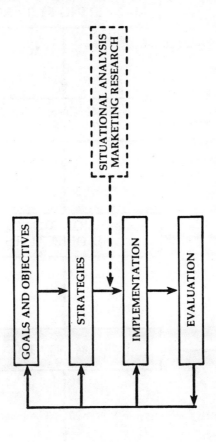

Figure 1 A Typical Health Planning Model

Figure 2 A Marketing Planning Model

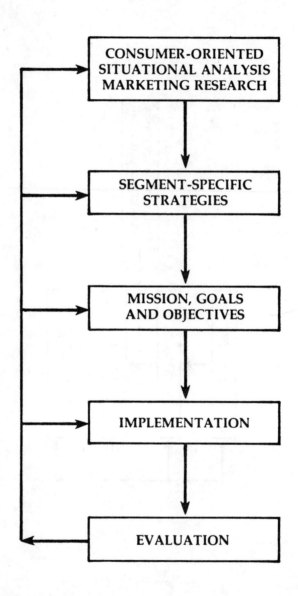

effective operation of any organization, the need for marketing audits in nontraditional businesses is increasing. As many health organizations begin to recognize the marketing function and to formulate marketing objectives, an early marketing audit is essential. This process provides a foundation on which to develop programs and standards for evaluation.

THE MEANING OF A MARKETING AUDIT

In its most basic sense, an audit is an evaluation of a firm's activities. Bell has suggested that "a marketing audit is a systematic and thorough examination of a company's marketing position." [8] Shuchman more precisely outlines this practice as:[9]

> . . .a systematic, critical, and impartial review and appraisal of the total marketing operation: of the basic objectives and policies and the assumptions which underlie them as well as the methods, procedures, personnel, and organization employed to implement the policies and achieve the objectives.

A variety of reasons for conducting a marketing audit exists. The dynamic nature of society and the health care industry, in particular, requires up-to-date information for the organization to operate effectively. One must periodically monitor the organization's position and activities to assess their responsiveness to market needs and preferences.

In this dynamic environment, a marketing audit has several purposes:[10]

- It appraises the total marketing operation.
- It centers on the evaluation of objectives and policies and the assumptions that underlie them.
- It aims for prognosis as well as diagnosis.
- It searches for opportunities and means for exploiting them as well as for weaknesses and means for their elimination.
- It practices preventive as well as curative marketing practices.

The Nature of an Audit

Conducting an audit can be an extremely complex task. In essence, it involves examining the entire scope of the organization's activities. Through a broad-based approach, certain cogent issues within each area of marketing operations (product and service design, promotion, price, location) can be

Figure 3 The Scope of the Marketing Audit

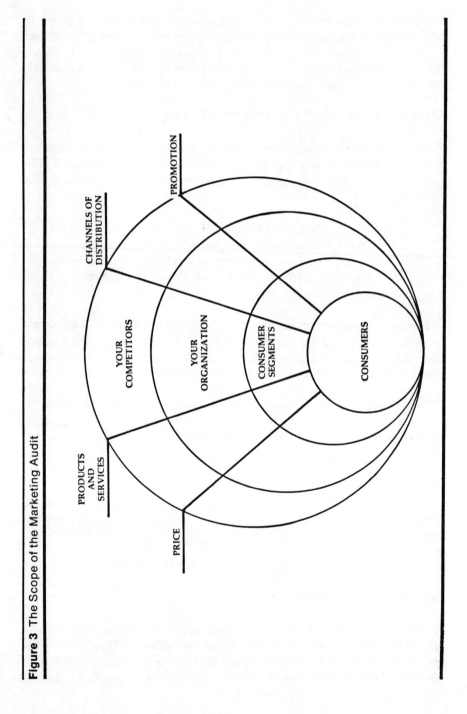

identified for analysis in greater depth. Figure 3 shows the scope of the marketing audit procedure.

The audit process is represented as a series of circles expanding outward from the consumer. One begins by looking at the size of the consumer market and the various ways that it can be divided or segmented. To this information must be added information concerning one's own health service organization. Often there are internal constraints that must be determined before devising marketing strategies. Beyond the organization, an assessment needs to be made of the competition, its strengths and weaknesses.

Cutting across each of these circles are the organizing or controllable variables that ultimately come together to define the marketing strategy. These marketing mix variables include the product or service offered, the price at which it is offered, the way in which it is promoted, and the channels through which the product or service is distributed.[11] At each stage of the marketing audit, these variables must be considered.

Areas of Inquiry in the Marketing Audit Procedure

For any organization, some factors may appear more relevant than others. The more important and common areas of inquiry for each circle represented in Figure 3 will be listed here in the form of questions to serve as a guide in the marketing audit process. These questions indicate that an audit is an information gathering process. Analysis will then depend on the audit team's foresight and management skills. (See pages 94-98.)

Summary

The marketing audit is the starting point. Examining the issues raised in these questions will allow a more viable, effective marketing strategy to be developed. For the health organization beginning its marketing plan, the audit process will establish parameters for the program and goals to be accomplished.

Many of the questions raised within the marketing audit already are being considered in some form by health planners. In this sense, marketing planning may seem no different from methods presently used. Yet the key difference is *when* these questions are examined. A marketing orientation begins with the consumers of the service. The audit process then continues internally after information is gained from the marketplace. This approach follows an external sequence, while traditional health planning methods proceed in the opposite direction.

Because the health care organization operates in a dynamic environment, the audit should become a part of the regular planning sequence. Each question should be reevaluated to highlight changes that may have important strategic implications for the organization in fulfilling its goals.

THE MARKET AND MARKET SEGMENTS

- How large is the territory covered by your market? How have you determined this?
- How is your market grouped?
  - Is it scattered?
  - How many important segments are there?
  - How are these segments determined (demographics, service usage, attitudinally)?
- Is the market entirely urban, or is a fair proportion of it rural?
- What percentage of your market uses third party payment?
  - What are the attitudes and operations of third parties?
  - Are they all equally profitable?
- What are the effects of the following factors on your market?
  - Age
  - Income
  - Occupation
  - Increasing population
  - ⎫
  - Decreasing birthrate ⎬ demographic shifting
- What proportion of potential customers are familiar with your organization, services, programs?
  - What is your image in the marketplace?
  - What are the important components of your image?

THE ORGANIZATION

- Short history of your organization:
  - When and how was it organized?
  - What has been the nature of its growth?
  - How fast and far have its markets expanded? Where do your patients come from geographically?
  - What is the basic policy of the organization? Is it "health care," "profit"?
  - What has been the financial history of the organization?
    - How has it been capitalized?
    - Have there been any account receivable problems?
    - What is inventory investment?
  - What has been the organization's success with the various services promoted?
- How does your organization compare with the industry?
  - Is the total volume (gross revenue, utilization) increasing, decreasing?

- — Have there been any fluctuations in revenue? If so, what were they due to?
- What are the objectives and goals of the organization? How can they be expressed beyond the provision of "good health care"?
- What are the organization's present strengths and weaknesses in:
  - — Medical facilities
  - — Management capabilities
  - — Medical staff
  - — Technical facilities
  - — Reputation
  - — Financial capabilities
  - — Image
- What is the labor environment for your organization?
  - — For medical staff (nurses, physicians, etc.)?
  - — For support personnel?
- How dependent is your organization upon conditions of other industries (third party payers)?
- Are weaknesses being compensated for and strengths being used? How?
- How are the following areas of your marketing function organized?
  - — Structure
  - — Manpower
  - — Reporting relationships
  - — Decision-making power
- What kinds of external controls affect your organization?
  - — Local?
  - — State?
  - — Federal?
  - — Self-regulatory?
- What are the trends in recent regulatory rulings?

COMPETITORS

- How many competitors are in your industry?
  - — How do you define your competitors?
  - — Has this number increased or decreased in the last four years?
- Is competition on a price or nonprice basis?
- What are the choices afforded patients?
  - — In services?
  - — In payment?
- What is your position in the market—size and strength—relative to competitors?

Continued on next page

PRODUCTS AND SERVICES

- Complete a list of your organization's products and services, both present and proposed.
- What are the general outstanding characteristics of each product or service?
- What superiority or distinctiveness of products or services do you have, as compared with competing organizations?
- What is the total cost per service (in-use)? Is service over/under utilized?
- What services are most heavily used? Why?
  — What is the profile of patients/physicians who use the services?
  — Are there distinct groups of users?
- What are your organization's policies regarding:
  — Number and types of services to offer?
  — Assessing needs for service addition/deletion?
- History of products and services (complete for major products and services):
  — How many did the organization originally have?
  — How many have been added or dropped?
  — What important changes have taken place in services during the last ten years?
  — Has demand for the services increased or decreased?
  — What are the most common complaints against the service?
  — What services could be added to your organization that would make it more attractive to patients, medical staff, nonmedical personnel?
  — What are the strongest points of your services to patients, medical staff, nonmedical personnel?
  — Have you any other features that individualize your service or give you an advantage over competitors?

PRICE

- What is the pricing strategy of the organization?
  — Cost-plus
  — Return on investment
  — Stabilization
- How are prices for services determined?
  — How often are prices reviewed?
  — What factors contribute to price increase/decrease?
- What have been the price trends for the past five years?
- How are your pricing policies viewed by:
  — Patients

— Physicians
— Third party payers
— Competitors
— Regulators

PROMOTION

- What is the purpose of the organization's present promotional activities (including advertising)?
  — Protective
  — Educational
  — Search out new materials
  — Develop all markets
  — Establish a new service
- Has this purpose undergone any change in recent years?
- To whom has advertising appeal been largely directed?
  — Donors
  — Patients
    — Former or current
    — Prospective
  — Physicians
    — On staff
    — Potential
- What media have been used?
- Are the media still effective in reaching the intended audience?
- What copy appeals have been notable in terms of response?
- What methods have been used for measuring advertising effectiveness?
- What is the role of public relations?
  — Is it a separate function/department?
  — What is the scope of responsibilities?

CHANNELS OF DISTRIBUTION

- What are the trends in distribution in the industry?
  — What services are being performed on an outpatient basis?
  — What services are being provided on an at-home basis?
  — Are satellite facilities being used?
- What factors are considered in location decisions?
- When did you last evaluate present location?
- What distributors do you deal with? (e.g., medical supply houses, etc.)
- How large an inventory must you carry?

The marketing audit provides guidance for improving the organization's profitability, competitive position, and overall performance. This is accomplished by clarifying the setting in which strategies, goals, and objectives related to future action can be intelligently generated.

REFERENCES

1. Ireland, R.C. "Using Marketing Strategies to Put Hospitals on Target." *Hospitals* 51 (June 1, 1977) pp. 54-58.

2. O'Halloran, R.D., Staples, J., and Chiampa, P. "Marketing Your Hospital." *Hospital Progress* 57 (1976) pp. 68-71.

3. Clarke, R.N. "Marketing Health Care: Problems in Implementation." *Health Care Management Review* 3:1 (Winter 1978) pp. 21-27.

4. Shapiro, B.P. "Marketing for Nonprofit Organizations." *Harvard Business Review* (September-October 1973) pp. 123-132.

5. Ireland. "Using Marketing Strategies." p. 55.

6. Hyman, H. *Health Planning*. Germantown, Md.: Aspen Systems Corporation, 1975, Ch. 3.

7. Keith, R.J. "The Marketing Revolution." *Journal of Marketing* (January 1960) pp. 35-38.

8. Bell, M.L. *Marketing Concepts and Strategies*, 2d ed. Boston: Houghton Mifflin Co., 1972, p. 428.

9. Shuchman, A. "The Marketing Audit: Its Nature, Purposes, and Problems." In *Analyzing and and Improving Marketing Performance, Report No. 32*. New York: American Management Association, 1959, p. 13.

10. Shuchman. "The Marketing Audit." p. 15.

11. McCarthy, E.J. *Basic Marketing: A Managerial Approach*, 5th ed. Homewood, Ill.: Richard D. Irwin, Inc., 1975.

7. Marketing Information and Market Research— Valuable Tools For Managers

ROBERTA N. CLARKE and LINDA SHYAVITZ

Clarke, Roberta N., and Shyavitz, Linda. "Marketing Information and Market Research—Valuable Tools for Managers." *Health Care Management Review,* Winter 1981.

The recent adoption of marketing as a management tool by health care administrators is often swiftly followed by the hiring of consultants to perform health-related marketing research. While many hospitals and health care agencies could ultimately profit from having this research done, they are often paying for general marketing information that could be collected by their own staffs. In these times of cost-containment pressures such unnecessary expenditures should be avoided. Specifically, the issue raised here is the spending of funds externally to collect marketing data that could, to a large extent, be collected internally.

To determine if a health care organization is spending money inappropriately, it is necessary to distinguish between *marketing information*—any data that can be used in a marketing analysis—and *market research*—original, objective, systematized (and usually professionally performed) research.

MARKETING INFORMATION: WHAT IS IT? WHERE IS IT FOUND?

Marketing information can be divided into internal data (about the hospital itself) and external data (about the hospital's competition, market, and general operating environment). Both types of data are important since a well-designed marketing program requires the successful integration of internal capabilities and limitations with external opportunities and constraints.

Any hospital (or other health care provider) intending to engage in marketing activities should systematically and regularly review and analyze these general marketing data. Some of the information, such as number of admissions and discharges, distribution by specialty of medical staff and raw patient data, is already collected, aggregated and organized within most hospitals. Other information, such as characteristics of the service area, profile data on physicians in the service area, and number and type of competitors, may require some effort to collect and organize. The significant advantage of this basic information is that most of it is currently available within the hospital or can be collected to a large extent by the hospital's own staff.

The challenge presented by the collection of basic marketing data is being able to look at familiar information from a new perspective. Many hospitals have a wealth of marketing information already available or easily accessible to management. The failure to use this information results primarily from a failure on the part of planning and management to recognize that the data *are* marketing information and should form part of the basic marketing analysis. Not only should this information help identify marketing problems and issues, but it should also aid in determining strategic responses.

No one problem or opportunity is likely to require the use of all the information given in Table 1. However, it is wise to have the information readily accessible so that it can be used when a relevant marketing problem arises.

Case Study—Marketing Information Applied

A community hospital in the Baltimore/Washington area with a respected reputation found itself with a declining census in its medical-surgical services over a four-year period. The decline of roughly 5 percent for the four years was not steep, but the long-term implications for the hospital were negative if the decline was not reversed or at least halted. Recognizing this, the hospital management immediately sought out the services of a consulting firm to perform a marketing survey of the community. The hospital presumed it would learn the causes of the declining census from such a survey. Moreover, it expected the research to suggest strategies for reversing the decline.

The hospital was first directed by the consulting firm to examine internally available marketing information that might shed some light on the situation. Patient satisfaction cards from the previous three years were studied to determine if satisfaction had decreased. It had not, suggesting that dissatisfaction of the "patient market" might not be the cause of the medical-surgical census decline.

Information on the "physician market" was then examined. Specifically, the hospital looked for trends over the four years in terms of numbers of physicians affiliated with the hospital, the age spread and distribution among specialties of the physicians, and admission by physician.

Table 1 General Marketing Information

Internal	External
Census—aggregate and by service	Characteristics of the hospital's service area
Admissions/discharges	
by service (medical, surgical, pediatric, etc.)	age distribution
by diagnosis within service	income distribution
by physician	level of education
by source of payment	by religion (if applicable)
by patient origin by community	by culture or ethnic background (if applicable)
by source of referral (medical staff, emergency room, outpatient department, etc.)	by medical service usage rates (inpatient, ambulatory, emergency room)
by patient age	market size and growth rate
by average length of stay	natality and mortality statistics
	membership in HMOs (number of members in each HMO)
Medical staff	Profile of MDs in hospital's market area
aggregate number and by department	age
by credentials	specialty
by specialty	practice setting
by age	office location
by practice plans	admission rates
by office location	affiliations
by use of ancillary services and operating room	patients' origins
by admissions by diagnosis	credentials
by other hospital affiliations and percentage use of each other hospital affiliation	
by total hospital revenue generated	
Emergency department utilization	Competitors
gross utilization	number of beds
by shift	occupancy by service
by time of year, day of week	service configuration
by source of payment	characteristics of population served
by patient origin by community	service expansion or alteration
by type of diagnosis	plans including major capital projects
time in waiting area until patient treated	medical staff makeup
percentage of EMS ambulance runs to emergency department	prices
patient origin by incidence of emergency	
by source of referral (walk-in, physician, fire, police, etc.)	
percentage of emergency department patients who are admitted as inpatients	

(Continued on next page)

Table 1 General Marketing Information *(continued)*

Internal	External

Ambulatory medical services utilization
   gross utilization
   by service
   by diagnosis
   by patient source
   by patient origin by community
   by source of referral
   by patient age
   percentage of ambulatory patients who
      are admitted as inpatients
	Planning, regulatory and hospital
	reimbursement trends
	
	Medical (clinical) practice trends (i.e.
	decreasing tendency to hospitalize
	children, increasing use of home health
	care, etc.)

Financial information
   revenues by department
   expenditures by department	

Gross index of patient satisfaction
with all services
   from patient cards
   from hospital ombudsmen	

Initially, the data were not enlightening. The number of physicians had remained roughly the same, with a small number retiring each year and a comparable number of young physicians joining the staff. The age spread of medical staff ranged from 28 to 70. And physicians were well distributed among the specialties and general practice.

It was discovered, however, that most physicians were admitting slightly fewer patients than they had been four years ago. And older physicians had experienced a somewhat greater decline in the number of admissions than had the younger physicians.

A further examination of these factors revealed a situation of which the hospital had been unaware, a situation that explained much of the decline in medical-surgical utilization. By cross tabulating two of the factors previously addressed, distribution of physician by age and by specialty, the hospital discovered that most of their general practitioners were at or near retirement age while most of their specialists were relatively young. As the general practitioners approached retirement, many were allowing their practices to decline. (See Table 2.)

The general practitioners themselves admitted patients to the hospital and were a major source of patient referrals to the hospital's young specialists. Consequently, the general practitioners' reduction in activity had also directly affected the specialists' activity. The cumulative impact explained the census decline.

Table 2 Distribution of Physicians By Age and By Specialty

		Age	
		Under 45 years	**Over 45 years**
Type physician	General practitioner	**Few**	**Most**
	Specialist	**Most**	**Few**

The hospital further discovered that this problem was likely to worsen. Within ten years, 65 percent of their general practitioners would be of retirement age. As explained above, this dramatically declining general practitioner physician base would not only directly affect the census but also seriously threaten the viability of the specialty practices.

Through the use of internally available marketing information, the hospital was able to save itself the cost of having the consultants perform a consumer research study that would likely not have identified the problem's cause. Moreover, once the cause and potential problem were discovered, the hospital was able to address it by recruiting and helping to place new young family practitioners in areas being covered by retiring general practitioners.

Advantages of Marketing Information

Marketing information collected and analyzed on an ongoing basis has the following advantages:

1. It is not expensive to collect compared to the higher prices associated with market research.
2. Once the baseline marketing information is collected, it can be easily updated to allow the rapid identification of trends.
3. Marketing information can be collected and analyzed by the hospital's own staff, particularly with the involvement of the planning staff. (For the initial collection and analysis effort, it is sometimes wise to hire outside marketing experts both to aid in the analysis and to transfer the skills of the experts to the relevant hospital staff.) By keeping the collection and analysis of the marketing information within the hospital, the hospital should be able to develop and internalize the marketing skills within its staff.
4. The results of the analysis of marketing information are necessary for

and invaluable in the development of marketing strategies for the hospital.

MARKET RESEARCH—ORIGINAL, OBJECTIVE, SYSTEMATIZED

Market research is original, objective, systematized research. Its value lies largely in providing information that is complementary to rather than duplicative of marketing information.

Information Generated

Specifically, market research can generate information on:

1. *Perceptions*—What does the consumer (physician, potential donor, etc.) think about this hospital and its specific services? What are his or her attitudes toward the hospital? The physical facility? The nursing care?
2. *Preference*—Which hospital would the consumer prefer (or intend to use) if he or she needs to be hospitalized? Does this preference vary by service or nature of the diagnosis? Or does the consumer's preference even matter since physicians admit patients?
3. *Potential demand*—For what new services is there a demand? In other words, what unmet health care needs exist in the community? In what way should the hospital structure services to meet these needs in terms of service policies, price (if any), location, access and promotion?
4. *Usage*—General marketing information should generate substantial usage information, but market research can complement significantly the hospital profile of its user (patient) base. It can better indicate past usage (as reported by the consumer, compared to future usage, as preference information would project) by identifying who went to which hospital for what service.

Clearly, market research, similar to marketing information, generates valuable information for strategic marketing planning and problem identification. However, the nature of the information generated differs. Moreover, due to its expenses, marketing research should be used only when information on specific issues is needed and such information cannot be obtained through the marketing information available internally.

INTERESTED IN MARKET RESEARCH?

Do you have the competence to do your own market research? You should answer "yes" only if you possess skills in such areas as:
—experimental versus nonexperimental designs
—sampling procedures (sample size, statistical inference, confidence limits, sampling error, sampling design)
—qualitative versus quantitative research
—questionnaire construction (scaling methods, question/item order, length and phrasing, interface between questionnaire design and the analytical methods to be used)
—interview techniques, interviewer qualifications
—various analytical techniques
—data analysis, processing and interpretation

If you are interested in learning about market research you might begin by:
—checking with your state hospital association to see if it has any market research skills or training to offer
—checking with local universities to ascertain what market research courses are offered and open to the public
—reading recommended market research texts [1-3]

---

1. Green, P. and Tull, D.S. *Research for Marketing Decisions* (Englewood Cliffs, N.J.: Prentice-Hall 1975).
2. Kinnear, T.C. and Taylor, J.R. *Marketing Research: An Applied Approach* (New York: McGraw-Hill Book Co. 1979).
3. Tull, D. and Hawkins, D. *Marketing Research* (New York: Macmillan Publishing Co. 1976).

Expertise Required

Market research should typically be performed with the aid of or by outside professionals with expertise in the area of market research. However, in an attempt to minimize costs, hospital managements have sometimes tried to perform their own market research through the use of internally available staff. This presents problems for several reasons.

Market research must be objective, which means that the research effort must be carried out in an unbiased manner. It is difficult for employees of any organization to be objective and unbiased in the way they ask questions and in the questions they choose to ask.

For example, one questionnaire designed by a hospital's administrative staff erred in encouraging the interviewees to respond positively by not allowing sufficient leeway for negative answers. They asked, for instance: "Do you think the medical care at this hospital is good? Yes _____ No _____."
Only those with a highly negative view of the medical care would check "no."
Yet it cannot be assumed that the respondents checking "yes" perceived the medical care to be good, only that they had no alternative answer. The

question could be better phrased: "How would you rate the medical care at this hospital?" (please check one)

☐ poor   ☐ acceptable   ☐ very good
☐ somewhat poor   ☐ somewhat good   ☐ don't know

By designing questions (and questionnaires, interview guides, etc.) that are objective and less likely to solicit desired responses, the professional market researcher is able to provide more accurate marketing information to the hospital.

Using outside expertise ensures that information is sought systematically rather than haphazardly. The systematizing of research, requiring professional training and experience, minimizes research bias. This is done, for example, through the careful application of sample design and nonresponse follow-up. In addition, systematization promotes the examination of a broad base of marketing variables, many of which the hospital may not have previously considered.

The real value in market research is not in collecting the data but in analyzing it. It is the analysis that identifies problems and opportunities as well as strategies for addressing both. Some health care organizations have found themselves with a wealth of data but without the skills necessary to perform a reasonable analysis of the data. Given this situation, one must ask: Why bother collecting data if they cannot be analyzed and productively used to develop marketing strategies and identify marketing problems?

Finally, using marketing research experts avoids a problem common to nonprofessional market researchers: the confusion of market research with promotion. The desire to economize has led hospital managements in the past to attempt to "sell" or promote the hospital to the same market they are trying to research. Unfortunately, the introduction of promotion into a market research effort is likely to ruin the integrity of the research: if the interviewee knows the sponsor of the market research, then a wide range of perceptions, attitudes and preferences become subject to bias and are no longer researchable. Market research professionals, unlike hospital administrators who have vested interests in gaining visibility for their hospitals, do not attempt to mix promotion with market research. They know that the purpose of market research is for the hospital to become educated about its market; the purpose of promotion on the other hand is to educate the market about the hospital. The two have little overlap.

Hospitals seeking to become proficient in marketing and the development of marketing strategies need to recognize that a broad array of marketing information is available to them, of which market research is only one part. The distinction between general marketing information and market research is that the former can be collected and analyzed internally at little cost on a continuing basis. In contrast, market research should be performed when needed information about specific issues cannot be obtained from the general marketing information.

Both marketing information and market research are valuable tools to hospital managers. However, to maximize their value to the hospital, they should be used appropriately, with an understanding of their benefits and limitations.

8. Marketing Research in Health Services Planning: a Model

WILLIAM A. FLEXNER and ERIC N. BERKOWITZ

Flexner, William A., and Berkowitz, Eric N. "Marketing Research in Health Services Planning: a Model. *Public Health Reports,* November-December 1979.

Health services have been defined as "all personal and public services performed by individuals or institutions for the purpose of maintaining or restoring health."[1] Decisions about the design and delivery of services by private clinics, hospitals, neighborhood health centers, and health maintenance organizations (HMOs) are made primarily by professionals. Yet consumer input into these decisions is increasingly being sought, even demanded. Generally this input has been obtained by four methods: (1) consumer representation on boards, (2) consumer advocacy (for example, Ralph Nader's Health Research Group), (3) a diagnosis of the community (the community being regarded as the patient) and assessment of the community's needs, and (4) behavioral and social science research.[2]

These four methods provide for firsthand contact between health professionals and the lay public and a medically objective review of health care requirements. Yet, in application, weaknesses in the methods may be revealed, such as presumed representation of the whole consumer population, a tendency toward professional domination of decisions, and ineffective integration of consumer input into the organization's planning. These weaknesses often preclude the creation of programs and services that are sensitive and responsive to all sectors of the population.[3]

The strengths of the four methods must be integrated into a managerial structure in order to produce programs and services that are satisfactory to health care consumers. To accomplish such integration, a framework is needed, and marketing research can provide it.

Marketing research is the organizational activity of systematically gathering, recording, and analyzing the information needed to make planning and implementation decisions that affect the quality or intensity of an organization's interactions with consumers.[4,5] We propose that a marketing research model and marketing research methods be incorporated into the health services planning process at the institutional level.

MARKETING: RESPONSIVENESS TO CONSUMERS

In business, marketing is the matching of a company's capabilities and resources with consumers' needs and wants.[6,7] Needs and wants are the things that are important to consumers and that underlie their behavior. Because consumers' preferences and expectations vary, companies provide many different products or services. Through marketing, management can foster mutually beneficial exchanges between the company and specified segments of consumers. Exchanges occur when something of value is given up for something of value received—goods, services, money, attention, devotion, ideas, and so forth.[8]

Defined in this way, marketing encompasses far more than the narrow activities of advertising or promotion in a traditional business setting. To be successful a business or any other organization must satisfy various consumer segments by providing appropriately designed products or services. Simultaneously, it must also achieve its internal goals and objectives, whether these be defined as profit, market share, health outcomes, or patient compliance. To reach these goals, a business or an organization has to offer the right product or service at the right price and deliver it at the right time and place. When planning is oriented toward the marketplace, effective and efficient exchanges are more likely to take place between the business or organization and its consumers. Such an orientation, however, requires an understanding on the part of management as to how and why consumers choose specific products or services in the marketplace.

MARKETING IN THE HEALTH SECTOR

In the health sector, consumers' needs are traditionally viewed as equivalent to their health or medical care requirements.[9-11] Health providers create "products" to respond to these requirements. These products (usually specific services) include the technical knowledge and skills of the provider, the technological capacity of the institution in which the provider functions, and the specific tests, surgical procedures, and regimens that are prescribed.

Health professionals primarily consider health services in technical terms.[12] Consumers, on the other hand, often use very different criteria when considering health services,[13,14] placing greater emphasis on the nontechnical components of service delivery from which they expect to derive values or benefits. These benefits become, in turn, surrogates in the consumers' minds for the technical components of the health service. Among the nontechnical benefits that consumers desire or expect in a medical facility are a pleasing appearance, physical comfort, an opportunity for effective communication with the staff, and ease in obtaining services.[15] Priority in program planning should be given to identifying the benefits that most influence consumers in deciding whether or not to use health services and where to obtain them. Consumers' choices of sources of health care are becoming increasingly important to health care management because consumers are beginning to shop around for care.[16] If services are to be responsive to consumers' preferences and expectations, the benefits that consumers seek have to be identified. Information on consumers' preferences and expectations also has to be made available to managers in a usable form before decisions are made about the service design.

TWO PLANNING APPROACHES

Collection of information from consumers should be a primary concern of any organization. The time of collection in terms of the planning sequence is also of great importance. Managers of clinics, hospitals, neighborhood health centers, and HMOs typically consider information about consumers' preferences and behavior only after they have set goals and objectives and decided on service strategy.[17] That is, they turn to consumers only after having already decided what they are going to do for them. And although the information about consumers collected at this stage may aid in selling the services being offered, it comes too late to be of value in helping managers determine whether the consumers actually want or need the services.

In a marketing approach, the planning sequence is different. Consumers are the focal point for the key decisions that determine the organization's success or failure (Figure 1). Therefore consumers are considered at the beginning of the planning process.[18] Information gathered from and about them provides the foundation for defining the organization's goals and objectives. Consumers are viewed in terms of sub-groupings, or segments, based on similar behavior or preferences. Each segment is profiled according to identifiable characteristics. In the initial analysis, both the organization's internal capabilities and the preferences of its current constituency are taken into account.

Once the initial analysis is completed, a strategy is devised for each segment of consumers. Only after consumers have been segmented does the organization specify its operational goals and objectives and the means that will be used to achieve them through control of the design, location, price, and promotion of services.

A marketing approach and traditional approaches in the health sector differ only in the timing of the steps in the planning process. This difference,

Figure 1 Models for Planning Health Programs

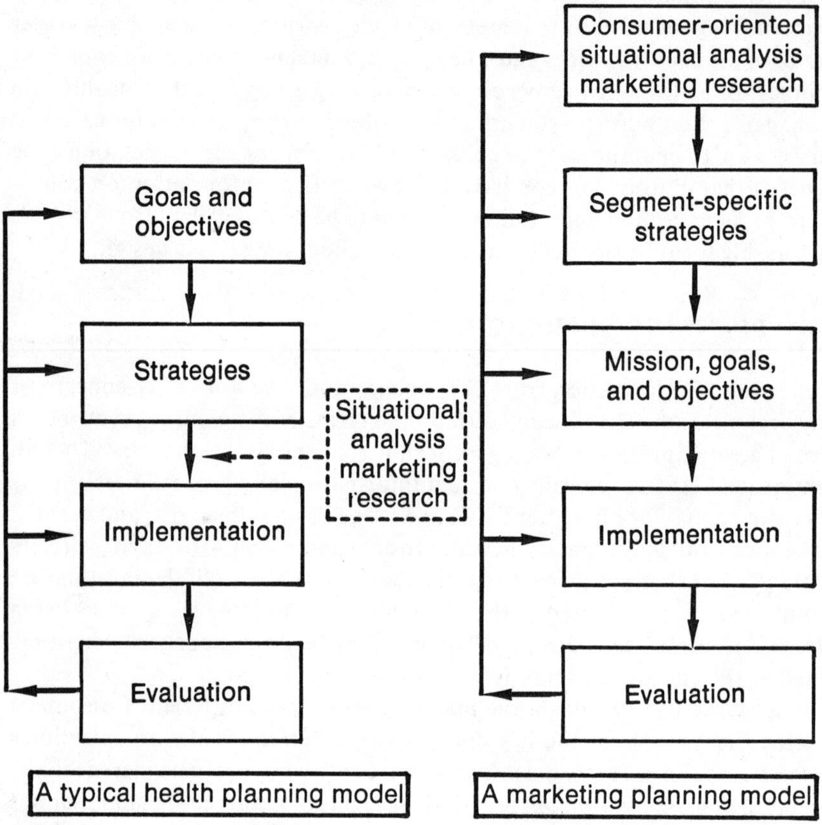

A typical health planning model

A marketing planning model

Source: Adapted from reference 18.

however, is critical to the design of strategies that are sensitive to consumers' preferences. Traditionally, the planning of health service organizations has been done from inside the organization out to the consumer. That is, the organization determines what the health professionals' needs are, what consumers should have, and how consumers' needs are to be filled. Current trends and pressures, however, such as those causing consumers to shop around for service alternatives, dictate a change from the traditional approach to one more responsive to the marketplace. Because planning begins with the consumer in a marketing approach, consumers' preferences and needs, particularly those not directly related to medical techniques, guide the organization's strategy. Consumer segments then form the basis on which appropriate and selective strategies, objectives, and goals can be constructed. Because information is available from consumers, programs and services can be made more responsive to them. Consequently, the levels of their satisfaction can be expected to be higher because of the greater congruence between their expectations and the actual service features.

INTEGRATING RESEARCH ON CONSUMERS

As the conceptual framework for market-oriented health services planning in Figure 2 shows, the essential link in such planning is between research on

Figure 2 A Framework for Integrating Consumer Research and Management Planning and Control

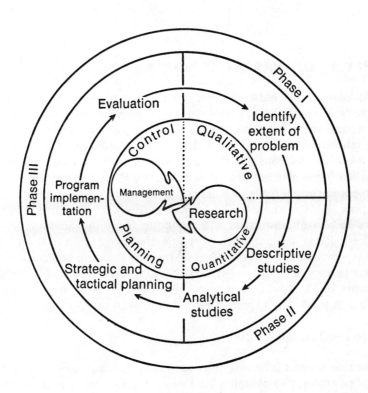

consumers and planning and control by management. To respond appropriately to consumers' preferences, an organization needs to have an information-gathering or research program that is well integrated into the management process. There are three phases in this process. The first two involve the research program. In the first phase, the extent of the problem is determined in qualitative terms. Management seeks to learn what factors affect relationships between the organization and its consumers. In the second phase, quantitative studies are conducted to identify the various consumer segments in the health care marketplace so that their future behavior can be forecast.

Upon completion of the research, the information must be disseminated, so that the results can be translated into programs that are sensitive to consumers' preferences and needs. This translation is done in the third phase. This management phase involves the formulation of plans incorporating the results of the research, implementation of these plans, and the evaluation of their results. As program outputs are observed and measured against the plans, new problems may surface, creating a need for additional information. Thus, for an organization to be effective, research has to be a dynamic process and an integral part of planning.

APPLYING THE MARKETING MODEL

Many hospitals are currently trying to broaden their target markets from primarily inpatient care to a wide range of noninpatient services. In one plan under consideration in a major midwestern metropolitan area, for example, hospitals would provide acute care through ambulatory (outpatient) services. (We use this plan throughout this paper to illustrate the actual application of a marketing model to health services planning.) The outpatient market in this metropolitan area already includes large fee-for-service multispecialty group practices, HMOs, and neighborhood health centers. Consumers also are served in part by hospital emergency rooms. As with traditional business services, successful expansion of hospitals into a new market—the outpatient market—requires an understanding on the part of the managers about consumers' perceptions of the hospital, as well as the identification of the potential segments of the market that would use hospital-based ambulatory care services. A marketing approach can aid in such an exploration.

Phase 1—Qualitative Studies

In the first phase of the investigation, the components of the problem or problems relevant to planning decisions are delineated. Often health care providers assume that they understand these components. However, because consumers may have different perceptions, an opportunity should be taken at the outset of planning to verify or challenge providers' conventional assumptions.[19]

Several qualitative research techniques are used in this phase of investigation. The first, focus group discussion, is used frequently in business to elicit consumer perceptions about a given subject.[20, 21] After a representative group of actual or potential consumers is brought together, a general subject for discussion is introduced by a moderator, who generates discussion by a few carefully selected "focusing" questions. In a focus group discussion, the aim is to elicit emotional and subjective statements revealing the participants' preferences in respect to the issues under discussion. The participants' statements are subsequently analyzed to identify the components of the research problem that seem worthy of more exact assessment. As opposed to other methods of qualitative group research, such a discussion is supposed to be as expansive as possible, so that the full range of participants' opinions are revealed. Group consensus is not a goal.

In our study in the midwestern metropolitan area, focus group discussions helped clarify key elements in consumers' perceptions of hospitals. In these discussions, four focusing questions were posed to determine what consumers—when new in a city—considered important about hospitals, what in a hospital indicated that the place was all right or, on the other hand, that they should never go back, and what influenced them in determining a hospital's reputation for quality. The discussions were held in the evening in the community rooms of a public library and a commercial bank. Participants were selected by telephone solicitation of households in the appropriate geographic area. Criteria for the participants' selection included having no exposure to a hospital in the previous six months and having no family member working in the health field.

In our analysis of the focus group discussions, we identified nine attributes related to consumers' perceptions of hospitals. Six have some face validity, since they have been cited in earlier studies as important dimensions in consumers' perceptions and choices of hospitals;[22-25] namely, the attitude of the staff; the quality, cost, location, and range of services; and the appearance of the facility. Interestingly, however, the focus group discussions elicited three other organizational attributes not mentioned in the literature, namely, the hospital's reputation, the hospital's cleanliness, and the hospital affiliation of the respondent's personal physician. All nine attributes were included in the quantitative phase of our analysis. Transcripts of the focus group discussions were of help in preparing attitude statements for the survey instrument that we used in the second phase of the research.

A second qualitative research technique, the individual depth interview, is often used to clarify issues that have been raised in focus group discussions, but in a form too vague for useful pursuit in quantitative research.[26] In individual depth interviews, the decision-making processes or reasoning of the participants is probed on a one-to-one basis through structured questionnaires, comprised primarily of open-ended questions. Although the responses to such questions are subjective, analysis of the responses can further clarify the problem under consideration.

A third kind of qualitative research, nominal group and delphi processes, is used when group consensus is desired.[27] In these processes, a highly structured format is used to minimize group interaction and, consequently, to help the group reach creative or judgmental decisions. By working within a group, the managers or planners can reach agreement on the critical issues related to future planning decisions.

Phase 2—Quantitative Studies

Once the components of the problem are defined, the second phase of research begins. The conditions that affect the relationship between the organization and its consumers are identified through descriptive studies.[28] The behavior and the demographic profiles of both the consumers and the providers are then assessed. The demographic profiles show who comprises the market and who provides services to the segments within it. Much of the data needed for descriptive studies can be found in secondary sources, both inside and outside the organization: patient origin studies, previous research studies, clinic or hospital discharge or case-mix records, county records, census data, and so forth. Secondary sources are used whenever possible since they speed data collection and reduce costs.

Figure 3 shows some of the data that a hospital might want to have available in its information system to improve the efficiency and effectiveness of a descriptive market analysis. The solid-line boxes indicate how data should be stored, namely, by patient, by physician, and by service. The two-way classifications that the manager should have available are also shown (broken-line boxes). In a case-mix analysis, for example, the number of patients by diagnosis and by physician, as well as by average length of stay, would be valuable information for managers to have to plan the organization's strategies.

Other sources of data for descriptive studies vary in terms of ease of access and the complexity of the data collection methods. In some cases, the data must be collected through survey instruments. Care in planning the questionnaire's design, selecting the sample, and administering the survey will prevent the introduction of systematic error through the data collection method. Distinct tradeoffs exist with each type of data-gathering approach—mail questionnaire, telephone interview, and personal interview—and therefore the kind of information required must figure in the selection of the correct

Figure 3 Information Needed to Formulate a Marketing Strategy in the Hospital Setting

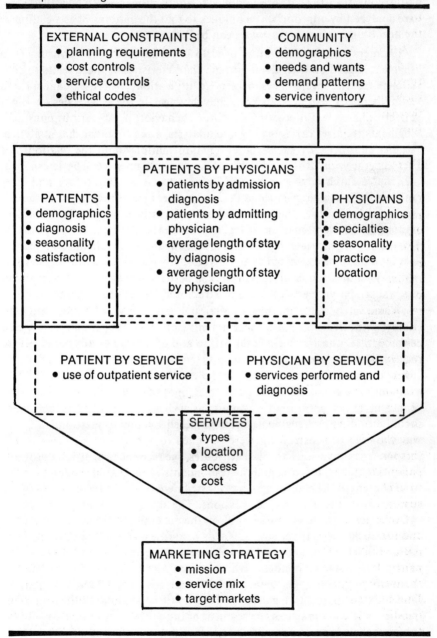

alternative. The criteria for this selection include the cost, timeliness, and sensitivity of the information that the method can be expected to provide. After collection, the data are compiled to address the research hypotheses and are analyzed by appropriate techniques so that the patterns of association or relationship among the variables can be determined.

Planners and administrators need to know how to group consumers in segments based on their demographic characteristics as these relate to consumers' service preferences or service utilization patterns. Planners and administrators also need to know how changes in the service design might affect utilization. Forecasting the future behavior of the various consumer segments requires careful study and analysis, a requirement that analytical studies can meet. By such studies, (1) information about the relationships between the variables that identify the consumer segments can be determined, (2) the research environment can be monitored so that before and after relationships can be specified, and (3) any other factors that might have been responsible for the phenomenon under investigation can be identified. Although a discussion of analytical approaches is not within the scope of this paper, it is appropriate to note that recent advances in multivariate statistics permit data to be examined in an operationally useful way. [29-31] For example, differences between several segments can be identified by discriminant analysis, and underlying attitudes can be structured by factor analysis.

Whenever possible, both the descriptive and analytical studies are conducted with the same survey instrument. But, when they are necessary and appropriate, quasi-experimental before and after studies are done. Before and after studies are particularly helpful if new services or new service features are available for testing before full implementation.

In our study in the midwestern metropolitan area, data for assessing consumers' perceptions of hospitals, as well as for identifying consumer profiles and market segments, were gathered by a mail questionnaire. The questions in this instrument were designed to elicit the importance to the respondents of various hospital attributes, the respondents' attitudes toward hospitals and health care, and the respondents' demographic characteristics. The content of the eight-page survey instrument was based on analysis of the content of the focus group discussions. The survey instrument was sent to 4,844 randomly selected households in the area, along with a postcard that, when returned with the completed form, made the respondent eligible to win a television set. There were 1,465 usable responses (response rate 30.2 percent). There were 1,446 respondents who answered the question, "Do you have a personal physician?" Of these, 1,213 (83.9 percent) responded affirmatively and 233 (16.1 percent) negatively. These results are similar to those in other studies in which the size of the segment of the consumer population with no physician has been estimated. [32, 33]

In the study, our overriding concern was what the potential was for expansion of outpatient services by the hospitals in the area. People in the area with no personal physician were viewed as the potential users of these services. Thus, the research problem was first to determine what attributes of hospitals were important to this group in choosing a hospital and then to profile this segment relative to consumers who had a personal physician. Table 1 shows how each of nine attributes (which had been identified as being important in Phase 1, the qualitative portion of the research) was rated in importance by the two groups. Although both groups rated all nine attributes as rather important, significant differences were observed for seven attributes. For example, the range of services and the reputation of the hospital were more important to consumers with a physician. Yet it is interesting that even this group of consumers rated the attribute of having one's physician affiliated with the hospital as only the sixth most important hospital attribute.

Table 1 Importance of Various Hospital Attributes to Consumers With and Without a Personal Physician

Hospital attributes	Values for consumers with a physician[1] X	Values for consumers without a physician[1] X	Pooled "t" significance level of difference
Location	2.30	2.43	Not significant
Cost of services	1.94	2.04	Not significant
Quality of care	1.09	1.17	0.005
Range of specialized services	1.76	2.03	<0.001
Attitude of staff	1.41	1.69	<0.001
Reputation	1.69	1.96	<0.001
Cleanliness of facilities	1.27	1.49	<0.001
Appearance and decor . . .	2.73	3.00	0.001
Hospital affiliation of consumer's physician	1.80	2.59	<0.001

[1] Values are mean responses on a 5-point scale on which "very important" = 1 and "not very important at all" = 5.

Once the existence of different needs is determined, each consumer segment is profiled. Hospital management can then determine whether potential or actual consumers who match the profile are present in the hospital's current service area in sufficient numbers to justify the establishment of appropriate outpatient services.

In our example, consumers with and without a physician differed significantly in respect to a variety of demographic and social characteristics (Table 2). Two distinct profiles emerged. The consumers with no physician tended to be younger, to be single, and to include more males than the other group. The respondents without a physician were more likely to rent than own their own homes, and, unlike the group with a physician, almost half had lived at their present address less than three years. Consumers without a physician were also more likely to have their medical expenses paid primarily through a prepaid health plan or through a mixture of Medicaid, self-pay, and other means. Analysis of the racial differences between the two groups suggested that minority respondents were less likely to have a personal physician. The small number of minority respondents in the study sample precluded more detailed analysis of the variable. However, even though the number was small, it reflected the proportion of minorities in the population in the survey area.

A third area of investigation focused upon the attitudes of the two consumer segments toward hospitals and health care. A profile of consumers' attitudes is often helpful, because an understanding of them may provide direction for explaining plans and encouraging acceptance of new services. Table 3 shows that the differences between the consumers with no physician and those with a physician extended beyond demographic characteristics to attitudes. For ease of discussion, the attitude statements from the survey instrument have been arranged by topical areas. The first set of statements relates to hospital systems in general. The consumers with a physician appeared to be more discriminating with regard to hospital systems. Some significant differences were observed between the two consumer segments in respect to four statements (No. 2, 3, 5, and 6). The responses of the consumers with a physician indicated that they did not believe that all hospitals were alike. They also apparently believed that better hospitals offered a wide range of services and were associated with medical schools.

Although no significant differences were observed in respect to the statements on the questionnaire relating to time, the two segments clearly differed as to whether they had an opportunity for personal choice. As expected, the consumers with no physician appeared to be more skeptical about allowing a physician to control hospital choice. They indicated that they would prefer a consumer rating service for hospitals. Also, this segment expressed the belief that it helps to find out about a hospital from someone who has been there and that advertising would provide an appropriate source of information about hospital services and rates. For six of the seven statements related to choice, differences between the two groups were significant at the 0.01 level or better.

On the price dimension, both segments agreed that if hospitals were run like a business, costs would decrease. Yet significant differences were observed between the two consumer groups as to the strategies for lowering costs. Although neither segment appeared to believe that advertising would raise costs, the consumers with a physician were not so sure. Both segments agreed that sharing services would lower costs, but the consumers without a physician were more positive about this strategy. The respondents with no physician seemed to have had more negative experiences in interpersonal relationships. For example, they were more likely to report that they felt intimidated by hospitals and did not have good feelings about them.

In the final area of investigation, hospital management and operations, there were significant differences between the segments on only one statement (No. 45). Both groups indicated that they felt billing mistakes were not unusual, but again this opinion was more strongly held by the segment without a physician.

The two groups had rather interesting differences in attitudes. The segment with no physician appeared to be far more critical and negative about hospitals and health care. Yet the commonalities between the two groups cannot be overlooked. Both segments expressed the belief that the current number of hospitals is sufficient. And as their ranking of hospital attributes revealed, neither group paid much attention to hospital ambience. Both groups expressed general agreement that hospitals do little to keep costs down and that government intervention in this area would help. Both segments indicated that they would prefer more surveys of patients and agreed that health care is big business.

Phase 3—Planning, implementation, and evaluation

In the final phase of the marketing research approach, the results of data collection are translated into feasible programs. At this point the concepts illustrated in Figures 1 and 2 can be integrated into the planning process. Following an outside-in approach, consumer-based research is conducted and specific segments profiled. Next, strategies and tactics must be devised. The information gathered in the qualitative and quantitative phases of the research is then used in conjunction with organizational expertise to devise program strategies and tactics. Such information can validate or challenge the subjective knowledge of the organization's managers. When different subgroups have different preferences and profiles, programs may have to be set

Table 2 Comparison of Demographic Profiles of Consumers With and Without a Physician

Demographic characteristics	Percent of consumers with a physician	Percent of consumers without a physician
Age group:		
20-29	20	37
30-39	24	29
40-49	18	12
50-59	17	14
60 and over	21	8
$x^2 = 49.4$, df = 4, $P < 0.001$.		
Marital status:		
Single	12	36
Married	74	55
Other	14	9
$x^2 = 86.2$, df = 2, $P < 0.001$.		
Sex:		
Male	31	53
Female	69	47
$x^2 = 39.3$, df = 1, $P < 0.001$.		
Children:		
0	51	59
1	16	15
2	20	14
3	9	8
4 or more	4	4
$x^2 = 6.4$, df = 4, $P <$ N.S.		
Home ownership:		
Own home	82	65
Rent home	18	35
$x^2 = 35.0$, df = 1, $P < 0.001$.		
Years at present address:		
Less than 1	6	12
1-3	16	31
3-5	15	16
5-10	19	21
10-25	31	15
More than 25	13	5
$x^2 = 61.2$, df = 5, $P < 0.001$.		
Occupation:		
Managerial	12	11

NOTE: df = degrees of freedom, N.S. = not significant. Percentages add vertically to 100 percent except when rounded.

Table 2—*Continued*

Demographic characteristics	Percent of consumers with a physician	Percent of consumers without a physician
Occupation—*Continued*		
Skilled trade	6	10
Laborer.........................	4	5
Office worker	14	13
Technical	4	5
Professional	24	30
Homemaker....................	22	10
Student........................	1	8
Retired	13	7
	$x^2 = 66.0$, df = 8, $P < 0.001$.	
Education:		
Less than 12 years..............	8	6
High school graduate...........	28	16
Technical-vocational school	12	11
Some college	19	22
College graduate	21	28
Graduate or professional		
degree......................	12	17
	$x^2 = 17.7$, df = 6, $P < 0.007$.	
Annual income:		
Under $8,000...................	11	18
$8,000-$11,999	10	10
$12,000-$15,999	12	20
$16,000-$19,999	15	15
$20,000-$24,999	18	13
$25,000 or more	34	24
	$x^2 = 28.2$, df = 5, $P < 0.001$.	
How medical expenses paid:		
self-paid	23	21
Mostly insurance	57	38
Mostly Medicare	7	3
Mostly Medicaid...............	1	1
Prepaid plan	8	27
Other.........................	5	10
	$x^2 = 92.0$, df = 5, $P < 0.001$.	
Race:		
Caucasian	97	94
Other.........................	3	6
	$x^2 = 6.93$, df = 1, $P < 0.001$.	

Table 3 Attitudes of Consumers With and Without a Personal Physician About Hospitals and their Services

Statements used to elicit consumers' attitudes	Values for consumers with physician[1] $\overline{X}$	Values for consumers without physician[1] $\overline{X}$	Pooled "r" significance level of difference[2]
Hospital systems			
1. Some hospitals are better than others	1.63	1.64	0.907
2. I prefer a hospital with my same religious affiliation	3.40	3.72	<0.001
3. The best hospitals have a wide range of services	2.45	2.67	<0.001
4. New teaching hospitals usually have all the services you need	2.83	2.87	0.512
5. Most hospitals are all alike	3.58	3.41	0.016
6. Hospitals associated with medical schools and universities are usually better	2.67	2.48	<0.008
7. There are not enough hospitals to care for the people who need them	3.79	3.83	0.570
8. People's faith in hospitals has gone down dramatically in the last 2 years	2.86	2.78	0.229
9. All hospitals should offer special services like diet workshops, stop smoking programs	3.02	3.13	0.216
10. It is important for hospitals to have plans for low-income consumers	2.03	2.05	0.767
Time			
11. It usually takes forever to check in for emergencies	2.89	2.80	0.289
12. Hospitals should find some way to help pass the time while you wait	3.02	2.92	0.203
13. It often takes days to learn of test results from hospitals	2.73	2.70	0.625
14. In an emergency it's best just to go to the closest hospital	2.35	3.31	0.627
15. I always choose the hospital that is closest to where I live for my medical needs	3.36	3.33	0.723
Having choices			
16. I don't choose my hospital, my doctor does	2.31	2.67	<0.001
17. It's easier to go to the hospital when I have a problem than to get an appointment with a doctor	3.57	3.24	<0.001
18. I don't trust my doctor's opinion about hospitals	1.90	2.32	<0.001
19. It would be nice to have a consumer rating service	2.13	1.94	<0.001
20. It's important to ask around to learn a hospital's reputation	2.70	2.59	0.108
21. Hospitals should advertise their services and rates	2.98	2.69	<0.001
22. Before choosing a hospital, it's best to find someone who's been there	3.27	3.09	0.010
Hospital ambience			
23. Most hospitals have a sterile, cold atmosphere	3.34	3.27	0.319
24. Cleanliness is one of the first things I check when entering a hospital	2.22	2.48	<0.001

Table 3—Continued

Statements used to elicit consumers' attitudes	Values for consumers with physician[1] $\bar{X}$	Values for consumers without physician[1] $\bar{X}$	Pooled "t" significance level of difference[2]
Hospital ambience—Continued			
25. The hospital building tells a lot about how people are cared for ...	3.36	3.39	0.647
26. When I enter a hospital, the first thing I do is look at how it is decorated ...	3.96	3.96	0.928
27. Hospitals should make their waiting rooms nicer places to sit ...	3.00	2.93	0.276
Price			
28. If hospitals were run like a business, costs would go down ...	2.72	2.81	0.225
29. Hospitals don't really try to keep costs down ...	2.50	2.54	0.603
30. If hospitals start to advertise, costs would go up ...	2.83	3.01	*0.014*
31. If hospitals were to share services, costs would be lower ...	2.18	2.04	*0.016*
32. Hospital costs seem to be rising for no real reason ...	2.74	2.85	0.172
33. Governments should be more active in lowering hospital charges ...	2.60	2.52	0.349
34. The best way to lower hospital costs would be to close some hospitals ...	3.32	3.21	0.104
35. The saying "you get what you pay for" is definitely true in medicine ...	3.64	3.68	0.593
Interpersonal relations			
36. I often feel intimidated in hospitals ...	3.36	3.15	*0.008*
37. The attitude of the hospital staff is one of the best ways to tell what the hospital is like ...	2.23	2.29	0.364
38. Nurses should show more respect for patients ...	2.55	2.69	0.051
39. Most people who work in hospitals forget patients are human ...	3.52	3.35	*0.019*
40. It's hard to get a straight answer when you ask a question in a hospital ...	2.83	2.84	0.888
41. I've had good feelings about the hospitals I have been in ...	2.10	2.43	*<0.001*
Hospital management and operations			
42. Hospital billing procedures are too complicated ...	2.64	2.54	0.248
43. I often wonder who is in charge when I enter the hospital ...	2.94	2.90	0.590
44. Hospitals should survey patients to see what their feelings are ...	2.08	1.99	0.154
45. It is very rare that hospitals make mistakes in billing people ...	3.52	3.67	*0.028*
46. Health care is big business ...	1.63	1.55	0.114
47. I feel that most hospitals have high ethical standards ...	2.25	2.33	0.179
48. It is irritating to be given medicine without being told the purpose ...	1.70	1.62	0.179

[1] Values are mean responses on a 5-point scale on which "strongly agree" = 1 and "strongly disagree" = 5.

[2] Italicized numbers are significant at < 0.05.

up for each of them. Criteria for evaluating program implementation are outlined, as is done in the present planning process. Program effectiveness, for example, is measured by analyses of service utilization, revenues and costs, consumers' compliance and satisfaction, and health outcomes. A program is more likely to be successful with a marketing research approach than with traditional health planning, because with a marketing approach, a monitoring system is designed specifically for each segment of consumers before implementation begins.

In our study, consumers with no physician differed from consumers with a physician in many respects. Particularly interesting were the results showing the importance that each consumer segment attached to various attributes in selecting a hospital. Consumers with no physician placed less importance on all nine hospital attributes on which they were queried than did consumers with a physician. Of particular note were the significant differences between the two groups in their rating of the importance to them of a hospital's range of services, reputation, and appearance.

Demographically, also, the two segments differed. The consumers with no physicians tended to be young, single males with relatively high levels of education. These consumers were more critical of hospitals and less concerned with a hospital's size or reputation. Their attitudes implied that the traditional association with a physician was not essential, indeed, was possibly not even desirable. The responses of these consumers showed that they preferred to maintain control and decide for themselves which health resources to use and when. Therefore, a hospital or other health care system seeking to respond to these values would need to provide access for these consumers to an organized, integrated system of health services that they could use as needed on a periodic basis. This conclusion does not imply that members of this segment might not align themselves with a specific physician if a long-term problem were to occur. Given their current health status, however, they consider a personal physician to be less essential than a comprehensive system to which they can have relatively immediate access. Managers of hospitals and other organized systems of health care should consider creating programs and services for this market segment. Following are some guidelines for making some of the necessary strategic decisions:

- Services should focus primarily on short-term acute care, not on emergency and nonacute chronic conditions. (The segment with no physician views an appropriate set of services more favorably than a wide range of them.)

- Services should be designed so as to provide consumers with alternatives in terms of the type of health manpower that they see, the times and places that services are offered, and the basis on which they are offered—walk-in visits or appointments. (The desire to have a choice and be in control of decisions seems to be a key characteristic of consumers with no personal physician.)

- Information about services should be made available in carefully targeted ways, such as by advertising and stimulation of word-of-mouth referrals. A consumer rating service might also be appropriate for reaching the target market. (Consumers with no physician seem to put a high value on having information about their available options.)

- Finally, management might want to survey actual and potential consumers to determine their feelings about the specific mix of services that should be offered and the best way to present them.

CONCLUSIONS

In a marketing approach to planning, problems are defined and studies are designed in the sequence that we have shown. First, the extent of the problem is determined by qualitative research. Second, the characteristics and current behavior patterns of the participants in the health care marketplace are described. Third, trends and relationships are analyzed in order to identify the various segments of consumers and to forecast their future behavior and future utilization of health care services.

Already widely used in business, the marketing approach is beginning to be applied successfully in the health care field. In a family practice clinic in the Southwest, for example, the results of personal interviews with clinic patients, as well as information from an adjacent hospital, helped to identify a segment of consumers who preferred to have access to nonemergency, acute-care medical services outside of the hospital on a 24-hour walk-in basis. Because of the estimated size of this segment, planning has begun at the clinic to add a 24-hour walk-in medical service to its existing appointment-based services. This new program will provide the clinic an opportunity for growth as well as remove a considerable portion of the current inappropriate demands on the hospital's emergency room.

In a 170-bed community hospital in a major midwestern city, individual depth interviews with private practice physicians were used to identify ways to increase the number of physicians affiliated with the hospital. This investigation revealed that physicians newly entering practice in the area had a need for help in setting up their offices. The hospital therefore appointed a management staff to assist private practice physicians who affiliated with the hospital to apply modern management methods in their offices.

The approach to planning presented here may seem in many respects obvious to health care providers. Yet the differences between it and the traditional approach, which are highlighted in Figure 1, are distinct. In a marketing planning model, Phases 1 and 2 of marketing research (Figure 2) take place before any strategies or tactics are decided upon. Marketing research is just that, an examination of the market, that is, of an organization's present and potential customers or users. Information about these groups (their attitudes, perceptions, needs, and wants) dictates the organization's strategic decisions.

Planning and research are not separate activities, each producing a distinct outcome. Rather, they are both part of a sequence of actions, beginning with consumer research and ending with the service mix appropriate to the organization's various publics.

Upon implementation of plans and feedback from evaluation or control procedures, this total sequence of activities becomes a dynamic process that enables the organization to adjust effectively and rapidly to the factors that determine the success or failure of its programs.

REFERENCES

1. Levey, S., and Loomba, M.P. *Health Care Administration: A Managerial Perspective.* J. B. Lippincott Company, Philadelphia, Pa., 1973, p. 4.

2. Scutchfield, F.D. "Alternate Methods for Health Priority Assessment." *Journal of Community Health* 1, (Fall 1975): 29-28.

3. Flexner, W.A., and Littlefield, J.E. "Comment on Alternative Methods of Health Priority Assessment." *Journal of Community Health* 2, (Spring 1977): 245-246. (Letters to the editors).

4. Green, P.E., and Tull, D.S. *Research for Marketing Decisions,* 3d edition. Englewood Cliffs, N.J.; Prentice-Hall, Inc., 1976.

5. Schoner, B., and Uhl, K.P. *Marketing Research: Information Systems and Decision Making,* 2d edition. New York: John Wiley & Sons, Inc., 1975.

6. McCarthy, E.J. *Basic Marketing: A Managerial Approach,* 5th edition. Homewood, Ill.: Richard D. Irwin, Inc., 1975.

7. Hughes, G.D. *Marketing Management: A Planning Approach.* Reading, Mass.: Addison-Wesley, 1978.

8. Kotler, P. *Marketing for Nonprofit Organizations.* Englewood Cliffs, N.J.: Prentice-Hall, Inc., 1975.

9. Fuchs, V. "The Growing Demand for Medical Care." *New England Journal of Medicine* 279, (July 25, 1968): 190-195.

10. Jeffers, J.R.; Bognanno, M.F.; and Barlett, J.C. "On the Demand Versus Need for Medical Services and the Concept of 'Shortage.'" *American Journal of Public Health* 61 (January 1971): 46-63.

11. Donabedian, A. *Aspects of Medical Care Administration.* Cambridge, Mass.: Harvard University Press, 1973.

12. Egdahl, R.H., and Gertman, P.M. *Technology and the Quality of Health Care,* Germantown, Md.: Aspen Systems Corporation, 1978.

13. Flexner, W.A.; McLaughlin, C.P.; and Littlefield, J.E. "Discovering What the Health Consumer Really Wants." *Health Care Management Review* 2 (Fall 1977): 43-69.

14. Stratmann, W.C. "A Study of Consumer Attitudes About Health Care: The Delivery of Ambulatory Services." *Medical Care* 8 (July 1975): 537-548.

15. Kasteler, J., et al. "Issues Underlying Prevalence of 'Doctor-Shopping' Behavior." *Journal of Health and Social Behavior* 17, (December 1976): 328-339.

16. Brooks, E.F., and Madison, D.L. "Primary Care Practice: Forms of Organization." In *Primary Care and the Practice of Medicine*, edited by J. Noble. Boston, Mass.: Little, Brown and Company, 1976, pp. 67-89.

17. Hyman, H. *Health Planning*. Germantown, Md.: Aspen Systems Corporation, 1975.

18. Berkowitz, E.N., and Flexner, W.A. "The Marketing Audit: A Tool for Health Service Organizations." *Health Care Management Review* 3 (Fall 1978): 51-57.

19. Flexner, McLaughlin, and Littlefield. "Discovering What the Health Consumer Really Wants," op. cit.

20. Reynolds, F.D., and Johnson, D.K. "Validity of Focus Group Findings." *Journal of Advertising Research* 18 (June 1978): 21-24.

21. Calder, B.J. "Focus Groups and the Nature of Qualitative Research." *Journal of Marketing Research* 14 (August 1977): 353-364.

22. Parker, B., and Srinivasan, V.A. "Consumer Preference Approach to the Planning of Rural Primary Health Care Facilities." *Operations Research* 24 (September—October 1976): 991-1025.

23. Ware, J. "Consumer Perceptions of Health Care Services: Implications for Academic Research." *Journal of Medical Education* 50 (September 1975): 839-849.

24. Ware, J., and Snyder, M. "Dimensions of Patient Attitudes Regarding Doctors and Medical Care Services." *Medical Care* 13 (August 1975): 669-682.

25. Wind, Y., and Spitz, L. "Analytical Approach to Marketing Decisions in Health Care Organizations." *Operations Research* 24 (September-October 1976): 973-990.

26. Kerlinger, R.N. *Foundations of Behavioral Research*, 2d edition. New York: Holt, Rinehart and Winston, 1973.

27. Delbecq, A.L.; Van de Ven, A.H.; and Gustafson, D.H. *Group Techniques for Program Planning: A Guide to Nominal Group and Delphi Processes*. Glenview, Ill: Scott, Foresman and Company, 1975.

28. Green and Tull, *Research for Marketing Decisions*, op. cit.

29. Kerlinger, F.N., and Pedhazur, E.J. *Multiple Regression in Behavioral Research*. New York: Holt, Rinehart, and Winston, Inc., 1973.

30. Sheth, J.N. *Multivariate Methods for Market and Survey Research*. Chicago, Ill.: American Marketing Association, 1977.

31. Frank, R.E.; Masey, W.F.; and Wind, Y. *Market Segmentation*. Englewood Cliffs, N.J.: Prentice-Hall, Inc., 1972.

32. Anderson, R.; Lion, J.; and Anderson, O.W. *Two Decades of Health Services: Social Survey Trends in Use and Expenditures*. Cambridge, Mass.: Ballinger Publishing Co., 1976.

33. "America's Health Care System: A Comprehensive Portrait." In *Special Report*. Princeton, N.J.: Robert Wood Johnson Foundation, 1978, pp. 4-15.

Section Three
Finance: An Overview

Manager A must make a decision. Two services have been identified as possible candidates for elimination. One has a relatively high volume but a low average price. The other has a low volume but a high average price. Intuitively, the manager wants to eliminate the low volume/high price service since it contributes less to the occupancy rate of the hospital. But before making the decision, the manager asks the finance director for an analysis of the cost of producing each of these services and their subsequent contribution margins. The response: "We have some financial data, but not in a form that will respond to your request. We can't determine the cost of each service without a detailed and lengthy special study."

This anecdote illustrates the critical role of financial management in strategic planning. All too often, the health care organization's financial system is little more than a budget and book of accounts, unable to be used effectively to respond to management's decision-making needs.

Although the anecdote above is fictional, it is based on the kind of decision raised in Figure 2 of Milch's article in Section 1 ("Product-Market Differentiation: A Strategic Planning Model for Community Hospitals"). Look at that figure and try to decide which service should be eliminated between numbers 10 and 16. It is difficult to make a decision without knowing the profit contribution of each service. And, just knowing the average price or charge does not provide this information. What is needed is cost and volume data for each service.

Thus, at the same time that health care managers are building a system to understand better the organization's market performance, they should also be creating a financial management system that permits them to understand the resource implications of market-oriented strategic decisions. The framework and issues related to creating such a system are the focus of the articles in this section.

The primary purpose of a financial management system is to ensure availability of adequate resources for implementation of the organization's plans. This relates to (1) adequate cash flow for effective service delivery and (2) realization of sufficient return on investment (or equity) to make the endeavor "profitable" in terms of the organization's goals and objectives and to produce sufficient slack to permit growth or adjustment to changing market conditions. In his article in this section ("Identity Crisis: Financial Management in Health"), Silvers notes that "it is this *future* decision orientation that is of central importance" to financial management.

In building a financial management system, certain management tools are required. Herzlinger ("Fiscal Management in Health Organizations") identifies the need for (1) an accrual accounting system, (2) a statistical system related to program/service/cost centers, and (3) a data processing system to facilitate the integration of the accounting and programmatic data. While most health organizations have these three tools already installed, they are often viewed as separate functional elements or, as Herzlinger says, "as a collection of chores to be delegated to subordinates and unworthy of [top management's] attention." They are seldom integrated into a management process (a financial management system) that aids the managers of the health organization.

The process required for effective financial management, according to Herzlinger, involves four sequential steps beginning with planning and ending with control. Readers may note the similarity between this sequence and Figure 2 in Flexner and Berkowitz's article in Section 2 on marketing research. Both emphasize the critical importance of broadening the data base for decision making from existing data to look for new opportunities. And each article identifies control (or evaluation) as a look backward to relate actual to planned results.

Herzlinger's article provides a sound basis for understanding the general tools and process that are essential in financial management. It is important, however, that the manager go beyond this level to develop an appreciation for the complexities of financial decisions. The article by Silvers ("Identity Crisis: Financial Management in Health") addresses these in two ways. First, Silvers describes the relationship between management decisions and financial results and notes the frequent difficulties that occur in making these linkages. Second, he shows how a framework for making financial decisions must be placed within the broader context of the organization's internal environment and the market forces that influence what should be produced. Consider how thìs more complex view of financial management relates to the general elements in the strategic planning process described by Thieme in Section 1. This same view is repeated in Section 4 when Roberts and Hirsch, and Stearns and his colleagues discuss strategic modeling as a means to integrate these various factors.

The article by Silvers is important in another sense. The need for health organizations to develop proactive rather than reactive financial decisions to survive and grow is highlighted. A further rationale for this more dynamic view of the allocation of scarce resources is given by Long ("Valuation as a Criterion in Not-For-Profit Decision Making"). Here, the author develops the case for the not-for-profit organization to focus on its return on investment to be maximally responsive to its ownership—identified as the range of recipients, donors, volunteers, and payers of services. Note the multiple constituencies again entering the discussion. The argument presented in this article expands on the service elimination/profit contribution anecdote presented earlier by recognizing the numerous factors—inflation, technological improvement, expansion, alteration of services—that affect the ultimate profitability or survival of the services and organization. Finally, Long provides the reader with a "finance catechism" that permits comparison of the financial management issues facing both for-profit and not-for-profit organizations.

Managing the health organization in the face of constrained reimbursements, supply equilibrium, and increased competition is not an easy task. To respond to these changes, many health care managers are turning to strategic planning, with its underlying market orientation, as a management framework. The articles in this section emphasize the dual importance of developing a sound financial management and integrating this framework into the overall strategic planning process.

9. Fiscal Management in Health Organizations

REGINA E. HERZLINGER

Herzlinger, Regina E. "Fiscal Management in Health Organizations." *Health Care Management Review,* Summer 1977.

Fiscal management is a key managerial activity. If properly executed, it ensures that the organization will have the resources to carry out its plans and that the plans will be administered in an efficient and effective manner.

It is in practice, however, an activity that rarely engages the attention and skills of the top-level administrators in health organizations. And, as a result, many health organizations find themselves unable either to marshal the resources they need to carry out their plans or to judge how well their plans are being carried out. The reason for this is that fiscal management is frequently viewed by top-level administrators as a collection of chores to be delegated to subordinates and unworthy of their attention: accounting, material management, management information systems, insurance, bonding, property and office management, and so on.

This inverted perspective of the fiscal management activity is symptomized by the problem of data inundation that plagues many health care organizations. The problem manifests itself via two simultaneous developments (1) a plentitude of statistics, numbers, journals, ledgers, and computer printouts; and (2) a dearth of meaningful managerial information. These two developments coexist because the data system has been implemented by lower-level managers in response to various outside requests for it; but, since top managers remain uninvolved in the process, the data system does not meet their needs for integrated, comprehensive information.

Using the framework developed by R.N. Anthony, the process of fiscal management can be viewed as consisting of two pieces: a *system* that provides data and a *process* that translates the data into managerial action.[1] The *system* is the basic information system of the organization that provides accounting and statistical data. The *process* of fiscal management uses these data for planning, programming, budgeting, and controlling the financial activities of the organization. Both the system and the process will be discussed in greater detail below.

THE FISCAL MANAGEMENT SYSTEM

A sound fiscal management system should always rest on the base of an accrual accounting system, whose transactions are recorded via double-entry bookkeeping. Accrual accounting was first codified by a 15th Century monk in a mathematics text and has lingered to plague a grudgingly compliant public ever since.

Accrual accounting is not only a very important concept but also a very slippery one. Essentially, it posits that the flow of income is not necessarily equal to the flow of cash; revenues are not necessarily equal to cash inflows and expenses are not necessarily equal to cash outflows. This makes sense; for example, if an organization buys $5,000 worth of office equipment that is going to last for at least ten years, it really doesn't make much sense to declare all of the $5,000 as being the current year's expense. But how much of the total $5,000 is this year's expense and, in general, how are revenues and expenses defined?

This is the most critical question in accrual accounting: the delineation of the decision rules that trigger recognition of revenues and expenses. (These decision rules are so complex that they have caused many budding business students to reconsider their choice of career.) Fundamentally, revenues are recognized at a point in time where there is objective evidence of their amount and where the work that generated the revenues has already been performed. For most service-delivering health organizations, this is the point of service delivery or billing. Expenses are the resources that were consumed to generate the revenues. For example, a community health organization that generates the bulk of its revenues by providing services will have revenues for a period of time, which consist of all the bills sent during that period, and expenses, which are the resources consumed to provide the revenues: salaries, benefits, rent, heat, light and power, depreciation, and so on.

The difference between revenues and expenses, defined in this manner, is income, and the income statement enables comparison of the two items over time. The other major financial statement, the balance sheet, enables examination of the sources of capital (the liabilities and fund balance accounts) and the uses of capital (the asset accounts). Under accrual accounting, both assets and liabilities may consist of nontangible items: for example, goodwill on the asset side and fund balance on the liability side. If the organization follows fund accounting practices, the income statement is prepared for the current funds, while the balance sheet is prepared separately for all the funds.

Of course, the question of recognizing revenues and expenses is a difficult one, and it is therefore difficult to understand clearly what the income statement and balance sheet are telling us. For example, depreciation expense is frequently thought of as the rate at which a capital item—like a car—is being used up or as an account for its replacement. But, in accrual accounting, depreciation is nothing of the sort. Rather, it is the process of allocating original cost. It does not necessarily measure the "true" costs of using up the item, because it measures on the basis of historical cost and not on the basis of replacement cost.

Yet, despite these difficulties in interpretation, accrual accounting is more useful than cash accounting in producing financial statements. It generates not only the financial statements just discussed but also cost accounting statements. In the excellent National League of Nursing's cost analysis method, for example, the items of expense—such as salaries, transportation, etc.—are collected through the fundamental books of accounts of the organization. They are then either traced directly to particular programs or allocated to these programs. The full costs—direct and indirect—of each program are thus calculated. In addition, using a statistical system, the programmatic costs are divided by relevant measures of output to calculate the costs per unit of output. This system, thus, uses the expense data to calculate costs of various programs, costs of various outputs, and costs of different types of line item expenses.

An additional component of the fiscal management system is the statistical system that collects data on how time is spent and on the various types of · output. If the organization is large enough, these financial and statistical data are stored and manipulated via a computerized data-handling system.

These then are the elements of the fiscal management system:

- An accrual accounting system which is used to produce financial statements;
- A statistical system which is combined with the accounting system to produce cost reports;
- An automated or manual data processing system which facilitates the manipulation of the data produced by the accounting and statistical systems.

These three systems are frequently regarded as being fiscal management. They are nothing of the kind. Rather, they are merely the tools used to effect the fiscal management process, which will be discussed in greater detail below.

THE FISCAL MANAGEMENT PROCESS

The process of fiscal management should enable the managers of the organization to ensure that they have the financial resources to enable them to carry out their programs. The process consists of four sequential steps: planning, programming, budgeting and controlling.

Planning

The process of planning consists of articulating the long-range goals and objectives of the organization and the steps that will have to be followed in order to accomplish those goals. The planning process is frequently depicted as a rational, systematic one where all opportunities are explored, costs and benefits are carefully assessed, and strategies are shrewdly and skillfully mapped out. The living analogue of this portrayal has yet to exist.

Rather, in most organizations, the planning process is fragmented, unsystematic, and inspired by random events and not by calculation. It cannot be otherwise. This is not to say that a plan shouldn't be carefully compiled. It should. But, the plan is never the product of a systematic, routine searching process—because the real world isn't systematic and routinized, and the planning process, which explores the relationship between the real world and the organization, can, therefore, not be routinized either.

The planning process can be partially guided by the output of the fiscal management system, which indicates the needs and strengths of the organization; the income statement and the program-based cost data are particularly useful for this purpose. However, the process should not rely primarily on *existing* data, but rather on externally provided data that inspire plans for *new* opportunities.

The most useful plans extend five years into the future and are quite specific and detailed. The first year of the five-year plan should consist of the next year's budget. The plans should be updated and/or revised as new information comes in. It is most important that they exist—not because they are part of the litany of what sound management is about, but because they crystallize the aspirations of the organization in an unambiguous manner, which enables all the members of the organization to understand and *share* in its future.

Programming

The programming process converts the plan, the output of the planning process, into a set of programs. This process, unlike the planning one, should be done in a careful, systematic way with the costs and benefits of existing and newly-created programs being carefully considered. The programming process is somewhat useful for interprogram comparisons but it is primarily useful for intraprogram ones: the process of evaluating alternative means of reaching the same goal.

In for-profit corporations, the process of programming is similar to traditional capital budgeting procedures, in which different investment proposals are ranked and, on a time adjusted basis, analyzed for their relative profitability. In nonprofit organizations, the criteria for success include dimensions not included in mere measurement of profits, and, of course, careful consideration of such criteria should be part of the process.

In the 1960s, the tendency was to attempt to overquantify these criteria, and, as a result, the analysis of benefits and costs received an unjustly poor reputation. This process is frequently neglected or performed in a cursory fashion. It is painstaking work and if done correctly involves a great deal of excruciatingly dull number pushing. Nevertheless, it is a very important job and in many ways determines the future of the organization.

The consequences of doing a sloppy job in the programming process are that the organization in the future won't necessarily be the one the current management wants it to be. This is because, once begun, programs take on a life of their own; additionally, unless they are carefully considered from their inception, these immortals may not even resemble their original model. Any governmental organization could provide many examples of the immortality of programs. And, it is particularly important for privately financed, non-profit organizations to avoid this particular problem.

One aspect of the programming process that is usually omitted is that of long-range consideration of programmatic consequences. It is important that programs be considered on a long-run basis, because the future is not a mere extrapolation of the present. Long-run consideration is particularly important for programs that are started by grants or gifts from outsiders to the organizations. The odds are good that the programs will be there long after the grants and gifts have run out; in this case, it is important to "look a gift horse in the mouth."

Budgeting

The process of budgeting must compete with the *Bible* in the quantity of words written about it. And the election of Jimmy Carter, and the likely advent of zero-based budgeting (or ZBB as its fans refer to it) has inspired yet another torrent of words.

Yet despite the deluge in most organizations, budgeting consists of pulling out last year's budget, adding five percent here, eight percent there, adding up the total, and labeling it next year's budget. This form of budgeting is called "incremental" budgeting. And although it is the most frequently practiced method of budgeting, it is viewed with disdain by professional budgeteers.

Does it deserve this? One reason for the disdain is that incremental budgeting is performed on a so-called "line-item" budget, which merely lists the different classes of expenses. The problem with line-item budgeting is that it doesn't inform the manager as to how the expenses were used and in what they resulted. The use of a "program" budget, which isolates the budgets for certain programs, is recommended for overcoming this problem.

It is worthwhile to devote a substantial amount of time to setting up a program structure that either collects the costs and budget for the organization's programs and/or one that collects these data for particular organizational units. The programs and organizational units do not necessarily coincide, and in some cases it is useful to collect these data for both entities. The program data are used to evaluate plans, while the responsibility-center data are used to hold organizational units responsible for carrying out their duties.

Nevertheless, critics of incremental budgeting still disdain this process, even if it is performed on a program budget. The reason for this is that incremental budgeting merely continues past activities and thus may be merely perpetuating past mistakes or mediocre performances. Rather, they recommend zero-base budgeting, which means literally starting the budgeting process with a base of zero, rather than last year's budget, as a starting point. What the ZBB adherents advocate is a complete, thorough analysis of the budget from the ground up. And President Carter, when he was Governor Carter, claims he did just that in the State of Georgia.

Of course, ZBB is impossible to do on a yearly basis. It is beyond the resources of any organization. What can feasibly be done is to perform a zero-base budgeting process for a particular program that needs close and careful attention. The remaining programs can be budgeted for on an incremental fashion as depicted above or can be budgeted for by isolating the amount of the increase in last year's budget that was brought about by:

- inflation

- changes in the *quantity* of output

- changes in the *quality* of output

Changes in existing programs that were not caused by one or more of these three reasons are changes that can't be justified.

There are two more noteworthy aspects of the budgeting process. First, it is important to start the process with an estimate of revenues and then to match expenses to the revenues. Most organizations reverse this process, budgeting expenses first and then matching revenues, wishfully, to expenses. In health organizations, the calculations of patient care revenues and expenses are interdependent, and care should be taken to ensure that all allowable avenues for maximizing reimbursement are explored. For hospitals, which are frequently reimbursed on a "cost or charges, whichever is lower" basis and whose full costs are calculated via a complex double distribution of overhead procedure (the famous or infamous "step-down" methodology), it is particularly important to devote a substantial amount of effort to budgeting revenues. And, for medium to large-size hospitals, it is recommended that a number of computer-assisted simulations of the step-down outcomes be used as an aid in the process of budgeting revenues.

In addition to patient care revenues, all other sources of revenues should be explored and budgeted for. Among these are revenues from endowments (in those organizations that have such sources of capital), gifts for operations, grants for various programs, and prices for ancillary activities. For endowed institutions, the pros and cons of a "total return" approach to declaring revenues from the endowment should be carefully considered.

Second is the issue of whether to do it in a "top-down" manner, in which instructions are disseminated from the top-down, or on a "bottom-up" basis, where the lower organizational units have full rein. There is no one best method, but it must be consistent with the style of the organization. Whatever is chosen, the costs and virtues of the chosen approach should be carefully considered. The budgeting process should not be a child of circumstance.

To summarize, the budgeting process should be closely linked to the planning and programming processes, be done on a programmatic basis, and should reflect carefully articulated incremental reasoning for most programs. It should be done for both capital and operating expenses and, for purposes of control, should be on an accrual—rather than a cash—basis.

Controlling

The last part of the fiscal management process is the one that controls the organization by comparing actual results to those budgeted. This step closes the loop between planning and accounting in that it measures the extent to which the plans (as articulated by the budget and other documents) are actually being carried out.

It is difficult to believe that New York City, a $9 billion enterprise, is unable to carry out this step. And until 1968, the Department of Defense, with a budget of about $80 billion, couldn't do it either. Why? Because the accounting system and the budgeting system measured different things, and the two systems were not reconciled.

So, if your organization doesn't measure actual results against budgeted ones, it is not alone. On the other hand, performing this function is the only formal way to measure whether the financial plans are being carried out. And, if it is not done, there is no way—as in the case of New York City—to know the extent to which the budget is being carried out.

Designing such an accounting system essentially involves going back to the chart of accounts and developing a programmatic accounting system that uses the basic revenue and expense accounts. Sometimes, new revenue and expense accounts must be set up.

In addition, it is useful to set up systems that measure the extent to which planned results were achieved and that, to the extent possible, measure the quality of those results. Our technical ability to produce meaningful output data of this sort is limited—particularly when compared with our ability to measure inputs via the accrual accounting process. Nevertheless, it is important that, in large organizations, systematic efforts to measure output be made.

Thus, the fiscal management process consists of four integrated steps of planning, programming, budgeting, and controlling. The role of the top manager is to ensure that the steps are carried out and to use the data for managerial purposes. It is *not* his or her job to get so deeply enmeshed in the mechanics of producing the data that the process of fiscal management is neglected.

REFERENCES

1. Anthony, R.N., and Herzlinger, R.E. *Management Control in Nonprofit Organizations.* Homewood, Ill.: Irwin Publishers, 1975.

10. Identity Crisis: Financial Management in Health

J. B. SILVERS

Silvers, J.B. "Identity Crisis: Financial Management in Health. *Health Care Management Review,* Fall 1976.

Everyone agrees that one of the most critical elements of the "health care crisis" in the United States centers on finance. This must be so since we are experiencing escalating costs, exorbitant capital equipment outlays, insufficient contributions, rate and expenditure reviews, new debt issues, Medicare cost reports, *ad nauseam*—and all of these are clearly financial. At least they all involve dollars and are reported in financial statements.

However, the real concern is not so much that the issues are somehow financial in nature but that they are not being managed. The problem is *financial management,* not just dollars. Furthermore, a recent survey in the hospital sector of the health industry revealed a surprising strength and unanimity of opinion regarding the need for more financial management education.[1] Of the hospital administrators, board chairmen, medical directors, and other nonhospital health executives polled, financial management was far and away the most important priority. Any number of other public statements by legislators, regulators, intermediaries, and providers bear out this notion. Finance is somehow both the implicit culprit *and* the expected savior of an industry rapidly approaching bankruptcy. And approaching bankruptcy it is—from the Social Security System[2] through to the institution.[3, 4]

But the transition is difficult in an industry where management traditionally has concentrated on personnel, facilities, medical staff, community relationships, accreditation, and regulation, while finance has been regulated to mere "bean counting"—or more politely, bookkeeping—after the fact. The financial man, usually a controller, reported what had happened. He did not play an important role in *making decisions* that had a critical impact on the finances of the health delivery program. Nor did he even provide much in the way of data or forecasts of potential financial results of alternative management actions to those who were in the decision-making role. In short, the "finance man" usually did not and often still does not make or even contribute significantly to most of the important decisions that determine the financial viability of the institution or program.

It is rather the top executive on whom this financial management responsibility falls. Of course, there still would be little problem with financial management if the top executive were skilled and educated in this area—but he often is not. As recently as 1972, a survey conducted by the Association of University Programs in Health Administration[5] revealed that only 13 graduate programs out of 33 in the United States offered required courses in financial management. While this glaring flaw has been partially corrected, generations of managers in the health field cannot even critically analyze a financial statement, to say nothing of marshalling data and using them to provide an analytic financial input to decision making.

Stated another way, the health care executive often does not understand *financial accounting*—public financial reports, to say nothing of *financial management*—the use of accounting data, and analytic methods to make financial decisions, in spite of the fact that he is often in reality the chief *financial* officer as well as the chief *executive* officer. He is asked to make judgments and decisions regarding investment (inventories, collection policies, equipment purchases, expansion, replacement, new services, and so forth) and financing (bank loans, mortgages, debt capacity, net income margins, contributions, leases, and so forth) without sufficient preparation. Even if someone else has made preliminary recommendations, he must make the final decision, sometimes, of course, with board concurrence.

Even more important, however, than these more obvious financial decisions are a host of nonfinancial choices with both direct and indirect financial implications. Hiring, for instance, is the responsibility of a personnel director or, for higher level medical staff, of a committee. But the financial implications of the hiring process can be critical. Often after being committed to certain staff, the institution is also tied to related capital outlays and operating expenses. For instance, a new radiologist or chief of medicine in the teaching hospital often constitutes such an "investment" decision. In a reverse situation, a major new piece of equipment, which might have been purchased through contributions, requires certain additional staffing and overhead expenses that add to the cost and have serious financing implications.

To take another example, the addition of a new service, or its elimination, has such strong financial management overtones that it is hard to imagine this evaluation except in these terms. However, in the past, medical considerations alone, rather than long range financial or strategic factors, have often dominated these decisions.

ACCOUNTING VERSUS FINANCIAL MANAGEMENT

Perhaps before we go on we should attempt to define further what is meant by *financial management* versus accounting or, more specifically, *financial accounting*.[6] The accountant's goal in preparing financial information is simply to present a picture of what has happened in the past. To guide him are the principles of consistency, materiality, matching, and conservatism that have more precise technical meanings but are generally self-explanatory. By applying a set of rules based on these principles, but slanted toward the needs of the particular user, the accountant prepares a balance sheet and an income statement, plus subsidiary notes.

However, in most settings the accountant uses the "accrual" system rather than a mere inspection of the checkbook entries, that is, "cash" accounting, in order to provide a clearer picture of the underlying economic activity. Thus, the sale of goods or services to a customer is counted as sales revenue during a period, even though the bill is not actually paid until the following period. In the meantime, until cash is received from the customer, the accountant keeps tally of the transaction as an "accounts receivable" on the balance sheet. The revenue is "accrued," even though it has not been realized in cash.

The upshot of this typical treatment of a transaction by an accountant is that financial statements, as presented, usually shed very little light on the cash generating ability or cash financing needs of a given economic operation. A particular enterprise can easily show very large profits but be severely strapped for cash, even to the point of bankruptcy, or it can show no profits and still generate a good deal of excess cash. And it is the cash position, current and future, that must be of central concern in financial management.

In short, the accountant, in preparing public financial statements is merely following, and sometimes interpreting, a set of rules that may provide a clear picture of the *past* period as a part of an ongoing economic enterprise. However, his data can be used as a *base* for financial planning, forecasting, and management of future periods' activities and cash flows. It is this *future* decision orientation that is of central importance to the financial manager. And the most important element of this future-oriented financial decision making is the movement of cash—from initial outlay, and thus financing need, through to the subsequent cash inflows, that is, the return of initial capital outlay plus any additional return on capital.

In this light, although the goal of this article is not to make an accountant out of the reader, some knowledge of the relationship between management action, reported financial statements, and the impact on the cash balance is beneficial in becoming a better financial manager. Of course, many management actions together produce these financial results. However, to the extent that the manager can identify the process, he can construct an overall financial simulation of various alternatives.

FINANCIAL SIMULATION

It is clear that in every organization there are some key decisions made by management that help to determine observed financial results.[7] If both inputs, that is, decisions and outputs, or financial and operating results, are stated in common financial terms, then we have the beginnings of a financial model that can be used to predict and analyze the financial consequences of various alternative actions. Unfortunately, getting from input to output in a logical, consistent way is no easier to specify on paper than it is to observe in reality.

The key problem in pursuing any framework from beginning to end lies in isolating the specific relations between management actions and financial results. For instance, while the decision to purchase new radiological equipment has obvious and direct implications for cash outflows, its effect on patient volume, mix, and revenue may be very real but indirect. To complicate the matter further, it is not even clear in many institutions what decisions are actually the prerogative of the management and which are purely involuntary.

However, in order to make any progress, we must focus in on some key decisions and estimate the sensitivity of various financial outputs to management changes in them. As an example, seven basic decision areas have been singled out in Figure 1. The nature of these decisions is critical to understand. As an example, the manager does *not* directly determine the work force in any given period. Rather, he makes hiring decisions that, when combined with employee turnover rates and the beginning worker level, jointly result in a certain number of actual employees. Certainly the process could be refined further to look at recruitment advertisements, interviewing procedures, beginning salary offers, and job descriptions and criteria as the relevant decision factors rather than hiring decisions taken as a whole. The point is simply that a value judgment is involved with each step back from the end result down a line of increasingly more detailed decision inputs. The list in Figure 1 is a mixture of some decisions under relatively tight control, such as material purchases, and others, such as patient volume and mix, that often might be controlled as much by environmental factors as by management decisions. Furthermore, in spite of the fact that this example is based on a hospital setting, similar relationships could be determined for any other health provider.

Although for purposes of illustration the list of decisions in Figure 1 will suffice, it may be useful to comment briefly about the most important variable

Figure 1 Financial Model of the Health Institution

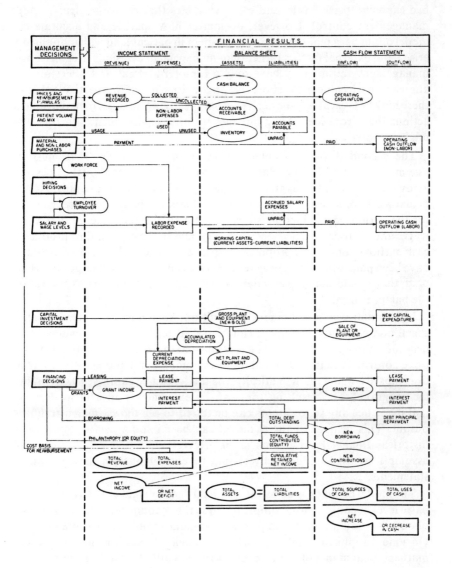

—patient volume and mix. Clearly this is *not* under direct management control. However, it will be influenced by a number of other decisions. In a more extensive financial model, one could even estimate the impact on patient volume and mix of staffing levels, equipment and plant expenditures, bed capacity, price levels, and other variables that *are* more clearly under management control. However, no matter how specific and accurate the model might be, a majority of any movement in patient load will undoubtedly arise from external factors rather than management decisions. Furthermore, management actions may have only a long-term effect and, therefore, be almost unnoticeable in the short run. In the situation of this particular input, there may be less value to be derived from specifying linkages to management actions than from identifying linkages to other environmental factors that might be forecast.

The second difficult problem arises from the linkages that must be assumed. Some of the key relationships have been indicated by the lines and arrows in Figure 1. For example, the salary and wage levels as applied to the actual work force result in a certain level of labor expenses that are recorded for the period on the income statement. Furthermore, while most of these wages and salaries will have been actually paid in the period, thus producing cash outflow, some small proportion—perhaps one week's worth—would not have been paid although they were counted as an expense for the period. Until paid, they would show up as a liability labeled "accrued salary expenses" on the balance sheet.

In a similar way, every financial result on the income statement, balance sheet, and cash flow statement can be traced back to a basic management decision. When environmental factors and external constraints, such as wage-price controls, are included and all of the judgmental and accounting relationships are stated mathematically, the model can be expressed as a computer program.[8] The resulting tool can be extremely powerful in decision making, since any set of inputs can be tested to see the estimated resulting output. This general financial model can be far more useful than simple historical financial statements alone. Nevertheless, the actual rules and assumptions used undoubtedly should be consistent with these historical statements.

The model could be used by the financial decision maker in two ways. At a basic level, it could be used simply to apply the accounting arithmetic to a set of output—volume, cost, and payment—assumptions to arrive at a forecast. On a more sophisticated level, with a great deal of guessing and analyzing, a mathematical model of the economic process could be constructed from the most basic decisions through to the intervening volume, cost, and payment results and, finally, to the resulting financial output as presented in income statements, balance sheets, and cost flow statements.

Using the example of Figure 1, when the inputs include variables such as patient volume and mix directly, the model is really nothing more than a way to translate physical output assumptions into financial output forecasts. When the intervening links from pricing, staffing, investment, quality, and other factors involved in patient volume and mix are mathematically estimated and included, then the model becomes a broader based simulation tool. In the first case, the many uncertain relationships must be resolved by the person making the volume forecast, while, in the second case, the modeler rather than the user specifies the linkages explicitly. Depending upon the situation, either might be more useful.

In any case, the point is that either an explicit model of this sort or an implicit model in the decision maker's mind is essential in identifying and analyzing all of the alternatives simultanteously and arriving at the "best" solution. The path from "management decisions" to "financial results" is not as straight as Figure 1 might lead one to believe.

A BROADER FINANCIAL MANAGEMENT MODEL

Reflecting on the concepts, techniques, and examples presented thus far, the reader might be tempted to conclude that financial management consists of nothing more than a series of separate decisions that can be made independently. The manager simply

- forecasts the financial need on the basis of expected volume, planned capital expenditures, and other cash flows;

- analyzes the various alternatives; and

- makes a number of financing and operating decisions that then are implemented.

The results show up in the income statement, balance sheet, and statistical report as well as on the accreditation review.

While this may be a useful analytic framework, the actual process is much more complex than this basic economic model. One goal of this article is to better integrate the separate pieces of this financial model of the health institution, but more importantly, to place it in the perspective of a more comprehensive decision-making framework.

In addition, it might be well to reaffirm the applicability of this structure to nonhospital situations, since many of the examples come from the hospital sector. As an example, most of the tools and concepts presented in a hospital context could be applied as well to the problems of a health maintenance organization. Forecasting, planning, financing, resource allocation, and the like may in fact be more critical in the HMO setting where cost recovery may not play such a central role. As the environment changes as a result of current legislation and other such influences, the numbers in our examples might change, but not the central concepts and techniques of analysis.

The basic decision-making process, as seen in purely financial terms, could be described as in Figure 2. Goals and objectives are somehow determined externally. These then serve as a foundation for the financial analysis process that explores the various legitimate sources of need and the underlying economic or quality justification for them. These, coupled with the various relevant characteristics, provide a basis for matching financing alternatives and a matching set of financing options.

The analytic process as outlined in Figure 2 might appear to imply that a set of optimal management decisions actually exists. This would of course imply a series of financial results. Of course, this is a somewhat naive view of the institution. At least two modifications are in order. First, the analytic process is nowhere near as purely financial as the preceding assumes. There are both system and organization effects that are critical. Second, the step between "management decisions" and "financial results" is often not direct at all.

A GENERAL DECISION-MAKING FRAMEWORK

Despite the usefulness of the financial view of decision making, it alone can never be self-sufficient, either as a way to analyze past actions or as a device for making institutional decisions that will affect the future. Financial analysis and simulation models can be of great assistance in assessing various options and projecting their results. However, as Figure 3 shows, the actual decisions are made in the context of a particular organization and a given health system. The latter context—the local and national health delivery system—is normally influenced very little by any single manager, while the former—the organizational context—should be somewhat within his partial control. In one case, the decision maker is exploring and assessing his *external* environment—political, economic, legal, regulatory, financial, technological, and so forth—in order to make judgments about its effect on his institution. In the other, he is assessing his *internal* environment with an eye toward identifying resources and restrictions and determining ways of changing the organization.

The control the manager has over his own organization may be partially of a direct authoritarian type—the stereotype behind most economic models of decision making—but is largely of a more indirect nature. He manages, to a great extent, by helping to form the *organizational context* within which the thousands of daily institutional decisions are made by others in the organiza-

Figure 2 Financial Framework for Decision Making

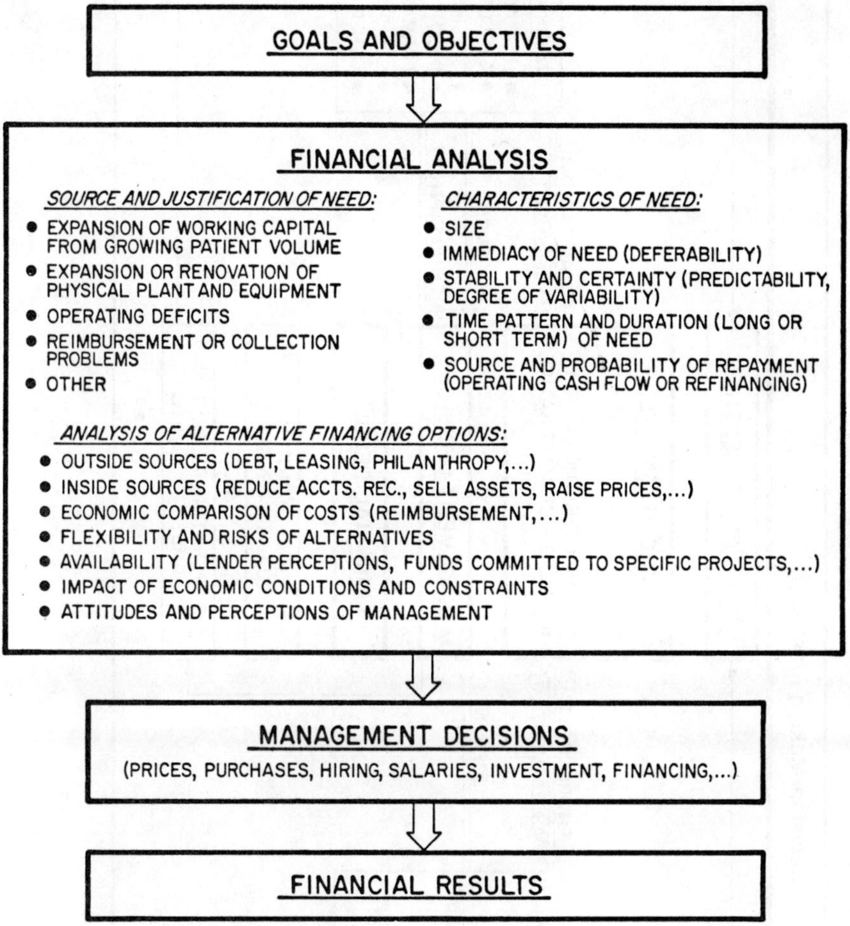

GOALS AND OBJECTIVES

⬇

FINANCIAL ANALYSIS

SOURCE AND JUSTIFICATION OF NEED:
- EXPANSION OF WORKING CAPITAL FROM GROWING PATIENT VOLUME
- EXPANSION OR RENOVATION OF PHYSICAL PLANT AND EQUIPMENT
- OPERATING DEFICITS
- REIMBURSEMENT OR COLLECTION PROBLEMS
- OTHER

CHARACTERISTICS OF NEED:
- SIZE
- IMMEDIACY OF NEED (DEFERABILITY)
- STABILITY AND CERTAINTY (PREDICTABILITY, DEGREE OF VARIABILITY)
- TIME PATTERN AND DURATION (LONG OR SHORT TERM) OF NEED
- SOURCE AND PROBABILITY OF REPAYMENT (OPERATING CASH FLOW OR REFINANCING)

ANALYSIS OF ALTERNATIVE FINANCING OPTIONS:
- OUTSIDE SOURCES (DEBT, LEASING, PHILANTHROPY,...)
- INSIDE SOURCES (REDUCE ACCTS. REC., SELL ASSETS, RAISE PRICES,...)
- ECONOMIC COMPARISON OF COSTS (REIMBURSEMENT,...)
- FLEXIBILITY AND RISKS OF ALTERNATIVES
- AVAILABILITY (LENDER PERCEPTIONS, FUNDS COMMITTED TO SPECIFIC PROJECTS,...)
- IMPACT OF ECONOMIC CONDITIONS AND CONSTRAINTS
- ATTITUDES AND PERCEPTIONS OF MANAGEMENT

⬇

MANAGEMENT DECISIONS
(PRICES, PURCHASES, HIRING, SALARIES, INVESTMENT, FINANCING,...)

⬇

FINANCIAL RESULTS

Figure 3 Proactive Decision-Making Framework

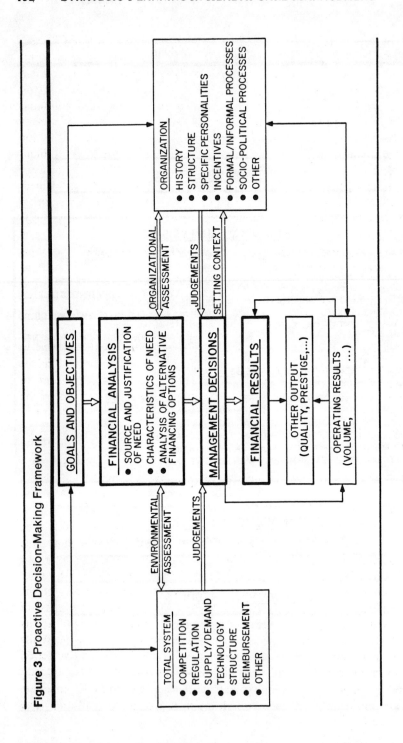

tion. Through hiring and promotion policies, compensation and reward systems, management information systems (feedback), interpersonal influence, and a variety of other organizational devices, the manager, we hope, can focus the large number of activities, which may be outside his direct control, toward some desired operational goals and objectives. It is really a combination of this context-setting activity plus more direct financial decisions—pricing and financing decisions, for example—that together produce the observed financial and operating results. It would be a mistake, even in an article directed at financial management, to consider only those portions of the operation with obvious and direct financial ramifications. In reality, there are no purely financial or purely organizational actions; there are rather management decisions with actions or results most readily expressed in terms of one or the other.

Clearly, all the preceding internal management assessments and decisions will be affected significantly by the external environment. Every organization must react to outside pressures. However, the usefulness of the decision-making framework highlighted in Figure 3 may lie more in fostering *proactive* rather than *reactive* decisions. By understanding and forecasting the relevant environmental variables, the manager in the health system may be able to devise anticipatory or proactive policies or actions rather than simply to react to the winds of change. Consider the movement toward health maintenance organizations (HMOs), for instance. The resistance of an existing insurer to cooperate with a new independent HMO shows a clear recognition of the threat of this sort of potential competition, but it is basically reactive in nature. The environment is changing and the company's response is an attempt to hold it back. On the other hand, the formation of a captive HMO by the insurer to complement his existing coverage might be seen as a proactive measure. The environment is changing, and, in anticipation of potentially unfavorable events, the company is attempting to pre-empt future HMO competition.

In a similar way, the response of a hospital to the HMO wave might be reactive or proactive. In the one case, the hospital might refuse to guarantee beds or services under a formal arrangement with an HMO. This represents a possible defensive reaction to the threat of decreased occupancy. On the other hand, it might negotiate an exclusive hospitalization arrangement with the HMO. This pre-emptive action might protect its revenues at the expense of other hospitals that formerly serviced subscribers. Finally, it might form its own HMO, starting with currently self-insured employees as a base. While preemptive in some respects, this might also be viewed as a creative action that both recognizes the trend and builds upon the institution's strengths.

Certainly, in general, a creative strategy that goes beyond the immediate threat or opportunity is desirable, although a pre-emptive solution may sometimes be the only possibility. Clearly, a continual posture of only reaction with little anticipation or foresight will be inadequate in the years to come, although it may have been acceptable in previous, less challenging environments. Unfortunately, all of the various elements of the health system listed in Figure 3 are increasingly dynamic. Assessments of these variables and constraints must be a major input into current decision making and future planning.

At this point, with the importance of environmental analysis firmly in mind, it may be appropriate to comment on change in the system. The potential for change can best be understood by first noting that the organizational context of higher levels of the system, such as the federal government, are for the most part the sum of the environmental context of each of the lower level organizations. For example, the Medicare reimbursement system is one formal organizational control mechanism and, as such, is a variable subject to management decision making by federal authorities. However, from the hospitals' viewpoint, the Medicare reimbursement formula is a part of the external environment. It makes up part of the context in which decisions must be made. Other factors, such as technology, might be part of the external environment for both levels of the system—federal authorities and hospital management. By recognizing and influencing those factors that are somewhat controllable variables in the organizational context of higher levels and, thus, in the environmental context of lower levels, it should be possible to stimulate change. In this light, the reimbursement structure can be seen as a key element in potential change. It is controllable by higher levels and is also a potent input into the decision making of lower levels. It should not be surprising then that the payment mechanism is the focus of a great deal of attention when potential changes in the health system are discussed. In a similar way, other financial variables that might be partially controlled—capital financing controls, incentives, or disclosure requirements—might come under increasing scrutiny as their importance in the decision-making context is recognized. Once again, by changing this context, regulators or reformers can change the system in ways that would be impossible by direct order.

USING THE INTERRELATIONSHIPS

The full decision-making structure contains much more than just financial results. Strategic factors, organizational constraints, and environmental assessments and inputs are all additional factors that must be included. To the extent that these inputs can be expressed in financial terms, they can be incorporated directly into the financial forecasting and analytic techniques discussed previously and thereby allow the financial decision maker—

whoever he might be—to function effectively. However, the health field, in large part, has been managed by professionals who often had a clear view of part of their external and internal environment without being able to relate these to the financial realities of the individual provider. Recognition of and action upon these relationships are the essence of financial decision making and management.

Until the real financial decision makers of the U.S. health system realize the implications of their "nonfinancial" management actions and address them squarely in the context of a comprehensive structure, such as that presented in Figure 3, the financial crisis at the provider level will continue. And the traditional "finance man" will be there to continue keeping score. What is needed is both an increase in the financial-management analytic support given the chief financial officer, including perhaps formal establishment of such a position, and a recognition of the financial nature of most of the management questions encountered.

REFERENCES

1. Boissonean, Robert. "No 1 Is Financial Management." *Hospital Financial Management*, February, 1976, pp. 14-16.

2. Spivak, Jonathon. "Social Security System Is on Its Way to Going Broke." *Wall Street Journal*, February 27, 1975.

3. Long, Hugh, and Silvers, J.B. "Health Care Reimbursement Is Federal Taxation of Tax-Exempt Providers." *Health Care Management Review*, Winter 1976, pp. 9-23.

4. Silvers, J.B. "How Do Limits to Debt Financing Affect Your Hospital's Financial Status?" *Hospital Financial Management*, February 1976, pp. 32-41.

5. Curriculum Task Force on Hospital Financial Management. *Summary of Financial Management and Related Courses Offered by Graduate Programs in Health and Hospital Administration.* Association of University Programs in Health Administration, Washington, D.C., December 1972.

6. To be fair to the accounting profession, the field of management accounting has as its focus an internal view and a goal of providing the relevant data for decision making. In many enterprises, this branch of accounting has evolved to the point where it is entirely consistent and, in fact, basic to financial decision making as discussed in this article. Unfortunately, in most health institutions, accounting is restricted to little more than generating data for use by outside reimbursement or review bodies rather than for internal decision-making purposes.

7. Portions of the remainder of this article are adapted with permission from J.B. Silvers and C.K. Prahalad, *Financial Management of Health Institutions,* Spectrum Publications, Holliswood, N.Y., 1974 (distributed by Halsted Division, J. Wiley Sons).

8. A computer model of this sort was developed by the author and has been used for several years in Harvard's *Program for Health Systems Management* with good success. Many other basic financial forecasting computer models are available commercially.

11. Valuation as a Criterion in Not-for-Profit Decision Making

HUGH W. LONG

Adapted from Long, Hugh W. "Valuation as a Criterion in Not-for-Profit Decision Making." *Health Care Management Review,* Summer 1976.

The U.S. health care industry, the largest in the domestic private sector, has failed to follow the lead of its smaller cousins like oil, chemicals, steel, and public utilities in using financial valuation as a management tool. Why is this so? The full answer is necessarily complex but probably reflects a number of health industry characteristics: the "not-for-profit" status of most of its institutions, the historic dependence on philanthropy as a source of capital, the consequent insulation of the industry from the discipline of the capital markets, the dominance of internal decision making by medical rather than managerial professionals, and a remarkable set of philosophical beliefs held by the industry's executives. These beliefs can be variously stated, but specifically include three major misconceptions:

1. Doing good is necessarily in conflict with doing well.
2. "Not-for-profit" (a technical legal term) corporations should not make money.
3. The concepts of value, ownership, wealth, and dividends have no place in a "not-for-profit" health care organization.

What is especially remarkable about the philosophy these misconceptions represent is that it is diametrically in opposition to any reasonable prospect for the economic survival of health care providers as a private-sector industry in this century. Time and again, one is chided with reminders that it is vaguely, if not blatantly, immoral to make money from people's illness, that the "bottom line" must be kept small if not zero, and that health care cannot be compared to "for-profit" industries. Yet, the very survival of health care activity as a private-sector industry depends on the abandonment of all these misconceptions and a modification of philosophy that recognizes economic reality.

What follows is the simple rationale for the applicability of the concepts of corporate finance to "not-for-profit" health care providers. In particular, the necessity for decision making based on valuation is explored.

VALUATION AS A FINANCE CONCEPT

Some notion of the value of assets has existed throughout economic history, but valuation as a *finance* concept is a relatively new idea. First stated intuitively less than 40 years ago,[1] financial valuation is still seen by many as a revolutionary approach to corporate management. This view of financial valuation largely reflects the fact that it is in substantial conflict with the generally accepted accounting model's view of value.

Since World War II, industry in free-enterprise economies, while still reporting to shareholders and outside parties via the accounting model, has gradually begun to adopt the finance model for internal decision making. This alteration of corporate philosophy and behavior, still in progress, was first applied to the asset-acquisition (capital-budgeting) decision in recognition of two facts: (1) capital is a scarce resource, and (2) rational allocation of scarce capital to obtain the most "bang for the buck" (the economist's "efficiency") is critical to corporate success and management tenure. This approach to decision making not only increases the wealth of the *corporate* ownership but also helps to ensure *national* economic survival in a world of international trade and capital flows.

NOT-FOR-PROFIT "BANKRUPTCY"

First let us examine exactly what it would mean to be literally not-for-profit— to have zero net income each and every period across time. To begin, we shall assume a very simplistic economy with no inflation, no technological change, no growth, and no expansion. Everything is stable; every period looks like every other period with respect to mix of service, payment categories, collection periods, and so forth. In this situation, zero net income, period after period, simply means the provider can continue to function indefinitely with sufficient positive cash flow so as always to be solvent, to meet payables, and to roll over real assets one-for-one as replacement is required. This is because the accounting model we use includes an inherent assumption of the recovery *of* capital; while there is no return *on* the capital employed, there *is* a recovery of the capital base itself. This is accomplished through an expense item on the income statement called a depreciation charge. As a noncash expense, it simply means that over the useful life of the assets generating these services, the original cost is recovered. In a perfectly stable system, at the end of the useful life of any particular asset, one has accumulated enough cash in the bank to go out and directly replace that asset.

Inflation

If we now complicate the picture and allow for some of the realities of the world, we shall begin to see why a literal "not-for-profit" situation is guaranteed bankruptcy. First, consider the impact of inflation. It is well established that we have an inflationary economy. Inflation may drop as low as 2 to 3 percent per year; it may go as high as 15 percent. It will probably average somewhere in the vicinity of 5 to 6 percent. Thus, there is a requirement for a bottom line that provides 5 to 6 percent return on capital invested in plant and equipment so that, when replacement time comes, the replacement asset can be acquired in current dollars at its new price and the stable state situation retained. With a zero bottom line, no replacement occurs. Quality is eroded with inferior replacement in real terms, and survival is threatened.

But, of course, plant and equipment are not the only areas impacted by inflation. To the extent current assets exceed current liabilities, this net working capital figure will also become a net drain of cash while inflation proceeds.[2] Normally, the book value of real assets (excluding land) plus net working capital is about equal to the book value of total capital employed, so that, in accounting terms, overall average return on capital must at least equal the average inflation rate just to maintain a stable state.

Technological Improvement

Next we add the reality of technological improvement in plant and equipment. The fact is that most old assets are *not* replaced with identical items but with improved versions that raise quality and provide better care. Technology may even cause wholly new equipment to be required that, though replacing no existing equipment, is absolutely required to maintain an institution's viability. Failure to stay abreast of technology has high costs related to licensure, accreditation, retention/attraction of medical staff, availability of malpractice/liability insurance, external funding, and so on. However, technology is not free and may, in the health industry, account for a 2 to 4 percent annual escalation in the cost of replacing/modifying real assets. Unlike inflation, the dollars devoted to keeping pace with technology show tangible results, mostly qualitative in nature. Nevertheless, dollars are dollars and must come from somewhere, and if plant and equipment represent over 90 percent of total capital employed, as is common in acute-care institutions, then over 90 percent of the annual rate of technological advance must show up as an accounting return on capital employed or as a financial cash flow.

Expansion

Then there is expansion. In the simplest case, shifting from 75 percent utilization to 85 percent utilization will require somewhere between a 10 and 15 percent increase in net working capital, depending on economies or diseconomies of scale. If capacity itself is to be expanded, then additional capital funds will be required, as well as significantly increased working capital. And capacity will need to grow, albeit gradually and carefully, even in our over-bedded cities. This is because (1) our population will continue to grow in aggregate for the remainder of the century, even if we can ultimately postulate zero population growth based on today's birth and fertility rates; (2) the changing age distribution of the population will need more health care; (3) most segments of the population, whether currently underserved or not, will probably demand more care in the future, probably in excess of need; and (4) the ultimate enactment of national health insurance of whatever type will enable large segments of the population to act on these needs and demands. In aggregate, the working capital needs alone associated with expansion may well require another 1 to 2 percent return on capital employed. And, of course, specific locales may experience much higher rates of expansion.

Alteration of Services

Next, consider alteration in the range of services and/or change in the nature of services offered. Transitional costs to types of service that are more ambulatory, primary, and/or preventive in nature may well involve large drains of cash reserves—assuming such reserves have been built. Zero bottom lines cannot fill such reservoirs.

Economics and Politics

Certain macroeconomic or political events may have major impact on cash flows as well. For example: (1) we can be virtually certain that economic controls like the Economic Stabilization Program's Phases II and IV will reappear sometime in the next decade; (2) we know that the collection period for accounts receivable may well lengthen more than the payables period during recessions; (3) specific components of providers' costs may escalate quite separately from the general level of inflation, as in the case of another energy crisis or the sudden need for significant escalation of fringe benefits in the face of unionization—premiums on malpractice/liability insurance are a perfect example of this type of phenomenon; (4) in the absence of effective industry lobbying, national health insurance may include payment mechanisms just as punitive as those under Medicare. It is imperative that liquid reserves be built in anticipation of such contingencies.

Required Return

In Table 1, all of the basic factors discussed above are brought together with the estimated average annual cash absorption of each, shown as a percentage of capital employed. Remember that these factors are what are required just to maintain existing operational activities in a real economic world. Recall also that they are "add-ons" to the basic historical costs covered by the cash masked by the depreciation expense item. Since each factor interacts with the others, a compound aggregate rate of return is formulated, with the addition of a 10 percent hedge factor to cushion against the fact that, for example, in some years any one or several of the basic factors might vary upward significantly. The specific rates appearing in Table 1 are, of course, arbitrary, but whatever rates are chosen, it is clear that some substantial positive rate of return on capital employed is essential for provider survival. The "not-for-profit" provider who literally produces a zero bottom line in accounting terms, or only replacement-at-historical-cost cash flows in finance terms, cannot and will not survive in the environment of the 70s and 80s. Having no profit presages having no provider, unless alternative sources of funds can be obtained.

CAN DEBT SUBSTITUTE FOR "PROFIT"?

So far, we have thought in terms of meeting the requirements arrayed in Table 1 with accounting "profit,"—the excess of revenues over expenses or, more correctly, with what finance identifies as operational cash flow—which includes the cash represented by depreciation expense but not, in fact, expended. Could not these needs be met through permanent borrowing?

"Rush to Debt"

For the provider with little or no debt currently, the answer is probably "yes" in the short term. But since the requirements noted in Table 1 are ongoing, since they continue to exist and compound year after year, the health care industry cannot look to debt as a long-run solution. This is because the use of debt is always subject to various constraints rationally imposed by suppliers of debt capital. When an institution or an industry moves from a position of little debt to a position of much debt, it moves increasingly close to these

---

Table 1 Required Return on Capital Employed

Basic Factors	Estimated Average Annual Rate of Return Required
Inflation	5.5%
Technology	2.0%
Expansion of Existing Services	1.0%
Alteration of Services	0.5%
Recession, Economic Controls, Oil Embargoes, NHI, etc.	0.5%
Sub-Total (Compounded)*	9.8%
Hedge (10%)** Against Variability in Basic Factors	0.9%
Total Required Return (Compounded)*** (τ)	10.8%

---

*(1.055)(1.020)(1.010)(1.005)(1.005) – 1 = 9.8%

** (1.098)^{10} –1 = 0.9%

*** (1.098)(1.009) – 1 = 10.8%

---

borrowing constraints. Once against the constraints, debt capacity is likely to expand very slowly, if at all, so that debt tends to be a one-time answer. Indeed, in its classic "rush to debt" of the last decade, the industry has virtually used up this one-time recourse.[3] Many observers feel that the industry's debt capacity may not only have been reached but already exceeded.

The specific constraints to borrowing most commonly include rule-of-thumb ratios relating the principal amount of debt to plant and equipment and to total capital, and total periodic debt service payments (principal and interest) to adjusted income or cash flow. These constraints are carefully discussed elsewhere, and it is clear that they mitigate strongly against the indefinite buildup of more and more leverage.[4]

We raise the question of debt as a substitute for "profit" only because this substitution has been the industry's response over the last decade to the erosion of "profit." Since the ability to maintain this response is clearly limited if not terminal, the only remaining option is to focus on production of internally generated cash flows.

Defense of Debt

Before turning to the production of internally generated cash flows in the next section, there are two points to be made in defense of debt. First, it should be noted that debt is a relatively inexpensive form of capital. Since debt's returns are contractual and senior, the risk that debt suppliers will not receive the returns promised them is less than the comparable risk associated with other classes of capital. Since we have very efficient capital markets, and since participants in those markets tend to be risk averse, we can observe a positive correlation in the marketplace between risk and return: higher risk requires higher return, and lower risk, such as debt, a lower return. Thus, the price paid for debt capital, namely interest, always makes debt relatively more attractive on a pure cost basis than other forms of capital. Furthermore, interest is an allowable cost under cost-based reimbursement and, as discussed in an earlier article, this produces a tax-subsidy effect that can significantly reduce the real cost of debt.[5]

The second observation about debt is that its requirement for interest payments should *not* be viewed as a constraint to borrowing vis-a-vis the acquisition of nondebt (equity) capital. The fact that interest payments *are* often viewed as a relative constraint is due to an unfortunate tendency in the health industry for management to behave as though equity capital were free and only debt need be paid for. The fact is that equity capital *also* requires a return. Debt's return (interest) is contractual and has legal priority, but equity is due no less a return, albeit noncontractual and subordinated, and in a noncash form. This argument will be developed in detail in the next section of this article. The point here is that *all* capital requires a return, so that debt is at no disadvantage to equity in this regard. Capital, regardless of type, will require additional returns over and above those referenced in Table 1. Hence, neither new debt nor new equity is particularly attractive or, indeed, viable as an ongoing substitute for operational cash flows. If an institution cannot produce the returns in Table 1, it clearly cannot produce those additional returns needed to attract new capital, be it debt or equity.

MAXIMIZING WEALTH OF THE "OWNERSHIP"

The factors contained in Table 1 present a strong argument for a positive return. By themselves, they can argue for maximizing operational cash flows, simply because, the larger the return, the less likely an organization is to face a short-fall of cash to meet any one of these factors. But taken as a whole, these factors only address the renewal of the provider organization in terms of real asset replacement and working capital needs. They do not reflect the real economic cost of the capital tied up in working balances and physical assets. That capital could be productively employed elsewhere, earning returns for its suppliers. And ultimately, in a world in which capital is a scarce resource, suppliers of capital will be willing to commit their resources only to users of that capital who can produce competitive returns.

The truth of this is already quite clearly demonstrated with respect to debt capital. The fact that health care providers "do good" has not, to my knowledge, caused the bond markets to supply debt to hospitals at zero percent interest. Rather, interest is charged at a rate that is competitive with alternative bonds bearing commensurate risk.

Equity Capital

And what about nondebt (equity) capital? Need no return be provided to equity suppliers, either because health care providers are nice people or because not-for-profit providers cannot pay cash dividends? Absolutely *not*. Return *is* required. Why is this so?

First, we need to identify the suppliers of equity capital. Depending on the individual case, the list may include recipients of services who themselves or via third parties pay more than costs for those services; private donors of cash, be they major philanthropists, private foundations, or persons contributing one dollar to the annual fund drive; volunteers who provide wage and salary expense relief to the institution or program; and payers of sales, property, income, or other tax monies that flow to the provider by grant, appropriation, or designation. These suppliers of equity capital, along with those who might supply such capital in the future, clearly constitute the provider's constituency. They are not only the suppliers of equity capital, they are the community served. Viewed either way, they are the "ownership."

Second, we know that the "ownership" requires a return *of* their investment. That is what Table 1 is all about: the renewal of the assets, the provision of working capital to accompany the renewal, and the maintenance of the capacity of the provider to remain an ongoing enterprise with the capability of providing basic, mainstream services to the community. And because of the economic realities of our world, we have seen that perhaps a 10 to 11 percent nominal return is required just to stay even, just to give the community stable health care capacity, just to give the "ownership" their return *of* capital.

Third, it is clear that the "ownership" expects much more than just return *of* capital, and rightly so. They expect return *on* capital—real return over and above all else. While that return is not required to take the form of cash payments, it is required to represent aggregate value at least commensurate with the average return that could be expected if that equity capital were committed to an alternative opportunity.

Alternatives

We shall discuss the specific form of such returns below. But let us first consider the nature of viable alternative opportunities for equity commitment. If we look to the long-run average performance of equity investment in major U.S. industries, we can certainly obtain a reasonable approximation of alternative returns. Careful empirical research has shown that from 1926 through 1965—including the Great Depression—the annual after-tax compound rate of return from equity investment in U.S. for-profit industry was about 8 percent.[6] "After-tax" here means after corporate *and personal* income tax, which is important, since we wish to make comparisons to health industry returns that are not subject to personal taxation.

Also, we need to make two other adjustments to the 8 percent figure. First, since it reflects values in current dollars and since we have already accounted for inflation in Table 1, we need to adjust for the average inflation rate from 1926 to 1965. Using the GNP deflator, this produces a *real* return in dollars of constant purchasing power of about 6 percent. Finally, we need to adjust the 6 percent downward to compensate for certain frictional or transactions costs. That is, we wish to compare the health returns *on* investment actually produced by the health care industry with what the recipient of that 6 percent alternative return could purchase directly. In order to use that 6 percent return, it would have to be converted to cash, which would require the sale of securities and payment of commissions and some costs of shopping for the services to be purchased. After these costs were paid, only a 4 to 5 percent return would actually be available for real consumption. But this is a vitally important 4 to 5 percent, and it is totally separate from, in fact is in addition to, the 10 to 11 percent return (Table 1) needed just to stay even. If "ownership" does not maintain the rational expectation of such a real net return from the health care industry, indeed if health management does not strive to generate such a return on its nondebt capital, then societal resources will have been misallocated to health care. In that event, the community is worse off than if it had originally invested its equity resources in the for-profit sector. For had it done so, the net cash returns therefrom could have been used to purchase directly the kinds of services that constitute the health care industry's dividends. And the community would be able to purchase *more* such services than the industry itself would provide if it failed to achieve the 4 to 5 percent required level of return. Hence, if that level of return is not achieved, one might reasonably expect society to allocate its equity resources elsewhere. This fact may, in part, explain the tendency of equity capital to avoid the health care industry in recent years. This flight of equity has occurred, for example, through (1) the mechanism of cost-based reimbursement, since the difference between charges and costs that is no longer received would have been a contribution to equity returns, and (2) the relative decline in philanthropy. To some extent, reversal of these trends depends on highly productive use of current capital, a topic we shall return to in the next section.

Return On Equity Capital

Specifically, then, what are the monies that constitute return *on* equity capital in the health care industry, and in what forms can this return be realized by the community, the "ownership"? As to the monies, the return on capital represents cash remaining from operational dollar flows *after* debt suppliers receive interest and principal, *after* replacement of assets and attendant working capital needs are accomplished, and *after* outlays have been made for totally new real investment. These residual monies are then expected to be available to provide dividends to the "ownership," to the community. But instead of sending cash payments to the "ownership," not-for-profit health care providers have an economic obligation to provide their return on equity investment in the form of spending money on *community* dividends. Specifically, this includes providing charity care, supporting medical and other teaching and research, conducting in-house training and educational programs, running an emergency room, providing other community service, and so forth.

The community, the "ownership," is clearly better off by virtue of such real returns—dividends—than it would be in their absence. Indeed, every management effort should be directed to providing more benefits to the "ownership" than they could independently provide for themselves. This is what constitutes maximization of wealth. Not only is such management behavior consistent with the long-run best interests of the community served, as well as the maintenance of management tenure, it also is central to the survival of the industry as a valued component of a private enterprise society.

IMPLICATIONS FOR MANAGEMENT DECISIONS

Since not-for-profit health care providers do, indeed must, pay dividends to their "ownership," and since continuing as an ongoing private-sector industry requires substantial cash returns of and on capital, the notion of maximizing organizational ability to accomplish these ends is relatively straightforward.

The guts of financial management is not only to maintain the capacity to deliver normal service for economic return, but simultaneously to generate sufficient return to guarantee future ability to attract new debt and equity capital when it is needed, by meeting or exceeding the return expectations of existing capital suppliers.

If we are careful to view not-for-profit health care delivery as a dividend-paying, income-tax-paying,[7] "ownership" wealth-maximizing, private-sector industry, then there is virtually no practical distinction between health care and any other industry having those characteristics. Concerns about quality of service delivered, maintenance of human life and health, external controls and regulations, and such are *not* unique to health care and do not present health care with any problems not already facing one or more other domestic industries. Economic parallels to rate setting, licensure, accreditation, independent medical staffs, certificate of need, and so forth are readily found outside of the health care industry.

Financial Criteria

Consequently, as is shown in Table 2, the "not-for-profit" hospital differs very little in financial terms from for-profit firms. Once ownership is properly defined, the only distinctions between profit and not-for-profit firms arise out of the forms of dividends—transfers of wealth to ownership—and the mechanisms for ascertaining the value of equity capital employed. We have already discussed the nature of not-for-profit dividends; the matter of equity valuation remains. It will be easier, however, for us to approach that subject after we have first considered, and drawn some powerful conclusions about, the correct financial criteria for operational decision making.

Future Cash Flow

We have already observed from the Table 2 Reponse to Question Number 9 that management should implement decisions that, in finance terms, will meet either of two criteria:

1. Increase or leave unchanged the amount of *every* future expected operational cash flow (as defined in the last footnote to Table 2) net of expected new investment, or
2. Cause *every* such future expected net cash flow to occur at the same time or sooner.

However, most management decisions will cause a decrease or a delay in at least one such net cash flow. For instance, the purchase of new equipment causes a cash drain now, reducing dividend-paying potential; the manager

Table 2 A Finance Catechism

Questions	For-profit Firm*	Normative Responses from Viewpoint of A: "Not-for-Profit" Hospital
1. What should management's fiscal objectives be?	Management should *maximize* the wealth of "the ownership."	Same.
2. Who is "the ownership?"	The stockholders or equity-holders own the firm.	The community served is the "ownership."
3. How is "ownership's" wealth increased?	*Management makes decisions* (see Question 9) *which increase the value of non-debt (equity)* capital.	*Same.*
4. What constrains these management decisions?	Generally, constraints include: Laws, Regulations, and Administration thereof (e.g. OHSA, FTC, PUC) Board policies The Marketplace	Same, including specific requirements of Licensure Accreditation Review under P.L. 93-641 Etc.
5. What about federal taxes?	Income taxes flow to government, collected by IRS as agent for Dept. of Treasury	Same, except collected by SSA as agent for Dept. of HEW
6. How is increased equity value transferred to "ownership?"	Cash Dividends Capital Gains realized in Capital Markets Social Dividends**	Provision of Charity Care Support of Educational and Research Activities On-the-job Training Programs Emergency Room Services
7. How is the value of equity determined?	This is determined in the capital markets by current and potential suppliers of equity capital trading shares of equity.+	This is determined by management (see text) subject to review by the board and ultimate judgment by the "ownership," the community.

(Continued on next page)

Table 2 A Finance Catechism (*continued*)

Questions	For-profit Firm*	Normative Responses from Viewpoint of A: "Not-for-Profit" Hospital
8. How is the value of debt determined?	This is determined in the capital markets by current and potential suppliers of debt capital trading units of debt.+	Same.
9. What management decisions may affect equity value?	Any decision which increases operational cash flows++ (or speeds their receipt), net of new investment outlays. This would include all basic finance decisions: A. Operational and Taxation Decisions B. Financing Decisions are (1) Capital Structure (2) Capital Acquisition and Disbursement C. Investment Decisions re Asset Acquisition and Divestment	Same.
10. Which of these decisions require management to ascertain value of both equity and debt capital?	All finance decisions require this information as input to rational decision-making	Same.

*E.g. General Motors, AT&T, the local hardware store.

**E.g. scholarships, charitable contributions. These, of course, accrue to others beside ownership, but may be argued to benefit ownership in the long run.

+These market participants are risk-averse, and act on their perceptions of promised future cash flows (interest and principal payments for debt: cash dividends and proceeds from share liquidation for equity). They arrive at a value for such promises in today's dollars which "clears the market" of buyers and sellers.

++Operational cash flows are total receipts less total expenditures (including income taxes) associated with the products or services sold, *prior* to the deduction or addition of:
(1) Any flows to or from capital suppliers like interest, principal, dividends, or proceeds from fund drives or new debt.
(2) Any reimbursement of any portion of interest expanse under cost-based contracts
(3) Any investment outlays.

hopes the new equipment will produce larger-than-otherwise-expected cash inflows later, increasing future dividend-paying potential. How can management properly evaluate such decisions, especially as they involve reductions of cash flows now in anticipation of larger flows later? The correct third criterion by which management should judge alternatives that do not qualify under the two criteria listed above is to undertake decisions that:

3. Produce either no change or an increase in the overall *value* of the organization. (It can be shown that any change in the value of the organization accrues wholly to the value of the organization's equity. That is, if the value of the organization increases by $100, the value of its equity will have increased by $100 simultaneously.[8]

Focus On Value

By focusing on value, we can simultaneously deal with (1) the returns required by suppliers of capital and (2) the economic fact that a dollar received (or expended) today is not equivalent to a dollar received (or expended) a year from today, even in the absence of inflation and other Table 1 factors. This "time value" of money is critical to most management decisions and central to implementing the third criterion. Specifically, the impact of any decision on organizational or equity value is determined by finding the value today of all expected—forecast—incremental changes in future cash flows.

When the value obtained is compared to changes in cash flows now, the *net present value* that results is the change in organizational value.[9] The actual value of the expected future cash flow changes is determined by applying the organization's overall *cost of capital* to the estimated cash flow changes across time.

This cost of capital (c*) is the actual nominal rate that the organization must return on the value of *all* of its capital (debt *and* equity) to meet the requirements for long-run economic survival we have identified. This cost of capital has three components. First, it includes the return we depicted in Table 1 as necessary for the organization just to stay even. That return (r) is required on the value of all capital, but includes no real returns compensating for the use of the capital.[10] Second, it includes the net percentage cost (d*) of that part (proportion) of the organization's capital supplied through the debt markets.[11] Third, it includes the real net return required to maintain the community's commitment of equity capital. This return (e*) is the 4 to 5 percent figure discussed earlier and applies just to that proportion of the organization's capital that is nondebt. The second and third components of c*, the cost of capital, are weighted by the proportion of total capital value to which they each apply. Since the proportion of debt plus the proportion of equity must equal one (all of the capital), we can designate the proportion of debt value as L (leverage), a number between zero and one. Then the proportion of equity value is given by 1-L.

When the leverage-weighted costs of debt and equity are added along with r, the "stay-even" return on all capital, the total sum is the overall cost of capital, c*. Thus

$$c^* = r + L \cdot d^* + (1-L) \cdot e^*$$

We have already estimated r in Table 1 and e* in our section on maximizing "ownership's" wealth. And d* is also known (see reference note 11) since each organization can (1) observe the organized debt capital markets and (2) estimate its own value of P, the proportion of total service revenue delivered to patients covered by cost-based reimbursement contracts. The exact value of L is, of course, a management decision,[12] so we can calculate each of the individual components of c*.

As a simple numerical example, let us use the numbers developed previously, namely, let r equal 10.8 percent and e* be estimated as 4.5 percent. We shall also assume that, after discussions with the organization's board, its bankers, its consultants, and/or its underwriters, management has decided that 60 percent leverage is the appropriate long-run target for the organization. If d is 8 percent and P is 30 percent then, by reference note 11, d* = 5.6 percent, and

$$c^* = 10.8\% + (.6) (5.6\%) + (.4) (4.5\%)$$

or, c*, the organization's cost of capital, is approximately equal to 16 percent.

Now, if the organization has the operational option of expending an additional $2,000 now with the prospect of increased cash inflows of $925 one year hence and $1,450 two years hence, it should decline the option. This is because the present value of those expected future cash flows at a 16 percent cost of capital is only $1,875.[13] By comparing the $1,875 value of the expected incremental future cash flows to the $2,000 outlay required, we see that exercising this operational option *decreases* the value of the organization and its equity by $125, leaving it *less* able to provide both ongoing service and/or dividends to the community it serves. To undertake this option would violate the third criterion.

Any decision that fails to meet one of the three criteria listed earlier leaves the community as a whole worse off financially. No other financial criterion may be substituted if management is to maximize the ultimate wealth of its "ownership," its community.

VALUATION OF NOT-FOR-PROFIT EQUITY

The manager of the large for-profit corporation need only pick up today's newspaper and look at the quotations in the finance section to ascertain the value of that firm's equity. In the not-for-profit setting, obtaining this information is more difficult and less certain. Essentially, the process involves forecasting future financial performance and is therefore a specific management responsibility. Conceptually, the value of equity is simply the value *today* of all *future* dividends as we have defined them, adjusted for future contributions of equity capital. The *only* reason any thing has value is that someone expects some future benefit to accrue to the owner of that thing; the fact that someone paid some particular number of dollars for that thing yesterday is no guarantee that it has value today. Historical costs and accounting values are irrelevant. A million dollars contributed over the years through community fund drives implies no particular value today, even if the organization's books reflect the million dollar amount.

Future Dividends

What management must do is make careful estimates of (1) the dollar values of expected future dividends to the community—dollar values as of the time the dividends are delivered—and (2) the dollar values of expected direct contributions to equity, such as from philanthropy, fund drives, and similar sources. Gross dividend amounts are then reduced by the amount of new contributions. The estimated annual net dollar amounts then need to be valued as of today. That is, the following question must be answered, what *should* the community, the "ownership," be willing to pay today for this promised stream of *future* dividends net of anticipated new contributions, the dollar values of which we have estimated?

The answer is really quite simple. All that we need to do is determine the present value of the estimated dollar values of future dividends to the community net of new contributions. To be able to ascertain that present value, the only additional tool needed is to determine that the *overall* required rate of return on equity, which we shall identify with the letter e, differs from e*, the *real* return required on equity. Note that e includes *both* the real return represented by e*, *and* the nominal returns required by the "ownership" to stay even. We have identified those nominal returns in Table 1 and have referred to them in aggregate as requiring a rate of return, r, on *all* capital. In the absence of any debt capital, all capital is equity, so the overall required return is simply the sum of e* and r. But what happens when there *is* debt capital?

Leverage

When we *do* have leverage (L greater than zero), debt requires and receives its returns in the form of interest and principal payments. That debt service departs the organization as cash and therefore contributes nothing to the maintenance of the organization as an ongoing institution or program. That is, if *any* of the returns listed in Table 1 are to be realized, they must come from returns accruing to equity capital. Hence, equity must earn a return large enough not only to produce its required real return e* but, in addition, large enough to produce a rate of return, r, on *all* capital, both debt *and* equity. This requirement that equity carry the burden of generating the nominal return for *all* capital causes the rate of return on equity to rise as leverage (L) increases and, at high levels of debt, to rise dramatically.

The exact relationship between leverage (L) and the required rate of equity (e) is that e is equal to e* plus the quotient of the nominal return on all capital, r, divided by one minus L. (The derivation of this relationship is found in the appendix to this article.) In our example, with e* given a 4.5 percent, r equal to 10.8 percent, and leverage at 60 percent (L = 0.6), the resulting e is 31.5 percent! To most, that is an amazing number, totally antithetical to old-line "not-for-profit" philosophy. However, if you stop and think about it for a moment, you should begin to understand the implications of economic reality coupled with high leverage in this industry. Equity must necessarily carry the burden of organizational survival, and the 31.5 percent is the return that, in this example, *must* be earned on that portion of capital that is nondebt if long-run viability is to be assured. The *overall* cost of capital, c*, has not changed; it is still about 16 percent as we calculated earlier, but it is important to recognize the differential overall return required by debt and equity that average out to c* of 16 percent.

With our ability to estimate e, the overall required rate of return on equity, we can now estimate the value of equity capital using the same approach we used to evaluate the operational option discussed earlier. The only difference is that instead of c*, we use e, and instead of estimated changes in future operational cash flows, we use estimates of future community dividends net of new contributions of equity.

Once our estimate of the actual value of equity is determined, management has one additional financial task: to ascertain whether or not the existing capital structure coincides with that desired by management. In other words, is actual leverage, L', about equal to desired leverage, L, that has been targeted by management?

Since we have estimated the actual value of equity, E, and since we can observe the actual value of debt, D, in the organized debt capital markets, we can calculate actual leverage, L', as D divided by the sum of D plus E. This actual leverage then can be compared directly to L, management's desired amount of leverage. Actual leverage may, of course, be too high or too low. Hence, it may become necessary for management either to increase or repay debt claims or to increase or decrease current dividends, or both, in order to adjust D and E so as to achieve the desired amount of leverage.

SURVIVAL REVISITED

From a normative viewpoint, management decisions in the health care industry, as in any other private sector industry, must rest solidly on the finance concept of valuation. Increasing or retiring debt, raising new equity capital, or altering community dividends to achieve a desired capital structure requires knowledge of the values of the existing structure. Making rational operational or asset acquisition/divestment decisions can only occur with knowledge of their impact on existing values. Continuing failure to make decisions thus based on economic reality can lead to only two results. First, the community served will be shortchanged, being left less well off because management failed to maximize the wealth of the "ownership." Second, the health care organization will become increasingly unable to provide dividends and, later, ongoing service to the community. Continuation down this path must end in bankruptcy. New York City hospitals provide a perfect example of an instance in which economic irrationality led numerous institutions to consume large endowments rather than make economically sound—though unpopular—decisions, such as deciding to terminate cost-based reimbursement contracts.

Only by giving much higher priority to the decision-making criteria presented here—much higher priority than *ever* before—is there any reasonable expectation that the private sector, not-for-profit health care industry will ultimately survive.

Appendix 11-A

We let e be the *overall* rate of return required on equity, e^* be the real rate of return required on equity, d^* be the cost of debt to the organization, r be the nominal rate of return on *all* capital, and L be management's desired proportion of debt to total capital (leverage). c^* is the overall cost of capital to the organization. In the main body of the article we argued that

$$c^* = r + L \cdot d^* + (1-L) \cdot e^*$$

But c^* can alternatively be specified by a similarly weighted average of d^* and e. This is because e properly incorporates the returns represented by r (Table 1) which e^* excludes. Hence, it is also true that

$$c^* = L \cdot d^* + (1-L) \cdot e$$

From these two expressions for c^*, it follows that

$$(1-L) \cdot e = r + (1-L) \cdot e$$

and

$$e = e^* + \frac{r}{1-L}$$

REFERENCES

1. Williams, John Burr. *The Theory of Investment Value.* Cambridge, Mass.: Harvard University Press, 1938.

2. Long, Hugh W., and Silvers, J.B. "Health Care Reimbursement is Federal Taxation of Tax-Exempt Providers." *Health Care Management Review*, Winter, 1976, pp. 19-22.

3. Silvers, J.B. "How Do Limits to Debt Financing Affect Your Hospital's Financial Status?" *Hospital Financial Management*, 29 (February, 1975): 32-33.

4. Ibid., pp. 33-41

5. Long and Silvers, "Health Care Reimbursement." p. 18.

6. Fisher, Lawrence, and Lorie, James H. "Rates of Return on Investments in Common Stock: The Year-by-Year Record, 1926-65." *Journal of Business* 41 (July, 1968): 291-316.

7. Long and Silvers. "Health Care Reimbursement." pp. 9-18.

8. This concept of value changes flowing to equity is discussed in Section 2 of a forthcoming text: Kenneth J. Boudreaux and Hugh W. Long, *The Basic Theory of Corporate Finance* (Englewood Cliffs, New Jersey: Prentice-Hall, Inc.), 1977.

9. *Ibid.* Discussions of the concept of net present value can also be found in most introductory finance texts.

10. Conceptually, all of r is *nominal* return rather than real return; e*, by contrast, is all real return. Some of the smaller components listed in Table 1 might be considered by some persons as elements of real return. While the exact categorization is debatable, the numerical difference implied is small.

11. If we use the letter d to represent the *rate of return* required by the external suppliers of debt, what we are really interested in here is d*, the *net cost of debt* (as percentage) to the organization after cost-based reimbursement effects. If P is the proportion of interest cost that is reimbursed under cost-based contracts, then d* = d(1-P). P is approximately equal to the proportion of total service delivered to consumers covered by cost-based plans and programs. (Long and Silvers, *op. cit.*, reference note number 1, p. 23—the use of P here is the same as that of C in the earlier article.) It is also worth noting that d (and, of course, d*) include some built-in nominal return to debt suppliers to compensate them for the effects of inflation on their principal.

12. Boudreaux and Long, *The Basic Theory of Corporate Finance*, Section 3, discusses the factors influencing this decision.

13. If management invested $1,875 at 16 percent per year, $2,175 would have accumulated at the end of the first year. If they paid the organization $925 (the first year's increased cash flow) from that accumulation, $1,250 would remain. At 16 percent, that $1,250 would grow to exactly equal the $1,450 second-year increased cash flow, thus exactly replicating the expected incremental future cash flows associated with the option. It is clearly not in the best financial interests of the organization to invest an extra $125 now ($2,000 less $1,875) and receive only the return expected by capital suppliers on $1,875; in effect, no return would be received *of* or *on* the $125, and that is obviously unsatisfactory.

Section Four

Perspectives on Strategic Planning

In recent years, health care providers along with traditional for-profit corporations have been attracted to the concept of strategic planning. This section contains several articles demonstrating not only the output of such plans but also guidelines to consider in developing them. Strategic planning requires two ingredients. First, one has to understand the opportunities that exist in the marketplace and the organization's capability to capitalize on those opportunities. Second, one needs to understand the financial implications of the decisions to meet these requirements.

The first article in this section by MacStravic ("Resource Requirements for Health Care Organizations") considers several important aspects to successful planning. First is the issue of *whom* do you serve. As MacStravic notes, patient origin data provide the major starting point in answering this question. The earlier article in Section 2 by Clarke and Shyavitz ("A Guide to Marketing Information and Market Research for Hospitals") emphasizes this same point, namely the value of internal data. MacStravic also notes that awareness of the competition is important. He discusses this concept from the perspective of market share (very similar to the approach in Milch and Martinelli's article in Section 2). Finally, MacStravic recognizes the need for accountability. Any good strategic plan must develop performance standards. In reading MacStravic's article, consider the five elements of any strategic plan as outlined by Abell and Hammond in their recent text on the subject:[1]

1. *Customers* must be analyzed to determine how the market can be segmented and what the requirements of each segment are;

177

2. *Competitors* must be identified and their individual strategies understood;
3. *Environmental trends* (social, economic, political, technological) affecting the market must be isolated and forecasted;
4. *Market characteristics,* in terms of the evolution of supply and demand, and the interaction of these characteristics must be understood; and
5. *Internal company characteristics* must be audited to establish how many company strengths and weaknesses relate to market requirements.

The integration of these elements is difficult. The natural question is, How can all these factors be intelligently integrated? The next two articles in this section provide one such approach. "Strategic Modelling for Health Care Managers" by Roberts and Hirsch and "Systems Intervention: New Help for Hospitals" by Stearns, Bergan, Roberts, and Quigley both provide some insight into the use of computer models for probing the interactions of organizational elements. The visual flow procedures described in each article were developed initially for industrial purposes by Jay Forrester.[2] His original models described how uncoordinated decision making could result in costly fluctuations in sales and production. While extremely complicated in application, the models are useful to show the consequences of different organizational policies.

Roberts and Hirsch note that the strategic modelling procedure, with its visual outlining of flows, forces the clarification of assumptions around which decisions might be made. Model development, however, is a difficult and time-consuming activity. Indeed, if viewed only as an "academic" exercise, model building is a useless activity. Stearns and his colleagues raise two key points to consider so as to minimize the dissatisfaction with strategic modelling.

1. Recognize that all units in the organization are involved in the organization's problems, causes, effects, and solutions.
2. The key people must be involved in the development of cause-and-effect diagrams.

Strategic modelling and planning requires the inputs of all departments and cost centers. More importantly, the key people (administrators, department heads, etc.) must be involved in the early stages. Only in this way will the outcome of any strategic modelling approach be accepted throughout the organization.

In reviewing these two articles, consider the steps that operations researchers go through in analyzing and developing a model:[3]

- defining the problem
- collecting data on the factors affecting results
- analyzing the data
- establishing a realistic criterion for measuring results
- developing a model (usually but not always a mathematical one)
- testing the model on sample problems to make sure that it represents the system correctly
- developing working tools, based on the model, to achieve the desired results
- integrating the new methods into company operations
- reevaluating and revising the model as it is used

Following these guidelines, problem definition must begin with top management participation. Collecting and analyzing data are marketing tasks. Establishing a criterion (similar to MacStravic's performance concern) is both a marketing and finance consideration. Model development and testing requires the entire organization's talents. Finally, implementation and integration must fall on top management. In essence, problem solving and strategic planning can only be done effectively by a comprehensive organizational effort.

The final article in this section describes the mandated long-range planning process conducted in Massachusetts. Recognize in these mandated procedures the attention given to *who* is being served: In marketing terms, we are asking, who is the customer? Also, note the similarity between Table 3 in the article by Mandel and Getson and the auditing questions posed in Section 2 by Berkowitz and Flexner ("The Marketing Audit: A Tool for Health Service Organizations"). The mandated planning approach may be the wave of the future. If so, greater sophistication and recognition of environmental flows will be required of health care managers.

REFERENCES

1. Derek F. Abell and John S. Hammond, *Strategic Market Planning* (Englewood Cliffs, N.J.: Prentice-Hall, Inc., 1979), pp. 47 ff.

2. Jay Forrester, *Industrial Dynamics* (Cambridge, Mass.: The M.I.T. Press, 1961).

3. Source: "The ABCs of Operations Research," *Dun's Review and Modern Industry*, part 2, September 1963, pp. 105 ff.

12. Resource Requirements for Health Care Organizations

ROBIN E. MacSTRAVIC

MacStravic, Robin E. "Resource Requirements for Health Care Organizations." *Health Care Management Review,* Fall 1979.

Determining the ideal amount of specific types of resources (facilities, equipment, labor) is a challenge to decision makers in hospitals and health care delivery organizations, as well as to officials in planning and regulatory agencies. The types of analysis useful in reaching resources decisions are likely to be similar for all parties, though their interests and perspectives may differ. Each resource decision can be analyzed by answering a series of four interrelated questions:

1. Whom do you expect to serve for any given service or program (e.g., obstetric inpatient care, outpatient surgery)?
2. How many units of service (e.g., admissions, days of care, clinic visits, operations) do you expect that population to use?
3. What kind of performance do you wish to achieve (e.g., cost, quality, occupancy, income, accommodation of demand)?
4. How many resource units (e.g., beds, physicians, employees, items of equipment) would be required to achieve the best performance mix?[1]

SERVICE POPULATION

Analysis of these four interrelated questions begins most easily with the issue of the service population.[2] There are two basic questions that must be answered about the population served by a health care delivery organization:

1. Who are the people who will require and use the kind of service being planned (markets or market segments)?

2. What portion of them will choose or be referred to this organization as a source of that service (market share)?

Major Markets

Analysis of current patient origin data[3] will identify current markets of significance. Depending on the depth of detail desired and the availability of current data plus future projections, individual market segments may be census tracts, zip codes, cities, countries, or any other convenient unit. A sample listing of current major markets is shown in Table 1.

Major markets are sources of significant numbers of admissions and visits. The identical analysis can be carried out concerning specific physicians. Such a listing would describe major admitting physicians or referral sources[4] and also describe the major market. Similar analyses can be made of market segments, such as

- classes of payment sources (e.g., Medicare, Medicaid, Blue Cross, other insurance, self-pay)

- age, sex, residence or other demographic factors

- diagnoses

Each of the preceding analyses represents a different way of describing the patient mix.[5] Upon examining this information, the decision maker may be perfectly satisfied that the mix of patients now served is optimal considering

Table 1 Current Major Markets

Market Segment	No. of Admissions	% of Total Admissions
A	400	20
B	200	10
C	600	30
D	300	15
E	500	25
Total	2,000	100

such factors as the facility's capacity and financial needs.[6] On the other hand, the decision maker may decide there is a problem and wish to alter the mix in the future. For example, a hospital administrator may feel it necessary to alter the proportion of self-pay patients in order to reduce bad debts or the proportion of surgical versus medical patients to generate more efficient use of the operating suites.

Market Shares

The analysis of the current service population is incomplete, however, without an identification of the health care facility's market shares.[7] To calculate market shares, the administrator uses the same information used to determine major markets, namely, the number of admissions or referrals from each segment, and compares this number to the total number of admissions or referrals available in each segment. Such an analysis is shown in Table 2.

This breakdown tells you how many patients out of the total number available in each market segment are coming to the health care facility for care. When the analyses of major markets and market share are combined, the administrator can determine where changes are desirable (e.g., large markets where the share is low), where change could be dangerous (e.g., large markets where the share is high), where change is unlikely (small markets where the share is high), or where change is possible but unlikely to be significant (small markets where the share is low).[8]

Table 2 Market Shares

Market Segment	No. of Admissions to This Facility	No. of Admissions to Any Facility	This Facility Market Share (%)
A	400	500	80
B	200	800	25
C	600	800	75
D	300	600	50
E	500	2500	20

The decision maker has the choice of trying to forecast future markets and market shares or trying to do something about either. For organizations with high shares in all existing markets, the only source of growth may be in identifying and attracting new markets[9] (e.g., geographic areas, income levels, physicians) or in developing new services for existing markets. Organizations with low shares in many markets may seek to expand such shares by making their existing services more attractive.[10]

Changing Market Position

Such changes in markets or shares involve changing the facility's market position.[11] This concept is probably one of the most critical notions in health services development. It entails identifying and pursuing the optimal union between a facility's capacity—what the facility is best able to do—and the needs of the community, that is, the services people will use if offered to them.[12] Market positioning must take place in the competitive environment of other organizations capable of providing the same services to the same population.[13]

Optimally, market positioning occurs naturally out of the desire of individual organizations to grow and the selection by consumers of the sources and types of services that best meet their needs. Organizations end up doing what they do best for a specific population because they grow in directions where services attract sufficient clientele and decline in directions where they do not. However, in the unique health care marketplace, where services are evaluated and demanded mostly through physicians, where prices are paid mostly by third parties, and where certificate-of-need laws prevent the growth of the successful and prolong the life of the unsuccessful, such positioning does not occur naturally.[14]

In effect, a new market has been created in which regulators decide which organizations survive, which services they can offer, and how much they will be paid for doing so. This situation, however, does not eliminate the need for marketing analysis or the usefulness of such analysis, since regulators deal mainly in preventing gross changes. Adjustments in occupancy or productivity may be critical to organizational survival,[15] and elimination of services is usually welcomed by regulators.

Where current markets, market shares, competitive realities, the strengths of the organization, and the needs of the community predict inefficient use of an existing service,[16] consideration should be given to eliminating it. Cooperative efforts among several organizations may result in each doing what it does best. Thus, effective market positioning can occur naturally through the marketplace, result artificially through regulation, or be arrived at jointly through coordinated developments that would be subject to antitrust prosecution in most other industries.[17]

FUTURE UTILIZATION

The purpose of analysis, forecasting and changing markets or market shares, is to determine what the use of a specific service will be. Whether future use is passively predicted[18] or specifically targeted for intervention, an estimate of future utilization should result. If change is expected, the factors that will cause such changes should be identified and analyzed.[19] If change is desired, the strategies that will effect such change should be selected and implemented based on their anticipated results.[20] If changes are feared, strategies to prevent them may have to be selected, implemented, and their effectiveness estimated.

Simple Estimates

There are numerous technical approaches to forecasting future utilization.[21] Simple estimates assuming no intervention may be made by trend extrapolation or correlation. Such techniques assume that whatever changes or relationships have existed in the past will persevere into the future. But unless the reasons for such trends are identified and understood, the trends should not be relied upon too heavily. A straight-line trend based on past numbers of admissions, visits, or census levels may level off or reverse itself if population growth stabilizes or reverses. Use rates by populations may alter with shifts in such factors as age levels, fertility rates, and emphasis on self-care.[22]

Complex Techniques

Compared with simple estimates, complex techniques such as multiple regressions and simulations may enable the organization to deal with more factors affecting utilization. Such techniques, however, are likely to be expensive and may not always be accurate. Multivariate equations for forecasting beyond next year require estimates of future measures for all the variables used to forecast utilization. Each such estimate is only a guess, so the result may be simply a more expensive and scientific-looking wild guess. A simulation offers the opportunity for the organization to estimate effects of specific interventions, though such effects can only be estimated.[23]

Nevertheless, multivariate quantitative techniques can be very useful as guides to provide insight into how change occurs. When used carefully, they should identify aspects of complex situations that are sensitive to changes in certain factors. Once factors have been identified and their linkage to utilization recognized, forecasts or strategies may be developed that incorporate changes in such factors and their anticipated effects. Sophisticated analytical and forecasting models should assist rather than replace reasoned judgment.

Accuracy of Forecasts

The only way to determine the accuracy of a forecast is to wait and see. Any forecast is a guess, hopefully a reasoned estimate of what the future will probably be like. Forecasting techniques that have worked in the past are not guaranteed against utter failure in the future. But by identifying the factors that are likely to change or that the facility intends to change, and by estimating the probable effects of each change by formal quantitative analysis or by informal group processes, the decision maker will be making as informed an estimate of the future as is possible. The future is always at least partially what people make it, so an administrator can partially correct forecasting errors.

The best forecasting of future use of health services should incorporate some recognition of at least the following:

- changes in the numbers of people in the service population;

- changes in the demographic characteristics of the service population (e.g., age, sex, race, income);

- changes in the attitudes and behavior patterns of the service population (e.g., fertility rates, preference for home care or self-treatment, ambulatory versus inpatient care);

- changes in the numbers of physicians serving the service population;

- changes in medical practice patterns (e.g., length of stay, preference for ambulatory versus inpatient care, new technology); and

- changes in the environment affecting utilization behavior (e.g., national health insurance, developments by competitors, employment levels).

RESOURCE PERFORMANCE

To decide what types and amounts of resources are appropriate for the level of utilization anticipated, the administrator must define and operationalize what is meant by *appropriate*. It is best at this point to avoid the concept of need or absolute necessity. The organization does not *need* a hospital bed to serve the *needs* of the community. Rather, it will *require* a certain number of beds *in order to* accommodate an expected level of use. What number of beds is *required* for a given level of use will depend on what performance is expected out of those beds.

The concept of program performance is as critical as that of market position and more useful than that of need. Whether or not a specific program is developed and maintained or how any resources are provided for a given level of utilization will determine how well the organization performs.[24] Therefore, the decision on whether to develop and maintain a program and how many resources will be provided should be based on what performance is expected.

Defining Performance

The first step in using the resource performance concept is to define what is meant by *performance*. As a minimum, performance should be measured in such terms as

- *cost*—per visit, per patient day, per case, fixed versus variable, and so on;

- *quality*—adequacy of staffing, training, experience, equipment, and so on; and

- *access*—ability to accommodate use when it is demanded or most appropriate for the patient.

The performance attributes that the organization considers important should be identified and operationalized. Perceptions of patients, physicians, employees, and the board of trustees may all contribute to developing a listing of the most important performance factors to consider. Ways to operationalize and estimate values for each must be developed. For example, providing access to patients is a fine rhetorical goal, but determining how frequently beds will be available when needed and how long people might have to wait for care or travel to it produce more useful operational measures.

Defining Standards

The organization may wish to define standards for the performance criteria it considers important. It might identify precise values for such factors as

- cost per patient day—$250;

- occupancy—85 percent;

- percent of time demand is met—100 percent; and

- average emergency room waiting time—30 minutes.

188   STRATEGIC PLANNING IN HEALTH CARE MANAGEMENT

The organization must recognize, however, that these performance factors can conflict with each other. For example, the demand for inpatient care varies—higher during the week than on weekends, higher during some seasons of the year than others, very low on holidays, especially around Christmas. How many beds should the hospital maintain considering its varying census? If it maintains as many as are used during peak periods, it can be proud of its access, but concerned about cost and quality. High fixed costs together with the times larger numbers of the beds are not used will raise the average cost per patient day. Staffing will either have to be geared to the high census, resulting in higher costs, or to the lower census with periodic under-staffing during peaks.

RESOURCE DECISION

The mix of performance that a given resource decision promises concerning expected utilization should be the basis for making each decision. Specific decisions will require compromising some desired performance factor (e.g., high occupancy, low cost) to further another (e.g., good access, high quality). Fortunately there are a number of formal techniques available to decision makers for analyzing performance mix. Many of these techniques are described in terms of preference analysis, value analysis, or priority setting, but all are designed to help select the optimal situation, considering multiple characteristics.

The basic approach of these techniques is to quantify the value of specific attributes as perceived by different people. One technique, cost-risk analysis, is designed to evaluate positive attributes as benefits and negative attributes as risks.[25] Another, multiple classification, compares distance, satisfaction, and utilization of clinic services.[26] Conventional operations analysis techniques, such as linear programming, may be used in some cases.[27] All that is necessary is that a way be developed to score alternative resource decisions according to each performance factor affected and to combine the scores into a meaningful total.

Although most of the techniques are likely to seem esoteric, they do have multiple applications and are worth an examination. Each is designed to rank or measure objectively preference for a series of choices that have multiple attributes. As such, each can potentially be used for

- evaluating patient or physician preference for possible new programs or changing attributes of existing programs;[28]

- establishing priorities among problems for attention, strategies for implementation, and objectives for pursuit;[29] and

- evaluating any specific action, whether proposed or implemented, based on anticipated or actual results.[30]

Considering the number of occasions when such functions are carried out with multiple outcomes or attributes, administrators could benefit from a familiarity with the class of preference analysis techniques. Fortunately, they range in complexity from sophisticated computer models[31] to relatively simple paper-and-pencil alternatives.[32] Somewhere in the array is likely tc be one appropriate for each application.

Resisting Single-Factor Decision Rules

It might seem preferable to make resource decisions based on specific objectives or constraints. Certainly this would make the job simpler. Hospitals could translate average daily census, for example, into bed need by dividing the census figure by desired occupancy, say 85 percent. This is an approach long preferred by governmental agencies. Other examples suggested in national planning guidelines are minimum resource units, such as 20 pediatric beds or 15 neonatal intensive care unit beds, and minimum utilization levels per resource unit, such as 2,500 CAT scans per year or 300 megavoltage radiation therapy cases per year.[33]

Use of such single-factor decision rules will simplify the decision process, but at the cost of ignoring the multiple consequences of each decision. If bed requirements for a given average census are calculated based on desired occupancy, the hospital will presumably end up with the desired occupancy. Unfortunately, no one will know what the costs will be, the number of times admissions may be delayed or denied for lack of beds, or whether the peak census will ever approach the bed supply. In some cases, a single performance factor may be of such overriding importance that a specific standard must be met that serves as a constraint on decisions. Even so, the decision maker should accept such a constraint knowing its impact on other performance factors and confident that nothing better can be achieved.

Single Performance Criteria and Planning Agencies

The imposition of controls based on single performance criteria and standards by planning and regulatory agencies certainly conflicts with the reality of resources performance. If such controls are to be resisted, two sources of objection are worth pursuing:

1. concern that the criteria themselves do not adequately incorporate important performance factors; and

2. concern that the standard will adversely affect other performance factors.

Both objections require examination of multiple performance attributes, either in general or in the context of specific cases. The appropriateness of considering additional attributes is specifically recognized in the national guideline. This recognition should be reflected both in the responses made by health care delivery organizations to the guidelines themselves and in the decisions each organization makes regarding its own resources development. Both the organization and the community it serves are affected in multiple, conflicting ways by resource decisions. The totality of such effects upon the community and the organization constitute the better, although more difficult, basis for making such decisions.

REFERENCES

1. MacStravic, R. *Determining Health Needs.* Ann Arbor, Mich.: Health Administration Press, 1978.

2. Zimmerman, J. "Service Areas and Their Needs Must Be Reassured." *Hospitals, JAHA* 49 (September 1975): 46.

3. Zuckerman, A. "Patient Origin Study Profiles Service Area, Evolving Patterns." *Hospitals, JAHA* 51 (July 1977): 83.

4. Creditor, M. "The Ecology of an Urban Voluntary Hospital: The Referral Chain." *Medical Care* 10 (January/February 1972): 88.

5. Suver, J., et al. "Patient Mix and Break-Even Analysis." *Management Accounting* 58 (January 1977): 38.

6. Hogan, S. "Your Patient Mix Affects Costs." *Hospital Financial Management* 8 (April 1978): 20.

7. Karr, D. "Increasing a Hospital's Market Share." *Hospitals, JAHA* 51 (June 1977): 64.

8. Ross, D., and Tripoli, F. "Fiscal Risks, Methods, Rewards Shape Community Outreach Success." *Hospitals, JAHA* 51 (July 1977): 86.

9. Deitch, M. "Should Health Care Providers Enter Marketplace?" *Health Care Week*, October 3, 1977, p. 1.

10. Roberts, S. "Improving Primary Care Clinic Effectiveness Through Assessment." *Hospitals, JAHA* 51 (November 1977): 123.

11. Seaver, D. "Hospital Revises Role, Reaches Out to Cultivate and Capture Markets." *Hospitals, JAHA* 51 (June 1977): 59.

12. Falberg, W., and Bonnem, S. "Good Marketing Helps a Hospital Grow." *Hospitals, JAHA* 51 (June 1977): 7.

13. Slom, S. "Ghetto Medicine." *Wall Street Journal*, October 21, 1977.

14. Enthoven, A. "Rx for Health Care Economics: Competition, Not Rigid NHI." *Hospital Progress* 59 (October 1978): 44.

15. Sachs, T. "It Takes a Sense of Survival." *Hospitals, JAHA* 52 (April 1978): 101.

16. Cowen, D., et al. "Problems in the Development of a Rural Primary Care Center." *Journal of Community Health* 2 (Fall 1976): 52.

17. McDaniel, J. "We Have Seen Rate Review and It Works." *Hospitals, JAHA* 52 (April 1978): 71.

18. Cunningham, R. "Hospitals Face Fewer Admissions, Shorter Stays." *Modern Healthcare* 128 (June 1977): 29.

19. Johnson, B. "Basic Assumptions Are Being Reviewed." *Modern Healthcare* 130 (January 1978): 54.

20. Schumer, J. "HMO Feasibility: The Market Decision." *Medical Group Management* 24 (March/April 1977): 37.

21. Harrington, M. "Forecasting Areawide Demand for Health Care Services." *Inquiry* 15 (September 1977): 254.

22. Ware, J., and Snyder, M. "Dimensions of Patient Attitudes Regarding Doctors and Medical Care Services." *Medical Care* 13 (August 1975): 669.

23. Roberts, E., and Hirsch, G. "Strategic Modeling for Health Care Managers." *Health Care Management Review* 1 (Winter 1976): 69.

24. Griffith, J. *Measuring Hospital Performance.* Chicago, Ill.: Blue Cross Association, 1978.

25. Fischhoff, B., et al. "How Safe Is Enough? A Psychometric Study of Attitudes Toward Technological Risks and Benefits." *Policy Sciences* 9 (April 1978): 127.

26. Brooks, C. "Associations Among Distance, Patient Satisfaction and Utilization of Two Types of Inner-City Clinics." *Medical Care* 11 (September/October 1973): 62.

27. Parker, B., and Srinivasan, V. "A Consumer Preference Approach to the Planning of Rural Primary Health Care Facilities." *Operations Research* 24 (September/October 1976): 991.

28. Koutsopoulos, K., et al. "Psychometric Modeling of Consumer Decisions in Primary Health Care." *Health Services Research* 12 (Winter 1977): 427.

29. MacStravic, R. "Setting Priorities in Health Planning: What Does It All Mean?" *Inquiry* 15 (March 1978): 20.

30. Shortell, S., and Richardson, W. *Health Program Evaluation.* St. Louis, Mo.: The C.V. Mosby Co., 1978.

31. Wind, Y., and Spitz, L. "Analytical Approach to Marketing Decisions in Health Care Organizations." *Operations Research* 24 (September/October 1976): 973.

32. Grimes, R., et al. "Use of Decision Theory in Regional Planning." *Health Services Research* 9 (Spring 1974): 73.

33. U.S. Department of Health, Education and Welfare. *National Guidelines for Health Planning.* Washington, D.C.: Government Printing Office, 1978, pp. 4-16.

13. Strategic Modelling for Health Care Managers

EDWARD B. ROBERTS and GARY B. HIRSCH

Roberts, Edward B., and Hirsch, Gary B. "Strategic Modelling for Health Care Managers." *Health Care Management Review,* Winter, 1976.

A dismaying number of health and social service programs fail, or stagger along at marginal effectiveness, because of basic flaws in their design—flaws that are all too obvious when viewed in retrospect. In today's complex health care environment, when a program proves incapable of delivering the urgently needed services it is supposed to provide, both the provider and the recipient lose. Money and people are wasted across the board. Such prolonged ineffectiveness or outright failure usually results from incomplete consideration by planners and administrators of the factors impinging on a program's success.

During the past seven years we have seen strategic modelling methods, developed initially for industry, effectively adapted to the needs of health executives. These versatile tools, based on practical applications of theories and computer techniques created at the MIT-Sloan School of Management,[1] allow simultaneous consideration of the complex factors that determine whether a health program will succeed or fail. For example:

- Models help to make decisions concerning program design, resource allocation, and the choice of program policies.

- Models can be used, before any resources have been committed to the program, to assess the impact of a health program on its sociomedical environment, and the effect of environmental changes on that program.

- Even before a program has been conceived, strategic models permit planners to study health problems and find leverage points where investment of health care resources brings the greatest return. When resources are limited—and they usually are—these leverage points are vital to accurate definition of the program.

PLANNING MODEL OF AN HMO

It is now apparent that the bright promise of prepaid group practice, especially health maintenance organizations (HMOs), has been dimmed by numerous problems of which staffing, marketing, and capitation setting are but a few. The difficulties encountered in the establishment of HMOs become clearer, and the interrelationships of various factors more obvious, when they are modelled in simple visual-tracing form. Let us see how cause and effect relate to each other in the development and operation of this type of health organization.

BASIC FLOWS

The subscriber population of an HMO grows as new subscribers enter and declines as dissatisfied subscribers leave. Subscribers have care needs that must be treated with outpatient services or by hospitalization. Since these needs cannot be dealt with instantaneously, a care backlog gradually builds up. The backlog is reduced at a treatment rate that is limited by the number of doctors employed by or under contract to the HMO. For any given number of doctors, the treatment rate can be increased to a degree by raising individual workloads and by employing paramedical people. Beyond that point, however, the care backlog begins to grow. These overall system elements and the relationships among them are shown in Figure 1.

As the subscriber population grows and its demands begin to exceed the treatment capacity of the available doctors, two mechanisms in the form of negative feedback control loops come into play to relieve the strain. The first, and more desirable, of the two is the adjustment of the number of doctors to conform to the care needs of the subscriber population. When care backlogs begin to grow, the number of doctors required also rises and motivates hiring. The rate at which new doctors can be hired may be dependent on the salary range offered by the HMO, as well as other influences. More doctors enable the treatment rate to be increased and backlog to be reduced. This adjustment mechanism is illustrated in Figure 2.

The negative sign on the dotted-loop arrow indicates a set of closed relationships that are goalseeking: As care backlog increases, doctor hiring rises to increase medical treatment rate, bringing care backlog down.

The other mechanism that reduces the strain of large care needs is less desirable because it all but defeats the purpose of the HMO. As the care

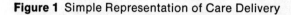

Figure 1 Simple Representation of Care Delivery

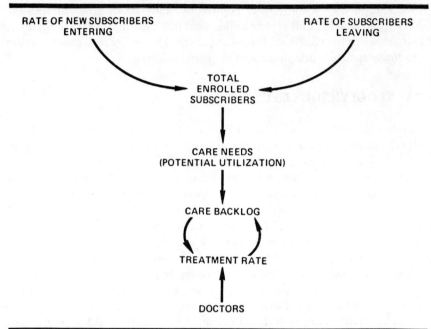

Figure 2 Medical Staff Expansion Loop

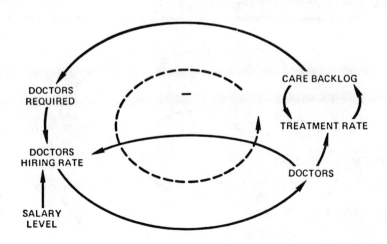

backlog rises, the delay in getting care also goes up and has a negative impact on subscriber satisfaction. Subscribers sensitive to poor service may leave the HMO, reducing the subscriber population. Care needs go down and the backlog is reduced. This second adjustment mechanism is shown in Figure 3. It is also a negative feedback loop—as care backlog increases, subscribers are gradually reduced, bringing down the care backlog.

BACKLOG: VICIOUS CYCLE

But the two mechanisms shown in Figures 2 and 3 do not always work. If the HMO's administration is very conservative about hiring or contracting for additional doctors, or if patients are insensitive to delays because of inadequate access to other sources of care, backlog continues to grow and creates increasing strain on the staff. A vicious cycle (positive feedback loop) may develop in which the overload causes doctors to begin leaving, and the number of doctors declines. Treatment rate goes down and leaves the remaining doctors faced with an even larger care backlog. This vicious cycle can lead to a steadily deteriorating situation in which fewer doctors are available for growing care needs. The factors underlying such a situation are shown in Figure 4. The positive sign on the loop arrow indicates a positive feedback loop, one that fosters self-amplifying change.

Such vicious cycles as in Figure 4, more typical of an urban public care program than a prepaid HMO, are clearly to be avoided by the management

Figure 3 Subscriber Dissatisfaction Loop

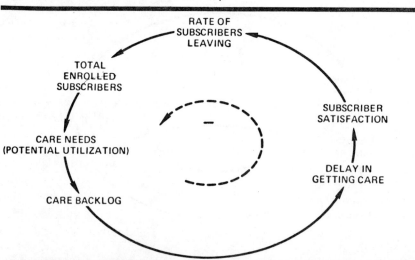

Figure 4 Doctors Leaving Due to Overloads

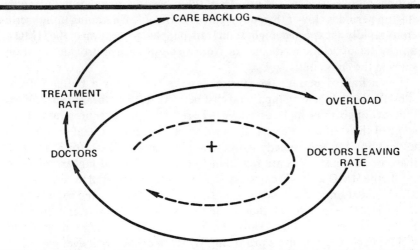

of the HMO. Limiting the growth of the subscriber population or having a temporary source of part-time doctors to provide flexible capacity during the growth phase of the HMO are possible preventive measures. Dealing with situations as they arise, however, is often not enough. By the time a problem becomes evident, anything less than drastic measures may be inadequate. As the subscriber population grows, the number of doctors available may seem sufficient. However, after subscribers have been with the HMO for some time, they become more knowledgeable of the range of medical services available to them and utilize them more frequently for health maintenance as well as for the treatment of illness. Once this phenomenon becomes evident, it may be too late to control workload by limiting new subscribers. Before any new doctors can be hired, the vicious cycle of doctors leaving and increasing workload per doctor may begin. If the HMO gets a reputation for having a very heavy workload, it will encounter difficulties in recruiting new doctors.

Another set of vicious cycles can also have serious detrimental effects on the HMO. Unlike a conventional medical insurance program that has no fixed overhead other than administrative costs, a large proportion of an HMO's expenses—salaries, rents, contracts—are fixed and must be paid regardless of the subscriber population. These large fixed costs imply some break-even point, some number of subscribers the HMO needs to operate without losing money. New HMOs usually set aside funds to deal with deficits during the startup period without unfairly burdening those who are among the first to become subscribers.

PREMIUMS UP, ENROLLMENTS DOWN

Suppose, however, that the growth of the subscriber population during the startup period is slower than anticipated. Difficulties in signing up subscribers as rapidly as expected might stem from peoples' perception of the HMO as a provider of "clinic medicine" or from well-established provider relationships in the community.

For a limited period, the startup reserve can act as a buffer between subscribers and the very high total cost per actual subscriber enrolled. Eventually, though, these high costs have to be reflected in higher premiums unless some of the staff are released. Because an HMO's professional staff is often under contract, this remedy is frequently not available or, for other good reasons, administrators are reluctant to apply it. Should higher premiums result, the HMO would become even less attractive compared to conventional arrangements, new enrollments would decline even further, and some of those in the HMO would decide that it had become too expensive and drop out. Remaining subscribers then would have still higher costs and premiums. This vicious cycle might cause a promising HMO to die before it ever got off the ground. The factors that could produce this cycle are shown in Figure 5, which includes a positive feedback loop affecting subscribers leaving.

Figure 5 Cost Increases Resulting From Slow Growth

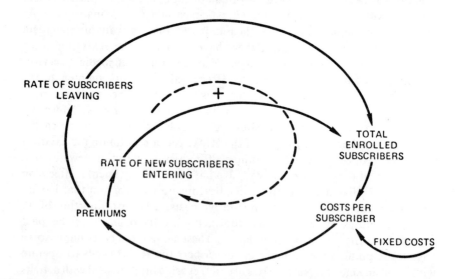

This kind of problem suggests a need for at least two measures to protect the fledgling HMO. One is the provision of a line of credit through governmental or private sources for HMOs that find their startup reserves inadequate to cover initial losses. The other measure is the gradual acquisition of staff and facilities by the HMO during its growth period. Both measures would help to prevent the HMO from falling into the vicious cycle described. Allocation of more resources to marketing activities would also help.

MORBIDITY FILTER

The last problem to be discussed in the context of this simple illustrative model is another vicious cycle that can affect an HMO in either its growth phase or its long-term phase of steady-state operations. If the efficiency of the HMO's operations begins to decline, more staff have to be hired and facilities acquired to serve the same number of subscribers. Costs per subscriber go up and are eventually reflected in higher premiums. People who are often ill and require care may not be bothered by the high premiums, feeling that they can still get their money's worth; but those who are healthier and get less use out of a health program would be less willing to join the HMO as its premiums rise. Similarly, healthier people already enrolled in the HMO may be motivated to drop out by higher premiums, while those who utilize services more frequently will be less sensitive to premium increases. The expensive HMO, in effect, becomes a filter, drawing in people who require more care while discouraging and driving out those who are healthier and would not utilize its services very frequently. Average morbidity of the subscriber population increases as a result of this filter effect, and care needs go up.

If the HMO raises benefits to compensate partially for the higher premiums, utilization can go up even further, and the HMO may become even more attractive to those who are very ill. Higher utilization creates larger backlogs and greater resource requirements, especially more doctors. As doctors are hired and other resources acquired, costs go up and force higher premiums to complete the cycle. The structure that produces this behavior is shown in Figure 6; dotted feedback-loop arrows are omitted here for simplification.

Two strategies can be employed to avoid or get out of this vicious cycle. The HMO should have a cost-accounting system that reveals whether excessive cost increases are due to operating inefficiencies or are caused by a rising average morbidity among the subscriber population. If inefficient operations are revealed as the cause of rising costs, a strategy should be used that focuses on cost control and allocates more effort to cost-saving studies, measures to improve efficiency, and the introduction of labor-saving technology.

Figure 6 Factors That Generate Higher Costs and Greater Average Morbidity

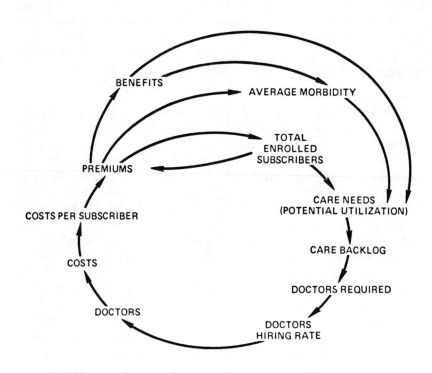

MARKETING: CAVEAT VENDOR

If the HMO's costs seem to be rising because it is serving a higher cost population, a strategy of selective marketing is in order. Selective marketing can be carried out in several ways. Efforts to stimulate new enrollment can be directed at groups that are expected to contain mostly low utilizers. Experience rating, under which low utilizer groups are offered lower premiums, is

another way of overcoming high utilization problems. Adjustment of the
benefit package in a way that would not affect low utilizers very much but
would discourage high utilizers is a third alternative. The use of at least one of
these alternatives may be necessary if the rising average morbidity-high cost
cycle is to be avoided. The complete model structure as developed thus far is
shown in Figure 7.

Figure 7 Complete HMO Model Structure as Illustrative Example

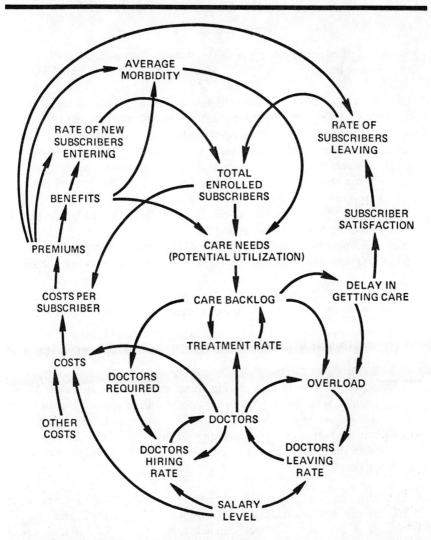

USING THE MODEL

The process of developing a visual cause-and-effect model of the type illustrated is immediately helpful for initiating a strategic planning effort. It helps to coalesce a multidisciplinary task force around the key goal, strategy, or policy issues that challenge effective program design. Seeing interrelationships among different functional areas of a health organization generates shared insights into common objectives and interdependencies.

DYNAMO

Visual modelling as the driving mechanism in conflict resolution and strategy development has now been applied successfully in several complex health settings.[2]

In many cases, the complexity will deserve further elaboration and detailing of the visual model and representation in computer language to enable more rigorous analysis. For the type of model illustrated in Figure 7, a special language has been developed, called DYNAMO,[3] that permits easy translation of the visual model into mathematical equations and computer form. The computer can then generate simulated time histories of the modelled health organization for a variety of hypothesized or expected scenarios. The simulated histories help to forecast the effects on the health care organization of using various management policies.

For example, even with the simple HMO model described, a set of DYNAMO simulations can help to answer some of the following questions:

- What problems (in addition to the ones discussed) are likely to arise during the growth phase or in steady-state operations of the HMO?

- What policy of hiring doctors will yield the lowest cost for the HMO while creating the highest possible levels of satisfaction for both subscribers and doctors?

- What policies for reflecting costs in premiums should be followed? Allowing premiums to lag very far behind costs will, of course, lead to bankruptcy. Adjusting premiums too quickly in response to rising costs may lead to the high cost-high morbidity vicious cycle. Simulations carried out with the model can indicate the proper balance necessary to avoid either situation.

Even this simple model can help the planners and decision makers in the HMO choose policies needed to enable its healthy growth and smooth operation. A more detailed model can help them to deal with a wider range of issues and decision.

In fact, a model reflecting many of the issues discussed above was developed as part of an HMO planning process for the Albert Einstein College of Medicine in New York.[4] The model contained far more detail, taking into consideration specific characteristics of multiple potential subscriber markets, as well as several treatment program alternatives. Development and computer simulation of that model helped to persuade the medical school that an HMO would be relatively ineffective and overly expensive under the then existing environmental conditions. The strategic decision resulted that the school should not proceed with the HMO. An earlier version of a similar HMO model was helpful in planning the development of the Harvard Community Health Plan, a medical-school-sponsored HMO in a very different setting.

DEVELOPING STRATEGIC HEALTH CARE MODELS

Models for solving strategic care delivery problems and for planning new health education or health service programs are most effective when they are developed by teams of senior managers and program leaders working collaboratively with model-building specialists. Active participation of the health organization's leadership group ensures greater accuracy of the model's representation of the real world system and improves the chances that the model will be used by planners and decision makers. Initially, this group of participants provides the model builders with a set of impressions, experiences, anecdotes, and intuitive feelings that, when combined with hard data and documented case studies, become the basis for a visual model structure.

As the visual cause-and-effect model evolves, those team members with health-problems expertise critique and modify its formulations until the model structure is acceptable. It is then represented by equations in the special-purpose computer language and "run" to determine its basic behavior under a baseline set of data and assumptions. The model's behavior is studied by the experts. If it is deemed unrealistic, the model's structure is further revised.

Effective strategic modelling efforts should usually try to avoid unnecessarily extensive data collection. Instead, they should focus, at least initially, on the relatively few parameters whose accuracy is important in explaining system behavior. Experience has shown that most of the parameters in a model can be varied over a wide range with little effect on system behavior. Usually only a few sensitive parameters impact heavily on behavior. Sensitive parameters are found by performing baseline runs with changes in only one parameter per run. The few that produce major behavior shifts when changed are then more carefully researched.

Once the model has been developed in this manner, the health services people in the modeling team help to raise research questions, develop hypotheses, propose experiments, and evaluate the implications of simulation results for program planning. Finally, the participation of these people plays an essential role in starting up the appropriate set of programs, organizational forms, policy sets, linkages among service units, and supportive services in an operating program.

Model building plays an important role in forcing the clarification of assumptions about the causes of service delivery problems. Where these assumptions differ, the model serves as a vehicle for achieving consensus. In the course of building a model, many interesting (and sometimes counterintuitive) hypotheses about the modelled system's structure and their corresponding effects on behavior are generated. These can then be tested within the context of the model. As a completed model emerges, its feedback loops become more apparent, and more elaborate behavioral hypotheses can be formulated.

The completed model has several uses. Primarily, it enables the health care manager or planner to ask "What if?" questions and perform simulations to get the answers. Simulation helps to avoid experimental tampering with existing programs or setting up new ones that may have critical flaws. Further sensitivity analysis can be done with the completed model to identify leverage points and generate additional research priorities. Operating models can also serve as a communications medium for people who were not involved in building the model. By observing the effects of changes in policies and parameters in behavior, these people can better understand the dynamic forces at work in the real-world system. The models are open-ended and can always be modified to support analyses of more detailed issues in system design. If a group of health program planners have a fairly good model of the operations and economics of their plan but are wondering about community reaction to the program, a community response sector can be added to the model.

APPLYING STRATEGIC HEALTH CARE MODELLING

Although health system dynamics models have been under development for only seven years, they have already been applied to management issues in academic medical centers, hospitals, and community care organizations; and they also have been used in several manpower planning and health policy areas. For example, in addition to the HMO planning models described earlier that were developed for Einstein and Harvard, efforts for three other medical schools have revealed a common set of causal factors relevant to all three schools and the problems they face:

- One of the three models focuses on future patient utilization of a medical school's teaching hospital and on problems that may cause utilization to decline below levels needed for teaching purposes.

- Another deals with the number of students that can be accommodated in the various programs at an academic health center without doing harm to the quality of training and of patient care provided by the health center. Problems associated with enrolling too many students are a central focus of that effort.

- A third model deals with difficulties encountered by a medical school in interacting with a number of its affiliated hospitals.

Despite the apparent diversity of problems and the great differences in the schools at which these problems are being modeled, the relationships diagrammed in simplified form in Figure 8 seem applicable in all three cases. In each of the medical center projects, the interplay between a medical school and one or more teaching hospitals was central to the principal problem analyzed. Work has been carried out in appraising strategic planning issues at several other hospitals as well. For example, reference note 2 describes the

Figure 8 Some of the Causal Relationships Affecting the Performance of Academic Medical Centers

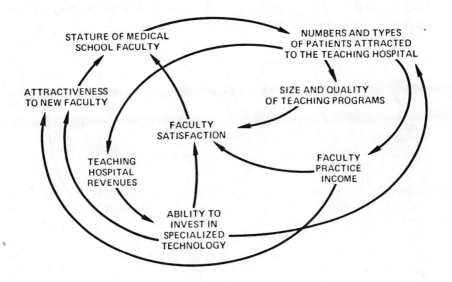

modeling of a community-based hospital facing decline in both outpatient volume and bed census, with serious threats to the viability of the whole organization.

CHECKING THE DOWNWARD SPIRAL

Figure 9 suggests part of the predicament faced by that hospital. The diagram indicates that if the outpatient department "dries up," the hospital census will decline and the acute services would eventually have to be closed—that is, a declining hospital census will make it harder to maintain ancillary support services such as lab and X ray and to justify the purchase of needed equipment. This will in turn reduce the attractiveness of the hospital to physicians,

Figure 9 Interdependencies Between Outpatient Department and Hospital Services

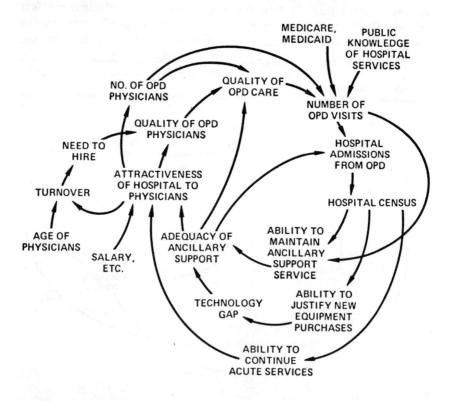

reduce the quality of OPD care, and, further, reduce the number of hospital admissions because OPD will have to refer more patients elsewhere. This downward spiral could result in the discontinuation of acute services, which would lead to further declines in the quality of OPD care.

In this hospital the modeling effort led to a broad program of institutional change, now largely implemented, that has reversed the downward spiral. The hospital is now past its crisis phase and is steadily improving in health. Other strategic models have focused upon mental hospitals,[5] community mental health centers,[6] ambulatory care,[7] and emergency care.[8] Our ready access to neighboring Boston-area institutions has also resulted in models dealing with issues at Massachusetts General Hospital, New England Medical Center Hospital, Boston City Hospital, and Cambridge Hospital.

MANPOWER PLANNING

Manpower planning has become the focus of two major current modeling projects that are seeking to understand supply, demand, and impact upon care in the separate areas of dental care and nursing. Earlier efforts in the dental area[9] have been expanded into the largest computerized system dynamics model yet developed, treating over 2,000 detailed variables relating to the future of dentistry. A similar effort in the nursing field is now underway in a collaboration between the Division of Nursing of the Western Interstate Commission on Higher Education (WICHE) and Pugh-Roberts Associates of Cambridge, Massachusetts.

In broader aspects of health policy, strategic modeling has attempted to cope with the complexities of comprehensive health planning, with the defensive practice of medicine,[10] and with the total system of urban heroin addiction, its consequences, and the multiple strategies for dealing with it.[11] The latter work exemplifies the type of comprehensive analysis that is possible using strategic system dynamic models. At a time when the nation was heralding the apparent end of the drug problem, that analysis concluded that drug abuse was persistent and would not soon be eradicated, an assessment now firmly supported by the latest nationwide studies.

As indicated above, strategic models can serve a number of useful functions for health program administrators and planners: problem diagnosis, resource allocation, decision making, cost-benefit analysis, evaluation of alternative program designs, and impact assessment for proposed programs. Several other specific areas to which models might be applied are:

- *Analyzing the relationship between living conditions and health ti identify high-leverage public health measures to help maintain good health.* This would involve developing models that relate such environmental factors as poor nutrition, crowding, inadequate prenatal and well child care, lead poisoning, and the tensions of living in areas of extreme poverty to the overall health of the client population. Such a model would allow planners to find the most effective allocation of resources among these public health programs.

• *Designing programs to deal with illnesses whose treatment is complicated by social designations of deviance.* Models representing the forces surrounding such problems as alcoholism and narcotics addiction—how people become involved, punitive societal response, and so on—help planners to design comprehensive programs that deal with every aspect of the problem, including prevention, treatment, rehabilitation, followup, and changing community attitudes about the problem.

• *Exploring needs for programmatic and technological development to determine high-priority research and development topics.* We can analyze the problems confronting the care delivery system, using models to find the points at which technological or program innovations would be especially useful in reducing the cost of care or improving its quality. This approach has been used in other industries but not yet in the area of health care technology.

• *Creating epidemiological models to help design comprehensive approaches to particular diseases and health programs.* These models can be used to evaluate the cost effectiveness of various strategies for intervention and to find high-leverage opportunities for prevention and mass treatment. [12,13]

As the HMO example demonstrates, models can be built to include the important factors that determine the success or failure and effectiveness of any program. With these models, steps can be taken to enable programs to be successful and avoid many of the pitfalls that spell the end of well-intentioned but poorly designed programs. Health care, as a business, is rapidly becoming aware of the wealth of sophisticated techniques available to it from industry. Providers, as their reluctance wanes to emulate their profit-oriented brethren, will derive an increasing amount of assistance from the hard lessons learned by competitive corporations. The opportunity is there to take advantage of this expertise, and we should not ignore it.

REFERENCES

1. Forrester, Jay W. *Industrial Dynamics.* Cambridge, Mass.: M.I.T. Press, 1961.

2. Stearns, N.S.; Bergan, T.A.; Roberts, E.B.; and Quigley, J.L. "System Intervention: A New Approach to Implementing Change in the Hospital Setting." Unpublished manuscript. Cambridge, Mass.: M.I.T. Sloan School of Management, 1975.

3. Pugh, Alexander L. III. *DYNAMO II User's Manual.* Cambridge, Mass.: M.I.T. Press, 1973.

4. Hirsch, G.B., and Miller, Sutherland. "Evaluating HMO Policies with a Computer Simulation Model." *Medical Care,* August 1974.

5. Hertzman, M., and Levin, G. "Empirical Confirmation of a Simulation Model of Mental Hospitalization." *International Journal of Social Psychiatry,* 1975, pp. 218-224.

6. Levin, G., et al. *The Dynamics of Human Service Delivery.* Cambridge, Mass.: Ballinger Publishing Co., expected 1976.

7. Hirsch, G.B., and Bergan, T.A. "Simulating Ambulatory Care Systems: The Relationship between Structure and Behavior." *Proceedings of the Summer Simulation Conference,* 1973.

8. Troup, S.B., and Van Niel, R. *Hospital Emergency Services: Modelling a Dynamic System.* Unpublished M.S. thesis. Cambridge, Mass.: M.I.T. Sloan School of Management, 1972.

9. Hirsch, G.B., and Killingsworth, W.R. "A New Framework for Projecting Dental Manpower Requirements." *Inquiry,* September 1975.

10. Twine, E., and Potchen, E.J. *Dynamic Systems Analysis of Defensive Medicine.* Unpublished M.S. thesis. Cambridge, Mass.: M.I.T. Sloan School of Management, 1973.

11. Levin, G.; Roberts, E.B.; and Hirsch, G.B. *Persistent Poppy: A Computer-Aided Search for Heroin Policy.* Cambridge, Mass.: Ballinger Publishing Co., 1975.

12. McPherson, L.F. "Urban Yellow Fever: An Industrial Dynamics Study of Epidemiology." Unpublished memorandum D-572. Cambridge, Mass.: M.I.T. Sloan School of Management, 1963.

13. Watanabe, M. "Cancer Population Dynamics." *Proceeding of the Summer Simulation Conference,* 1974.

14. Systems Intervention: New Help for Hospitals

NORMAN S. STEARNS, THOMAS A. BERGAN,
EDWARD B. ROBERTS and JOHN L. QUIGLEY

Stearns, Norman S.; Bergan, Thomas A.; Roberts, Edward B.; and
Quigley, John L. "Systems Intervention: New Help for Hospitals."
Health Care Management Review, Fall 1976.

When the chief of medical services at the Lawrence Quigley Memorial Hospital announced his decision to resign, the hospital director knew he could expect trouble in finding a replacement. Salaries at the Chelsea, Massachusetts hospital complex were simply not competitive. Without a highly qualified chief of medicine, the quality of the hospital's medical residency program would drop. Should the residency program be withdrawn, the hospital would soon be unable to recruit staff physicians interested in teaching opportunities in spite of the hospital's low salaries. The hospital might be forced to drop some services. Inevitably, patient care would suffer. To head off this spiral of decline, the director suggested to the board of trustees that Quigley Memorial set up a "systems intervention" project. He explained that systems intervention is based on the assumption that all units within an organization are involved in the organization's problems—their causes, effects, and, ultimately, solutions. The board supported his proposal.

Within four months, a systems intervention task force composed of senior hospital staff, a consultant, and key persons from outside the hospital had set in motion a course of action that strengthened Quigley Memorial's residency program and enabled the director to recruit five new staff physicians, to improve coordination of inpatient and outpatient services, to heighten staff awareness to problems in the delivery of ancillary services, and—not the smallest of achievements—to convince the chief of medicine to withdraw his resignation.

DYNAMICS AND TECHNIQUES

Systems intervention is a process that uses systems dynamics[1] and behavioral science techniques[2,3] to overcome barriers to change. By involving those key players who could prevent change in the process of planning and directing change, the systems intervention process goes right to the heart of the issue that ordinarily stymies hospital administrators—the rivalry and personal conflict among "autonomous" departments and service chiefs.

System Flow Diagrams

Systems intervention relies on system flow diagrams. These visual models help policy makers to analyze current problems, to see how the problems have evolved over time, to design potential solutions, and, most important, to understand the implications of each possible solution for each affected department of the hospital. Models focus on (1) the relationships among services within the hospital and (2) the behavioral factors that are central to both problems and solutions. In the process of developing their own models, participants come to understand the root causes of personal and professional conflicts and can discuss these conflicts within a structured context. Structure provides safety; it promotes openness and a new sense of mutual trust.

Team Commitment

Once they perceive avenues for change together, key hospital leaders are committed to the "team" approach. This commitment does not end with the preparation of a list of recommendations. It continues into the implementation, monitoring, and reevaluation stages of problem-solving activities and can lead to a new awareness of the hospital as an organic unity.

BARRIERS TO CHANGE

Separatism

Most hospitals are organized into separate departments along functional lines, for example, medicine, surgery, outpatient, nursing, laboratory. The delegation of substantial power and authority to each department chief instills in each a sense of autonomy. Within each department, this sense is heightened for staff by an intense, and exclusive, identity with their immediate peer group. Few staff members in any one department understand how other departments operate. Separatism is nourished by a common assumption that other departments are competing for scarce resources—money and people—and by a history of interdepartmental rivalries. There is seldom agreement among departments on the causes, or even the nature, of problems that affect them all, and certainly not on the solutions. Half-hearted and, therefore, unsuccessful attempts to work together to solve problems breed frustration and resignation—"it can't be done." Long-standing problems are often deal with only when they become too critical to put aside, and then usually by a handful of administrators rather than key members of all affected groups.

Primary Responsibility

The facts of life are that all the functions within a hospital are interrelated and interdependent. But few hospitals have a permanent structure for solving problems that takes this interdependence into account. It is rare to find a committee composed of department heads who see their *primary* responsibility as working *together* to solve the hospital's problems.

SYSTEMS INTERVENTION KNOCKS DOWN BARRIERS

Four tactics are basic to systems intervention: the formation of a *broad-based task force of key hospital staff,* a *focus on specific problems,* the preparation of *flow diagrams,* and an *orientation toward implementation.* Task force members must have sufficient authority among themselves to ensure that a consensus would be tantamount to an authorization for action. A specific focus provides a structure within which to resolve personal and organizational problems. Flow diagrams promote a dynamic view of a problem situation by showing past changes over time; they also provide a framework for future change by projecting the impact of change on all affected departments. Since flow diagrams, or models, show the attitudinal and behavioral changes that must accompany changes in activity, the task force can prevent conflicts *before* they occur. And finally, task force members are encouraged to participate in every stage of change, to oversee as well as to recommend new policies and activities. This is the most crucial aspect of systems intervention. The people most likely to resist change take responsibility for seeing that it happens.

SYSTEMS INTERVENTION IN ACTION

In the remainder of this article, we shall demonstrate how the systems intervention process works by describing how the Lawrence Quigley Memorial Hospital complex (QMH) put it to work.

The Quigley Memorial complex consists of a large general medical and surgical outpatient department, a 305-bed domiciliary unit, and an inpatient unit that includes 100 acute medical and surgical beds and 200 extended-care and chronic-care beds. All patients are veterans who are not directly charged for the services they receive. The hospital is supported financially by the Commonwealth of Massachusetts. Medical and surgical services at the hospital are staffed in part by residents from two Boston community hospitals with medical school affiliations: St. Elizabeth's Hospital and the New England Deaconess Hospital. (St. Elizabeth's Hospital also provides clinical and laboratory services to support its residency program.) The two residency programs are vital to the operation of Quigley Memorial's medical and surgical services. Thanks to the presence of residents, QMH can operate with fewer salaried physicians and, despite its low salaries, can recruit full- and part-time physicians.

When Quigley Memorial's chief of medicine decided to resign, the hospital director chose to address the major issue—how to make QMH more attractive to full-time and part-time physicians. Toward this end, he solicited suggestions for ways to improve the medical residency and patient care programs. From a source within the hospital, he received a document entitled: "A Proposal for Development of an Expanded Patient Care and Teaching Medical Service." This proposal called for a restructuring of the medical service, more emphasis on teaching, and development of a new program called "Teaching Teachers to Teach." Key staff people who reviewed the proposal were favorably disposed, but they argued that it would put an unbearable strain on certain supporting services (e.g., nursing, laboratory, and radiology). Further discussion revealed that relations among members of these services were already strained to the breaking point. It was clear that *no* plan to improve the medical service would succeed unless something was done to deal with this basic barrier to change.

What happened next is described below in tandem with the basic steps of the systems intervention process.

Step 1. Defining the Rules

Before a systems intervention project is launched, it is essential that the key actors—the hospital director, the consultant (who may be a systems intervention expert from within the hospital), the task force chairman (in some cases, the hospital director), and potential task force members—reach agreement on three subjects. These are (1) the project's objective, (2) the initial problem focus, and (3) the steps involved in the project (i.e., *all* the steps, herein discussed, essential to the systems intervention process).

Once the QMH trustees approved a systems intervention project, a consultant was appointed and the key staff people were able to reach an agreement in all three areas. The objective was to improve the medical residency and patient care programs. The immediate task was to evaluate the specific proposal received by the hospital director.

Step 2. Forming a Task Force

The systems intervention task force must be broad-based. This means that membership must include all senior staff people, and others from outside the hospital, who have the power to prevent change in the areas directly involved in the problem under consideration. At Quigley Memorial, the task force was composed of the medical director, the chief of medicine, representatives from the surgical services, the director of the outpatient department (OPD), the director of the nursing service, and representatives from St. Elizabeth's Hospital and its teaching affiliate, Tufts Medical School.

Step 3. Conducting the Research

In order to analyze the problem at hand, the systems intervention consultant must interview all task force members and may also decide to question other persons whose knowledge and opinions are germane. (In addition, the consultant may prepare and distribute questionnaires.) He or she then prepares a list of the problems and an issue-by-issue synopsis of interviews (and survey results). Although the consultant need not check the validity of data received from interviews and questionnaires (unless conflicting information is received), he or she must inform all those who are asked for information that data will be discussed openly at task force meetings.

At QMH, the consultant began his interviews immediately after the first task force meeting. He asked questions relating to (1) the interviewee's role in the hospital and the relation of his or her function or department to other areas in the hospital; (2) current problems confronting Quigley Memorial, their causes, and possible solutions; (3) other internal and external trends and changes that might affect the hospital; and (4) the proposal for expanded teaching programs, the interviewee's view of changes needed to implement the proposal, and the potential benefits and drawbacks of the proposal and associated changes. The consultant then prepared an issue-oriented synopsis of all his interviews with hospital staff and members of the larger community.

Step 4. Preparing the Flow Diagrams

After the interviews are conducted, the consultant prepares a set of cause-and-effect diagrams that describe the current problems, how the situation has evolved over time, and the possible opportunities for change. As more information is gathered and as the task force, on the basis of these initial diagrams, changes its perceptions or redefines problems, the consultant prepares new diagrams that express the relationships among actors and issues. The QMH consultant presented his initial diagrams at the second task force meeting. These are shown here as Figures 1-5.

Figure 1 set out the factors affecting the quality of the hospital's residency program and illustrated that the expanded-teaching proposal might help the hospital to attract new physicians, as well as improve residents' motivation. It also demonstrated that the poor quality of some supporting services and a decline in the hospital census could undermine an expanded teaching program. The proposal for the new program did not address these problems. Figure 2 revealed that services dependent on technology at QMH were not competitive with other hospitals' services. This technology gap affected staff in these services, and residents were unsatisfied. St. Elizabeth's Hospital, as a result, might decide to terminate its residency program and withdraw its supporting services. Figure 3 showed that the hospital's low salaries and inadequate support services had weakened its ability to recruit staff physicians. If these problems continued, staff turnover would increase and the residency program would suffer. An expanded emphasis on teaching, however, could revitalize QMH's acute services, especially if ancillary services were improved. Figure 4 suggested that the several problems together could cripple the hospital's ability to function, unless steps were taken to intervene in the "vicious cycle." Figure 5 brought the outpatient department into the hospital picture.

Step 5. Discussing the Diagrams

Once the consultant has prepared models that diagram the dynamic, cause-and-effect relationships among problems, the task force members have a framework for discussion. The diagrams enable them to redirect their attention from individual problems to the situation as a whole. They may then decide to narrow, expand, or shift the problem focus of their project.

At the second task force meeting, members discussed the diagrams prepared by the consultant. They focused on the inadequacies of certain ancillary services, the lack of equipment in some services, and the need for more professional personnel. They agreed that the specific problems were

- lack of round-the-clock laboratory and blood bank services;

- limited availability of x-ray services and radiologists;

- inadequate pulmonary and coronary-care equipment;

- the hospital's inability to recruit full-time physicians in the OPD, part-time physicians in the inpatient units, and registered inhalation therapists, laboratory technicians, and nurses (particularly RNs with specialties);

- disagreements among OPD staff and medical and surgical staff regarding admission criteria and procedures, preadmission tests, and the use of medical service residents in the OPD; and

Figure 1 Factors Affecting the Quality of QMH's Residency Program

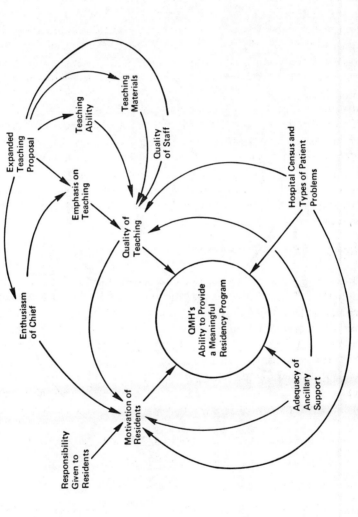

Figure 2 A More Complete View of Some of the Factors Influencing the Adequacy of Ancillary Services and the Quality of Teaching

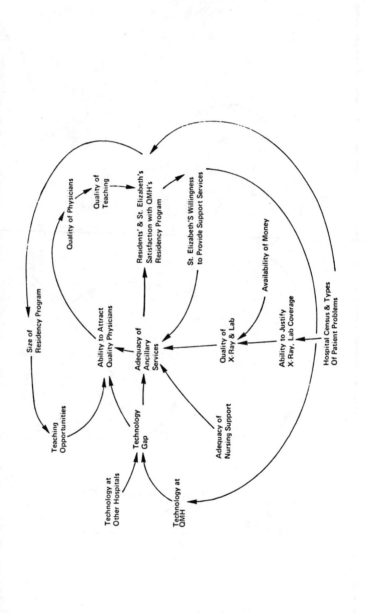

Figure 3 Attractiveness of QMH to Physicians and the Need to Hire Physicians

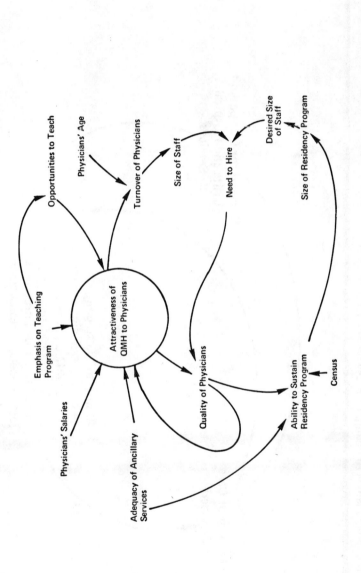

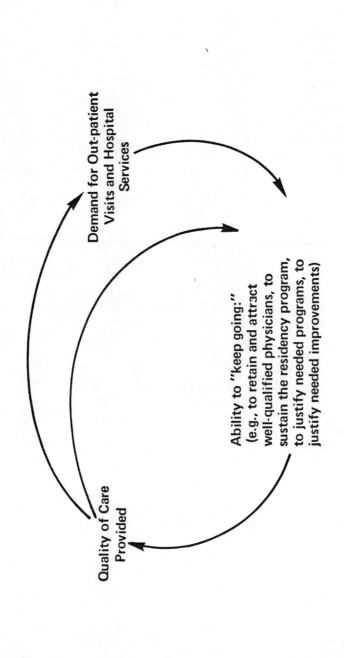

Figure 4 Overall Relationships Affecting the Evolving Situation at QMH

Demand for Out-patient Visits and Hospital Services

Quality of Care Provided

Ability to "keep going:" (e.g., to retain and attract well-qualified physicians, to sustain the residency program, to justify needed programs, to justify needed improvements)

Figure 5 Interdependencies Between OPD and Hospital Services

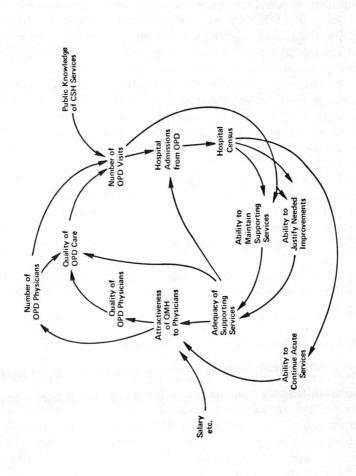

• long delays for patients using the area veterans hospital for diagnostic procedures.

Task force members were especially sensitive to problems in the OPD, as shown in Figure 5. Most patients at Quigley Memorial are admitted through the OPD which, for its part, depends on the hospital for laboratory, x-ray, and other services. During the year prior to the task force project, the number of physicians in the OPD had declined and the volume of OPD patients had dropped as a result. Figure 5 demonstrated that if this trend continued, the OPD would soon be unable to provide adequate service to its patient population and that there would be fewer hospital admissions as a result. A decline in the hospital census would, in turn, make it even more difficult to maintain an adequate level of ancillary services, to justify the purchase of equipment needed for chronic and acute patients, to support a residency program, and, therefore, to provide quality hospital care as a backup to the OPD. This would further diminish the hospital's ability to recruit physicians for the OPD and the inpatient units.

The fact that all these problems were interrelated suggested, on the one hand, that deterioration in every crucial area of the hospital affected the rest of the hospital, and, on the other, that improvement in any one area would upgrade other areas. For example, improvements in ancillary services would improve the quality of care and the quality of the residency program, thus making it easier to retain and recruit physicians of high quality. This, in turn, would improve the residency program and would persuade St. Elizabeth's Hospital to maintain the program and to continue to provide supporting services.

Step 6. Discussing Differing Perceptions

The systems intervention consultant helps the members of the task force discuss differences of opinion about the interpretation of data and variables in the models and to handle personality conflicts. Questions about validity of data may refer to material facts (costs, numbers of people, spatial dimensions, etc.) or behavioral perceptions. Material facts are easy to check. Validation of behavioral perceptions may be less "clean-cut," but this is the sine qua non of the systems intervention process.

In the discussion that followed the presentation of the consultant's models, task force members at Quigley Memorial agreed that the problems revealed were critical. They also admitted that these problems had been the major source of conflict among hospital departments and, in the past, among the task force members themselves. The chief of medicine said these problems had influenced his decision to resign. The diagrams convinced them that each department, not just Medical Services, would benefit if the problems were solved, and that it would take the cooperation of all task force members to solve them. Despite their past disputes and their apprehension about working together, they agreed to these key points.

Step 7. Sharpening the Focus

Once the first diagrams have been analyzed and discussed, task force members may ask the consultant to collect additional information and, if necessary, to prepare new diagrams. This may happen several times during the course of a project. The task force may also decide to authorize the development of a computer simulation model, based on the diagrams, to enable them to analyze problems involving a larger number of variables. On the basis of new diagrams and / or a computer simulation model, the members may decide to redefine the project by concentrating on fewer problems or expanding the ground to be covered.

As a result of its initial findings, the QMH task force decided to focus on the specific problems that were adversely affecting patient care, relationships among departments, and the quality of the residency program. This was a significant redefinition of objectives. Before the end of their second meeting, task force members developed a list of specific problems to be addressed, made recommendations for analyzing and solving them, and established priorities. Members also distributed responsibility among themselves for following up on these priorities.

Step 8. Studying Potential Solutions

After the task force members have become accustomed to using models for analyzing the causes and effects of current problems, it is a small step to the use of models for studying the impact of each proposed solution to a specific problem. Members will find that they have become proficient in preparing and using these models for further discussion and analysis.

During their third and fourth meetings, QMH task force members examined several specific problems and potential solutions. Each of these meetings was task-oriented. Diagrams were prepared beforehand that showed the causes and implications of each problem; other diagrams helped members to analyze the impact of proposed solutions. As before, the visual models helped to structure discussion and to defuse hostilities. Participants at these meetings discovered that they could discuss differences of opinion without rancor. Discussions almost always led to a consensus of opinion on how to solve commonly recognized problems. Some members found that the recommendations they most ardently championed could not be implemented without causing new problems and were willing to seek new answers.

Step 9. Preparing an Action Plan

As soon as the task force members have reached a consensus on how to solve the problems they have been studying, they should prepare a plan that will translate recommendations into actions. This plan should be shown to a broad range of staff within the hospital, and, where necessary, modifications should be incorporated into the final report.

During its fifth meeting, the QMH task force consolidated its findings, developed preliminary recommendations for change, drew up plans for implementing recommendations, identified areas needing further research or analysis, and assigned responsibility for following up on these activities among themselves. The draft report they prepared included recommendations for solving current problems, proposals for development of several new specialized programs, and several portions of the original proposal for a "Teaching Teachers to Teach" program. Task force members next discussed the draft with the hospital director, and held a sixth meeting to make appropriate revisions. They then distributed the report throughout the hospital and, after a short time, held a staff meeting to discuss their recommendations. They found that most of the resistance to their proposals came from key staff who had not been invited to participate in the task force, confirming the importance of involving all persons who are important to the implementation of change into the systems intervention process *from the beginning*. After this broad review, the task force made further revisions and submitted a final report to the hospital's medical executive committee and the board of trustees. This report emphasized the interdependencies among hospital departments and the need for cooperation to affect change. Both groups approved the report.

Step 10. Continuing the Commitment

Task force members should begin to implement their recommendations as soon as they receive the necessary approvals, and even before where approval is not in doubt. All members must take responsibility for monitoring progress and taking whatever actions are necessary to follow each proposal through to its successful conclusion. As often as necessary, task force members should reconvene to analyze and resolve unforeseen setbacks. It is this continuing commitment, beyond the preparation of a "final" report, that will make accomplishment of project goals possible.

The achievements mentioned at the beginning of this article suggest that Quigley Memorial is already beginning to reap the benefits of its commitment to the systems intervention process. It is a process that can be used successfully by service chiefs, hospital directors, and other administrators with major organizational responsibilities.

REFERENCES

1. Forrester, Jay W. "Market Growth as Influenced by Capital Investment." *Industrial Management Review* 9: 83-105.
2. Beckhard, R. *Organizational Development: Strategies and Models.* Reading, Mass.: Addison-Wesley, 1969, p. 100.
3. Kolb, David A., and Frohman, Alan L. "An Organization Development Approach to Consulting." *Sloan Management Review,* Fall 1970, pp. 51-65.

15. Mandated Long-Range Planning for Hospitals— Where Is It Going and Why?

MARK D. MANDEL and JACOB GETSON

Mandel, Mark D., and Getson, Jacob. "Mandated Long-Range Planning for Hospitals." *Health Care Management Review,* Winter 1979.

Why should hospitals plan five years in advance? What systematic problems in state certificate of need (CON) programs can be remedied through annual submissions of hospital short- and long-range plans? How can hospital planning be integrated with institutional budgeting to foster capital and program development consistent with rate-setting formulas and health systems plan (HSP) and state health plan (SHP) visions?

The Commonwealth of Massachusetts has successfully answered these questions while developing the Massachusetts One and Five Year Hospital Plan system.

HOW MASSACHUSETTS IMPLEMENTED LONG-RANGE PLANNING

Massachusetts had long sought to (1) constrain the rising cost of health care, (2) equalize the distribution of medical services, and (3) improve its citizens' health status. In all these attempts, however, no direct mechanisms were available to capture the creativity of hospital providers and focus the economics of the industry on a stable and sustained long-range health policy.

In January 1977, the Massachusetts Office of State Health Planning (OSHP), the Department of Public Health (the designated state health planning and development agency [SHPDA] under PL 93-941), the six Massachusetts HSAs, the Massachusetts Rate Setting Commission (RSC) and the Boston University Center for Health Planning (one of the ten national technical health planning centers established under PL 93-641) joined forces to design, implement, and evaluate a short- and long-range hospital planning system. The system was to link

- advances in health systems planning, such as mandated one- and five-year hospital plans;

- design of an interactive computerized forecasting model for acute-care bed need based on the state's acute care standards and criteria; and

- research findings from the state's prospective reimbursement experiment on production functions for hospital cost centers.[1]

The Standard Development Process

In order for the Massachusetts One and Five Year Plan system to be focused on achievable health systems change, the agencies first had to develop a statewide process for the evaluation and planning of institutional health services. In the process established, findings and recommendations developed by task forces on standards development flow to different agencies for different purposes but, in sum, form the procedure for long-range health policy development. In general, any task force, such as the One and Five Year Hospital Plan task force, follows decision-tree flows in four directions:

1. through the Department of Public Health's regulatory process for incorporation into legal language and consideration by the State Public Health Council (state CON program);
2. to the HSA boards for review and comment on the specific regulatory recommendations and consideration for the appropriate health system plan component;
3. to the Health Policy Group (an informal committee of all state commissioners with responsibility for aspects of health policy) so that appropriate state agencies understand and can support task force recommendations; and
4. to the Statewide Health Coordinating Council for consideration in the State Health Plan and State Medical Facilities Plan.

The overall statewide health policy development and coordination process for the One and Five Year Hospital Plan process is shown in Figure 1.

As a result of these efforts, on July 11, 1977 the Massachusetts Public Health Council adopted the hospital One and Five Year Plan submission format.

Quantifying Acute-Care Hospital Bed Need

The adoption of a rigorous 3.4 acute-care hospital beds per 1,000 population planning target by 1985 under the state's CON program provided the second

Figure 1 Massachusetts One and Five Year Hospital Plan Design and Adoption Process

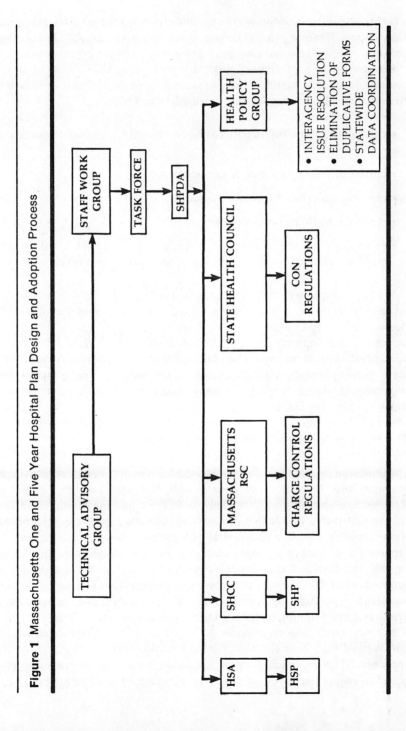

state health policy initiative for the promulgation of the state's hospital planning system. Reaching this planning target meant closing 4,472 acute care beds at a potential annual savings of $89.4 million to the commonwealth.[2]

Because of the participatory process for adopting Massachusetts's acute care standards and criteria, a listing of exceptions to the arithmetic norms was also created. These exceptions included adjustments for

- changes in patient origin patterns based on facility mergers, closures, and new services;

- impact of regulatory code enforcement;

- case mix differences from the standard;

- elective scheduling capacities; and

- variances from minimum size for services and facilities based on geographic isolation, economic efficiency, and quality assurance.

With the adoption of these quantitative standards and criteria, each hospital and service could plan within a specified capacity. One of the roles of the Boston University Center for Health Planning was to design the software to forecast the bed capacity by major clinical service for each of the 130 licensed, nonfederal, short-term hospitals in Massachusetts over the next decade. With these specific planning targets available, the One and Five Year Hospital Plan system could serve as a vehicle for negotiating compliance over time with the statewide planning target.

The Prospective Reimbursement Experiment

The third step taken to forge a long-range health policy was the enactment of Massachusetts General Law, Chapter 409, "An Act Further Regulating Health Development and Care Delivery in the Commonwealth." This law created rate-review mechanisms authorized to analyze total hospital revenue, charge modifications, and hospital comparisons based on size, service, department, and other appropriate criteria. Along with the passage of Chapter 409, the Health Care Financing Administration awarded a multiyear contract to the RSC. Several of the research projects funded under this grant focused on coordinating institutional planning, certificates of need, and health systems planning with hospital budgeting and rate setting.

These research projects provided an important conceptual framework for the One and Five Year Hospital Plan submission format—the "cost-center approach." This approach assumes that planning and budgeting must be integrated to ensure that both are driven by the same set of imperatives.

The common denominator between strategic planning, management control, and operational control in hospitals is the formal array of governing relationships and responsibilities known as the organizational structure.[3] The American Hospital Association states that a hospital's organizational structure should be expressed in its chart of accounts (cost centers).[4] Hence, it appears logical to establish the cost center as the baseline unit of measurement in forecasting, managing, and evaluating hospital growth or redeployment.

State Regulation Consolidation

Finally, no comprehensive health policy should be expected to achieve its goals within hospital operations unless an equal effort toward policy integration occurred within state government. Thus pressures arose within the task force to consolidate hospital reporting requirements from state agencies, define minimum data sets, and issue consistent regulations that affect related areas of hospital behavior.

Together, these four steps offered an opportunity for the hospital industry to respond to an integrated state health policy through a single, internal process—the One and Five Year Plan (see Table 1).

DESIGN CHOICES

Before designing the format and content of the Massachusetts One and Five Year Hospital Planning System, the state studied similar mandated institutional planning in New Jersey and Rhode Island, based on investigations conducted by the Boston University Center for Health Planning.

Lessons Learned from New Jersey

New Jersey was selected for detailed analysis because it has had a regulation requiring hospital plans since July 9, 1975. In addition, New Jersey resembled Massachusetts in its history of strong state health policy initiatives, particularly standards and criteria setting and rate regulation. Table 2 presents major achievements and shortcomings for New Jersey in 1977.

However, based on a 1977 analysis of the New Jersey long-range hospital plans, James B. Webber, management consultant, characterized New Jersey hospital values in planning and change as follows: 60 percent "don't rock the boat," 35 percent "roll with the punches," five percent "plan or dream ahead." In addition, 30 percent of the hospitals in the state "have a long range planning committee in name only; there are no full-time 'policy' planners; and, few if any established long range planning processes."[5]

Table 1 Trends in Selected Acute Hospital Indices, Massachusetts, New Jersey, Rhode Island and the United States, 1960–1975

Selected Indices	Massachusetts				New Jersey				Rhode Island				United States			
	1960	1965	1970	1975	1960	1965	1970	1975	1960	1965	1970	1975	1960	1965	1970	1975
Hospital Expense Amount Per Capita	46	67	143	268	27	42	83	171	38	54	123	212	31	47	95	155
% of increase since 1960	—	46	211	483	—	56	217	533	—	42	224	458	—	151	307	497
Indices of Utilization — Admissions Per 1,000 persons	137	144	149	154	108	113	118	137	113	124	141	141	127	136	143	156
Average Length of Stay	8.4	8.4	8.8	8.5	8.1	8.5	8.9	8.7	8.9	8.7	8.6	8.0	7.6	7.8	8.3	7.8

Table 1 *Continued*

Indices of Employees Service Intensity																
Per Bed	1.9	2.3	2.8	3.3	1.8	1.9	2.2	2.4	2.0	2.2	3.0	3.4	2.3	2.5	2.9	N/A
Assets Per Patient Day	85	107	154	249	67	77	100	160	113	143	192	279	62	72	101	145

Indices of Bed Per 1,000 Hospital Capacity																
Persons	4.2	4.3	4.6	4.5	3.0	3.3	3.5	4.0	3.6	3.7	4.0	3.8	3.5	3.8	4.1	4.4
Occupancy Rate	76	78	80	79	78	79	83	82	76	80	84	82	75	76	78	75

Sources: *Hospitals J.A.H.A. Guide Issue* (August 1975). Statistical Abstract of the U.S. (1975).
McClure, W. "Reducing Excess Hospital Capacity." Department of Health, Education and Welfare Contract No. HRA 230-76-0086 (October 15, 1976).
Webber, J.B. and Mandel, M.D. *The Institutional Planning Experience in New Jersey—A Preliminary View* (Boston: Boston University Center for Health Planning, April 15, 1976).
Webber, J.B. and Mandel, M.D. *The Institutional Planning Experience in Rhode Island—A Preliminary View* (Boston: Boston University Center for Health Planning, March 15, 1977).

Table 2 Comparative Analysis of the 1977 New Jersey Hospital Planning Process

Major Achievements	Key Shortcomings
(1) development of five year forecast of potential certificate of need applications;	(1) use of demand or utilization-based planning rather than measurements of medical need;
(2) encouragement of institutional dialogue around multi-institutional arrangements;	(2) institutional self-interest represented the driving force in many plans; hospitals were not considering alternative health systems; and problems of lack of coordination among other health and social service providers in the institutional service area;
(3) increase planning capability in hospitals in terms of policy rather than facilities;	
(4) positive, supportive role of the New Jersey Hospital Association;	(3) lack of specific context or selected quantitative goals for institutional planning issued by State or HSAs;
(5) apparent increasing competition among hospitals for service area franchises;	(4) once a state (or hospital) embarks on a major institutional planning system, significant revisions in format, scope, or context are extremely difficult;
(6) creation of a map of the diversity of the institutions within the state which provides insight into how to move the system; and,	(5) information in plans were extremely difficult to aggregate, cross-tabulate and reformat for purposes of SHPDA and HSA planning;
(7) ability to estimate early the maximum capital expenditure and incremental operating cost changes resulting from certificate of need proposed in plans over a five year period.	(6) the data base used in plans did not adequately assist in the hospital's goal determination process by analyzing community health needs; definitions of hospital service areas were inconsistent among institutions with little guidance from the state or HSAs;
	(7) cost containment did not show up as a real concern in most plans; growth as opposed to consolidation, or shrinkage or limits on proliferation of specialized services appeared the major goals of most institutions; concern over lack of consumer participation.

Sources: Holohean, M. A. *The New Jersey Hospital Planning Experience* (Syracuse, N.Y.: Alpha Center for Health Planning, August 31, 1977) p. 1-78.
Webber, J. B. and Mandel, M. D. *The Institutional Planning Experience in New Jersey—A Preliminary View* (Boston: Boston University Center for Health Planning, March 15, 1977) p. 25-48.

By analyzing how New Jersey developed its program, Massachusetts health planners learned several lessons:[6]

- The minimum data requirements involve five fundamental steps in planning. These steps and their relationship to the New Jersey Hospital Planning Guide[7] are illustrated in Table 3.

- During the early phases of development there was a debate as to how comprehensive to make the planning requirement. The choice was between "start small and general" (Who are you? Where are you going?) and "start comprehensive and specific and live with the lag between institutional capability versus requirements to plan." The latter approach was selected, and a process-oriented, evolutionary thrust to the planning requirement resulted.

- The design of the planning guide incorporated requirements of PL 92-603, Section 234, and PL 93-641. The design was based on the goal-oriented approach first used in the "Comprehensive Health Plan for New Jersey 1973-1974."

- After the planning guide had taken shape, a one-page regulation with the principal headings in the planning guide was drafted and approved. This one-page regulation enabled the planning guide to be written in instructional and descriptive terms rather than in regulatory terms.

Lessons Learned from Rhode Island

Rhode Island is using its institutional planning system to create a regionalized system with each hospital having a specific mission and role. The mission, to be defined in detail at the subspecialty level, includes both what a hospital will offer and what it will not. Through institutional planning, a line is drawn between the powers and the discretion of the state and the discretion of the institutional governing body.[8]

As stated by the commissioner of the Rhode Island Department of Health in a March 10, 1975, letter to the chief executive officers of Rhode Island hospitals:

The Rhode Island Department of Health has consistently identified the mechanism of the hospital, board approval, long and short range plan as the proper vehicle for the expression and considers omissions from such plans a demonstration of failure to comply with statutory or regulatory requirements.

Table 3 Planning Steps Required of Institutions Related to Fundamental Steps of Planning

Fundamental Steps	Descriptive Questions	Steps Outlined in Planning Guide for Hospital Long-Range Plans
1. PLAN FOR PLANNING	What are we about? What did we learn from last cycle?	Step 1. Organize for Planning Step 2. Create the Capacity for Planning
2. SYSTEM INVESTIGATION	Where are we? How did we get here? Where are we heading? What problems do we have? What problems do we see ahead?	Step 3. Collect and Organize Data Step 4. Forecast Important Data Step 5. Analyze External Forces Affecting the Hospital
3. ENDS ESTABLISHMENT	Where do we want to go?	Step 6. Develop Mission Statement Step 7. Develop Goals Step 8. Set Priorities Step 9. Develop Measurable Objectives
4. MEANS SELECTION	How do we get there? (The "plan" is the chosen means.)	Step 10. Identify Alternative Courses of Action Step 11. Select Recommended Course of Action Step 12. Identify Implementation Strategies Step 13. Identify Actions Requiring CON Step 14. Develop a Capital Resources Plan
5. INTERVENTION EVALUATION	Did we get there? (The learning component of planning)	Step 15. Develop an Evaluation Procedure

Sources: Waters, W. J. *A Process Appraisal of CHP at the State Level* (unpublished doctoral dissertation at Ohio State University 1974).

Webber, J.B. and Mandel, M.D. *The Institutional Planning Experience—A Preliminary View* (Boston: Boston University Center for Health Planning March 1977). Reprinted with permission.

In addition, the institutional planning process in Rhode Island is linked· with the prospective reimbursement process, the annual review of medically related programs, and the CON processes (See Table I).

Rhode Island has had four submissions of hospital plans since 1973, with each set of plans improved in quality and specificity. However, as shown in Table 4, several lessons can be learned from the Rhode Island approach to institutional planning.

THE HOSPITAL PLANNING SYSTEM

After careful review of lessons from other states with mandated institutional planning experience, the Massachuestts task force deliberated over many design choices.

After the participatory process outlined in Figure 1, the task force recommended the following six submission requirements as the state's regulatory requirements for short- and long-range hospital planning.

The Annual Planning Process. The state requires a brief description of the annual planning process, including a general timetable of significant planning activities. Also requested is an organizational chart with titles and names of the key individuals and committees in the planning process, including consultants and their role.

Statement of Purpose. In the statement of purpose, the institution describes its mission. In stating purpose, the institution must consider population services, education, research, community involvement issues, and the effects of any anticipated changes on its purpose over the next five years.

Statement of Goals. The institution's major goals over the next five years should be described in the purpose statement. The institution's goals must be ranked in priority over a five-year horizon and identified with specific national health priorities of Section 1502 of PL 93-641. Accompanying each goal should be a discussion of proposed major programs and resources necessary to reach the goal.

Physical Plant Description. A description is required of each building in the physical plant. Contents should include (1) age of buildings, (2) general construction characteristics, (3) floor space, (4) principle usage, and (5) current building deficiencies.

CON Monitoring Report. There are three phases of monitoring: (1) projects where CON was granted, but the construction is incomplete and the project is nonoperational; (2) projects where a CON application was submitted but has not been acted upon or is under appeal; and (3) projects where a CON application is anticipated during the One or Five Year Plan period but has not been formally filed with the Department of Public Health (DPH).

Table 4 Comparative Analysis of the 1977 Rhode Island Hospital Planning Process

Major Achievements	Key Shortcomings
(1) The Rhode Island Department of Health now requires hospital to relate future plans submitted to plans previously filed.	(1) Hospitals had no formal guidelines to assist them in their planning in the first year, resulting in plans of uneven quality and a lack of consistency between plans.
(2) The approach to institutional planning in Rhode Island stressed that health manpower and health facilities planning should not be conducted in a separate and categorized manner but rather should be conducted in an integrated and systematic manner.	(2) First year plans did not include rate impact estimates, specific timetables for implementation, or prioritization among objectives.
(3) Rhode Island Department of Health's stated policy emphasizes the necessity of using the short- and long-range hospital planning process to effect reallocation of existing resources from underused programs to programs required additional resources within an overall limit on total hospital expenditures.	(3) A lack of internal consistency in most hospitals' plans from year to year hindered examination of a hospital's progress in achieving goals and objectives.
(4) The Department of Health prepared a "Hospital Board Approved Long and Short Range Plans Authorized Summaries" document. The summaries of plans, which average three-and-one-half pages, show directions the hospitals are pursuing with specific time phased implementation strategy. In the aggregate, these summaries provide a short- and long-range profile of hospital direction and impact on delivery. From such summaries, a statewide comparison of policy objectives between the private and public health sectors is possible.	(4) The estimates of costs provided in the institutional plans were of uneven quality.
	(5) Institutional plans reflected trends in the health care system. In 1971 and 1972 a great many hospitals proposed establishing ambulatory care networks. Many hospitals never referenced these proposals again, although others submitted successful CON applications.
	(6) Although over $153 million in estimated expenditures were proposed in the institutional plans over the five-year period of existence, only $55 million worth of expenditures finally received CON approval during the same period.

Source: Webber, J.B. and Mandel, M.D., *The Institutional Planning Experience in Rhode Island—A Preliminary View* (Boston: Boston University Center for Health Planning, March 15, 1977).

This report links institutional goals to programs relating to the National Health Planning Priorities (Section 1502 of PL 93-641). It also identifies each CON project in these programs in terms of the specific cost centers where the capital and operating costs are projected.

Other concerns of the CON monitoring report are (1) anticipated impact on operating costs of the project; (2) options explored for proposed project; (3) anticipated impact on employment by job title; (4) estimated gross and net usable square footage; and (5) status reporting on each phase of the project, including the amount of cost overruns (if any) beyond the estimated capital expenditure approved by the state.

Cost-Center Report. The original design of this report stipulated that, for 34 high-priority cost centers, each hospital should file an annual report (designed for electronic data processing) that includes the following provisions:

- allocation of each cost center's activity or revenue to the programs and goals in the other submissions;

- analysis of statistical indicators that justify volume projections for the cost center;

- description of the driving force influencing the cost center's future, including plant and equipment obsolescence, space and functional layout problems, and substitution of technical advances;

- anticipated benefits to be generated by any programs proposed in the One and Five Year Hospital Plan; and

- description of mechanisms for evaluating the output of the plan on the cost center.

For each proposed project in a cost center, the hospital should analyze the feasibility of (1) doing nothing, (2) changing staffing patterns, (3) phasing in the project, (4) introducing improved construction techniques, (5) changing the schedule, and (6) sharing services.

For hospitals in Massachusetts, completion of the cost-center report could mean reviewing existing major hospital services for primarily (1) *availability,* as measured by service capacity and service use; (2) *quality,* examined in terms of staff, equipment, physical plant, and program; (3) *cost,* detailed in terms of productivity, cross subsidization and per diem charges; and (4) *accessibility* for users by ease of travel, responsiveness in delivering service, and scheduling.

To foster an institutional planning process based on population needs, each cost center should specify its service area communities.

The implementation of these provisions has been delayed until hospitals gain experience with the mandated planning process. Nevertheless, in 1978, all Massachusetts nonfederal acute care hospitals have filed a cost-center report that includes a detailed description of operating expense and capital expense for the current year, base year, and each of the five planning years, with corresponding workload forecasts based on the indicators published by the Massachusetts Rate Setting Commission.

PRELIMINARY RESULTS AND STRATEGIES

Defining Hospitals and Services at Risk for Multi-Institutional Arrangements

Four basic approaches were used to identify which hospitals and services should enter into discussions with the HSA and SHPDA about future bed complement levels, service configurations, and referral patterns. These four approaches were:

1. the development of a variable computerized acute-care bed forecasting model;
2. a computerized routine that displayed by medical-surgical, pediatric, and obstetric inpatient services which institutions served the same communities for similar services and what various combinations of mergers, closures, and expansion of services among these hospitals would reach the planning targets for the service area;
3. highlighting the key sections of each HSA's health system plan for goals, objectives, and recommendations for multi-institutional arrangements; and
4. analysis of each hospital's One and Five Year Plan submission for 1978.

Table 5 illustrates a basic report in the variable computerized forecasting model for acute-care bed need.[9] Three data sources were required for this report:

1. University of Massachusetts population projections, which included appropriate age, sex, and year of planning target;
2. the Massachusetts Hospital Association 1975 patient-origin study, which included a full year's analysis of discharges from each Massachusetts nonfederal general hospital by service and residence of patient; and
3. a set of algorithms specifying (a) age and sex categories for each service's population at risk; (b) the definition of towns within a hospital's primary service area; (c) number of admissions per 1,000 for populations at risk for medical-surgical, pediatric, and obstetric inpatient services; and (d)

Table 5 "X" Hospital—Town 87—Maternity 1985 Bed Need Projections

Primary Service Area Community	1985 Population Projection age 15-44 (Females)	Town's Market Share % to Hospital	Service Area Population	Use Rate	Patient Days Projections	Bed Need Estimate	Hospital % Dependence on Towns
Town # 101	15,348	16	2,429	0.203	493	2	18
115	8,336	7	569	0.203	115	0	0
123	9,941	23	2,331	0.203	473	2	18
154	5,736	20	1,139	0.203	230	1	9
102	11,417	39	4,398	0.203	892	3	27
Total Primary Service Area			10,866		2,203	8	72
Total Secondary Service Area					843	3	28
Total Service Area					3,046	11	100

Indications of Referred Hospital Status:
Ratio of Discharges: Primary Service Area = 0.72
Secondary Service Area = 0.28

Bed Need Based on Modified Population Projections = 11

Impact of Queuing Equation Bed Need Formula:
Maternity Project Projection at .95 Level (Implied Occupancy Rate) = 13
Maternity Project Projection at .99 Level (Implied Occupancy Rate) = 15

Occupancy Rate Applied = 0.75

occupancy rate or queuing equation for determining the minimum annual capacity for those services.

The forecasting model for acute-care bed need currently generates 17 different reports including individual hospital projections for medical-surgical, pediatric, and obstetric inpatient services; HSA and subarea aggregate projections by service; matrices of inflows and outflows of patients among HSA and neighboring states; and listings of institutions with projected bed size capacity levels below the state's minimum size for such services or facilities.

In addition, the model is programmed to accept and issue new reports based on revised population projections, modified use rate standards, updated patient origin data or any other change in the state's or HSA's standards for acute care bed need.

Mapping of Overlapping Service Areas

The second approach employed in defining hospitals and services that serve the same populations and must expand or reduce acute care beds was a mapping of overlapping service areas among all licensed nonfederal general hospitals within the commonwealth. The mapping involved identifying communities in each hospital's primary service area and then displaying all other hospitals that also included these communities in their primary service area. By matching hospitals with other hospitals that provide the same towns with the same clinical services and identifying the difference between 1975 actual operating bed complements and projected 1985 bed need by service for each hospital serving such service area, the state and HSA can suggest various optional bed reorganization plans. Figure 2 shows recommended changes in bed capacities for hospitals with overlapping service areas.[10]

Figure 2 Recommended Changes in Hospital Bed Capacities to Meet 1985 Community Health Needs

		A	B	C	D	E	F	G
ALL SERVICES	+	15				12		3
	−		30	33	9		30	
MED/SURG	+	45			3	33		3
	−		21	24			15	
PED	+							
	−	12	3	9	6	9	15	3
OB	+							
	−	18	6		6	12		

HSA Health Systems Plan

The third approach to planning multi-institutional arrangements was to abstract goals, objectives, and recommendations from the 1978 regional HSA plans. The special needs of local populations could be documented and the individual hospital's circumstances analyzed to identify exceptions to the state's acute care standards and criteria.

Only one HSA 1978 health system plan gave details about individual hospitals and, therefore, met the expectations explained above. All HSA 1978 plans, however, specified by service area-wide need projections for acute-care hospital beds.

Reporting System

The fourth approach to defining multi-institutional arrangements was the Massachusetts One and Five Year Hospital Plan reporting system. By analyzing the hospital's description of its mission, goals, and achievements in the planning process, the state highlighted patterns of emerging multi-institutional arrangements.

These four approaches are bringing planners, regulators, and providers around the negotiating table to decide who shall grow, who shall shrink, and who shall look like what in the future.

Pending and Anticipated CON Projects

Future CON applications are identified in the hospitals' One and Five Year Plan. The listing of anticipated CONs in the one-year plan is a prerequisite for CON submission. Thus, it is likely that hospitals will list CONs in numbers equal to, or more than, those actually submitted to the State Department of Public Health for approval. Therefore, the number of CONs anticipated in year one (fy78) is expected to be inflated.

Although hospitals are required to list those CONs to be filed in the first year, they are not required to list CONs anticipated in years two through five. Therefore, any conclusions about years two through five (fy79-82) will be based on conservative data.

Table 6 shows the clinical areas potentially affected by CON applications for fy79. Because a single CON will affect one or more clinical areas, the figures shown do not represent the number of discrete CONs. For example, one CON from Hospital X might include changes in the laboratory, administration, and long-term areas.

During one year (fy78), the hospitals of Massachusetts are planning to submit approximately 250 CONs, affecting 391 clinical areas, and costing more than $245 million in capital investment. During years two to five

Table 6 Projected Distribution of Anticipated CON Applicants by Clinical Area Impacted*

Based on the Massachusetts One and Five Year Plan Submissions: Anticipated in Year 1 (FY79) and HSA Region

Col.	1	2	3	4	5	6	7	8	9	10	11	12	13	14	15	16
HSA	Med/ Surg	OB Ped	Psy Alc	ICU CCU PICU	LTC	RR OR DR	CAT	Oth X-Ray	Endo EEG ECG	LAB PATH BB	Dialysis	OT PT Rehab	Other Anc Sv	Amb Care ER/OPD	Prof Adm Gen	Total
I	2	3	7	3	—	1	1	3	—	3	1	1	1	10	21	57
II	3	2	3	4	1	3	—	5	1	2	—	2	1	9	9	45
III	3	4	2	1	—	2	1	3	—	1	1	1	—	3	9	31
IV	6	6	7	9	3	13	5	18	6	12	4	10	17	22	53	191
V	1	—	2	1	—	—	—	2	—	—	—	1	2	—	9	18
VI	4	—	3	1	2	3	2	9	1	3	1	3	2	4	12	49
Total	19	15	24	19	5	22	9	40	8	21	7	18	23	48	113	391

* Note: The figures above do not represent the number of discrete CONs, but rather the number of major clinical areas impacted by potential CON applications. For example, one CON from Hospital X might include changes in the laboratory, administration and long term care areas.

(fy79-82), hospitals list about 265 anticipated CONs, affecting 393 clinical areas, costing more than $268 million.

The most anticipated projects are planned for the professional-administrative-general areas. Projects include heating, ventilating, and air conditioning overhaul; business computers; telecommunications updates; and structural changes to comply with regulatory codes.

The number of expected CONs for clinical areas shown in Table 6 provide the state and HSA with insights into priority services for future standards and criteria development as well as indications for compliance with the 3.4 nonfederal acute care beds per 1,000 population planning target.

DEVELOPING INSTITUTIONAL PLANS

Regulatory Assumptions

Health care regulation in Massachusetts, and increasingly nationwide, has been based on three assumptions:

1. Patient demands for medical care delivery can be forecast by hospital service areas.
2. Hospitals are responsible for the medical outcomes of patients in their service area where outcomes are measured by relative per capita hospitalization, surgery, and expenditure patterns.
3. As the managers of medical outcomes, hospitals require uniform information to establish charges, evaluate internal operations, and plan for the future.

Unfortunately, no prior adequate set of state regulations or reporting forms has been designed to integrate these three basic health regulatory expectations.

Need for an Industry Approach

Although the format for the Massachusetts One and Five Year Hospital Planning System is specific, detailed, and direct, significant analytic responsibilities are placed on the hospital management team. The hospital management team must consider:

• How can existing information systems in the hospital be integrated and revised to generate a uniform data set for rate-setting submission, One and Five Year Plan submissions, and internal management performance reports?

- How can quantitative measures of physical plant obsolescence be collected and analyzed to program replacement, modernization, and conversion of space and equipment to support departmental workloads and objectives?

- What routine analyses and special studies are required to forecast future morbidity, mortality, and unmet medical needs in the hospital's service area?

Institutional planning has a relatively short history. These three major issues represent significant technical, philosophical, and perhaps survival concerns for hospitals in Massachusetts and eventually the nation. In some states, health care regulations have formally requested a response, but there is not a proven method of investigation to ensure reasonable replies. Each hospital must choose either to put extensive effort into systems development or to undertake a strategy of political or data gamesmanship.

Managerial Objectives

The following discussion outline may help each hospital review its existing data systems and experience with long-range planning and formulate a strategy for addressing these new management concerns.

Objective 1: To design a program management information system (PMIS) that provides the necessary data base for reviewing programs and for making short- and long-term planning and budget allocation decisions.

The system is built up from a series of indicators for each department or subprogram element. These indicators attempt to measure, where possible, four aspects of health care: (1) the need for services, (2) the quantity of services being provided, (3) the efficiency with which services are provided, and (4) the quality of these services. It is clear that no program indicator or set of indicators can ever provide a complete understanding of a subprogram; an indicator must be supplemented by other information and subjective judgment.

For example, a low cost of food per patient may result from a high level of purchasing efficiency or from low-quality food. Thus program indicators only provide clues for understanding program performance and will raise more questions than they answer. Nevertheless, even these clues are an important beginning in obtaining program decision information.

Objective 2: To identify approaches and recommend strategies for assembling, analyzing, and publishing hospital service area community profiles of existing and five-year forecasts of morbidity, mortality, and unmet need characteristics.

Institutional planning requires investigations of the health status of the population served by the hospital. Significant deviations in mortality, morbidity, and other indicators over time or between hospital service area, regions, and states may be related to defects or imbalances in the allocation of resources by the institution. Assembly of such trends and appropriate analysis offers the hospital the soundest bases for its mission within a cost-effective and cost-benefit framework. In addition, plans for department change and identification of a hospital's appropriate classification for rate setting and planning could soon be determined by the relative health status of the population in its service area.

The Challenge for the Industry

Two major new systems of long-range institutional planning can help hospital management achieve these objectives: a PMIS and profiles of expected mortality and morbidity (PEMM) by hospital service area community. These systems will formulate (1) a uniform data base for generating hospital rate-setting submissions, internal management reports, and cost-center-based one- and five-year plans; and (2) expected hospital admissions by diagnosis over the next five years or decade.

The overall impact of these systems will be to help hospitals to better manage and plan their services based on timely, accurate, and meaningful information for the administrator, physician, trustee, planner, and regulator.

REFERENCES

1. Department of Health, Education and Welfare. *Centers for Health Planning.* Contract HRA 203-76-0078, Consultation Task Order MM/MASC-1 (1977).

2. Schneer, E., and Fielding, J. "Quantifying the Need for Hospital Beds." *New England Journal of Medicine* 297: 1087.

3. Anthony, R.N. *Planning and Control Systems: A Framework for Analysis.* Boston: Harvard University, 1965.

4. American Hospital Association. *Chart of Accounts for Hospitals.* Chicago: AHA, 1976.

5. Webber, J.B., and Mandel, M.D. *The Institutional Planning Experience in New Jersey—A Preliminary View,* Boston: Boston University Center of Health Planning, March 1977, p. 7.

6. Health Care Administration Board. *Regulation Requiring Hospital Planning.* New Jersey: New Jersey Department of Health, July 1975.

7. New Jersey Health Planning Council. *Planning Guide for Hospital Long Range Plans.* Trenton, N.J.: HPC, March 1975.

8. Webber, J.B., and Mandel, M.D. *The Institutional Planning Experience in Rhode Island—A Preliminary View* Boston: Boston University Center of Health Planning, April 1977, p. 10.

9. Mandel, M.D., and Cohen, H. *Development of an Interactive Hospital Bed Need Forecasting Model by Clinical Service,* DHEW No. HRP-0018744. Washington, D.C.: National Technical Information Service, 1977, pp. 1-32.

10. The authors thank Ms. Diana Chapman Walsh and William J. Bicknell, M.D., for their insights on this topic. See Walsh, D., and Bicknell, J. "Forecasting the Need for Hospital Beds: A Quantitative Methodology." *Public Health Reports* 92: 199-210.

Section Five

Perspectives on Marketing

This section provides greater detail on and several examples of the use of marketing in health care settings. A central theme is the foundation of each article—*understand the consumer's needs as the first step in developing plans.* Consumers, however, can be any and all of the diverse groups that have contact with a health organization. The article by Hughes ("Can Marketing Help Recruit and Retain Nurses") is an example of one such consumer group. Those readers involved with the recruiting dilemma in their own organization will find this article presents an orientation much different than the job-fair approach so often followed in the quest for nursing staff. Hughes applies the marketing research approach and selected techniques discussed in the article in Section 2 by Flexner and Berkowitz ("Marketing Research in Health Services Planning: A Model").

As noted in earlier sections, the marketing orientation to planning is different. Reexamine the planning model in Figure 2 of "The Marketing Audit: A Tool for Health Service Organizations" (Section 2). This framework is articulated in Section 5 by Kovner and Smits ("Consumer Expectations of Ambulatory Care"): "Consumer preferences will begin to be satisfied only when they are taken into direct account in both the planning and delivery of health services." Each of the articles in this section underscores this important focus.

Several of these articles point up another aspect of health planning that deserves reexamination. For too long, health providers have tried to be all things to all people, and the organization has operated with a "continual growth" philosophy. Readers should note the cautions of a changing health scenario put forth by Clarke ("Marketing Health Care: Problems in Implementation") and Rynne ("The Third Stage of Hospital Long-Range

Planning"). Rynne's article reveals the continual growth perspective always maintained in health planning. Both Clarke and Rynne discuss the possibility and rationale for deletion of services and redefining the portfolio of the organization's offerings. From where then does more revenue derive? Consider Hughes' discussion on brand loyalty at the beginning of his article.

Whether one focuses on new consumers or retaining present ones (physicians, nurses, patients), the perspective is back to the consumer. Yet, several questions exist. In what ways must we know the consumer? What could be the possible scope of their inputs for developing strategic plans? Several articles in this section provide some answers. Recall the article in Section 2 by Clarke and Shyavitz ("A Guide to Marketing Information and Market Research for Hospitals") in which were outlined the many uses of demographic data available internally to the organization. In Section 5, Sapienza ("Psychographic Profiles: Aid to Health Care Marketing") presents an additional perspective by which consumers may be defined. Her message is important—consumers should be described by more than their demographic profiles. Motivational, attitudinal, and emotional factors must be considered. Traditional business concerns have recognized this psychographic dimension for almost 20 years. And, in identifying these dimensions of consumers, effective managers will recognize that consumers view the world differently from people who provide the services they use.

Whether it be nurses desiring to be part of a patient-care team, consumers wanting to avoid unpredictable out-of-pocket medical expenses, or women seeking a more natural maternity setting (all scenarios presented in the following articles), consumers see the world differently. Kovner and Smits write that consumers cannot evaluate quality. We may disagree with that statement, or we might rather qualify that view. After reading these articles, one might prefer to say "Consumers cannot (do not) evaluate quality (in the same way as the provider, but they have a view of quality)."

In fact, Kovner and Smits provide us with some of these dimensions—privacy, humaneness, access, continuity, and so on. Check back to the article in Section 2 by Flexner and Berkowitz on the differential importance of these attributes between two groups of people and their attitudes toward health systems. These are the nondemographic elements discussed by Sapienza that contribute to and shape consumers' views of their world. Refer to the next to last paragraph in Rynne's article for a key phrase: "Finally, the marketing approach avoids the pitfalls of defining quality in isolation from community need and providing services which no one will use or already have too much of."

How do we fit this discussion into the planning and finance perspective? Clarke provides us the clue by noting that effective marketing and good marketing research take money. The financial implications are evident.

Moreover, as services may be added like ambulatory care (Kovner and Smits), deleted (as suggested in some cases by Rynne and described by Clarke), or altered (Sapienza, Hughes), the interactive nature of the organization comes back into focus. The systems perspective highlighted in the previous section must be brought into play. First, the consumer-based research suggests direction; then the marketing and financial perspectives assess the implications of these directions; and, finally, strategic plans are developed.

16. The Third Stage of Hospital Long-Range Planning: The Marketing Approach

TERRENCE J. RYNNE

Rynne, Terrence J. "The Third Stage of Hospital Long-Range Planning: The Marketing Approach." *Health Care Management Review,* Summer 1980.

Formal long-range planning began to gain more widespread acceptance in hospitals during the middle 1960s. In fact, the fall 1969 issue of *Hospital Administration* was the first major journal in the hospital administration field to devote an entire issue to the subject. Then, and in some places even today, long-range plans were usually developed "from the top." The board of directors or the chief executive officer of a hospital commissioned a consultant, architect, or senior administrator to develop a formal long-range master plan.

Long-range planning developed further as hospital administrators realized that the process of planning was as important to the future of a hospital as the plan document. Administrators began to see the value of the hospital leadership working together to chart a future course. The first national training sessions on institutional planning in the health field were held in September of 1974, sponsored by the Association of American Medical Colleges, and in February 1975, sponsored by the American Hospital Association.[1] Those sessions, as well as subsequent literature, stressed that planning should not be delegated to only one person within the hospital, but that it should be the responsibility of the entire leadership group directed by the chief executive officer. Above all, the responsibility should not be delegated to an outside consultant. These influences led to the development of formal processes that systematically involved senior management, medical staff, and department directors in the now familiar rhythm of top-down-bottom-up planning.

Long range planning has become so common in hospitals that in January 1979 over 500 hospital representatives formed the Society for Hospital Planning of the American Hospital Association.

DIFFICULTIES WITH CURRENT LONG-RANGE
PLANNING SYSTEMS IN HOSPITALS

Today most hospital administrators are convinced that they should develop long-range plans. Those who have not been convinced are required by Medicare regulations to develop three-year capital plans. Furthermore, many administrators have taken the second step of implementing formal long-range planning systems. The benefits for those hospitals have been real and acclaimed.

Many articles have appeared promoting and praising planning, but few articles have identified the practical difficulties of hospital long-range planning. Evidently, hospital planning is still too new and tender for anything but praise and promotion.

Articles criticizing long-range planning in the industrial sector appear frequently. Undoubtedly, critical evaluations of hospital planning will soon appear in the professional literature.

A basic critique of hospital planning as currently and commonly practiced can be constructed. There are three major difficulties with the way hospital planning is being conducted today. However, there is a marketing approach that brings some resolution to these difficulties. Those conducting hospital planning will recognize the problems.

The Bigger-Is-Better Syndrome

The formats used by hospitals in their long-range planning processes have encouraged growth projections, to the neglect of no-growth, pruning, or modification strategies.

The departmental planning worksheet in the *Workbook for Short Term Planning,*[2] a popular format widely distributed by the Chicago Hospital Council, exemplifies the problem. Further examples of widely used planning formats in the expansionist mode may be found in *The Practice of Planning in Health Care Institutions*[3] and *Planning For Health Service.*[4] Departmental history is described in terms of past major physical changes or construction projects; future improvements are described in similar terms. Improvements for a department are presumed to call for larger expenditures, ever-expanding space, and increased numbers of full-time staff. Improvement equals growth. On the other hand, business knows that planning cannot be based on the presumption of linear growth. Effective planning has to be sensitive to no-growth situations and their implications.

Actually, no-growth conditions, not necessarily related to economic recession, are always present They are a normal component of the business environment. They occur when the economy surges ahead as well as when it stagnates or actually declines. They may happen any time, in any industry, any company, any market, and with any product. And they have enormous impact on any business.[5]

A linear growth presumption not only prevents hospitals from anticipating no-growth situations, but it also prevents hospitals from eliminating some services, functions, and products that have outlived their usefulness.

The entire *Workbook for Short Term Planning,* as well as other common planning formats, omit mention of cutting, scaling down, or eliminating any services.[6] As a result, hospital planning usually focuses on what is new and does not give adequate attention to what is old, in decline, or no longer productive. Other businesses know that the decision to prune is as important as the one to plant.

A recent article in *Business Horizons* described the planning process of a successful plastic maker. "It focused on the sectors of highest potential yield ....By pruning unprofitable products and consolidating product recipes, the division reduced its line to thirty-three items that had above average performance characteristics."[7]

Planning with the bigger-is-better syndrome fails to give adequate attention to no-growth and pruning strategies and hinders the development of creative strategies for customer satisfaction. With all attention focused on new construction and programs, planning energy is diverted from analyzing current services. Scrutinizing current services has simply been outside the purview of the expansionist planning approach.

> Whether the physician, the house staff member or the nurse, the wait in X-ray or emergency room, the admitting clerk who is rude, the maid who bumps the bed while cleaning, the parking lot attendant who is less than helpful when the lot is full, the cafeteria that turns away visitors, the pharmacy that has limited hours for outpatients—all of this suggests that hospitals operate for their own convenience and not that of the patient, his family and friends.[8]

The changes that would make the real difference in the future success of a department are overlooked due to the overemphasis on the next new, larger, and therefore presumably better service. An approach to hospital planning is needed that gives adequate attention not only to new programs and construction strategies but also to the development of no-growth, pruning, and customer-satisfaction strategies. To improve the long-range planning process in hospitals, an approach is needed that goes beyond bigger-is-better and places proportional store on growth, no-growth, pruning, and customer satisfaction.

Middle Management Dropout

Few hospitals develop a long-range plan, say for five years, and live by it for five years. Today, many systematically update and revise their long-range plans every year, recognizing that the hospital environment changes very quickly. Many of these hospitals have consistently involved middle managers in the yearly planning process, recognizing that department directors frequently know more about developments in their particular fields than anyone in senior management. By encouraging "blue sky" dreaming from department directors, hospitals have generated many new ideas from the "bottom up." The more creative the dreaming evoked, the more fecund the ideas percolating upward in the organization.

Those hospitals with the more sophisticated approaches to planning that involve middle management in the planning process and in systematic long-range planning updates are experiencing middle-management dropout. Frequently these approaches have the surprising effect of deadening creativity and fostering apathy in middle management. Why? Because middle managers know that only a few good ideas will survive and become realities. Most of the ideas will fall by the wayside as the process of establishing priorities, assessing feasibility, and budgeting proceeds. Once managers realize that year after year their ideas feather away into nothing, they become less interested in dreaming fresh dreams for the planning process.

An approach to planning is needed that encourages dreaming by department directors and that ties that dreaming from the beginning to realistic possibilities for the hospital. This approach calls for dynamism, not in the blue sky, but in the current concrete.

Corporate business planners have already wrestled with the problem of middle managers who make unrealistic projections and consequently lose heart for planning. For example, a recent article in *Long Range Planning* stated that "nine out of ten companies at which interviews were conducted currently employ a top-down-bottom-up planning procedure." And "the executives interviewed pointed to the existence of planning problems both at the top management and the divisional management level—the setting of unrealistic plan targets (often overoptimistic) by division managers. . . ."[9]

Dearth of User Input

Planning formats in hospitals have traditionally depended almost exclusively on provider/experts to decide on, design, and develop the new products that are offered. User input concerning potential new services or programs has not been seriously sought. The presumption is that users as nonexperts have little to say about a field as technical and sophisticated as today's medical care. In fact, it has seemed irresponsible to even consider allowing anyone but the most technically competent person to decide on or design a new hospital service.

Business calls this orientation *the product concept.* In companies that use the product concept, decisions about the future are made by experts in the product. In manufacturing firms using the product concept, engineers would probably make the critical decisions about the future. Furthermore, firms that use the product concept leave definitions of product quality up to the experts.

Many firms have recognized the faults of the product concept. The first fault comes to light when product experts make the decision to offer the product. Experts may know all of the technical facts about the product; they do not know whether anyone will buy it. Many firms have awakened to the fact that there can be no effective planning without consulting the eventual consumers about what they need from the product. The decision about whether or not to offer a product should be triggered by the user. Many firms have discovered that, even if their product is the finest of its kind, if users have no input in the planning process, no one wants to buy it.

The second flaw in the product concept is that experts define product quality without reference to the user. The classic case is the Edsel. Ford Motor Company permitted its engineers to design a quality car, a masterpiece of expert engineering. Unfortunately, the engineers' dream car was a marketing disaster—customers did not find it appealing and therefore did not buy.

Quality cannot be defined by experts alone. They only have half the picture—what makes something work in the abstract. Planning must consider how the product works in reality.

Until now, hospitals have planned with the product concept approach, being overly reliant on decisions of provider/experts regarding new services, additional beds, additional equipment. Little interest has been shown in the opinions of users about whether or not they wanted or needed the proposed services, beds, or equipment. The product concept approach to planning has resulted in unnecessary duplications of services and a surplus of hospital beds.

Kotler describes a hospital in southern Illinois that decided to establish an adult day care center as a solution to its underutilized space. "It designed a whole floor to serve senior citizens who required personal care and services in an ambulatory setting during the day, but who would return home each evening. The cost was $16 a day and transportation was to be provided by the patient's relatives. About the only research that was done on this concept was to note that a lot of elderly people lived within a three-mile radius. The Center was opened with a capacity to handle thirty patients. Only two signed up."[10]

Hospital planning systems have often defined quality in terms abstracted from the user. Recently, a recognized leader in the planning field developed a proposal for a planning system.[11] (See Figure 1.) It is a very complicated and sophisticated system. However, it begins and ends with the intrahospital structure. The plan defines the future by consulting with every possible expert within the institution but it never breaks outside the circle of experts to consult with the users.

An approach to hospital planning is needed that will distill both provider input and user input. More specifically, hospital planning needs to provide accurate advance assessments of product usage by integrating user input with definitions of quality.

A SOLUTION TO THE DIFFICULTIES: A MARKETING APPROACH TO LONG-RANGE PLANNING

The answer to all three of these current difficulties with hospital planning is to take a marketing approach to long-range planning. A marketing approach puts the consumer at the beginning of the planning process. In the typical planning approach, understanding the hospital's environment and market-place usually occurs after the services have been designed. Using the market-ing approach, the sequence is reversed.

Marketing Approach Defined

"A marketing approach starts the planning process with the consumer, letting the consumer's needs and wants guide the strategy of the organization."[12] With a marketing approach, participants in the long-range planning process, from department director to chief executive officers, would

- know their customers so well that they would not only know what the customers want but also the customers' deeper needs;

- design services so that they precisely and effortlessly match the needs of the customers; and

- present the services to the customers so that they can see how the services satisfy their needs.

A hospital planning format using a marketing approach would have five main steps.[13]

1. Define carefully who the customers are, group them accordingly (seg-ment the market), and analyze what is satisfying them.
2. Analyze the current mix of services in terms of particular customer needs: (a) specify the services that are growing, those that are holding

Figure 1 Sequence of Planning Interactions

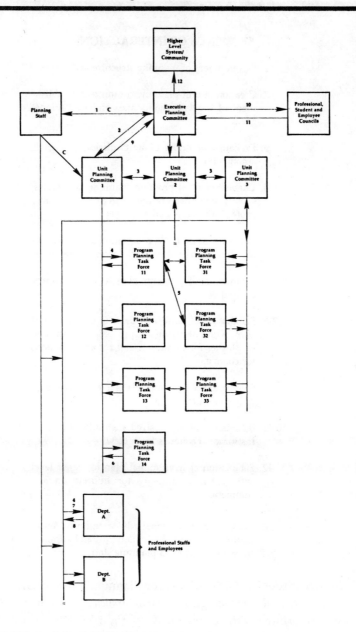

Figure 1 *Continued*

SEQUENCE OF INTERACTIONS

1. Development of planning structure and process

2. Creation of unit planning committees; establishment of timetable, guidelines and institutional goals

3. Exchange of drafts of unit mission and goals among all units

4. Establishment of program planning task forces; submission of draft of unit plan to departments, professional staffs and employees

5. Exchange of drafts of program plans among related program planning task forces in other units

6. Submission of program plan to unit planning committee

7-8. Submission of semi-final draft of complete unit plan to unit departments, professional staffs and employees for comments and recommendations for change

9. Submission of final unit plans to executive planning committee

10-11. Submission of synthesized institutional plan to institutional councils for review

12. Submission of institutional plan to higher level system and community for information and comments

---

C. Continuous professional advice, technical information and conceptual, analytical and administrative support from planning staff

Source: Stuehler, G. "A Model for Planning in Health Institutions." *Hospital and Health Services Administration* 23 (Summer 1978) p. 8. Reprinted with permission. Copyright © 1978.

steady, and those that are declining; and (b) describe the characteristics of the services that are satisfying the customers (differential advantages), and promote those advantages.
3. Identify the major opportunities and threats in the environment.
4. Analyze the competition; note the reasons for their success in satisfying customers and compare their share of the market.
5. Change, prune, and plan the services accordingly.

Most consumer-goods companies in the United States have abandoned exclusive reliance upon the product concept. They now balance their internal focus on materials and methods with an external orientation toward users. The engineers have given way to the marketers.

> The reorganization of the General Electric Company in the early 1950s signaled the ascendancy of a corporate philosophy which came to be known as the marketing concept. It was at once enthusiastically acclaimed as a new frontier in corporate development and attained a status comparable to an article of faith; few questioned its validity, both in business and academic circles. The GE approach to marketing was widely emulated and, notwithstanding a handful of detractors, has maintained almost absolute sway.[14]

Resolving the Three Difficulties

Figure 2 shows an overall schema of a hospital long-range planning process using a marketing approach.[15]

A marketing approach to long-range planning shifts hospitals away from the presumption of linear growth, the first difficulty with current long-range planning systems. Plans that begin by asking what the customer is really seeking put a premium on analyzing current services to improve the match between benefits offered and benefits sought. Such an analysis can lead to increased profit even in a no-growth situation. This kind of analysis targets certain services for discontinuance if in the light of benefit analysis they are no longer meeting a need. Furthermore, this kind of analysis can lead to adjustments of services increasing customer satisfaction and frequently saving costs rather than increasing them. A form similar to Exhibit 2, "Benefit Analysis of Services," can help hospitals segment their markets.[16]

Also, a marketing approach obviates the problem of middle-management dropout because it situates dreaming squarely in the real world of a department's actual and potential customers. Plans emerge from an in-depth appraisal of one's own situation and not from out of the blue. As a result, plans are more closely tied to real feasibility and have a better chance of being implemented.

Figure 2 The Marketing Approach to Long-Range Planning

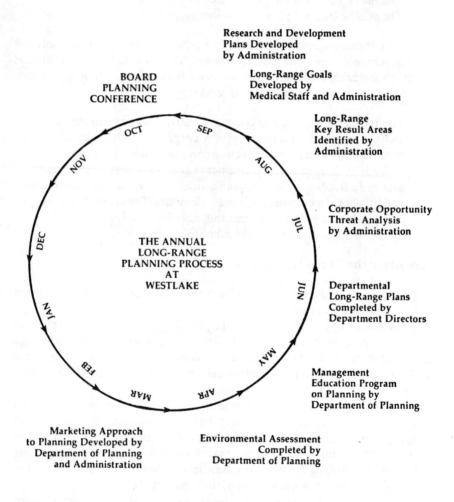

Source: Rynne, T.J. *Westlake Community Hospital Planning Handbook* (Melrose Park, III.: Westlake Community Hospital 1979) p. 3. Reprinted with permission.

Exhibit 2 Benefit Analysis of Services

DEPARTMENT_____

SEGMENTING YOUR MARKET

Step 1

List your major *customers*

1. _____

2. _____

3. _____

4. _____

5. _____

Step 2

List your services and *match* with customer

1. _____

2. _____

3. _____

4. _____

5. _____

Step 3

State basic *need* of customer met by the service

Service 1 _____

Service 2 _____

Service 3 _____

Service 4 _____

Service 5 _____

Step 4

List the prime *benefit(s)* of the service to the customer

Service 1 _____

Service 2 _____

Service 3 _____

Service 4 _____

Service 5 _____

Prepared by _____ Date _____ Reviewed by _____ Date _____

Source: Rynne, T.J. *Westlake Community Hospital Planning Handbook* (Melrose Park, Ill.: Westlake Community Hospital 1979) p. 3. Reprinted with permission.

Finally, the marketing approach avoids the pitfalls of defining quality in isolation from community need, which frequently leads to the implementation of unneeded services. Problems of overlapping and oversupplying services are avoided by using the marketing approach. Instead of designing a product and then looking for customers, the customers are consulted and then the product is designed.

The development of hospital long-range planning systems has produced significant benefits for participating hospitals. There are some major difficulties, however, with planning formats currently in widespread use. Use of the market concept and following a marketing approach will help hospitals further refine their planning systems.

REFERENCES

1. Stuehler, G. "A Model for Planning in Health Institutions." *Hospital and Health Services Administration* 23 (Summer 1978): 8.

2. Birchfield, R.W., and Keaton, H.F. *Workbook for Short Term Planning.* Chicago: Chicago Hospital Council, 1973.

3. American Hospital Association. *The Practice of Planning in Health Care Institutions.* Chicago: American Hospital Association, 1973.

4. California Hospital Association. *Planning for Health Service.* Sacramento, Calif.: California Hospital Association, 1969.

5. Guido, S., and Cooper, D. "Marketing and Distribution Planning for No Growth." *Management Focus* 2 (January/February 1979): 18. Reprinted with permission.

6. Birchfield and Keaton. *Workbook for Short Term Planning.*

7. Bales, C.F. "Strategic Control: The President's Paradox." *Business Horizons* 20 (August 1977): 19.

8. Lachner, B.J. "Marketing—An Emerging Management Challenge." *Health Care Management Review* 2 (Fall 1977): 27. Reprinted with permission.

9. Naor, J. "A New Approach to Corporate Planning." *Long Range Planning* 2 (April 1978): 2. Reprinted with permission.

10. Kotler, P. "Strategies for Introducing Marketing into Nonprofit Organizations." *Journal of Marketing* 43 (January 1979): 40. Reprinted with permission.

11. Stuehler. "A Model for Planning in Health Institutions," pp. 18-19.

12. Berkowitz, E.N., and Flexner, W.A. "The Marketing Audit: A Tool for Health Service Organizations." *Health Care Management Review* 3 (Fall 1978): 52.

13. Rynne, T.J. *Westlake Community Hospital Planning Handbook.* Melrose Park, Ill.: Westlake Community Hospital, 1979: 3.

14. Cachs, W.S., and Benson, G. "Is It Time to Discard the Marketing Concept?" *Business Horizons* 21 (August 1978): 68. Reprinted with permission.

15. Rynne. *Westlake Community Hospital Planning Handbook,* p. 3.

16. Ibid.

17. Marketing Health Care: Problems in Implementation

ROBERTA N. CLARKE

Clarke, Roberta N. "Marketing Health Care: Problems in Implementation." *Health Care Management Review*, Winter 1978.

The advent of PSROs, Utilization Review Committees, and the general decline in patient days have led to a problem of overbedding in hospitals and other institutional health care facilities. In addition, the availability of "easy" money in the 1960s allowed both the development of a large number of health facilities, such as neighborhood health centers, and the expansion of existing hospitals, which had not been forced in their early stages to consider whether sufficient demand existed to keep their organizations alive when soft money was no longer available.

MARKETING: ONE SOLUTION

The soft money is gone and some health care organizations are now faced with the problem of empty beds and vacant waiting rooms. One solution that has been suggested to alleviate this problem is marketing: marketing to attract patients, marketing to attract physicians, marketing of the more profitable health care services.

Discussions of marketing as an appropriate component of health care management have now reached the stage where health care professionals rarely ask, Is or is it not appropriate? Most health professionals who have cast a sideways glance at marketing have recognized its value, and rather than asking, "Should we or shouldn't we?" with regard to the use of marketing, are now posing two different queries: (1) What exactly is marketing as applied to health care? and (2) How does one implement marketing in a health care organization?

Marketing Applied to Health Care

The first question has been addressed in a number of articles, in marketing textbooks, and in conferences and symposia. Much of this explanatory literature addressing marketing in health care has been written by marketing academicians with limited exposure to the health care system rather than by practitioners. It therefore tends to assume a pedagogical tone with a traditional marketing emphasis on product, price, promotion, place, and so on. The academic approach notwithstanding, this appears to be the most reasonable way to explain the concepts of marketing as they apply to health care.

Implementing Health Care Marketing

The second question—How does one implement health care marketing?—is the more difficult one to answer. The difficulty lies not so much in the answer itself as in the practical problem of implementation. The implementation of a marketing strategy for any health care organization is dependent, in each case, upon the specific situation (the particular organization, consumer population, competing providers, etc.). However, there are certain practical problems that are readily generalizable across most health care organizations when it comes to the inclusion and implementation of marketing in health care management.

PROBLEMS WITH MARKETING IN HEALTH CARE

Lack of Training and Background

There are few health care managers (excluding some in HMOs) with any training or background in marketing. The traditional professional degrees that were supposed to provide preparation for entry into health care management positions were the masters of public health (MPH), of hospital administration (MHA), and the like, none of which include marketing in their curricula. Additionally, managerial positions in health care are often filled by physicians whose formal training not only lacks a marketing component but often includes a chastisement of those availing themselves of the promotional benefits of marketing. (The value and the future of the AMA antisolicitation rule has been the subject of much controversy.) The results have been, at worst, a distrust of marketing and, due to a lack of understanding of just what marketing is, a failure to recognize the value of marketing to health care institutions. More frequently, health care managers with no marketing training have learned from brief explanations that marketing would be a useful function within their organizations, but they do not know how to incorporate marketing expertise into their organizational structure.

No Administrative Position for Marketing

In community hospitals and neighborhood clinics representing a major portion of the health care providers in this country, where top nonmedical management is the administrator—and middle management consists of the administrator's secretary—there is no administrative position into which a health care marketer fits. Even in major hospitals of substantial size, the various managerial positions have been allocated to individuals with traditional health care management skills; marketing has not been one of these skills. To force-fit a marketer into an organizational structure not designed with a marketer in mind would be disruptive. (This is not to say that this is impossible, but rather likely to be avoided.)

Because health care managers rarely have a marketing background and cannot easily acquire marketing expertise within their organizations, the outcome is that they may not recognize a marketing problem when they are faced with one and that they may not recognize the value of the marketing function to health care management. If they do, they may have difficulty incorporating marketing into their organizations.

Solutions

There appear to be three solutions to this problem on an immediate basis. One is to make available to health care managers marketing courses, seminars, or conferences geared to their organizations or to the health care system. There are few of these courses yet offered; most existing marketing courses do not make applications to the health care field. However, the number of health care marketing courses and seminars are on the increase.

Secondly, health care organizations may seek to hire experienced managers from outside the health care field for their managerial positions. These individuals, in addition to offering managerial experience, are also likely to have training, experience, or both in the field of marketing. The quality of this second solution is highly dependent upon the skills and abilities of the individual manager. The drawback to this solution is that experienced managers from outside the health care field will need a substantial amount of time to acquaint themselves with the peculiarities of the health care field (third party payment, regulations and regulatory agencies, the division of medical tasks between various types of providers, etc.) before being able to manage effectively.

Thirdly, one may temporarily hire marketing expertise on a consulting basis. This solution is primarily effective in addressing a specific marketing problem or set of problems.

Outside Consultants Can Help

For example, a medical rehabilitation center with a spinal cord injury unit found a long-term trend of underutilization of this unit. Therefore, the rehabilitation center called in an outside consulting team to make recommendations to increase the unit's utilization. The consulting team ascertained (1) the number and nature of competitive spinal cord injury units in the same geographical area and the number of patients served by these units; (2) the nature of the spinal cord injury services offered by the center and the satisfaction with these services on the part of former patients, referring physicians, and third party payers with some influence on the patient's choice of service unit; (3) long-term trends in primary demand (total size) of the market; and (4) the referral mechanisms by which potential patients were or were not referred to the specific spinal cord injury unit.

The consulting team was able to discover declining primary demand, a large number of other spinal cord injury units that were also underutilized, and a competitive service unit nearby with superior resources, equipment, and facilities, a higher staff/patient ratio, and an excellent referral system. Therefore, the consulting team recommended an action that the center itself may not have seen as quickly, had the recommendation been generated internally: that the center close its spinal cord injury unit since it would be unlikely to counteract its underutilization trend; and that the center focus its resources on other offered services that faced less competition and for which there was yet unmet demand.

The use of outside marketing consultation can be very helpful in many situations, but its drawbacks must be recognized. The hiring of marketing expertise on a consulting basis can be costly. The consulting project for the rehabilitation center just described cost in the range of $6,000 to $8,000. Also, this alternative does not make the marketing function a part of the internal management structure, as it should be, but allows it to remain external to the organization.

The ideal but long-term solution, of course, is to educate future health care managers in the field of marketing during their professional training.

Function of Marketing Misunderstood

It is not yet understood within most parts of the health care system that marketing is a major policy-making function and therefore belongs in a top management or equivalent position. As it is, in profit-motivated businesses, marketing should be on an equal footing with the financial, planning, budgeting, labor management, and operations management functions. In most health care organizations (again, to the exclusion of HMOs' prepaid group practices), it is not.

Often, marketing is lumped together with the public relations function under the mistaken assumption that marketing is equivalent to public relations. The public relations office is never a top management office. Because of their lack of familiarity with it, health care providers tend to view marketing as a "neat idea" with interesting potential—but as peripheral to top management decisions.

Contrary to this belief, marketing involves decisions basic to the nature of the organization: what services to offer (product policy), whom to serve and how (market segmentation, product/market match), and issues of pricing referral and access. It is marketing, for example, that may be the function best able to address an issue facing many hospitals today: whether to close down departments within the hospital due to decline in demand, to attempt to stimulate selective demand, or to negotiate with competing hospitals for certain departments in exchange for others ("We'll take all of maternity and give you pediatrics").

Failure to Position Marketing Properly

An illustration of the failure to position the marketing function properly within the organization is that of a large city hospital that made the mistake of assigning the organization's marketing to a mid-level supervisor already overloaded with administrative tasks. Not only was the supervisor unable to spend adequate time analyzing the hospital's major markets and competitive stance, but also the supervisor found that he was unable to obtain support for the few (quite reasonable) marketing actions he recommended. Because no one in top management had initiated the analysis from which the recommendation came and no top level manager was responsible for the marketing function, no one with power to implement the recommended marketing actions would support them. The result was a frustrated supervisor who spent a good deal of his overallocated time on a nonproductive task and a hospital that missed out on two substantial market opportunities.

An Interim Solution

It will be difficult in the short run to incorporate marketing into top management. The best alternative at present to facilitate the proper use of marketing is to invite marketing expertise in whatever form possible into the policy-making office within the organization on a consistent basis. On the other hand, a great disservice will be done to furthering the acceptance of marketing if it is inappropriately used on a patchwork and inconsistent basis by managerial levels without the authority to implement marketing strategy.

Local Political Conflicts

Marketing-based strategy decisions are frequently at odds with local politics and community and individual desires. Speculation as to why this is so would probably focus on individual and community subgroup goals versus the organizational goals of the health care institution.

Community Desires Dictate Product Management

A currently common conflict and a classic marketing issue when translated into product management terms is the hospital that is torn between maintaining or closing its underutilized maternity ward. Almost every community thinks it should have a full service hospital. Having a full complement of community services plays a significant part in community pride and image. It also plays a role in the spirited competition between some neighboring towns; no town wants to place its real estate agents in the position of having to say to a prospective buyer, "We have a good hospital here, but you'll have to go to the neighboring town to have your baby." The desires of the community would thus dictate keeping an underutilized maternity ward open.

A marketing approach, on the other hand, would point out that a poorly used maternity service results in a higher mortality rate (with highly negative marketing implications in terms of word-of-mouth and bad publicity as well as low repeat purchase), a higher overhead cost per birth, poor space utilization (particularly if another service is cramped for space), and very possibly an angry local health planning agency.

This is not to say that a decision based on a marketing analysis would necessarily advise closing the ward. There are marketing-based product managers, for instance, who have elected to maintain a losing product because it is · one of the many products under a family name. In these situations, the product managers have concluded that it is more important to maintain a full complement of family-branded products than it is to rid themselves of one losing product—and be incompletely represented in the market (i.e., Kraft Salad Dressings with no Kraft Blue Cheese Dressing). The hospital with an underutilized maternity ward represents a strangely analogous situation.

Nonetheless, in the case of the hospital, a cost/benefit analysis performed on the advantages of keeping versus closing the maternity ward would more· than likely result in a consideration of closing the ward. The marketing implications in terms of lost business to the other services of the hospital as a result of the closing of the maternity ward, if judged to be insignificant, would suggest that the hospital might find it advantageous to put the maternity ward space to other use—and would also place a marketing-based decision at loggerheads with the community board of directors and local politics.

Interference with Marketing Strategy

A second example of conflict between a marketing versus a community subgroup orientation that interferes with the implementation of marketing strategy in a health care setting is the introduction by a hospital of a primary care unit into the community. From a marketing viewpoint, it may be clear that the community is underserved, that there is not a sufficient number of family or general practitioners in the area, and that many people, lacking other access to the health care system, resort to inappropriate usage of the hospital emergency room as a source of noncrisis medical care. To return its emergency room to its proper purpose—the provision of emergency care—and to provide better nonemergent medical care for people with no other access to care, the hospital, making a rational marketing strategy decision, proposed to introduce a primary care unit.

The conflict within the community, as has been seen to happen in similar circumstances in the past, arises from local physicians who fear loss of their patients to the primary care unit. They perceive the primary care unit as representing a major competitive threat to their individual practices, even though the supply for primary care services is known to be far less than the demand. The conflict is made more complex by the possible presence of these physicians on the hospital's board of directors and by the fact that the physicians are likely to have staff privileges at the hospital, thereby representing a major source of patients for the hospital. Needless to say, in a situation such as this, significant problems arise in attempting to implement the desired marketing strategy.

Compromise Is the Only Solution

No easy answer or trite response can deal satisfactorily with conflict of this nature. Given other steadily growing pressures upon health care organizations that threaten the organizations' very existences, it will be necessary under conditions of conflict for a compromise to be made between marketing and community politics, with survival of the organization being the ultimate goal. While not a totally satisfactory solution to either party in the conflict, the necessity to meet ever larger challenges to its survival will require a health care organization to call increasingly for compromises on all sides from all interested parties.

Market Research Necessary but Costly

Marketing costs money. The marketing concept, a basic tenet of marketing philosophy, proposes the consumer population or the market as the basis for the development of all marketing strategy. Therefore, if better knowledge of the consumer is needed in order to determine product policy (programs to be offered), access problems, price sensitivities, unmet consumer needs, and so on, then market surveys or consumer behavior/market research would be recommended. And good market research is costly.

Alternatives

The tendency of many health care organizations, when they learn of the expense involved in market research, is either (1) to stop right there—to continue managing as they have always managed without the advantage of the insights provided by marketing—rather than incur the expense of market research; or (2) to try to perform the necessary market research cheaply, through the use of volunteers, teenagers, or work-study students and by decreasing population sample size, quality of survey, instrument design, and so on. The problems inherent in this approach are manifold: there is enormous opportunity for bias to invade the development of a market research instrument; individuals without the expertise to recognize their own biases might elicit the results they want through exclusion of certain areas of questioning or by asking questions in biased ways.

Volunteers, lowly paid teenagers, or students are generally poorly if at all trained; again, the opportunity for bias to enter the research exists, and, at the very least, the collection of raw data is likely to be inconsistent and questionable. Lack of sufficient commitment on the part of volunteers and others, whose responsibility it is to knock on doors or conduct telephone interviews results in their not putting in a sufficient number of hours to allow the research to be performed in a reasonable time period. At worst, a not uncommon result is that research projects remain unfinished.

An Unsatisfactory Research Attempt

One example of this approach, of attempting to produce good extensive market research cheaply with typically unsatisfactory results, is a community hospital that intended to do a survey of its service area. In the hopes of saving money, the hospital enlisted the aid of an undergraduate work-study student with little training in the market research area to direct community volunteers in the performance of the survey. Fewer volunteers than had originally voiced interest actually became involved in the survey, which thus lost momentum, not only because of an inadequate number of volunteer surveyors to cover the neighborhood but also because the work-study student spent little time on the project, recognizing that his commitment was over at the end of the semester, regardless of the state of the completion of the project.

An effort to complete the survey the following year, using teenagers sponsored by a federally funded antipoverty program as surveyors, also produced dismal results due to lack of commitment, training, and ability of the teenagers. The newest plan of the hospital is to send a survey force of nuns into the neighborhood to administer the research questionnaire on a door-to-door basis. Such a survey force will eliminate some of the problems (commitment, interest) of the earlier volunteer groups but will necessarily introduce bias into areas of the questionnaire dealing with alcoholism, venereal disease, abortion, and birth control, at the very least.

The survey that this hospital wanted done could have been performed well and quickly by a consulting or market research firm experienced in this type of research. The cost for a survey of this nature varies according to the size and nature of the area to be surveyed as well as the firm involved. A reasonable estimate for this research effort is $15,000 to $25,000.

Negative Consequences of Unsatisfactory Research

Unfinished or questionable research results have negative consequences of their own. Having once performed poor market research, it might be more difficult to persuade those with funding power in the hospital to support a second (more expensive), better designed market research project; the consumer population might also be less willing to open their doors a second time, as most market research represents an invasion of privacy.

Furthermore, it is reasonable to ask whether it is better to have no market research rather than to refer to dubious research results. Market research results often take the form of statistics that tend to have an implied legitimacy regardless of the nature of their birth. Most people, professionals included, view statistics as representing truth, soon forgetting that they questioned the method by which the statistics were produced. To have health care managers making major policy decisions based on misleading market research would seem to be less wise than to have them manage according to information gathered through their own informal management information systems.

No Reimbursement for Marketing Costs

Market research—as well as other marketing—costs are not reimbursed by third party payers. As the major financing mechanisms (Blue Cross, Medicaid, Medicare) introduce progressively more stringent reimbursement policies, it will become increasingly difficult for health care organizations to cover existing overhead, without even giving consideration to new and unprecedented marketing costs. It has become obvious to the most casual observer of the health care system that the financial squeeze upon all health care organizations is both great and growing; there is little "hidden" money available in most health providers' budgets to apply to experimentation in marketing.

Until the major financing mechanisms recognize the value of marketing through their reimbursement policies, health care organizations will be reluctant to expend funds on marketing-related costs.

SUGGESTED READINGS

1. 1977 National Forum on Hospital and Health Affairs, Duke University. "Marketing the Hospital." Edited by B.J. Jaeger. May 13-14, 1977.

2. Kotler, P. "Marketing for Hospitals." Presentation at the 19th Congress on Administration, American College of Hospital Administrators, Chicago, Ill., Feb. 20-21, 1976.

3. Kotler, P. *Marketing for Nonprofit Organizations.* Englewood Cliffs, N.J.: Prentice-Hall, 1975, Chapter 16.

4. Kotler, P. "Marketing Tools and Guidelines for Public Agencies." Paper presented at the Workshop on Governmental Effectiveness, Annapolis, Md., July 13-15, 1976.

5. Lovelock, C.H. "Marketing for Social Change: Tools, Concepts and Strategies for Health' Care Marketers." Paper presented at a conference sponsored by the American College of Hospital Administrators and the Academy of Hospital Public Relations, Philadelphia, Pa., April 29-30, 1976.

6. "Marketing Aspects of Preventive Health Care." Proceedings of Conference on Marketing Aspects of Preventive Health Care, University of Virginia, April 1977.

7. Jerry Mechling Associates. "The Uses of Marketing and Citizen Involvement." A report for the National Center for Productivity and Quality of Working Life, July 1976.

8. Rathmell, J.M. *Marketing in the Service Sector.* Cambridge, Mass.: Winthrop Publishers, 1974, Chapter 10.

18. Can Marketing Help Recruit and Retain Nurses?

G. DAVID HUGHES

Hughes, G. David. "Can Marketing Help Recruit and Retain Nurses?" *Health Care Management Review,* Summer 1979.

Four years ago, a member of the medical staff of a large hospital asked the author, "Can marketing help us to recruit and retain nurses?" He explained that his hospital, like others, had a nurse staffing problem. A study and a follow-up study were conducted at this hospital to determine the answer to this question.

ASKING THE CRITICAL QUESTIONS

To answer a question on nurse staffing, marketing, or any question for that matter, it is necessary to break the question into components. To do this, the critical questions behind the main question must be asked. It is useful to think of the critical questions as subproblems or causes of the main problem to be solved.

To identify the critical questions, the researcher had focused group (small group) discussions with the medical, nursing, and administrative staff of the hospital. The discussions indicated clearly that recruiting was only 25 percent of the problem, that most of the effort should be on the problem of retention. In marketing terms this is the problem of brand *loyalty.* Keeping customers once they have been attracted may be cheaper than attracting new ones. Similarly, it may be cheaper to retain nurses than to recruit and train new nurses continuously.

The author acknowledges with gratitude the assistance of Ms. Faye D. Pickard, Associate Professor, School of Nursing, University of North Carolina, during the design of the study reported in this article.

To illustrate how the marketing process may be translated into the dual problems of recruiting and retaining nurses, the critical questions were stated in terms of nursing problems, with the marketing counterpart noted in parentheses. Four critical questions were identified as follows:

1. What personal needs do nurses (customers) wish to fulfill in choosing among hospitals (brands)? How important are these needs to nurses?
2. What sources of information do nurses use when choosing a hospital (brand) as a place to work?
3. Do the attitudes of present nurses (customers) within the several nursing services (market segments) indicate problems that may produce a high turnover rate (low brand loyalty)?
4. What job (brand) benefits should be added to attract new nurses (customers) and retain the present ones?

To answer these questions for the client hospital, it was necessary to conduct local field research, because there were no generalizable answers in the published literature. The research proceeded in two stages. The first stage consisted of focused group interviews with the client hospital administrators, house staff, supervisors, and nurses at the client hospital and at three hospitals in the adjacent county. These interviews helped to refine the definition of the problems and to identify items that needed to be included in the questionnaire.

After the results of the focused group interviews were completed, the client concluded that it would be necessary to survey nurses to get more precise answers than can be generated in focused group interviews. A list supplied by the state board of nursing provided the sample base for a stratified random sample totaling 300 nurses. A preliminary phone call to each potential respondent was used to gain cooperation prior to mailing the questionnaire. The response rate was 65 percent.

A detailed analysis of the responses permitted the following questions to be answered. The data reported are limited to the nurses in the client hospital.

What Needs Do Nurses Wish to Fulfill?

Respondents were asked to assign a weight to the criteria that were used when selecting a hospital. The 12 criteria and their weights are shown in Table 1. The focused group interviews generated a longer list that was then reduced by the client and the researcher. These weights reveal that the most important criterion was the fact that the spouse was in the area. This finding suggests that nurse recruiters will want to work with the personnel offices of local companies and graduate school admission officers to identify nurses whose spouses will be moving into the area.

Table 1 Weights Assigned to Criteria

Criteria	Number of Respondents*	Average Weight
1. Workload	59	8.1
2. Opportunity for university courses	57	5.8
3. Teaching hospital	57	6.1
4. Research hospital	22	4.4
5. Pay	81	11.3
6. Fringe benefits	72	7.6
7. Assigned to the service of my choice	84	14.2
8. Social life	26	6.1
9. Spouse working/studying in the area	42	16.2
10. Reputation of the hospital	66	5.2
11. Responsibility consistent with my training	74	10.4
12. Modern equipment	50	4.6
	Total	100.0

* Ninety of the respondents worked at the client hospital.

The second most important dimension, and more important than pay, was the desire to be assigned to the service of one's choice. Closely related to this dimension, and only slightly less important than pay, was the desire to have a responsibility that is consistent with training. The career dimensions of the job are clearly important to the nurse during the *selection* of a hospital. They are also important considerations for *staying* with the hospital, as will be seen later. These findings are important for recruiting, placing, and training nurses.

What Sources of Information Do Nurses Use When Choosing a Hospital?

Answers to this question become important when the nurse recruiter is planning a recruiting campaign. Which media should be used? Should there be an open house for graduating nurses? Should teachers and counselors be kept informed because they are influential? Table 2 shows the percentage of nurses in the client hospital choosing various information sources as the most

Table 2 Percent of Nurses Choosing Information Sources

Information Source	Percent
Family, friends	8
Other nurses	4
Nursing school counselors	0
Nursing school teachers	3
My own personal feelings	49
Professional journals	0
Convenience of location	22
Hospital recruiter	3
Employment agency	0
Radio, TV advertising	0
Newspaper advertising	1
Direct mail advertising	0
Other	10
	100

influential when selecting a hospital as a place to work. As can be seen, the source "my own personal feelings" dominated the information sources. This suggests that an open house or a tour of some kind is extremely important to the recruiting process.

What Are the Problems that Produce Nurse Turnover?

Potential turnover problems may be identified by measuring the attitudes of nurses toward job attributes. Attitudes toward 36 attributes were measured. These situations had been identified as potential problem areas during the focused group discussions. For simplicity, only 3 of the services and 18 of the attributes are reported in Table 3.

A comparison of the percentage of favorable responses for all of the services in the hospital with the percentages for these three services identified problems. For example, a comparison of the percentages for Service 1 with the average for the hospital revealed that there were problems in the dimensions of clarity of responsibility, task consistency with training, advance

Table 3 Percent of Favorable Attitudes Toward Specific Services (The Higher the Number, The More Favorable the Response)

Attitude*	Hospital Average	Services** 1	2	3
Staff nurse/intern responsibility clear	73	86	50	92
Tasks consistent with training	73	57	33	75
Schedule known in advance	78	43	50	100
Orientation program effective	86	57	100	83
Clinical supervision effective	66	29	67	75
Good management of personnel by RNs	59	14	67	58
Good nurse team leadership	76	29	83	83
Care more important than research	57	14	33	75
Care more important than teaching	48	29	33	42
RN part of a team effort	79	57	50	75
Nurse leadership effective	67	29	83	75
Good in-service education	89	71	100	100
Good attitudes between:				
RN/residents	82	71	67	75
RN/physicians	66	57	50	42
RN/LPNs	71	43	83	75
Good communications between:				
RN/physicians	60	71	50	42
RN/LPNs	74	43	83	58
RN/housekeeping	43	57	50	42
Probability of recommending as place to work (0.60 or greater)	66	14	67	83

*The questionnaire gave a fuller description of 36 attributes that were to be evaluated. These descriptions will generally be unique to each hospital.

**Percent of client hospital nurses scoring attitudes four through six and scoring probabilities 60 through 100. (A scale value of six was most favorable.) Services are not identified to preserve confidentiality. A total of nine services were examined.

knowledge of schedules, effectiveness of the orientation program, management/leadership, patient care versus research and teaching, and communication problems with supervisors. It comes as no surprise, therefore, that only 14 percent of the respondents in this department reported at least a 0.60 probability of recommending the client hospital as a place to work. In contrast, 83 percent of the respondents in Service 3 would make such a recommendation.

The training program for Service 1 was greatly expanded. Furthermore, a team approach was used when staffing this service.

Which of the 36 attributes are the most important in the minds of the nurses? To answer this question, an attitude model was built using multiple regression. This technique identified four variables that were statistically significant in contributing to the probability of the client hospital being recommended as a place to work. These variables were RN/intern responsibility, the relationship between patient care and research, communications between RN and housekeeping, and the feeling of being part of a team effort. These four variables accounted for 47 percent of the variance in the probability of recommending the hospital as a place to work.

Attitude models may be used to predict the effect of administrative action. In this case, an improvement of 0.5 scale point along each of these dimensions would change the probability of recommending the hospital as a place to work from 0.66 to 0.77. These models are simple to construct, but they are powerful because they locate precisely those areas that require immediate attention. (Here, an SPSS step-regression was used. Variables entered at a probability of 0.05 or less. The coefficients were 0.72, 0.53, and 0.46 respectively. Numbers must be multiplied by 0.1 to transform scale values into probabilities.)

What Job Benefits Should Be Added to Attract and Retain Nurses?

Many job benefits that seemed to have the potential of reducing turnover were identified during the focused group interviews. The research problem was to measure the importance of these benefits in terms that could be communicated readily to a hospital administrator. Frequently used scales, such as the semantic differential or the Likert scale, do not translate into the budget language of an administrator. There was a need to transform the nurses' perceptions of benefits into dollar terms.

Several existing scaling techniques were considered, tested, and rejected for a variety of technical and practical reasons. Finally, a unique application of a 1927 technique was used. One version of Thurstone's case V requires the respondent to rank order preferences.[1] The nursing questionnaire listed 13 job benefits and monthly pay increases of $10 and $40. Respondents were asked to rank these 15 benefits. The frequences of these rankings were then transformed into a monetary value using a computer routine. The result was the magnitude of pay increase that would be required to make the nurse indifferent between the increase in pay and the improved job environment. In economics, this concept is known as the indifference theory.

The results of this analysis, which appear in Table 4, have several important implications for the hospital administrator. First, it is important to learn that the top four benefits were social psychological, not physical benefits such as equipment or environment. The attitudinal model discussed above also identified the benefit, "feeling part of a team," as an important need. It is clear that recruiting and training methods should focus on this personal need. Second, the monetary values form the basis for establishing priorities when developing means to meet these needs.

The monthly individual values in the first column in Table 4 may be translated into annual benefits by multiplying first by 12 to attain a yearly figure and then by the average number of nurses to determine the total for the hospital. These calculations are summarized in the second column of the table. "Feeling that I am part of a patient care team" has the equivalent value of a $244,800 increase in pay. Figures such as this one are more meaningful than an abstract number from an attitude scale.

Nurses' perceived need for additional training appears in Table 1. To plan for in-service training, it was necessary to estimate the demand for various training programs. Respondents' first choices are reported in Table 5. It will be noted that the demand for training differs according to whether the nurse has a diploma, an associate degree, or a bachelor's degree. (Variations in demand across segments are common in marketing.) These data will make it possible to make an estimate of the number of nurses who would take each training opportunity if it were offered.

Some nurses wanted courses for which they could receive college credit. The demand for these courses also varied according to the basic training that the nurse received. These data were also collected so that arrangements could be made with nearby universities.

HOW WAS THE RESEARCH USED?

Six months and then several years after the research report was submitted, the author conducted follow-up interviews to see if the findings had been applied. The feedback was heartening. A team approach was being used to staff the services. In-service training was decentralized to the level of specific nursing services. The monetized utility data had been used to support budget requests. Turnover had been reduced. While marketing research cannot take all of the

Table 4 Perceived Benefits by Client Nurses*

Benefit	Client Hospital Nurses ($)	Annualized Perceived Value** ($)
Feeling that I am part of a patient care team	68	244,800
Working the shift of my choice	54	194,400
Assignments consistent with my training	54	194,400
Availability of nurse precepters at the clinical unit level	44	158,400
Knowing my work schedule a month in advance	41	147,600
Improved cleanliness	37	133,200
Better equipment	34	122,400
Better parking facilities	29	104,400
Better supervision of my work	23	82,800
A minibus that picks me up at home and returns me after work	3	10,800
Day care services for my children at no cost to me	3	10,800
Better social life	0	0

* Number of respondents = 90. Dollars are equivalent monthly pay increases.
** The annualized perceived value of a benefit for client nurses is computed by multiplying the monthly pay equivalent shown in Table 4 times 12 to yield an annual rate per nurse. This figure is then multiplied by the average number of client nurses.

Table 5 Estimated Demand for Various Training Programs

First Choice Training/Experience	Nurse Training Program(%)			
	Diploma	Associate Degree of Nursing	Bachelor's Degree	Total
Practice/Experience				
Anesthesia	0.0	0.0	2.7	1.2
Emergency room	7.7	28.6	2.7	7.2
Inhalation therapy	7.7	0.0	2.7	4.8
ICU/CCU	2.6	0.0	5.4	3.6
Nurse clinics	0.0	14.3	0.0	1.2
Ob/Gyn	0.0	0.0	5.4	2.4
Operating room	5.1	14.3	0.0	3.6
Pediatrics	0.0	0.0	2.7	1.2
Pediatric ICU	0.0	0.0	2.7	1.2
Psychiatry	2.6	14.3	0.0	2.4
Public health	2.6	0.0	2.7	2.4
Other	0.0	0.0	10.8	4.8
Practitioners				
Family nurse practitioner	7.7	0.0	5.4	6.0
Midwife	2.6	0.0	0.0	1.2
Pediatric nurse	0.0	0.0	8.1	3.6
Other	0.0	0.0	5.4	2.4
Further education				
MS	0.0	0.0	8.1	3.6
Other	5.1	14.3	2.7	4.8
Training				
Cardiac	15.4	14.3	10.3	13.3
Leadership	12.8	0.0	2.7	7.2
Management	2.6	0.0	2.7	2.4
Pharmacy	0.0	0.0	2.7	1.2
Physical assessment	5.1	0.0	2.7	3.6
Renal	2.6	0.0	0.0	1.2
Other	15.4	0.0	5.4	9.6
Miscellaneous				
Other	2.6	0.0	5.4	3.6
Sample size	39	7	37	83
Percent in each program	47.0	8.4	44.6	100.0

credit, it did provide important information for the decisions that produced the results.

In conclusion, the success of this application of marketing research techniques was in seeing the parallels between the critical questions in marketing and those in the recruiting and retention of nurses. These parallels made it possible to apply or adapt research techniques with known properties. Using known techniques lowers the costs and increases the probability that research will improve decision making.[2]

REFERENCES

1. For a detailed description of the approach, along with other methods for monetizing utilities, see Hughes, G.D. "Monetizing Utilities for Product and Service Benefits," in Woodside, A.G.; Sheth, J.N.; and Bennett, P.D., eds. *Consumer and Industrial Buying Behavior* (New York: North-Holland, 1977) pp. 179-189.

2. For a detailed discussion of the process of marketing planning see Hughes, G.D. *Marketing Management: A Planning Approach* (Reading, Mass.: Addison-Wesley Publishing Co., 1978).

19. Psychographic Profiles: Aid to Health Care Marketing

ALICE M. SAPIENZA

Sapienza, Alice M. "Psychographic Profiles: Aid to Health Care Marketing." *Health Care Management Review*, Fall 1980.

A marketing analysis—for purveyors of goods or services—always includes the question, Who is our consumer? Despite the growing sophistication of health care managers in the use of marketing tools, however, they rarely answer this question in full. Instead, many describe their population demographically but stop short of including psychographic information.

Unlike the determinants of many other "products," determinants of health care quality and outcome are highly subjective. Consumer satisfaction is never attributable to medical excellence alone. Thus managers of health care services must be especially sensitive to psychographic information. Programmatic, staffing, and facility planning will be wasted unless the entire constellation of consumer descriptors is taken into account.

Patients will not return to a practice, nor will they recommend it to others, if it does not meet their expectations. If the environment in which the care is offered or the philosophy behind the program is inimical, no persuasion will be sufficient to keep these patients.

The burden on ambulatory facility managers to understand and meet consumer expectations is particularly heavy. Because most ambulatory services are elective, and because facilities such as health maintenance organizations (HMOs) depend on a stable patient base, managers must know the needs and preferences of their consumers in order to attract and keep them.

Effective use of marketing tools in the health care field requires an understanding of the factors constituting demographic and psychographic profiles, a knowledge of the "market mix" affected by psychographic data, and a matching of patient and practitioner attitudes on key issues.

DEMOGRAPHIC VERSUS PSYCHOGRAPHIC DATA

All consumers may be described along two axes: demographic and psychographic. Demographic data include such categories as age, sex, and residence. For example, the average patient in an obstetrical group practice may be described as 28.3 years of age, with 1.2 children, living in a metropolitan area within a seven mile radius of the facility. This information is extremely important to health care managers and practitioners. Equally important, however, is information along the second descriptive axis: psychographic information.

As the name implies, psychographic data describe what the consumer thinks and feels about issues relevant to the goods or services being offered.[1][2] Psychographic data complete the description of the consumer. For health care managers, psychographic profiles

- reveal what patients expect from a facility,

- clarify patients' motivation in choosing a facility,

- determine the characteristics of practice style, and

- enable more effective marketing strategies to be designed and implemented.

For example the average patient in an obstetrical group practice might feel strongly that (1) she is to be involved in all decisions about her health care, (2) her labor and delivery should be as natural as possible, and (3) her partner should be present at the delivery, even if a Caesarean section is indicated.

Demographic and psychographic information complement each other. Demographic data describe physical characteristics of the consumer; psychographic data provide insights into motivational, intellectual, and emotional characteristics of the consumer and facilitate the consumer orientation so necessary for patient satisifaction.[3] Table 1 lists some questions that demographic and psychographic data can answer.

MARKETING MIX

Each element of the so-called marketing mix—product, price, promotion, place—is affected by psychographic data.

In health care, *product* comprises the services offered. If psychographic data indicate that the patient population wants to be involved in health care decision making, the range of services a facility offers might be broadened to include educational sessions on specific topics, such as childbirth preparation and women's health.

Table 1 Questions Answered by Demographic and Psychographic Data

DEMOGRAPHIC	PSYCHOGRAPHIC
How old is the consumer?	What is the consumer's stated and perceived health status?
Where does he/she live? (inner city, urban neighborhood, suburban, etc.)	What does he/she expect from a health care facility?
How many members in the family?	What has the consumer's prior experience of health care been?
What is the consumer's educational background?	What did the consumer like or dislike about that experience? Why?
What is the consumer's financial status?	What did the consumer like or dislike about this facility? Why?
Where does the consumer work? What does he/she do?	What are the explicit and implicit health care needs of the consumer?
What health care facilities has the consumer used?	
How long has the consumer used this facility?	
Are there known indicators of the future health status of the consumer?	

Price, or the cost of the health care services, might at first glance appear irrelevant. Certainly most people are covered by some form of insurance. However, price also includes the cost in time and inconvenience to the person using the health care services. A patient survey might reveal that one of the gravest inconveniences for women was finding someone to watch their children while they kept a medical appointment. If space permitted, a health care facility manager might design a children's corner in the waiting area and staff it with volunteers. Working parents coming to the facility in the evening might also find the children's corner reduced the inconvenience of seeking care.

Psychographic data are also vital to effective health care marketing communication or *promotion.* If people find out about a facility through friends or relatives who have used it, then a mailing list of patients might be an excellent means of distributing promotional material. The message of any promotional campaign must also speak to the psychographic characteristics of the audience. If the patient population prides itself on making an informed choice of medical services, this characteristic might be key to the contents and style of a marketing brochure.

Finally, as every HMO manager knows, the location or *place* of the facility is one of the most important planning decisions. It is a truism that people will choose health care services within reasonable access from their home or work.

Although managers of established health care facilities might not have the freedom of choice of those in the planning stages, they probably have more flexibility than they realize. Some health care services can be offered at satellite locations. In addition, place entails atmosphere. A facility might be advantageously situated but be perceived as having an unpleasant atmosphere (as evidenced by a patient survey). This could result from uncomfortable waiting areas, drab offices, or less than spotless corridors and bathrooms. The facility must be more than accessible for the people it hopes to attract and keep: it must also reflect a concern for patients' comfort.

ORGANIZATION CONCERNS

Health care managers must pay special attention to the "fit" between practice style and patient population. Practice style, in the context of this article, means the general attitudes of practitioners toward such issues as self-help, level of clinical interference, and patients' rights and responsibilities. It is thus analogous to psychographic data on how the consumer thinks and feels about similar issues. A manager must be able to describe the staff's style in order to determine its attractiveness to patients.

If the psychographic profile of a target population indicated they were less interested in health care self-determination, then the style of practitioners who would serve that population must be consonant. Conversely, if the psychographic profile indicated patients' eagerness to use self-help methods, facility staff must share that desire.

Health care managers can attempt to strengthen or change the characteristics of staff to meet consumer expectations. A useful technique in this process is psychographic mapping. In Figure 1, patient and staff characteristics along two continua (interaction and involvement, or any others that appropriately describe the two groups) can be simply defined and placed in the correct quadrant. For example, a staff that preferred to interact highly with patients would not fit (third quadrant) with a patient population that preferred to remain essentially uninvolved in health care issues. To change staff character-

Figure 1 Patient and Staff Characteristics

NONINVOLVEMENT	INVOLVEMENT
LOW INTERACTION	
FIT	NO FIT
1	2
3	4
HIGH INTERACTION	
NO FIT	FIT

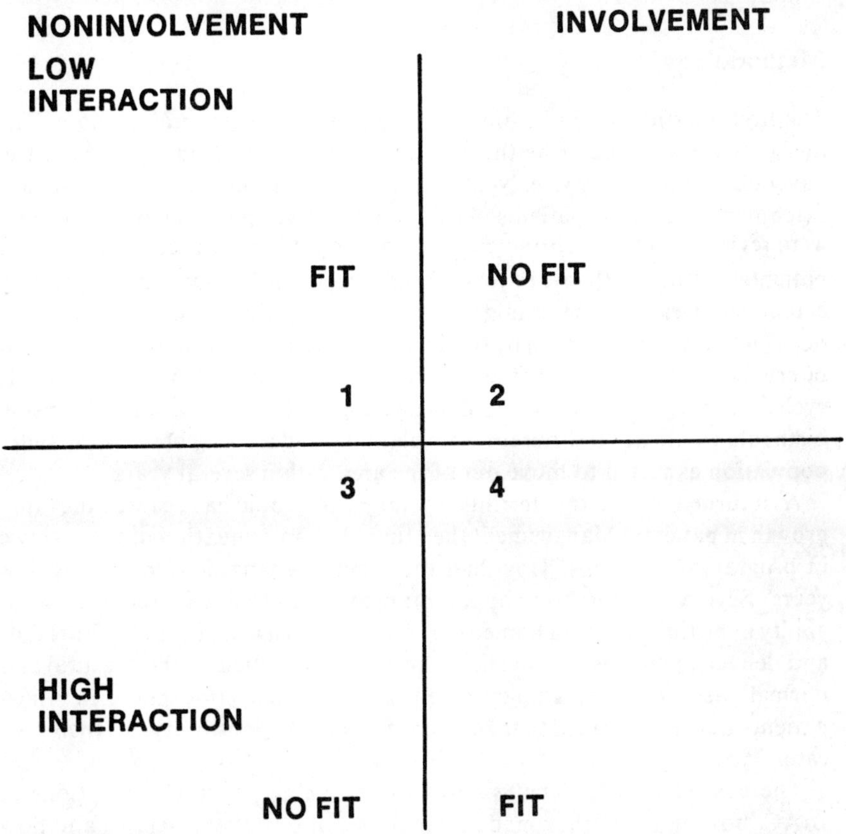

istics, of course, requires judicious hiring, training, and reinforcement techniques on the part of the manager and full cooperation of the medical leadership.

ILLUSTRATION

Problem

The obstetrical unit of Beth Israel Ambulatory Care Center (BIAC), the primary care group practice at Boston's Beth Israel Hospital, a major teaching hospital of Harvard Medical School, was faced with a 25 percent increase in patients in 1978. For planning and staffing purposes, management needed to know if this growth was a result of (1) environmental factors beyond its control, (2) programmatic changes in the services being offered by the facility, or (3) both.

Methodology

The first question could be answered by analyzing demographic data. The initial task was to describe the current patient population: age, residence, payer class, and family size. Next, based on the determined age and primary catchment area of the patients, fertility and migration trend data in the state were reviewed. Two environmental factors could have caused the growth in patients: a rising birth rate in general and/or a rising birth rate in the primary catchment area because of migrations of certain ethnic groups. If either or both factors were evidenced by the data, then the age of the population would be crucial, to determine if patients were at the beginning or end of their fertile cycle. Planning and staffing based on a young, stable population with a rising birth rate would be far different from planning and staffing based on an older population expected to move out of the area within several years.

As it turned out, neither fertility nor migration could have caused the rapid growth in patients. Management then turned to an evaluation of the practice in programmatic terms. How had the practice changed over the past few years? Several answers were apparent: provision of midwife services, availability of birthing room (a homelike room in which a woman could both labor and deliver), new obstetrical staff who were committed to the "natural and normal" aspects of pregnancy care, and a relaxed atmosphere in which patients were encouraged to take interest in, and responsibility for, their own care.

The next step in the analysis was to determine patients' perceptions of BIAC, how and why they made their choice of obstetrical service and how satisfied or dissatisfied they had been with previous obstetrical care. The practice evaluation contained implicit psychographic information. Explicit information could only be determined by survey.

Problems of respondent bias in the survey were minimized by using an interviewer who was not from the practice staff. In addition, the questionnaire was designed to eliminate as much bias as possible, given the purposes of the survey and the fact that it was conducted on site. Of course, if the practice had seen significant *decline* in patients, an onsite survey would have been totally inappropriate. Current patients are, by definition, satisfied. Those who are not, who have left the facility, will be found at competing institutions. In this case, a professional consultant would have to be called in to do a marketing analysis and off-site survey.

Some of the questions asked of patients at their first prenatal visit were:

- How did you find out about this practice?
- Did you find out about other practices before choosing this one? How? Which ones?
- What did you like/dislike about other programs?
- Why did you decide to come here?
- How important were the following issues to you in making your choice: location, midwife services, cost?

Results

About 50 percent of the women interviewed found out about BIAC from friends or relatives, about 20 percent through physicians' referrals (principally from neighborhood health centers), and about 10 percent by "shopping around." Most of the patients (70 percent) had received ob/gyn care at other sites before coming to BIAC, although only 58 percent identified the source(s) of care.

Patient satisfaction was evaluated by determining the criteria that women used to (1) judge their previous care and (2) choose BIAC. Most of the women who had changed their source of care did so because they were dissatisfied. Specifically, these women stated that their care had been impersonal, that the staff had been unprofessional, or that the atmosphere had been unpleasant. In fact, these perceptions were often coupled with the judgment of "poor quality." The women who chose BIAC did so because of Beth Israel Hospital's reputation, because they were confident of the care they would receive (a corollary of the first reason), or because they were highly recommended by friends or relatives. By analogy, these perceptions could be coupled with the judgment "high quality."

Table 2 Consumer Segments for BIAC Obstetrical Service

	TYPE 1	TYPE 2
Average age	20.5 years	27 years
Residence	Two urban neighborhoods	60+ cities and towns
Payer class	Welfare	Blue Cross/commercial
Source of referral	Friends/relatives	Friends/relatives
Perceptions of prior care	Not professional or impersonal	Not progressive
Basis for choosing BIAC	Recommendation of friend or relative	Confidence in hospital
Elements of satisfaction with BIAC	Personal attention of providers	Confidence in care and provision of midwives
Importance of:		
Location	Not important	Not important
Midwives	Not important	Important
Recommendation	Very important	Very important
Cost	Not important	Not important, important
Percentage of patients	42	58

Finally, responses to the question, "How important were the following issues to you in making your choice?" included, in increasing order of importance, comfortable environment, midwife services, confidence in the care, personal attention, and feeling at ease with the obstetricians and midwives.

When demographic and psychographic data were combined, two types of women emerged. The first was in her early 20s, from one of the two major urban areas close to the hospital, and attracted primarily by the personal attention she received from providers and staff. The second, and reflective of the larger group, was in her late 20s to early 30s from urban or suburban areas not necessarily close to the hospital, and attracted primarily by the progressive reputation of the practice (i.e., availability of midwife services and the birthing rooms, and the fact that this was a group practice). Table 2 illustrates the salient characteristics of these two consumer segments.

Most of the patients were articulate women who evaluated other obstetrical services before choosing BIAC and were highly influenced by the recommendations of other women who had used the practice. The referral network, in other words, consisted of friends, acquaintances, and relatives of former BIAC patients. Women who sought progressive obstetrical care (however idiosyncratically defined) were attracted by this practice, satisfied with their care, and forthright in their recommendations.

REFERENCES

1. Kotler, P. *Marketing for Non-Profit Organizations*. Englewood Cliffs, N.J.: Prentice-Hall, 1975.

2. Wells, W., ed. *Life Style and Psychographics*. Chicago: American Marketing Association, 1974.

3. Flexner, W.A.; McLaughlin, C.P.; and Littlefield, J.E. "Discovering What the Consumer Really Wants." *Health Care Management Review* 2 (Fall 1977).

20. Point of View: Consumer Expectations of Ambulatory Care

ANTHONY R. KOVNER and HELEN L. SMITS

Kovner, Anthony R., and Smits, Helen L. "Consumer Expectations of Ambulatory Care." *Health Care Management Review,* Winter 1978.

In the current national debate over how to modify our health care system, much lip service is paid to health consumers. Provision for consumer membership on governing boards and consumer participation in grievance machinery is common in new and proposed health care legislation.[1]

Underlying these provisions is the assumption that, through such structural mechanisms, consumers can make their needs felt and create a system responsive to their demands. Those associated with large health care organizations, however, are apt to view skeptically the notion that even a consumer majority of board members can, by themselves, radically alter the way in which an organization behaves.

Consumer preferences will begin to be satisfied only when they are taken into direct account in both the planning and delivery of health services. Consumer desires must be determined in the context of our existing system, recognizing that consumer expectations and demands vary among individuals and can change rapidly and often unpredictably.

Whether and when to seek care, whether to undergo diagnostic testing, whether to take pills, whether to return for follow-up visits—all of these decisions lie within the control of the ambulatory care consumer. Patients confined to bed are not in a position to make many, if any, consumer demands regarding the care they expect to receive. Therefore, the consumer preferences of the ambulatory care patient are more relevant to general consumer behavior.

On the other hand, it is surprisingly difficult to discover what the ambulatory care customer does want. Little effort has been made to study the attitudes of consumers toward the services they are now using. The few exceptions, such as the work of Stratmann and colleagues in Rochester, New

York, are local and, in the national context, based on too small a sample.[2-6] (See Table 1 for a comparison of key elements of consumer expectations as compiled by various authors.) From our point of view, ambulatory care patients have definite expectations regarding the delivery and the quality of care they consume.

BENEFITS OF HEALTH CARE SERVICE

Access

Everyone wants to know who will take care of them when they are sick or when they are in pain. Everyone wants a health care system that will respond quickly and with sensitivity when their own ability to cope ends. Consumers place a high value on knowing that access to care is always available in emergencies. While health care providers are apt to emphasize access at odd hours *only* for true emergencies, it is important to remember that the consumer, frightened by a new symptom, may need some help in deciding just what an emergency is. Such access may be brief and simple: a phone call often suffices. Serious and tragic mistakes can result when individuals feel that they are unwelcome during evening and weekend hours.

Humaneness

Humaneness is an important part of medical care. Consumers want to feel they are welcome, encouraged to come back. Consumers are individuals with important feelings about their health and their bodies. They want to see that providers understand the differences between their situation and that of other similar individuals.

In all fairness, the delivery of humane service is not as simple for the providers of health care as it is for those in many other kinds of service in our society. A day spent communicating with cancer patients, severe diabetics, or even patients with ordinary ambulatory problems can be totally draining. One aspect of a humane health care system is the way in which it deals with its own providers—the mechanisms provided to "heal the healers."

Privacy

Seldom mentioned as a criterion in evaluating medical care is the customer's desire for privacy. Everyone wishes not to be exposed, either in body or mind, more than is medically necessary. Consumers are wary of providers who might share information about them with neighbors, other family members, or employers. "Community-based" services may be considered undesirable by the community if the strictest attention is not paid to confidentiality.

Table 1 Service Aspects of Medical Care: Various Lists

	KOVNER/SMITS	KINDIG/SIDEL[1]	SHEPS/MADISON[2]	ADAY/ANDERSON
BENEFITS				
Access	Yes	Yes	Yes	(see Convenience)
Humaneness (Courtesy)	Yes	—	Yes	Yes
Privacy	Yes	—	—	—
Continuity	Yes	Yes	Yes	—
Quality	Yes	Yes	Yes	Yes
Information	Yes	—	—	Yes
Input	Yes	Yes	Yes	—
Eligibility	n/a	Yes	n/a	n/a
Comprehensive	—	Yes	Yes	—
Availability	(see Access)	Yes	—	—
Research and Demonstration	—	Yes	—	—
Coordinated	(see Continuity)	—	Yes	Yes
Family-centered	—	—	Yes	—
Understandable	(see Information)	—	—	—
Convenience	—	—	—	Yes
COSTS				
Money	Yes	Yes	n/a	Yes
Time	Yes	—	—	(see Convenience)
Uncertainty	Yes	—	—	—

[1] Developed to evaluate national health insurance proposals.
[2] Developed to evaluate neighborhood health centers.

Continuity

The mythic importance of the physician/patient relationship is probably overrated by many providers; it appears relatively less important to consumers, although it is certainly important to some. Consumers want continuity of care, in that their previous medical history and condition are taken into account by the provider caring for them; they want care that is appropriately coordinated among providers. Consumers do not wish to be retested or requestioned more than is appropriate. Since a large percentage of the population changes their residence every year, the expectation of continuity may often depend upon adequate record keeping and good communication among physicians rather than on a consumer's long-term relationship with an individual physician.

Quality

Everyone expects medical care of adequate quality. But there is ample evidence that consumers cannot effectively evaluate quality; most consumers base their evaluations of quality upon irrelevant factors, such as the degree of humaneness of their providers, their perceived status in the community, or even the cost of the service. Consumers desire information that indicates that their provider bears somebody else's stamp of approval, namely, licensure, specialty board approval, or, more important, community acceptance.

Although quality often has the highest priority of all factors with consumers, consumers are apt to judge all care they receive as being of high quality, and quality of care may not be a significant reason for choosing one provider over another.

Information

One health ombudsman noted that the bulk of complaints reaching her office has to do with the consumers' sense of receiving inadequate advance information about a service. More often, the problem concerns financial issues, but many other questions arise as well: Why did the strange consultant visit me in the hospital? Why did the "simple x-ray" take all day and hurt so much? What does my insurance cover? Why am I still so incapacitated if the operation was really a success? The doctrine of informed consent, properly observed, could answer some questions, but others will be answered only if providers and intermediaries are sensitive to patients' needs to be fully informed participants in their own care.

Most consumers are much less concerned about receiving information regarding how they can prevent illness by changing behavior. Many, for very understandable reasons, dislike being given information they do not wish to use.

Input

Few consumers are willing to take the time to become involved in trying to change the medical care system. Those who wish to work for change may be chronically ill or lack the ability to involve themselves effectively. Many would prefer to switch providers than to take the trouble to change the way service is delivered. Perhaps part of the problem is that consumer involvement is often an "all or none" phenomenon, demanding time or expertise. It may be that providers must develop new methods—"marketing techniques" in a real sense—that make consumer input easier.

Consumer Expectations Vary

Since consumers are not an amorphous mass but a group of unique individuals, the importance placed by consumers on the various factors of service will vary. The urban poor, all too familiar with bureaucratic clinical care, may place an extreme emphasis on access and humaneness; the dying are very likely to desire personal continuity; busy executives may accept an impersonal system that never keeps them waiting; the chronically ill may accept inconveniences in order to guarantee emergency care at all times. Any decision relating to what consumers want must, of necessity, refer back to who the consumers are. That is why the development of ongoing dialogues between consumers and providers is, in many ways, more important than static research into consumer attitudes.

In selecting and buying any product or service, there are two aspects to consider—benefits and cost. Three factors are considered in cost: money, time, and uncertainty.

COSTS OF HEALTH CARE SERVICES

Money

There are three main expenditures that health care consumers must consider: out-of-pocket costs, premium expenses, and taxes, in descending order of visibility to consumers. Those who are sick place a high value on minimizing out-of-pocket costs and a low value on premium expenses and taxes; those who are healthy have, for the most part, a reverse ordering of values. All consumers wish to avoid large, unpredictable out-of-pocket outlays for health care expenses, and, if they can afford it, many will purchase insurance to protect themselves against such outlays, even if this is not a "good buy" according to the economists. For example, half the people under Medicare have taken out policies that fill in the deductibles and coinsurance.[7]

Time

Consumers place different values on their time, depending usually on what else they want to do. For a small minority—the lonely, the chronically ill, some of the elderly—seeing the health care provider is a social event, a benefit in nonmonetary terms rather than a cost. Most consumers, on the other hand, would prefer not to spend their leisure time in the physician's office. Time comprises more than just the wait in the office and the minutes with the provider; it includes time spent finding out which medical care resources to use, making appointments, and getting to and from the health care providers.

Uncertainty

A final cost for consumers, which is difficult to translate into monetary terms, is uncertainty—not knowing "what is wrong with me, what will it cost, will I get better, whom do I talk to if I don't understand, did they really hear what I said, and will they respond appropriately?" Uncertainty applies to many of the factors already mentioned. It is particularly important as related to access and cost. Consumers want to know both whom to call in a perceived medical emergency and approximately what it will cost. These are not unreasonable demands to make on the medical care system, and yet they are often not met in practice.

Table 2 illustrates how consumers would rank these aspects of care.

Table 2 Importance of Ambulatory Medical Care Service Aspects to Customers

SERVICE ASPECT	IMPORTANCE TO MOST CUSTOMERS	NUMBER OF CUSTOMERS TO WHOM IT IS IMPORTANT
Access	high	most
Out-of-pocket cost	high	most
Humaneness	high	most
Episode information	high	most
Uncertainty	high	many
Privacy	high	some
Time	high and low	most
Quality	high	all
Continuity	low	few
Health information	low	few
Input	low and high	few
System cost	low	few

RESPONDING TO CONSUMER NEEDS

What can organizations do to ensure that they respond to consumer needs? Tables 3 and 4 illustrate what managers should look for and how key elements can be measured in better meeting consumer expectations for ambulatory care.

Suggestions for a Prepaid Group Practice

Here is what two organizations, a large midwestern prepaid group practice plan and an eastern teaching hospital, could do to better meet consumer expectations for ambulatory care. For the group practice plan:

- All plan members should know what access is regularly available to them for different types of ambulatory care. Standard waiting times for first and subsequent appointments and for waiting in the facility prior to receipt of service should be set and communicated periodically to each plan member. When longer waits are necessary because of unpredictability of staff, this should be communicated quickly to members who will be affected.

- Plan members should be informed that they are expected to indicate when standards of access are not being met and to make suggestions for improving access. Complaints should be welcomed, and information about complaint resolution should be regularly communicated to all members.

- When the organization cannot provide access according to program standards on a regular basis, plan members should be informed of the reasons and of programs being developed whereby the delivery system may be adjusted or the standards changed.

Suggestions for a Large Teaching Hospital

For the ambulatory services of a large teaching hospital, improved communications is the first priority:

- As much as possible, all costs should be made known to customers before receiving service. This should include an explanation of charges for ancillary services as well as the coverage provided by the most common insurance plans.

- Means for obtaining emergency care should be posted, as should methods of obtaining further information concerning after-hours service.

Table 3 Meeting Consumer Expectations of Ambulatory Care: Benefits of Service

SERVICE ASPECT	WHAT TO LOOK FOR	HOW TO MEASURE IT
Access	Customers can get into the system when they expect service.	Availability of general physicians for new patients; waiting time for first and subsequent visits.
Humaneness	Staff are polite and warm; they smile and listen.	Satisfaction questionnaires; patient letters of appreciation or criticism; observation on rounds.
Privacy	Privacy of examining facilities (sight and sound); adequate systems for confidentiality of records.	Testing the system by "dummy" patients; observation on rounds.
Continuity	Adequate integrated record system for all parts of the institution, transfer forms between institutions; low staff turnover.	Audit of record system for continuity; requirements for adequate information in transfer records; staff turnover rates.
Quality	All customers receive service which they perceive to be of adequate quality; key staff officials are held accountable for quality.	Satisfaction questionnaires; formal accountability of key officials; focus on key areas which need improvement and periodic measurement of progress.
Information	Customer receives adequate and accurate information on availability and cost of service; providers explain diagnosis and therapy to patients.	Interview with sample of customers; observation of providers by peers.
Input	Growth in demand for services; positive feedback on service delivery.	Interviews with sample of customers; market surveys to improve services; organized advisory groups.

Table 4 Meeting Consumer Expectations of Ambulatory Care: Costs of Services

SERVICE ASPECT	WHAT TO LOOK FOR	HOW TO MEASURE IT
Money	Price charged for the services is competitive with alternative sources of supply; customers understand in advance what services cost and the extent to which insurance covers the fee.	Identification of characteristics of customers served and comparisons of fees with alternate providers; patient satisfaction questionnaires; signs and handouts concerning financial policy; credit arrangements as appropriate.
Time	Amount of time the customer waits prior to receiving service should be no greater than that for other personal services; total time in the facility per diagnosis or treatment should be competitive with alternate providers.	Regular audit of waiting time and of total time in facility for key "package" of services; periodic comparison with other facilities.
Uncertainty	First contact person informs the customer of what he can expect during his first visit to the facility and as desired during subsequent visits; the provider should do likewise during each episode of care.	Interviews with a sample of customers; adequate clerical supervision related to basic standards of behavior; observation of providers by peers.

- Lack of continuity should be minimized where possible; when physicians change, prior treatment plans should be continued without repeating unnecessary tests and procedures.

- A joint consumer/provider board should be developed to hear complaints and monitor their resolution.

Suggestions for Third Party Payers

Insurance agencies (third party agencies), both public and private, can also make a vital contribution to meeting consumer expectations of ambulatory care. Many of the areas mentioned as presenting problems to customers are profoundly influenced by the means of payment. No effort on the part of health care providers can be completely successful as long as an impersonal, unresponsive, and bureaucratic insurance agent mediates between providers and patients. For third party agencies, the priorities are:

- Clear, readable information regarding benefits and exclusions should be made available to all covered persons.

- Simple mechanisms should be communicated to those covered if they wish to file a grievance with a clear-cut definition of the time frame and manner in which the insurers must respond.

- A sampling of customer preferences should be used by government and private insurers (and group purchasers) in the development of new benefits and the alteration of current benefits programs.

Need for Taking Consumer into Account

The common themes of these suggestions are easily apparent. Customers should be told a great deal more about the services they have bought or may buy. Health care providers and third party agencies should take customer preferences more directly into account in the development and delivery of medical care service and reimbursement plans related to such services.

Governmental support is essential. On the one hand, individual organizations will need research and development funds if they are to develop innovative methods for improving provider/consumer relations. On the other hand, the government is itself an active participant in health care delivery and must take the lead in ensuring that even massive federal insurance programs have mechanisms for responsiveness to consumer preferences.

Health care is one of the most personal human services. Humane, individualized medical treatment *is* possible, even under a system of national insurance, as long as the customers' viewpoints help to determine how that system works.

REFERENCES

1. See, for example, PL 89-749 and PL 93-222.

2. Stratmann, W.C. "A Study of Consumer Attitudes About Health Care: The Delivery of Ambulatory Services." *Medical Care* 13 (July 1975): 537-548.

3. Kindig, D.A., and Sidel, V.W. "Impact of National Health Insurance Plans on the Consumer." In *National Health Insurance*, edited by R.D. Eilers and S. Moyerman, pp. 15-61.

4. Sheps, C.G., and Madison, D.L. "Evaluation of Neighborhood Health Centers." Report for the Office of Economic Opportunity. Washington, D.C. Mimeographed.

5. Stratmann, W.C., et al. "A Study of Consumer Attitudes about Health Care: the Control, Cost and Financing of Health Services." *Medical Care* 13 (August 1975): 659-688.

6. Aday, L.A., and Anderson, R. *Access to Medical Care*. Ann Arbor, Mich.: Health Administration Press, 1975.

7. Ball, R. *Implications of Guaranteeing Medical Care*. Washington, D.C.: National Academy of Sciences, 1974, p. 39.

Section Six

Perspectives on Finance

This final section on finance presents some additional complexities facing the health care manager. As in the preceding section, the same dirge of difficult times for health providers is echoed in these articles. Vraciu and Griffith ("Cost Control Challenge for Hospitals") underscore one more time that the "fat" years are over. Does any manager really remember them?

The difficulties of finance and financial management are a day-to-day concern. Yet, nowhere is the more long-term macroproblem more clearly presented than in the article by Long and Silvers ("Health Care Reimbursement Is Federal Taxation of Tax-Exempt Providers"). This article elaborates on an earlier concern voiced by David Ricardo, the English economist: "Taxation under every form presents but a choice of evils." It is disconcerting to realize the existence of the subliminal form of taxation described in this article. Moreover, as the authors note, not-for-profit organizations do not have the risk reduction options of carrying back/forward losses. Calculations aside, the thrust of this article relates directly to the earlier piece in Section 3 by Silvers ("Identity Crisis: Financial Management in Health"). Managers must be cognizant of this subliminal tax code and incorporate its implications within the framework of an integrated financial management system.

As we have noted, recognition of this subliminal tax system is disconcerting. The second article by Cleverley ("Cost/Volume/Profit Analysis in the Hospital Industry"), however, suggests additional aspects for close attention by managers. Cleverley describes one of the more conceptually simplistic but relevant approaches in financial planning—break-even analysis. It is essential for a health organization to recognize that only the patient who pays full charges contributes to break-even and a positive cash flow. Recognition of this aspect of break-even analysis is of particular importance in pricing

309

decisions. Initially, one might consider Cleverley's point about full-paying customers to be obvious. Note the study, which is cited in his article, conducted among 22 hospitals. None of these institutions accounted for their two different types of customers. As a result, the break-even is severely understated. Break-even analysis, while conceptually simple and mathematically easy, requires both good marketing research (which develops accurate forecasts) and detailed accounting procedures (which can correctly allocate fixed and variable costs). As organizations add new services, consider prepaid alternatives, or try to reverse existing charges, the break-even approach should be an integral component of the financial management framework.

A changing environment, a repressive tax system, two classes of customers—how can these elements be managed? The article by Boldt describes a way of handling these complexities. Financial management encompasses the planning for and utilization of cash. Yet for managers to be able to do this effectively, they must be able to play the "what if" game. Recall this use described in Section 4 by Roberts and Hirsch ("Strategic Modeling for Health Care Managers"). In modeling terminology, we might call this sensitivity analysis. Managing in any organizational setting necessitates an ongoing understanding of the environment or, as termed earlier, the "industrial dynamics."

Boldt suggests several alternative computer models for making financial projections. One should recognize the natural linkage between finance and marketing that is built into these financial models. The general model presented in Boldt's article discusses the addition of a new facility, while the budget model posits a scenario based on projected patient days. Marketing research and subsequent forecasting models must be developed in order to create these financial models. Again, the integration of decisions in functional areas is obvious. Turn back to the article by MacStravic in Section 4 ("Resource Requirements for Health Care Organizations") for a detailed discussion of forecasting techniques and accuracy considerations.

Modeling is an effective, useful exercise. It forces the participants to think through the interactions of their decisions. This process alone can help develop a more insightful managerial decision process. This text has presented several such computer oriented models other than Boldt's. For example, in Section 3, review Silvers' conceptual model in Figure 1 of Chapter 10. Complicated, yes! Complete, maybe not? Any model, computer-based or conceptual, needs to have every box, equation, assumption, and parameter closely examined. Does the relationship make sense? Is it sequential? Do cause and effect actually exist? Not all answers will be available. But the procedure should be conducted to force close inspection of the process. Then, upon completion of an organization model, strategies can be intelligently specified.

Specific strategies in light of one financial model are presented in the next to last article by Vraciu and Griffith ("Cost Control Challenges for Hospitals"). Reduction alternatives under MAI formula are described along with their potential results. As the authors note, the key objective is to reduce cost increases without a reduction in service quality. At this point, we recognize the complexity of this task. For we must ask, "Quality as defined by which groups?" Short-term reductions presented by Vraciu and Griffith focus on reducing employee benefits. But, recall the earlier discussion in Section 5 on perspectives on marketing. If we view employees as a market, haven't we reduced quality? Tougher contract negotiation is recommended, along with greater production efficiency. Review Hughes's finding in one organization of the nurses' desire for a patient-care team strategy. Operationalizing this need within that organization led to reduced turnover. This program improved efficiency by diminishing the need for new recruiting efforts, training costs, and so on. Again, we can see the marketing-finance interface in planning. As a final offering, Vraciu and Griffith pose volume reduction as a cost-control strategy. One could term this a "demarketing" approach with very positive financial implications. That is, discourage the use of inpatient facilities among certain groups. This message is similar in many respects to Rynne's caution in Section 5 against a continual growth philosophy ("The Third Stage of Hospital Long Range Planning: The Marketing Approach").

Regardless of the specific strategies, the implications are clear. Tighter times require a better understanding of the hospital environment. Not-for-profit seems to be a meaningless distinction if subliminal taxation is one element of the definiton. Cost reimbursement effects clearly must be recognized in pricing strategies. Computer models may aid in deciphering the interactions for sound fiscal strategies.

To end this text, what article could be more appropriate than Neuhauser's contribution, "The *Really* Effective Health Service Delivery System." Has he provided us with the ultimate macromodel for health care managers? Are the modeling approaches and demarketing strategies inappropriate for health providers? Is Neuhauser a thorn in the side of the philosophy or approach in this text, or should we, in the final analysis, agree that the present system is best? Most of the articles presented suggest that "the system we all know and love" (to quote Neuhauser) is no longer in our control. Budget constraints are realities, planning is a necessity; but recognize that the need for health services will never be eliminated.

21. Medicare Reimbursement Is Federal Taxation of Tax-Exempt Providers

HUGH W. LONG and J.B. SILVERS

Adapted from Long, Hugh W., and Silvers, J.B. "Health Care Reimbursement is Federal Taxation of Tax-Exempt Providers." *Health Care Management Review,* Winter 1976.

"The marvel of all history is the patience with which men and women submit to burdens unnecessarily laid upon them by their governments."—William Edgar Borah, on the floor of the U.S. Senate

What U.S. economic unit is often subject to the highest rate of federal income taxation? An industrial corporation? A multitentacled conglomerate? A millionaire in the maximum 70 percent personal income tax bracket? No—it is the provider of acute inpatient care: the private, voluntary, not-for-profit or investor-owned hospital delivering a high percentage of its services to individuals who, through third parties, particularly Medicare intermediaries, pay less than full charges for those services. In the health care industry, many institutions face effective taxation rates in excess of 90 percent of full revenue less expenses. These high tax rates are the direct result of a reimbursement system that pays less than full charges for service delivered in the form of payment on the basis of "allowable costs" or at less than 100 percent of charges.

The actual tax impact of a less-than-full-charge reimbursement system on an institution depends on

- the varying administration of the Medicare program by different intermediaries,

- the extent to which the state programs and private group insurance plans such as Blue Cross pay less than full charges, and

- the proportion of total care delivered to consumers covered by cost-based or discount-from-charges reimbursement contracts.

Such variation aside, a conceptual understanding of these taxation impacts is crucial for resource allocation and financing decisions made by all health care administrators. Every policy analyst or operating manager must understand this mechanism, whether the task at hand is a national health priority or the formulation of operating strategies for an individual health-care institution or program. Further, where taxation exists, tax-type incentives to minimize taxation must also exist. They are present under our current, primarily cost-based system and they will be present in one form or another under a prospective reimbursement system, a network of maximum reimbursement limitations, or any other sort of price control system.

The basic federal reimbursement system and its impact on decision making by health providers lie at the heart of the problems. Unlike earlier years when financial considerations were relatively secondary, today's milieu of tightening fiscal controls and the squeeze on availability of funds require the manager to incorporate actively these fiscal factors into the decision-making process in order to survive, let alone prosper. So, leaving national health policy where it belongs—in the hands of legislators, regulators, and other public decision makers—we should identify the important elements of *any* reimbursement system, which, in turn, will largely determine whether national health policy will be implemented in a manner consistent with stated goals.

THE TAX-PAYING CORPORATION

To understand the tax-like aspect of a less-than-full-charge reimbursement system, compare it to a tax-paying business corporation. Table 1 provides a simplified income statement for a hypothetical corporation over three periods. Revenue is a function of price and volume. For each additional unit sold, total revenue goes up by the amount of the unit price. Cost, on the other hand, reflects total fixed cost, which is independent of volume, and total variable cost, which is a multiple of the number of units sold. Finally, net income (or profit) after tax is the excess of revenue over cost (expenses) reduced by the required tax payment, calculated here at a rate of 45 percent for purposes of illustration, although the current federal corporate income tax rate is 48 percent.

Part (a) of Figure 1 shows corporate income and what the operating results would be if there were no taxes to be paid. By contrast, Part (b) presents the same situation under federal income taxation: The profit is cut by the 45 percent tax rate, but the loss is reduced by 45 percent as well. This results from the provision of the tax code that allows corporations either to carry back losses against prior profits, thus restating reported taxable income in earlier years, or to carry them forward as an offset against future profits. As long as

Table 1 Volume, Revenue, and Cost For a Tax-paying Corporation (Nonhealth Care)

	Period		
	1	**2**	**3**
Unit Volume (000)	90	100	115
Total Revenue $100unit	$9,000	$10,000	$11,500
Fixed cost*	6,000	6,000	6,000
Variable Cost $40unit	3,600	4,000	4,600
Total Cost	$9,600	$10,000	$10,600
Net Income (Loss) Before Tax	(600)	0	900
Less: Tax Payment (Refund) at 45%	(270)**	0	405
Net Income (Loss) After Tax	$ (330)	$ 0	$ 495

*Including interest and depreciation charges.

**IRS (Department of Treasury) regulations allow for tax refunds against taxes paid during the immediately preceding three tax years, or alternatively, a tax credit carried forward for up to five years.

there were profits made and taxes paid in prior periods, the government will cushion the net loss by actually providing a cash refund to the tax-paying corporation. In the absence of prior years' profits, the firm has the option of carrying forward the tax loss and offsetting it against future profits, thereby paying a lower tax in succeeding periods. The economic philosophy expressed in this mechanism is that, due to the loss, income over the *total* period, including both loss and profit years, would be "overtaxed" were it not for the

Figure 1 Taxable Corporate Revenue and Expenses (Breakeven Chart) Under 0% and 45% Income Rates

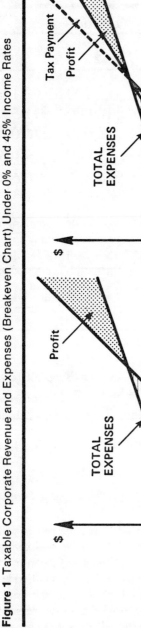
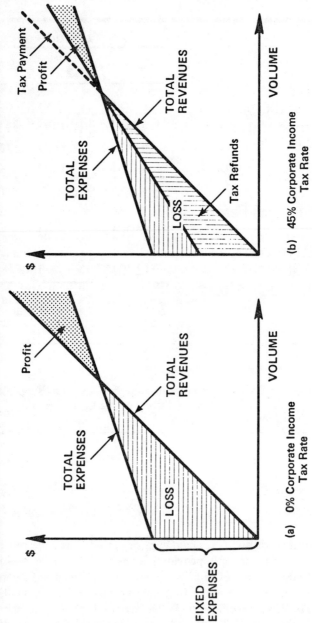

refund or future tax loss carry-forward. This provision of the tax code is important and will come up again as we dig deeper into our subject.

The balance sheet of our hypothetical tax-paying corporation is shown in Table 2. It reflects some important consequences of the growth in its volume or output over the three periods of operation. Aside from its normal business activity, the firm must meet its needs for additional working capital, new fixed assets, tax payments, and debt repayments.

Focusing on the working capital requirements, note in Table 2 that current assets and current liabilities rise as a result of the increasing volume in the normal course of business. The initial source that finances the increase in current assets is the increase, if one exists, in current liabilities. During our hypothetical firm's second period, $60,000 of the $300,000 increase in current assets is financed by the increase in current liabilities. The excess of $240,000 is the increase in *net* working capital—equal to the *change* in current assets less current liabilities from the beginning to the end of the period—and is particularly important, since it is this change that requires additional financing from an operational or outside source. Part of this growth financing is typically provided by flows from operations that are retained internally by the corporation rather than being paid out as dividends to the stockholders. The remaining financing comes from external sources of capital, often debt suppliers.

TAXES AND DECISION MAKING

Let us now consider some of the impacts of the tax system on the decision-making process of the corporation. For example, in the absence of income taxes, the corporation would require an *additional* $270,000 in new debt in Period 1 ($5,430,000 instead of $5,160,000), which is exactly the amount of the tax refund in that period. Conversely, if there were no income taxes in Period 3, $40,000 of debt principal could be retired rather than $365,000 of new debt being added, the difference reflecting the $405,000 tax actually paid at that time, so that external capital needs relate dollar-for-dollar to income tax flows.

Looking further, income taxation also has a detrimental impact on new investment. Consider a $1,000 investment outlay that results in a decrease in cash costs of $200 per year. The net effect of this cash saving alone is to increase the cash available to the firm by $200 each year if no income taxes are due. With taxes, however, this cash saving, by itself, reduces to only $110 per year—$200 savings less 45 percent tax payment. Taxes obviously make all investments less attractive.

Table 2 Balance Sheet for Tax-Paying Corporation

	Start of Period 1	End of Period 1	End of Period 2	End of Period 3
Current Assets Including Inventory, Accounts Receivable, Etc. (30% of Revenue)*	$ 2,700	$ 2,700	$ 3,000	$ 3,450
Plant and Equipment (Net)	$12,000	$12,000	$12,000	$12,500
Total Assets	$14,700	$14,700	$15,000	$15,950
Current Liabilities Including Accounts Payable (15% of Total Cost)*	$ 1,440	$ 1,440	$ 1,500	$ 1,590
Debt	$ 4,830	$ 5,160	$ 5,400	$ 5,765
Net Worth	$ 8,430	$ 8,100	$ 8,100	$ 8,595
Total Liabilities & Capital	$14,700	$14,700	$15,000	$15,950

*These ratios and other similar relationships are chosen to be representative of many businesses.

However, the analysis cannot stop here since there are additional cash-flow implications arising from the noncash charges associated with an investment—the most important being depreciation. Table 3 outlines the combined impact of cash savings and depreciation for our hypothetical $1,000 investment. You can see that, with taxes, the decrease in after-tax cash savings is offset to some degree by the reduction in taxes due to the deductibility of depreciation charges. This effective reduction is often referred to as a "depreciation tax subsidy." Noncash charges such as depreciation are very important in preserving cash for the tax-paying corporation. Depreciation is a critical factor in cash-flow generation and therefore in the investment decision-making process. On the other hand, in the absence of taxes, depreciation would be meaningless, since it would have no effect on actual cash flow.

Financing costs are also affected in an important way by the tax system. This impact is fairly straightforward. For instance, the additional 10 percent interest payment before tax means that taxable profits are reduced by the amount of the interest, and so taxes are reduced. The result in our example is that 45 percent of the interest payment is offset by reduction in taxes due; the net cost to a tax-paying corporation of 10 percent debt is only 5.5 percent after taxes are paid and the effect of the government's interest tax subsidy is felt. This factor obviously increases the relative desirability of debt financing.

The income tax system has a large operational impact on U.S. corporations in determining their general business strategy. Most obvious, perhaps, is the encouragement given to certain tax-favored business activities. For instance, the investment tax credit for specific classifications of new investment allows a direct reduction in corporate taxes and therefore provides very large incentives for the corporation to make qualifying purchases of productive assets. Accelerated depreciation has a similar impact by reducing taxes in the early years of the ownership of an asset, therefore increasing near-term cash flow. The tax system also encourages other sorts of behavior, such as exploration for new mineral and petroleum resources through depletion allowances, worker training through certain tax credits, particular plant location by establishing certain tax havens (such as Puerto Rico), philanthropic endeavors by allowing contributions as tax-deductible expenses, and so forth.

Finally, the tax system has an important influence on corporate risk-taking. Since losses can be cushioned by the tax carry-back/carry-forward provisions, corporations may be more inclined to undertake risky activities resulting in either large gains or losses. Risky ventures may be further encouraged by the fact that capital gains, in contrast to ordinary operating income, are taxed at a lower rate, while capital losses sometimes can be used to reduce taxes at the higher ordinary tax rate. The point is simply that the tax system has a major impact on corporate behavior in terms of investments, financing, operational strategy, and risk-taking.

Table 3 Impact of a $1,000 Investment on Tax-Paying Corporation

	0% Tax Rate		45% Tax Rate	
	Accounting Statement	Impact On Cash Account	Accounting Statement	Impact on Cash Account
Investment Outlay	(1,000)	(1,000)	(1,000)	(1,000)
Yearly Income & Cash Flow Effects:				
Reduction in Cash Cost (i.e. Labor)	200	200	200	200
Increase in Depreciation Expense ($1,000 investment ÷ 10 year life)	100	0	100	0
Increase in Profit Before Tax	100	0	100	0
Increase in Tax Payment	0	0	100	(45)
Increase in Profit After Tax	100	0	55	0
Increase in Cash Available per Year		+200		+155

"TAXING" THE NONPROFIT PROVIDER

What, then, is the relevance of discussing the tax-paying corporation? After all, isn't the typical provider of health care a not-for-profit, income-tax-exempt, voluntary corporation? Unfortunately we will see that an income tax by any other name is still an income tax, even if that other name is something so complex as "a third party reimbursement contract providing for payments that are less than full charges." Here again, we are working with the same numerical example we developed for the tax-paying corporation—the same unit and total dollar volume, costs, and identical structure and amounts. As before, we assume away bad debts and other complexities. The differences are that our health care provider pays no income tax to the IRS and delivers 45 percent of all service to consumers covered by a Medicare cost-based reimbursement contract. We use pure cost-based reimbursement rather than cost-plus or charges-minus to keep the arithmetic simple. Similarly, we assume all costs are allowable—reimbursable by Medicare. We also assume for simplicity that the service rendered to the two payment categories is homogeneous throughout in variable cost. However, to the extent that reimbursement systems force the provider to calculate its percentage of cost-based volume by department rather than on an overall basis, it may be subject to as many equivalent "tax rates" as it has departments if cost-based service utilization varies by department. This has obvious and important impacts on decision making. For example, it may encourage different types of decisions in different areas of the institution or program, resulting in some unintended and undesirable effects.

Tables 4 and 5 present the health care provider's income statement for a volume level of 115,000 units, the level of our tax-paying corporation in Period 3 of its operation. Table 4 uses a standard format, which may be compared to Table 1, while Table 5 breaks out the statement for cost-based and charge-based service segments.

The basic concept of cost-based reimbursement produces a total net revenue quite unlike that of the tax-paying corporation. Here, net revenue is a function of stated charges, actual costs, and the volume mix by payment source—private insurance, Medicare, Medicaid, Blue Cross, self-pays, and so on, as well as the specific rules of each third party governing allowable cost. With our assumption that all accounting costs are allowable, the third party allowance, or discount, that defines the difference between gross and net revenue is relatively easy to calculate. If 45 percent of the provider's service volume is covered by third party reimbursers who pay on the basis of cost, then approximately 45 percent of the total cost will also be paid by them. Table 6 presents a provider's income statement as it often appears in hospital financial statements: revenue is calculated at full charges and the allowance

---

Table 4 Volume, Revenue, and Cost for a "Tax-Exempt" Health Care Provider

---

Unit Volume*	115,000
%of Service Delivered to Consumers Covered by Cost-Based Reimbursement Contracts (e.g. Medicare)	45%

		$(000)
Gross Revenues with Charges $100/unit consisting of:		
Service to Charge-Based Consumers (55% x 115 units x $100/unit)	$6,325	
Service to Cost-Based Consumers (45% x 115 units x $100/unit)	5,175	
		$11,500
Less: Third Party Allowances**		405
Net Revenues		$11,095
Fixed Cost***		$6,000
Variable Cost at $40/unit		4,600
Total cost (Expenses)		$10,600
Net Income (Excess of Revenues over Expenses)		$ 495

---

*For example, patient days.

**The allowance to third parties can be determined as the difference between full service charges for the 45 percent of unit volume covered by the third parties less the allowable cost of providing that service (i.e., 45 percent of total cost if all costs are allowable for reimbursement purposes). In this case, 45 percent of the $11,500 total full charge revenue ($5,175) less 45 percent of the $10,600 total cost ($4,770) gives the third party allowance of $405.

***Fixed cost includes interest and depreciation charges.

Table 5 Volume, Revenue, and Cost for a "Tax-Exempt" Health Care Provider (Restatement of Table 4)

	$(000)		
	45% Cost Based Portion	**55% Charge Based Portion**	**Total**
Units of Service	51,750	63,250	115,000
Gross Revenues at $100/unit	5,175	6,325	11,500
Less: Third Party Allowances*	405*	0*	405*
Net Revenue	4,770	6,325	11,095
Total Expenses	4,770	5,830	10,600
Net Income	$ 0	$ 495	$ 495

*The allowance to third parties represents the difference between their share of costs and their share of charges. It also can be calculated as the percentage of the gross margin of the provider (total gross revenue less total costs) attributable to service volume covered by the third parties.

(or discount) to cost-based third parties is subtracted from it to obtain the net revenue.

Ultimately, however, both the health care provider and the tax-paying corporation show "bottom lines" of $495,000, even though the former is income-tax-exempt. Or is it? In fact, it is not. The health care provider's $405,000 tax bill has been in the form of a withholding tax retained by the Social Security Administration's intermediary in contrast to the tax-paying corporation's check that is mailed to the Internal Revenue Service.

Table 6 Volume, Revenue, and Cost for an "Income-Tax-Exempt" Health Care Provider $(000)

	Provider A 0% Cost-Based Service			Provider B 45% Cost-Based Service		
	Period			Period		
	1	2	3	1	2	3
Unit Volume (thousands of patient days)	90	100	115	90	100	115
Total Revenue Full Charges ($100/unit)	$9,000	$10,000	$11,500	$9,000	$10,000	$11,500
Less: Third Party Allowances*	0	0	0	0	0	405**
Net Revenue..................	$9,000	$10,000	$11,500	9,000	$10,000	$11,095
Fixed cost	$6,000	$6,000	$6,000	$6,000	$6,000	$6,000
Variable Cost ($40/unit)	3,600	4,000	4,600	3,600	4,000	4,600
Total cost (Expenses)	$9,600	$10,000	$10,600	$9,600	$10,000	$10,600
Net Income (Loss)	$ (600)	$ 0	$ 900	$ (600)	$ 0	$ 495

*Under the "lower of costs or charges" rule, when the provider is functioning below breakeven volume, reimbursement is calculated at the lower average charge per unit of service level rather than at the higher average cost per unit of service level.

**As noted in Table 5, the amount of the third party allowance or discount is equal to the third party service proportion of total gross margin. Total gross margin is, of course, exactly the same as Income Before Taxes for the tax-paying corporation (See Table 1), and the percentage of service delivered to consumers covered by cost-based reimbursement contracts is an exact equivalent to the corporate income tax rate.

Table 7 Revenue and Cost for a "Tax-Exempt" Health Care Provider
(Restatement of Table 4)

	$(000)
Total Revenue at Full Charges	$11,500
Fixed Cost	6,000
Variable Cost	4,600
Total Cost	$10,600
Net Income before Allowance	900
Less: Third Party Allowance (45%)	405
Net Income	$ 495

ONE HUNDRED PERCENT TAX ON MARGIN

This withholding on third party allowance can be viewed as a 100 percent tax on the margin (excess of revenues over expenses) associated with cost-based services. Table 5 emphasizes the fact that all of the provider's net income is generated by charge-based service because of the cost-based services being subjected to the 100 percent tax rate. A 100 percent tax on 45 percent of the activity averaged with no tax on the remaining 55 percent of the provider's charge-based services results in an overall 45 percent effective tax rate.

Nevertheless, regardless of how it is presented and who administers it, a tax is a tax! Table 7 dramatizes this point by recasting the health care provider's income statement once more to look precisely like that of Period 3 in Table 1 for the tax-paying corporation. The effective income tax rate levied by the federal government against "tax-exempt" health care providers is approximately equal to that proportion of dollar volume of health services delivered to consumers under federal cost-based coverage. Hence, a provider delivering 80 percent of all services to cost-based consumers (as do a number of central-city, acute care hospitals) is, in effect, paying income tax at an 80 percent rate. Perhaps this provides a key insight into the health care financial crisis.

As if it were not enough that the "tax-exempt" health care sector is often subject to the highest rates on income taxation, other subtleties effectively increase the rate of taxation even further. One of these facets is illustrated if we expand our provider example to three time periods analogous to our original tax-paying corporation.

Table 6 shows our 45 percent, cost-based provider as Provider B over three periods embracing the same growth in volume across time shown in Table 1; and Provider A as delivering 0-percent, cost-based service, but also facing identical aggregate service growth, unit and total revenues, and total costs, including the same fixed and variable cost structure. As before, we continue to assume that all accounting costs are allowable for cost-based reimbursement and that total costs are homogeneous in each payment category.

Provider A's results over the three periods confirm that the absence of cost-based service is precisely equivalent to having no income taxes for the for-profit corporation depicted in Table 1. This is evident since Provider A's net income is exactly equal in all instances to Table 1's net income before tax.

Provider B, however, is less well off than our tax-paying corporation, even though both face an overall tax rate of 45 percent when above a break-even volume of 100 units. The difference occurs *below* break-even volume where Provider B runs into the common rule, used by Medicare, that allows reimbursement of only the *lower* of cost or charges and makes the hospital absorb the full loss if it operates below the break-even point. Note that below break-even, the institution, by definition, suffers losses, thus implying that average costs are greater than average charges. Unlike the tax-paying corporation, there is no carry-back of underreimbursement of prior costs to cushion the blow of current operating losses (and only limited carry-forward under Medicare). Thus, Provider B faces the worst of all possible worlds: high taxes when doing well and few or no subsidies when not.

Figure 2, parts (a) and (b), present graphically the numbers in Table 6. Part (c) of Figure 2 carries the cost-based phenomenon to its logical extreme.

In summary, then, a health care provider with 90 percent of its total dollar volume of service reimbursed on the basis of cost is *exactly* equivalent to a tax-paying corporation with a 90 percent tax rate having no loss carry-back or carry-forward provisions. What is the effect of this phenomenon on decision making by management?

DILEMMA OF HEALTH CARE DECISION MAKING

Not only does this system *look* the same as a tax system, it *is* the same—that is, it has an identical impact on managerial actions. For instance, the financing needs that were increased under a high tax rate for the corporation are also increased by a high level of cost-based reimbursement for the health care provider, assuming, of course, that the provider is able to keep its charges above its average cost. For many institutions in which this assumption may not hold, the tax-like impact is even more dramatic.

Table 8 provides balance sheets for Providers A and B in the same format as Table 2 to facilitate comparison with our tax-paying corporation. Both

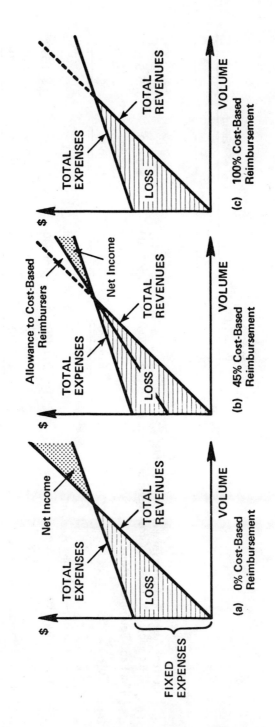

Figure 2 Tax-Exempt Hospital—Revenue and Expenses (Break-even Chart) With 0%, 45%, and 100% of Total Patient Volume Under Cost-Based Reimbursement

Table 8 Balance Sheet for Provider A   0% Cost-Based Service $(000)

	Start Period 1	End of Period 1	End of Period 2	End of Period 3
Current Assets including Inventory, Accounts Receivable, Etc. (30% of Gross Revenue)......	$ 2,700	$ 2,700	$ 3,000	$ 3,400
Plant and Equipment (Net)	12,000	12,000	12,000	12,500
Total Assets................	$14,700	$14,700	$15,000	$15,950
Current Liabilities including Accounts Payable (15% of total cost)	$ 1,440	$ 1,440	$ 1,500	$ 1,590
Debt................	4,830	5,430	5,670	5,630
Net worth (Funds Balance)	8,430	7,830	7,830	8,730
Total Liabilities and Capital	$14,700	$14,700	$15,000	$15,950

(Continued on next page)

Table 8 *Continued* Balance Sheet for Provider B   45% Cost-Based Service $(000)

	Start Period 1	End of Period		
		1	2	3
Current Assets including inventory, Accounts Receivable, Etc. (30% of Gross Revenue)............	$ 2,700	$ 2,700	$ 3,000	$ 3,450
Plant and Equipment (Net)	12,000	12,000	12,000	$12,500
Total Assets.....................	$14,700	$14,700	$15,000	$15,950
Current Liabilities including Accounts Payable (15% of total cost)	$ 1,440	$ 1,440	$ 1,500	$ 1,590
Debt............................	4,830	5,430	5,670	6,035
Net Worth (Funds Balance)............	8,430	7,830	7,830	8,325
Total Liabilities and Capital	$14,700	$14,700	$15,000	$15,950

providers must borrow $270,000 more in Periods 1 and 2 than the tax-paying corporation—in Period 1, $5,430,000 versus $5,160,000; in Period 2, $5,670,000 versus $5,400,000. B is just as bad off as A, since the presence of reimbursement taxation with no carry-back or carry-forward provisions does nothing to cushion the $600,000 loss experienced in Period 1. In Period 3, however, we discover a dismaying fact: *Provider B is in an economic situation which is worse than that of either Provider A or the tax-paying corporation.*

In Period 3, the tax-paying corporation pays its income taxes and sustains total debt of $5,765,000. Provider A, paying no income taxes and suffering no cost-based reimbursement, more than makes up for larger previous debt and is able to reduce debt outstanding to $5,630,000. Provider B, however, un-cushioned earlier in Period 1, must now in addition face the full impact of reimbursement taxation. The combination of not receiving the $270,000 cushion in Period 1, and having to pay effective taxes of $405,000 in Period 3, causes Provider B to top the debt levels of the other two corporations. At the end of Period 3, Provider B's outstanding debt is $6,035,000.

INVESTMENT DECISIONS

Another parallel between cost-based reimbursement and income tax impacts on managerial behavior is found by looking at the investment decision. Table 9 depicts the cash flow impact of a $1,000 cost-saving investment that is depreciated over a 10-year life and that results in a $200 reduction in cash costs as a result of efficiency increases. The results, not surprisingly, are exactly parallel to those for a similar investment reported in Table 3. A higher level of cost-based reimbursement decreases the cash impact of the cost reduction and increases the cash impact of the depreciation charge. At higher levels of cost-based reimbursement, all investments in equipment on a fixed depreciation schedule tend to look more and more alike to the health care manager, regardless of their actual impact on service volume or operating costs before reimbursement. In fact, at a 100-percent, cost-based reimbursement level, the only net cash flow to the institution from this cost-saving investment would come from depreciation reimbursement. Furthermore, the maximum amount of return a hospital could expect over the life of the equipment is simply recovery of the original cost as reimbursement is received for the annual depreciation. This has an important implication in an infla-tionary environment, as we will see in a moment.

It is also not surprising to discover that cost-based reimbursement's subsidy impact on financing costs is exactly the same as that of federal income tax. In particular, at the hypothetical 45-percent patient volume under cost-based reimbursement, a 10 percent interest rate is subsidized to look like only a 5.5

Table 9 Impact of Cost-Based Reimbursement on a $1,000 Investment By a Tax-Exempt Health Care Provider

	0% Cost Based		45% Cost Based	
	Accounting Statement	Impact on Cash Account	Accounting Statement	Impact on Cash Account
	($1000)	($1000)	($1000)	($1000)
Investment Outlay	($1000)	($1000)	($1000)	($1000)
Yearly Income and Cash Flow Effect				
Reduction in Cash Cost (i.e. Labor)	$200	$200	$200	$200
Increase in Depreciation Expense ($100 Investment: 10 year life)	(100)	0	(100)	0
Reduction in Total Allowable Cost	100	0	100	0
Decrease in Cost-Based Reimbursement	0	0	(45)	45
Increase in Net Income	$100		$55	
Increase in Cash Available		+ $200		+ $140

percent rate on an unreimbursed basis. At a 90 percent level of cost-based reimbursement, almost any interest rate, net of cost-based reimbursement, looks reasonable. Such a subsidy obviously has a tendency to encourage the use of debt. This, coupled with the rapid growth of the industry and its low overall margins, both of which inflate the financing need, makes it easy to understand why debt has grown so dramatically for health institutions during the last ten years.

COSTLY CREDIT RATING

Furthermore, the availability of this debt has largely been dependent on the cost-based reimbursement system itself, because that system has changed the nature of the income stream. It could be argued, for instance, that the debt capacity of health institutions has been increased substantially by the stability and certainty of payment from third party reimbursement sources. Obviously, there have been some exceptions to this rule due to payment delays, retrospective denial of allowed costs, or other forms of nonpayment, particularly evident in Medicaid, in some states. However, in general, lenders have been quite happy to advance debt funds to health institutions, not because of their excellent management or inherently solid fiscal prospects, but rather due to the good credit of Blue Cross, Aetna, the U.S. Government, and other payers. Debt suppliers are lending against the third party promises to pay. It is obvious, however, that, at some high level, an institution's debt must be regarded as excessive due either to the absolute dollar volume outstanding or to uncertainties about the ability or willingness of third party reimbursers to pay. In fact, with maximum cost reimbursement limitations, which are now appearing in legislation such as Public Law 92-603, there is no question that the debt capacity of health institutions will decrease.

INFLATION COMPOUNDS INFLATION

In the providers' balance sheets in Table 8, we looked at financing needs under cost-based reimbursement. In today's environment it is important to modify this approach to include the effects of inflation. Inflation induces an exceptionally large additional financing need for working capital—current assets less current liabilities—and for additional investment in fixed plant and equipment.

Table 10 illustrates this impact on working capital. A provider who starts out with no debt could find itself with debt growing to over one-sixth of its net worth (funds balance) within ten years under a simple assumption of 10 percent inflation and financial break-even (zero net income) and assuming no

Table 10 Impact of Inflation on Hospital Working Capital Needs

	Base Year	1	2	 10
Unit Volume (Patient Days)	100	100	100	100
Average Charge (with 10% inflation)	$100	$110	$121	$259
Average Cost (with 10% inflation)	$100	$100	$121	$259
Income Statement				
Total Revenue	$10,000	$11,000	$12,100	$25,900
Total Cost	10,000	11,000	12,100	25,900
Net Income	0	0	0	0
Balance Sheet				
Inventory, Accounts Receivable & Other Current Assets (at 30% of Total Revenue)	3,000	3,300	3,630	7,781
Plant & Equipment	12,000	12,000	12,000	12,000
Total Assets	15,000	15,300	15,630	19,781
Current Liabilities (15% of Costs)	1,500	1,650	1,815	3,891
Funds Balance (Net Worth)	13,500	13,500	13,500	13,500
Subtotal	15,000	15,150	15,315	17,391
External Debt Required	0	150	315	2,390
Total Liabilities & Capital	15,000	15,300	15,630	19,781

increase in actual patient volume. In the last three or four years, a large part of the difficulty of American hospitals, and American industry in general, has been a result of inflation-induced financing need in the absence of real growth.

The impact of inflation in the prices of plant and equipment can be even more dramatic. For instance, a piece of equipment that had a $100.00 original cost and lasts five years would have to be replaced with a new piece of equipment costing $161.05 if inflation were ten percent per year over the five year period (the price grows from $100.00 to $110.00 to $121.00 and, ultimately, to $161.05 by the fifth year). If inflation has been proceeding at a steady rate for some time (i.e., steady state has been reached), then each $1.00 of depreciation requires a substantially larger dollar amount of replacement investment just to keep the hospital at the same level of service. This assumes, of course, that the depreciation schedule for accounting purposes is approximately the same as the actual economic depreciation. If the equipment lasts a considerably shorter or longer time than is assumed for reimbursement purposes, then the inflation effect on financing need will be altered.

An example may help illustrate this. In Table 10, we considered a provider with a constant $12,000 depreciated productive asset base. Assume that steady-state inflation of 10 percent yearly has affected the replacement cost of all capital assets in the years leading up to the present. In this situation, the provider must also increase new fixed assets by 10 percent each year on the average, just to maintain the existing level of services. In year one, $1,200 of additional new money for capital expenditures must be found over and above the amount assumed to be reinvested in Table 10. Even worse, this incremental amount will itself increase by 10 percent in each subsequent year ($1,320 additional required in year two, $1,452 more in year three, etc.). Combining this with the figures in Table 10, the actual new debt required in one year by this provider becomes $1,350 rather than $150. By the tenth year, again with no real growth in patient volume, the external financing need would have grown to $21,516, in addition to the $10,000 supporting original assets. If this is all raised from borrowing, then debt begins to dwarf the nongrowing net worth, or funds base of $13,500, so that, at the end of year ten, the institution would have over 60 percent of its capital in the form of debt. Viewed another way, that is almost $1.60 in debt for each dollar of funds balance. All of this is for a provider that had no initial debt outstanding and is providing the same volume of service.

The magnitude of this debt accumulation is astounding. However, this phenomenon is basically what has happened over the last five to ten years in the U.S. health care industry. Fund balances, or net worth accounts, have grown very little in proportion to the growth in dollar value of assets. Net income retained and reinvested has been low, and philanthropy has not kept pace. As a result, a huge amount of additional debt financing has been required.

Inflation, besides increasing the cost of medical care to each person in the country, either directly through charges paid or indirectly through increased insurance premiums, has created extremely large financing demands on the health system. This is due in part to the inability of cost-based reimbursement to provide sufficient internal financing, thus forcing institutions to the capital markets. This has resulted in the issuance of an unprecedented amount of new debt. Probably no other industry in the country has undergone such a dramatic change in the composition of its financing over such a short period of time.

Some of the decision-making implications resulting from cost-based reimbursement effects are fairly clear. For instance, at high levels of cost-based reimbursement, such as a high "equivalent tax rate," there will be less emphasis on cost savings. It is easier for health care providers not to resist demands for new technology and new services since asset growth, which could include cost saving, quality improvement, or service expansion, tends to look the same in terms of its impact on depreciation reimbursement. There is little incentive for cutting or controlling cost.

Furthermore, when forced to cut costs under some sort of controls, there may be little incentive to cut service volume as a means of achieving this, since total revenue could well fall further than total cost. In addition, the institutional manager may not want to cut his investment plans, assuming financing is available, since these produce extra reimbursement through added depreciation. The likely place to cut costs is through reductions in the labor force, since such costs are a direct pass-through to the reimbursement source. Such a cut could have either of two results: First, it could lead to more efficiency through the greater use of capital equipment of a labor-saving nature. This sort of capital intensity has been seen recently in a number of service industries ranging from fast-food preparation to banking services and grocery checkouts. A reaction of this type could have a positive impact on quality of care and/or health care costs.

Alternatively, it would be easy to imagine a cut in nursing services without a parallel increase in compensating capital equipment or other efficiency-producing changes. This could produce lower quality of care. Even with additional automatic equipment, the quality of patient service may deteriorate under some sort of cost or price control.

Another major place where decision making may be influenced is in the area of working capital management. It may be more difficult for an institution to finance working capital than fixed plant and equipment. The latter produces depreciation, which generates a positive cash flow from reimbursement, while working capital has no parallel reimbursable noncash expense.

The cash flow from depreciation reimbursement can be used to obtain and to serve a high level of debt financing secured by fixed assets.

SHORT-CHANGED WORKING CAPITAL

On the other hand, working capital investments, although they are technically short-term in duration, actually will remain outstanding as long as the patient level stays at the same rate, thus producing an additional long-term financing need. Without something equivalent to depreciation to provide cash flow, an investment in working capital can never be recovered in the same way that an investment in fixed plant and equipment is recovered through depreciation over its life. The only source of ultimate repayment of a working capital loan is through net income retained, and for most hospitals that is very close to zero. As a result, one might expect managers to bias their decisions away from projects that require additional working capital and toward projects that involve financible fixed assets.

In a similar way, investments whose returns depend upon reimbursement by a slow-paying third party may be short-changed in favor of other projects that provide services to patients with more rapid-paying reimbursement sources. For instance, projects to improve the services to Medicaid recipients might be deferred since payment in many states is notoriously slow.

Another influence discussed briefly above has to do with the encouragement of debt financing. In particular, there is little reason to assume that managers would not continue to borrow up to the limits of availability as opposed to imposing some limitation on growth or service. This is certainly the course of least resistance. However, at some point less than 100 percent debt, lenders will decide that the institution in question has too much debt financing. This is where financing sources will become a real constraint of growth. Then the remaining options for management are either to strive for more efficiency or simply to let quality drop to meet the demands. In addition, the implications of regional or institutional planning dictated by the capital markets rather than by planning agencies may or may not be a good idea. In fact, all government planning efforts could conceivably be ineffectual in the face of the discipline of more efficient capital markets refusing to fund some projects while providing financing for others.

CORPORATE SHELLS

Finally, the present reimbursement system may encourage organizational forms to take advantage of this system. The time honored principle of tax benefits flowing to the party to whom they are most valuable will certainly have a parallel in the health system. Cost will be allocated to the participant in the system who has the maximum reimbursement advantage. The interaction between reimbursement considerations for the provider and tax considerations for the lender will increasingly play a part in organizational decision making and structure. If this legitimate economic goal is recognized by all parties involved, then there should be no damage done. On the other hand, this economic behavior may encourage the formation of health care corporate shells that are cost-based reimbursed but that contract all activities out to independent suppliers of goods and services. The implication is that a positive net income could be captured by the independent suppliers of services (ranging from management to food to pharmacy to laundry to nursing), and the profit of these contractors would become a part of the cost base of the shell provider.[2] Thus, the health system would be able to capture needed net income to finance growth and provide incentives for investment while the central hospital would always be at breakeven. Such behavior might not necessarily be evil at all, but simply the response to a lack of alternative economic incentives and financing sources.

IMPLICATIONS FOR NATIONAL HEALTH POLICY

In order to see the advantages of any sort of reimbursement system, one must first acknowledge the tax aspects of the system. As stated at the outset, all reimbursement systems will have some tax-like impacts on the behavior of the institutional decision maker. Once this is acknowledged, it can then be used as a positive economic incentive. Rather than curse institutional managers who find ways to get around the intent of regulators, planners, and policy makers, the natural economic incentives to the manager can be used to fulfill national policy goals set at a high government level.

Along with recognizing the tax aspects of this system, some simple things, such as allowing carry-back and carry-forward provisions like those of the U.S. corporate income tax code, would have important impacts in cushioning providers in economic downturns or retrenchment periods. In effect, this means that the provision for payment on the *lower* of cost or charges should be eliminated in favor of a pure cost-based system. It is simply inequitable to restrict prices greatly, to force institutions into volume levels below breakeven, and *then* to reimburse them on the basis of their artificially low prices.

An effective national health policy will also have to recognize the legitimate capital need of providers that are now funded by debt. In the face of their dwindling unused debt capacity, if there is any inflation at all, continued financing for plant, equipment, and working capital is essential, even at constant levels of service and quality. This can be done through the allowance of some level of net income and retention of margin. Alternatively, it may be necessary to create better advance payment systems for reimbursement to include, perhaps, payment even *before* service is rendered; or a depreciation equivalent for working capital may be the answer.

Finally, once the system is recognized for what it is, policy makers and regulators can actively manage this "tax code" to encourage whatever health policy is deemed appropriate. This is a vital point, since, if this "code" is *not* managed, it may simply evolve randomly as the result of independent regulations written by SSA or HEW, interspersed with court decisions resulting from provider litigation. However, as is implied above, regulators, by incorporating incentives parallel to the tax system, could encourage, for instance,

- capital investment which would lower costs while maintaining quality;
- certain types of treatment, such as outpatient modes;
- location decisions—inner-city or rural; and
- worker training—M.D., Medex, nursing, and so forth.

All of these types of incentives have existing parallels in the federal tax code.

MEETING NATIONAL HEALTH CARE NEEDS

The fact that the U.S. health care industry faces higher effective federal income taxation than any other economic sector need not necessarily lead to the conclusion that the system places an impossible burden on providers or reflects evil intentions of policy makers or private third parties. Properly developed, with open recognition of reimbursement systems as the taxation codes that they are, there is obvious potential for third-party payment mechanisms to solve, or at least to serve as an equitable tool to address the health care needs of the nation. For better or worse, the reimbursement system, with or without conscious forethought, will have an important impact on what health care is delivered by what kind of provider to what segment of the population. Internal provider decision making can be attuned to national goals with careful system design. The potential for such design exists. Whether or not it will take place remains in question.

REFERENCES

1. In general, if i is the interest rate charged by debt-suppliers, T is the income tax rate, and C is the proportion of health service delivered under cost-based reimbursement, the effective cost of debt is given by the following expressions:

Tax-paying nonhealth corporation .... $i\,(1-T)$
Tax-exempt health provider .... $i\,(1-C)$

And for the investor-owned provider of health care who gets to be taxed twice, once by SSA and once by IRS, the effective cost of debt is i $(1-T-C+TC)$.

2. Certain interpretations of somewhat ad hoc Internal Revenue Service, Medicare, and Medicaid regulations would make achieving this extreme situation rather difficult. However, the national tendency is clearly to move in this direction, and specific instances very close to the extreme already exist and are receiving "cost-based" reimbursement where provider cost includes suppliers' contracted profit.

22. Cost/Volume/Profit Analysis in the Hospital Industry

WILLIAM O. CLEVERLEY

Cleverley, William O. "Cost/Volume/Profit Analysis in the Hospital Industry." *Health Care Management Review,* Summer 1979.

The use of marginal analysis (or cost/volume/profit analysis) in general industry is extremely widespread. It has been used to provide relevant information for a variety of decisions. Among these are selecting product lines, pricing individual products, developing marketing strategies, and using facilities. In short, marginal analysis has proven to be a powerful method of analyzing and improving profitability in many firms.

Simply stated, marginal analysis involves studying the interrelationships between prices, variable costs, fixed costs, and volume to aid management decision making. A key relationship is the difference between product price and per unit variable costs, or the so-called contribution margin. In situations of unrestrained resource availability, profit-maximizing decision makers will elect to produce all the product that they can as long as their marginal revenue (MR) exceeds their marginal cost (MC). Most accounting textbooks assume both linear revenue and cost functions. This implies that price is equal to MR and variable cost is equal to MC. With limited resources, profit-maximizing decision makers will select those products for market expansion with the highest contribution margins. By so doing, total profit is maximized.

Marginal analysis has not been used extensively, if at all, in the hospital industry for at least two reasons. First, profitability has not been a major concern for the large number of nonprofit hospitals. The primary objective for those institutions has been the delivery of needed services at a high quality level to the community. However, increasing fiscal pressures on hospitals have radically changed the orientation and involvement of hospital administrators in the financial area. To the extent that financing, be it from operations or other sources, is not sufficient to meet normal plant replacement and expansion needs, reductions in both services and quality are necessitated.

This changed economic equivalent has forced hospital administrators and financial managers to pay increasing attention to the profitability aspects of hospital operations.

Second, the methodology and formulas used in marginal analysis for general industry were recognized as being inappropriate for hospital profitability analysis. Specifically, the criticism is directed at the nature of the marginal revenue function. In general industry, marginal revenue is usually defined as a constant, namely the price or charge for the product or service. In the hospital industry, marginal revenue is more complex because of the existence of two major types of purchasers. One class of purchasers pays charges or posted prices while another class pays cost. Since price and cost are not usually identical, the amounts paid are not identical for the two purchaser groups. Furthermore, the rate paid by the cost purchaser group is not constant over various ranges of output because of the existence of fixed cost. As volume expands, the rate paid by cost payers declines because the fixed costs are spread over more units.

Although the formulas used in general industry for marginal analysis are inappropriate for hospital industry, these formulas can be adapted for hospital use.

REVENUE/COST RELATIONSHIPS IN THE HOSPITAL INDUSTRY

The first step in this development is to define formally the total cost (TC) function of a hospital or one of its departments (see Table 1). The next step is to define the revenue functions, both gross patient revenue (GPR) and net patient revenue (NPR) (see Table 2).

Table 1 Calculation of Total Cost Functions of a Hospital or One of Its Departments

$$TC = F + V \times Q \dotfill [1]$$

where:
TC = Total cost function
F = Level of fixed costs for the period
V = Variable cost per unit of output or service
Q = $Q_c + Q_{ch}$
Q_c = Number of cost-paying units
Q_{ch} = Number of charge-paying units

Table 2 Calculation of Gross Patient Revenue and Net Patient Revenue

$$GPR = P \times Q \dots\dots\dots\dots\dots\dots\dots\dots\dots\dots [2]$$

$$NPR = GPR - \text{Contractual adjustments} - \text{Allowance for bad debts} - \text{Allowance for charity care}$$

$$= P \times Q - \left[P \times Q_c - \frac{Q_c \times TC}{Q} \right] - CHAR \times P \times Q_{ch}$$

$$= P_n Q_{ch} + \frac{TC}{Q} \times Q_c. \dots\dots\dots\dots\dots\dots\dots [3]$$

where:

GPR	=	Gross patient revenue
NPR	=	Net patient revenue
P	=	Gross price or rate charged per unit of service
$CHAR$	=	Average percentage write-off for charity care and bad debts for charge-paying patients.
P_n	=	Net amount realized on the average for charge-paying patients $(1-CHAR)P$.

In Equation 1 (Table 1), total cost is represented as a linear cost function with a fixed and variable cost parameter. For short periods of time, one year or less, this linear representation has been found to be quite accurate, especially at the hospital department level. The GPR function, shown as Equation 2 in Table 2, simply defines the calculations performed to determine GPR, which is an account required in all audited hospital financial statements. It is a measure of overall activity, ignoring the implications of patient payment mix.

Net patient revenue, shown as Equation 3 in Table 2, adjusts GPR for deductions that must be made in the computation of income from operations or net patient income. There are two major deductions from GPR that must be made to arrive at NPR, the amount of monies actually realized by the hospital. The allowance for contractual adjustments is in most cases the difference between the rates billed to cost payers and the actual cost of the services. Actual cost of services to cost payers is represented in Equation 3 as the average total cost *(TC/Q)* times the number of cost patient units billed *(Q_c)*. There is an implicit assumption in this equation that rates for all services are set at levels higher than their anticipated average total cost. If they were not, the effective rate paid by many third parties, Medicare included, would be the posted price or rate. This is the so-called "lower of costs or charges". rule. In many cases, a cost payer, such as Medicare, Medicaid, or Blue Cross, may reimburse ancillary departments based on the ratio of charges to charges times cost. If the department has only one unit of service for which it bills or if its price markups are uniform in multiple service departments, the formulation in Equation 3 is accurate. However, in a situation of a multiple service department with unequal price markups, this formulation may not be totally accurate. There is no simple solution to this problem, but Equation 3 should still be useful, especially when contrasted with current methodology.

The second major deduction from GPR is for charity care and bad debts usually incurred on self-pay patients. In some cases, writeoffs may be made for patients with insurance who have significant copayment or deductible provisions. In almost all cases, the patients are charge payers. While Medicare does have a deductible and copayment provision, Medicare reimburses the provider for any bad debts incurred for Medicare patients. However, Medicare does not reimburse bad debts for patient services that are not covered. For calculation purposes, these service units would be treated as charge units of service because the individual patient is responsible for payment. Thus, the writeoffs for charity care and bad debts are limited almost, if not totally, to charge-paying patients. This explains why the allowance is limited to just charge-paying patients in Equation 3.

BREAK-EVEN ANALYSIS

One of the most useful analytical models developed for operating analysis has been the break-even model. This model permits managers to project quickly the amount of profit at various levels of prices, volumes, and costs (see Table 3). The only difference between the break-even formula of the hospital industry and that of general industry is the division of desired net income by the proportion of charge patients. This recognizes that any contribution to net income must come from patients who pay charges. Cost-paying patients will not in general provide anything toward the attainment of income objectives. However, there are a limited number of Blue Cross plans that do pay cost plus and thus would contribute to income.

The most useful purpose of break-even analysis in the hospital industry is as a decision-making aid in pricing. Hospitals typically are committed to providing services at whatever level demanded. They are thus less interested in selecting profitable product lines than their industrial counterparts. They are, however, extremely interested in pricing their products so as to recover their costs and to provide an operating surplus necessary for replacement and modernization.

Table 3 Break-Even Models for General Industry and Hospital Industry

General Industry

Break-even in units = $\dfrac{\text{Fixed expenses} + \text{Desired net income}}{\text{Contribution margin per unit}} = \dfrac{F + NI}{P_n - V}$

Hospital Industry*

To reflect the impact of cost reimbursement, the standard break-even model must be adjusted in the following manner:

$$Q = \frac{F + NI/PROP}{P_n - V} \quad \dotfill \quad [4]$$

where:
NI = Desired net income
$PROP$ = Proportion of charge-paying patients, assumed to be constant for all relevant values of output.

*The break-even model in Equation 4 is derived by setting net patient revenue less total costs and net income equal to zero and solving for Q.

$$NPR - TC - NI = O \quad \text{or}$$
$$P_n\,Q_{ch} + \frac{TC}{Q} \times Q_c - TC - NI = O$$

When there is no adjustment for the effects of cost reimbursement found in the hospital industry, a serious understatement of break-even volume occurs. The results of this understatement may directly affect pricing decisions. To the extent that hospital managers do not adjust for cost reimbursement in their present pricing decisions, they may seriously understate the price necessary to attain their income objectives at budgeted or projected output.

Using the Break-Even Model

To see this more clearly, consider the following hypothetical case. Assume that the intensive care unit expects 2,990 patient days during the coming budget year. Further assume that the total budgeted cost at this level of output is expected to be $328,900, with approximately 60 percent or $197,340 of this total cost fixed and the remaining 40 percent or $44.00 per patient day variable. If the hospital has 75 percent of its patients using the intensive care unit on cost formulas and 25 percent paying charges, with only 80 percent of the billed charges to be collected, what rate must be set to generate a 10 percent markup from cost?

To solve this problem, many hospital financial managers would adopt some derivation of the average cost pricing rule. This might mean that a selling price set at ten percent above cost would be set (see Table 4). Modification for the estimated bad debt allowance should inflate this further. Ideally, the rate should be divided by one minus the proportion of bad debt writeoffs. In this case, this figure would be 0.2, which implies a gross price of $151.25. From prior discussions, it is obvious that this price of $151.25 will not produce the desired net income level. A higher price is required to meet the stated profit objective.

A reformulation of the break-even model presented in Equation 4 (Table 3) can be used to solve for the required rate under conditions of cost reimbursement. As shown in Table 4, substituting the information from the hypothetical case into this equation yields a gross price of $154.00. Dividing by 0.8 to produce the rate that needs to be charged to reflect bad debt results in a rate of $192.50.

Income statements for this example under the two rates are presented in Table 5. They illustrate that, while the difference in rates may be only 27.3 percent, the difference in net income is 300.0 percent. This is not an atypical finding; small changes in prices can and do create significant changes in net income.

Current Use of Break-Even Model

The adapted break-even formulation of Equation 5 may represent a valuable decision-making aid in pricing hospital services. However, it may be that

---

Table 4 Two Approaches to Rate Setting

A. Derivation of average cost pricing rule

$$P_n = \frac{TC}{Q} \times 1.10 = \frac{\$328,900}{2,990} \times 1.10 = \$121.00$$

Modification for estimated bad debt allowance
$$P = \$121.00/.8 = \$151.25$$

B. Break-even cost model

$$P_n = V + \frac{F}{Q} + \frac{NI/PROP}{Q} \dots\dots\dots\dots\dots\dots\dots\dots\dots\dots\dots [5]$$

Substitution of case statistics
$$P_n = \$44 + \frac{\$197,340}{2,990} + \frac{\$32,390/.25}{2,990} = \$154.00$$

Modification for estimated bad debt allowance
$$P = \$154.00/.8 = \$192.50$$

---

hospital rate setters already establish rates in a manner consistent with this formulation. Murphy tested this hypothesis on a sample of 22 hospital administrators and fiscal officers from above-average-sized hospitals.[1] His results indicated that they did not adjust their rates for the effects of cost reimbursement. While this sample of 22 individuals may not be representative of the hospital industry at large, it does indicate that some method for pricing hospital services in a cost-reimbursement environment is needed. The formula developed in Equation 5 (Table 4) provides a reliable framework for developing and analyzing hospital prices.

Table 5 Intensive Care Unit Income Statement

	PRICE = $151.25	PRICE = $192.50
Gross patient revenue	$452,237.50	$575,575.00
Less contractual adjustment	92,503.13	185,006.25
Less bad debts & charity care	22,611.88	28,778.75
Net patient revenue	$337,122.49	$361,790.00
Less expenses	328,900.00	328,900.00
Net income	$ 8,222.49	$ 32,890.00

INCREMENTAL ANALYSIS

Break-even analysis as developed in the last section can be of great value to hospital managers in making all types of decisions that affect profitability. Perhaps pricing is the most important application. However, there is an explicit assumption in the prior adaptation of break-even analysis that may limit its utility in some situations. Specifically, it was assumed that any change in volume would keep the relative proportion of charge patients to total patients (PROP) constant.

When Proportions Are Constant

The likelihood of this assumption being valid is probably good in most normal situations. For these circumstances, the change in profitability for a given change in output can be stated as Equation 6 in Table 6. There is a striking similarity between Equation 6 and the traditional contribution margin used in conventional and incremental analysis. In fact, they are identical if PROP is replaced by the complement of the effective income tax rate, that is, one minus the tax rate. Long and Silvers have pointed out the similarity of cost reimbursement to income taxation.[2] For operating analysis purposes, a 75 percent cost-reimbursement factor in a nonprofit hospital is identical to a 75 percent income taxation.

When Proportions Are Not Constant

For situations where constant proportions of charge and cost patients are not realistic, some modification is necessary to develop an incremental profit estimator. Two general cases where this may be necessary are evaluating charges in patient mix in new or existing departments. Some specific examples where this is likely to occur include the following: development of a kidney dialysis program where all patients are expected to be reimbursed by Medicare; development of an ambulatory care program where a much greater proportion of patients are expected to be self-pay and thus charge payers; or discontinuance of a nearby hospital's obstetrical service, which is expected to increase demand for this service and result in a higher proportion of charge-

---

Table 6 Calculation of Change in Profit as Output Changes

$$\text{Change in profit} = (P_n - V) \times PROP \times \text{Change in volume} \dots \dots [6]$$

paying patients. In short, many planning situations could be hypothesized where the proportion of cost and charge patients would change. Note that while a change in output may initially be centered in one department such as obstetrics, the interdepartmental consumption of other services, especially ancillary services like laboratory and radiology, will produce a ripple effect. The change in profitability can only be assessed by accounting for all of these changes in volume.

Since there are two major classes of purchasers, marginal or incremental profit may be specified for each of the two classes. The derivation of these two values is accomplished by taking the partial derivative of the revenue and cost equations (Equations 1 and 3) with respect to number of cost-paying units (Q_c) and number of change-paying units (Q_{ch}). The marginal profit for a cost-paying patient (MP_c) is calculated in Table 7 as is the marginal profit of a charge-paying patient (MP_{ch}).

The marginal profit for a cost-paying patient is the product of the proportion of charge patients to total patients (Q_{ch}/Q) and average fixed cost (F/Q). To better understand this process, assume that there are currently no cost patients so that Q_{ch}/Q is equal to one. This means that the marginal profit of the first cost patient is average fixed cost F/Q. Remember in Equation 3 (Table 2) that the revenue of a cost patient was equal to TC/Q or average total cost. Average total cost can be restated as variable cost per unit of output (V) plus F/Q. Thus, this first cost patient in this example increases total cost by V, variable cost, but reimbursement to the hospital will be average cost, or V plus F/Q. As the proportion of charge patients decreases, the MP_c *declines.*

Table 7 Calculation of Marginal Profit for Cost-Paying and Charge-Paying Patients

---

Cost-Paying Patients

$$MP_c = \frac{Q_{ch}}{Q} \times \frac{F}{Q} \dots\dots\dots\dots\dots\dots\dots\dots\dots\dots\dots\dots\dots\dots [7]$$

Charge-Paying Patients

$$MP_{ch} = [P_n - V] - \left[\frac{Q_c}{Q} \times \frac{F}{Q}\right] \dots\dots\dots\dots\dots\dots\dots\dots [8]$$

where:

MP_c = Marginal profit for cost-paying patient
MP_{ch} = Marginal profit for charge-paying patient

An additional cost-paying unit still pays V plus F/Q; but, if there are significant numbers of existing cost-paying patients, then the average fixed cost that the existing cost-paying units pay is reduced because fixed costs are now spread over an additional unit of volume. The net effect is reflected in Equation 7.

MP_{ch} is equal to the contribution margin (P_n-V) less the product of the proportion of cost patients to total patients (Q_c/Q) and average fixed cost (F/Q). The inclusion of the contribution margin is easily understood, since it reflects what the charge patient will pay on the average (P_n) less the incremental cost required to service that patient (V). However, another factor $[(Q_c/Q) \times (F/Q)]$ is subtracted to derive MP_{ch}, which may not be understood at first. Assume this time that Q_{ch} is currently zero so that Q_c/Q is one. Then the average fixed cost is subtracted from the contribution margin to determine MP_{ch}. The addition of the first charge-paying unit spreads fixed costs over one more unit and reduces average fixed cost. Since there is the same number of cost-paying units (Q_c) and the average fixed cost has decreased, total revenue from cost-paying patients is reduced. The net effect when charge patients are present already is the product of the proportion of current cost patients to total patients and the average fixed cost.

The derivation of these two incremental profit values may be interesting, but, if they are used alone, they may be of little value. Hospital managers are not often interested in changes of output limited to one unit. Typically, the changes are expected to be much larger.

However, these marginal profit indexes are valuable in the development of an incremental profitability index that can be used in situations of nonconstant proportions. If estimates of the change in expected volume can be broken down into cost and charge patients, the incremental profitability index may be defined (see Table 8). The profitability index (PI) is accurate only for the specific volume change under consideration, and the effects of alternative changes in volume must be recomputed. However, the sensitivity of PI is such that if the proportion of change in payment mix $[\Delta_c/(\Delta_c + \Delta_{ch})]$ is known with reasonable accuracy, but the total volume change $(\Delta_c/ + \Delta_{ch})$ is less certain, the value of PI is reasonably accurate over a significant range of volume.

With the development of PI, it is a simple matter to project the estimated change in profit. The change in profit attributed to a change in volume can be simply calculated as shown in Equation 12 of Table 8.

Projection of the profit implications of various management decisions should now be improved with Equations 6 to 12. For situations of constant proportions, Equation 6 may be employed. Where the constant proportions assumption is expected to be invalid, Equation 12 may be used. Reliability

---

Table 8 Calculation of Incremental Profitability Index and Change in Profit

---

Incremental Profitability Index

$$PI = \frac{\Delta_c}{\Delta_c + \Delta_{ch}} \times MP_c + \frac{\Delta_{ch}}{\Delta_c + \Delta_{ch}} + MP_{ch} \dots\dots\dots\dots [9]$$

where:

PI = Profitability index

Δ_c and Δ_{ch} = Expected change in cost patient and charge patient units

MP_c and MP_{ch} = Revised marginal profit values for cost and charge patients defined as follows:

$$MP_c = \frac{(Q_{ch} + \Delta_{ch})}{Q_{ch} + \Delta_c + \Delta} \times \frac{F}{Q} \dots\dots\dots\dots\dots [10]$$

$$MP_{ch} = (P_n - V) - \frac{(Q_c + \Delta_c)}{Q + \Delta_c + \Delta_{ch}} \times \frac{F}{Q} \dots\dots\dots [11]$$

Change in Profit

Change in profit = $PI \times (\Delta_c + \Delta_{ch})$ ----------------------------[12]

---

and accuracy of profit projections should be improved significantly in the hospital industry if these decision tools are utilized.

CASE ILLUSTRATION

The formulas derived earlier can be applied in the following hypothetical case. Assume that the local public health department has contacted a hospital to explore the feasibility of purchasing a large quantity of laboratory services. Specifically, the public health department wants to purchase the equivalent of 300,000 relative value units (RVUs) of hospital laboratory services. They will reimburse on the basis of average cost compound at year end. The hospital laboratory's present cost and rate structure is shown in Table 9.

Most of this information is readily available; however, there are two major exceptions. In most situations, measures of fixed and variable cost are not normally available. However, estimates for these variables can be developed using existing techniques.[3]

Table 9 Data and Calculations for Case Illustration

Hospital Laboratory's Present Cost and Rate Structure

Yearly volume (RVUs)	1,200,000
Volume accounted for by cost payers	900,000
Volume accounted for by charge payers	300,000
Total cost	$3,000,000
Fixed cost	$1,200,000
Variable cost/RVU	$1.50
Fixed cost/RVU	$1.00
Average cost/RVU	$2.50
Rate/RVU	$3.00
Collection rate on charge patients	$ .90

Conventional Incremental Analysis
Incremental Profit: ($2.50 − $1.50) × 300,000 = $300,000
or Incremental Profit: ($2.30 − $1.50) × 300,000 = $240,000

Reimbursement Modified Incremental Analysis—Constant Proportions
Incremental Profit: $(Pn - V) \times PROP \times$ Change in volume
Before Acceptance: $90,000 = ($2.70 − $1.50) × .25 × 300,000
After Acceptance: $72,000 = ($2.70 − $1.50) × .20 × 300,000

Reimbursement Modified Incremental Analysis—No Constant Proportions

$$PI = MP_c \; \frac{Q_{ch}}{Q + \Delta_c} \times \frac{F}{Q} = \frac{300,000}{1,200,000 + 300,000} \times \$1.00 = \$.20$$

Incremental Profit: $.20 × 300,000 = $60,000

Assume that this cost and rate information will be reflective of future operations during the period of this proposed contract. Further, assume that there are no legal or reimbursement problems presented by the hospital's acceptance of this contract. What should the hospital do?

If the hospital's only objective in pursuing this contract is profit, how should they analyze this offer? There are at least four basic sets of calculations that different hospital financial managers might make to analyze profitability. Two criteria for evaluating the utility of the calculations for this specific case are accuracy of profit forecast and ability to select the proper decision.

Average Cost Basis

Many managers have estimates of variable cost, but they either do not believe them or do not know how to use them. Whatever the reason, some managers simply assume that costs will increase by $2.50/RVU, the current average cost. Since revenue will also increase by the same $2.50/RVU, there is no incremental change in profit. If no other reasons exist for accepting this contract, such as improved public relations, there is no incentive for the hospital to accept it. In fact, given even modest additional capital expenditures, there is reason for the hospital to reject the contract. Unless variable cost actually equals average cost, incremental profit is understated.

Conventional Incremental Analysis

In contrast to the financial managers, who use the average cost basis, there are many financial managers who might employ some form of conventional incremental analysis. Since the variable cost is given, the only unknown is price. But since the contract calls for payment of average cost, why not use the current average cost of $2.50/RVU or the expected average cost if the contract is accepted, which is $2.30/RVU. Incremental profit under this approach would be either $300,000 or $240,000 (see Table 9). These sets of calculations might provide the proper financial inducement to stimulate contract acceptance. However, both sets of calculations overstate profit because they disregard the lower price or average cost that all present cost volume payers will reimburse when volume is expanded.

Reimbursement Modified Incremental Analysis—
Constant Proportions Requirement

A modification of conventional incremental analysis is defined in Equation 6 (see Table 6). This formula is valid only for cases of constant proportions in payment mix. Such is not the case here, as all of the incremental volume is coming from a cost payment source. Nevertheless, to illustrate the use of this one adaption of conventional incremental analysis and to verify its inaccuracy, it will be applied in this case. Since PROP is not constant in this case, it may be useful to calculate incremental profit using the percentage of charge patients both before and after the contract acceptance. The calculations in Table 9 show $90,000 incremental profit before contract acceptance and $72,000 incremental profit after acceptance.

It is not possible to determine generally if incremental profit will be overstated or understated when this formulation is used inappropriately. In this specific example, incremental profit is overstated in both cases. However, had the net price been reduced only slightly, an understatement of profit would have occurred.

Reimbursement Modified Incremental Analysis — No Constant Proportions Requirement

The model presented in Equation 12 (Table 8) is the appropriate one for use in this case. Incremental output changes will not maintain the current proportion of charge to cost payers. In fact, all the incremental volume will be from cost payers. As shown in Table 9, the profitability index (PI) of Equation 9 (Table 8) in this case reduces to $0.20. Incremental profit should be $60,000. This fact is verified in Table 10, which contains pro forma income statements for the laboratory with and without the public health contract for 300,000 additional RVUs.

As shown in the case illustration, the concept and techniques of cost/volume/profit analysis can be adapted to the cost-reimbursed hospital industry. As cost/volume/profit analysis is currently discussed and utilized in general industry, it cannot be employed with any degree of reliability in the hospital industry. But, with modifications, this method of analysis should prove of value to hospital managers and financial managers.

Table 10 Pro Forma Laboratory Income

	Without Contract	With Contract
Gross patient revenue	$3,600,0000	$4,500,000
Less contractual adjustment	450,000	840,000
Less bad debts & charity care	90,000	90,000
Net patient revenue	$3,060,000	$3,570,000
Less expenses	3,000,000	3,450,000
Net income	$ 60,000	$ 120,0000

REFERENCES

1. Murphy, F. "A Study of the Effect of Cost Reimbursement, Bad Debt and the Percentage of Fixed Costs on Rate Setting in Health Care Institutions." Thesis, Ohio State University, 1977.

2. Long, H., and Silvers, J. "Health Care Reimbursement is Federal Taxation of Tax Exempt Providers." *Health Care Management Review* 1 (Winter 1976): 9-23.

3. Horngren, C. *Cost Accounting: A Managerial Emphasis.* 3d edition. Englewood Cliffs, N.J.: Prentice-Hall, 1972, pp. 806-834.

SUGGESTED READINGS

American Institute of Certified Public Accountants. *Hospital Audit Guide.* New York: AICPA, 1972.

Cleverley, W. "Profitability Analysis in the Hospital Industry." *Health Services Research* (Spring 1978), pp. 16-27.

23. Financial Modeling: A Must for Today's Hospital Management

BEN I. BOLDT, JR.

Boldt, Ben I., Jr. "Financial Modeling: A Must for Today's Hospital Management." *Health Care Management Review,* Summer 1978.

As the administrator or financial manager of your hospital, have you ever considered the implications of your institution's capital project programs for the future financial success or survival of your institution? Do you understand how your hospital's cash flow requirements will be affected if the newly initiated renovation project incurred a 20-percent cost overrun? Have you taken time to analyze the financial implications of securing that new CAT scanner, but obtaining only 60 percent of the expected patient utilization?

If the answers to the above questions are "no" or "not recently," perhaps you are not providing the appropriate level of service to your institution. Capital projects bring about top major problems facing hospital management today: the planning for and utilization of cash. A one-time evaluation of a project may be adequate to reach a decision to proceed; but, since most capital projects span a number of months or even years, a continuing analysis is also necessary to reflect the impact of program changes on hospital operations.

The analysis and evaluation of capital expenditure programs are not the only areas that require close and continuing attention. The requirement to provide sound financial planning for overall hospital operations is increasing almost daily as a result of new legislation and the continual change of reimbursement programs.

For example, the trend for hospitals and hospital groups to share services—both administrative and medical—encourages strong financial and operational planning. Shared services seem to be a good idea; but, without careful planning and a program of continued analysis, today's cost-effective idea might result in unnecessarily high or unreimbursed costs tomorrow.

To meet the increasing demand for planning, the hospital administrator or financial manager will have to use financial planning techniques, such as flexible budgeting (adjusting budgeted expenses and revenues to reflect actual versus planned volumes before determining actual to budget variances), preparation of quarterly or even monthly cost reports to estimate the year-end reimbursement situation, and multiyear financial projections to analyze the long-term impact of construction programs or changes in patient mix. However, even though the need is recognized and the desire to implement these planning techniques is sincere, one of the major stumbling blocks to the success of these techniques has been the amount of time incurred to perform the required calculations either initially or when changes are made to the assumptions.

The financial model is an important tool that can relieve managers and their staff from the task of performing the repetitive mathematical calculations required for thorough financial planning. Simply stated, a financial model is a computer program that simulates, either in whole or in part, the financial operations of the hospital. It can perform predetermined calculations required by a flexible budget, a cost report, or most other types of financial analyses. The financial model provides its user with two distinct groups of advantages:

1. Clerical efficiency.

  • It reduces the time necessary initially to prepare or revise the financial projections.

  • It reduces the cost of preparing and revising the financial projections.

  • It eliminates the arithmetical errors of manually prepared projections.

2. Planning improvement.

  • It improves the planning process since it allows more time to be directed at analyzing the problems encountered.

  • It provides an insight into hospital operations by identifying (or forcing someone to identify) how factors within the hospital interact.

  • It provides an ability to try quickly numerous alternative strategies to find or identify those that provide optimum results.

Financial models can be classified into three major categories: general, industry or specific function, and custom.

THE GENERAL MODEL

General models include those models that provide pro forma financial statements and are not restricted to any one industry or purpose. The principal output of these models includes an income statement, balance sheet, and statement of cash flow or change in working capital.

Within the general category, two types of financial models can be identified: unstructured and structured.

The *unstructured* model can be thought of as a matrix programmed on a computer in which the user has the ability to define the number of columns and rows to be used for calculations and the mathematical relationships between these columns and rows. The level of detail and sophistication of the calculations can be as simple or complex as the user wishes to make it. The unstructured general financial model allows maximum flexibility in integrating modeling into the planning process; however, it also demands a substantial amount of technical know-how.

The *structured* model is similar in concept to the unstructured model except that the number of columns and rows that can be used within the matrix is fixed and many of the relationships between columns and rows are predefined and cannot be changed by the user. This type of financial model requires the user to input data in a specified format and identify the variable values to be used in the projections in a set manner. The model processes the input data and prepares output reports in a predetermined format.

The structured model provides an excellent tool for the less experienced user, while providing most of the modeling capability found in the more sophisticated unstructured model.

An income statement comparing the beginning condition of an unstructured and structured model before data are entered for analysis appears in Table 1. As illustrated, the unstructured model requires the user to define the number of rows (revenue and cost elements) and columns (years or other time periods) to be used in the projections. The structured model has these items defined (in the illustration, 10 rows and 4 years, respectively), as well as a defined type of data to be entered in the rows (Rows 1 and 2 are for revenue items, Row 8 is for general and administrative expenses, etc.).

The general category of financial models has many applications in the area of multiyear financial projections. For example, it can be used to answer types of planning questions such as: What is the expected impact on operating costs due to the planned renovation program? Can the hospital generate the necessary cash flow to undertake a $12 million construction program? What happens to the hospital's financial position if pediatric services are phased out and a seven percent average occupancy is lost over the next five years?

These questions are answered by changing the projection variables affected by the criteria of the question. For example, when answering the first or

Table 1 Comparison of Unstructured and Structured Financial Models

Unstructured

Line No.	Title	Time (Years)						
		Y_1	Y_2	Y_3	Y_4	Y_5	...	Y_n
1								
2	Must be							
3	defined							
4	by user							
5								
6								
7								
8								
9								
10								
...								
n								

Structured

Line No.	Title	Time (Years)			
		Y_1	Y_2	Y_3	Y_4
1	Revenue (1)				
2	Revenue (2)				
3	Total Revenue				
4	Variable Cost (1)				
5	Variable Cost (2)				
6	Fixed Expense (1)				
7	Fixed Expense (2)				
8	G & A Expense				
9	Other Expense				
10	Net Income				

second question above, users should ask themselves, What items of my present plan are affected by the renovation or construction program? The "simplified" answer might be, for the income statement:

- interest expense will increase since monies are to be borrowed and repaid over a period of 20 years;
- salary expense will increase since more nursing staff will be required;
- fixed expenses will increase as a result of higher depreciation charges; and
- heat, power, and light will decrease because of the installation of more efficient systems.

For the balance sheet, the "simplified" answer might be

- long-term debt will increase as a result of additional borrowing;
- short-term debt will be incurred to finance construction payments between long-term debt take-downs;
- fixed assets will increase to reflect the new facility being put into service; and
- accumulated depreciation will increase as a result of the depreciation charges.

After identifying the known or estimated value of the variable changes, the user can input the data and run the model to reflect the effect of these changes on the income statement, balance sheet, and cash flow statement.

The third question presents a situation where the principal variables affected are contained in the income statement. The number and type of changes will depend a great deal on the level of sophistication originally incorporated into the model. For example, a complex relationship might relate specific ancillary serices (laboratory tests, x-ray procedures, etc.) within the hospital to the types of patients (general, medical, surgical, pediatric, obstetric, etc.) serviced. Alternatively, a simple case might relate only the overall average revenue or average cost per patient day to total patient days regardless of the type of patient. To illustrate, the income statement projection might change for the simplified case as follows:

- patient days will decrease because of the loss of pediatric patients;
- average revenue day will decrease, since pediatrics has a higher average revenue/patient day that will be lost;

- average cost/day will decrease, since pediatrics has a higher average revenue/patient day that will be lost; and

- average cost/day will decrease as a result of the reduction in staff serving pediatrics.

These changes would be reflected in the input data and the model run to ascertain the effect on operating income, balance sheet, and cash flow to answer the "what happens if" question.

THE INDUSTRY MODEL

The industry category of financial models is structured and has two principal applications within the health care industry: flexible budgeting, and the preparation of cost-reimbursement reports.

The Budget Model

The budget model provides a hospital with the ability to develop departmental budgets based on a desired level of service and expected occupancy rate. When all department-level assumptions are input, the model executes the calculations necessary to determine each department's budget and also consolidates all departments to obtain the budget for the total hospital. Once the budget is established, the model provides the user with the ability to recalculate rapidly the budget to reflect varying conditions such as changes in occupancy and labor costs, increases in radiology service charges or other departmental revenue, or cost changes. Depending on the degree of sophistication used, this type of model offers to the hospital financial manager complete flexible budgeting capability.

The features that distinguish a forecasting model from a budget model are the length of time covered by the projections and the level of detail included. Typically, a budget model is designed to cover a one-year period by month and provides for totaling the months for each line item entered to obtain the budgeted amount for the year. Additionally, this type of model provides for not only revenue and expense data but operating statistics at the department level. The overall level of detail utilized in a budget model should correspond to the hospital's chart of accounts. This chart of accounts detail is desirable since it facilitates easy comparison of the actual result versus budgeted data throughout the year.

To illustrate the level of detail available, one operating budget model provides for

- nineteen service cost centers;
- seventy ancillary cost centers;
- one hundred general and administrative cost centers;
- eighty expense classifications within each cost center; and
- nine methods for computing contractual allowance.

A major benefit of a budget model is the ability to develop meaningful departmental detail and be in a position to analyze quickly the impact of alternative courses of actions on the affected department(s) and the hospital in total. Examples of the types of options available within budget models for projecting financial and statistical data follow.

Predetermined Budgeted Amounts. With this simple option, predetermined budgeted amounts are entered for each budget period. This option may be used to enter constant value items, such as depreciation, rental expense, or other items that are relatively constant over the budget period. Research grants would also be entered using this option.

Constant or Varying Percentage of Another Budget Item. This type of option allows the user to interrelate budget line items. For instance, in many laboratories a professional fee is incurred as a percentage of the revenues derived from that department. If it is known that a change in the professional fee rate is to take place during the budget year, the user can incorporate this option into the budget to reflect the specific percentage change and month in which the change will occur. Additionally, if the laboratory revenue is related to patient activity (patient days or admissions) the user can quickly see the professional fee expense to be incurred at the new rate for various levels of patient volume.

Constant or Varying Unit Increases. With this type of budget option, the user can prepare a budget reflecting dollar amount changes in a patient revenue or other items budgeted on a dollar amount per unit of services basis. For example, if patient days are budgeted by month, the effect of increasing the charge for a particular type of accommodation (semiprivate, private, ward) by five dollars beginning in a specific month during the year can be quickly computed or analyzed.

By utilizing these types of budget options for either the revenue or expense for a unit of service, the user can "string" budget line items together to develop a detailed flexible budget. For example, the following types of calculations can be constructed:

- Patient days can be calculated by entering the occupancy percentage expected each year, the number of beds available, and the days per year.

- Routine service revenues can be calculated by multiplying patient days by accommodation or by type of service (which could also be entered as a percentage of total patient days) times the anticipated average daily charge for that accommodation or service. The daily charge may be budgeted using other projection options.

- Ancillary service revenues can be calculated using procedures and rate per procedure, or using average ancillary service charges per patient day or per outpatient visit for that department. Provisions are often available to accommodate general intensity of service factors applying to all ancillary departments or specific intensity factors applying only to specific departments.

- Operating expenses can be calculated based on cost per unit times number of units. Units may represent patient days, visits, procedures, meals served, employee hours, or any other projection options. Professional fees (radiology, pathology, etc.) may be expressed as a percentage of the revenues of a department. Employee fringe benefits may be expressed as a percentage of wages and salaries.

- Contractual allowances can be calculated automatically based on a number of cost-reimbursement and prospective-reimbursement methods. These methods can include the standard Medicare, Medicaid, and Blue Cross cost-reimbursement formulas with cost ceilings, if applicable, or prospective-reimbursement contracts that call for payment on an admission basis, per diem/visit basis, or percentage of charge basis.

The Cost-Reimbursement Model

The second type of application of the structured industry model is the cost-reimbursement model. As the title implies, this model is specifically designed to prepare or recalculate a hospital's cost-reimbursement report. The more advanced models allow for rapid recalculation and comparison of alternative allocation formula and reimbursement strategies. This capability allows the hospital financial executive to evaluate which of a number of allocation bases will provide the maximum reimbursement to the hospital or, alternatively, which is capable of answering the question, What impact will that new Medicare regulation have on my expected reimbursement?

Following are some of the capabilities provided by this type of model:

- The model provides the user with the capability to experiment with various statistical bases, cost center composition, and sequence of allocation alternatives. The effect of these alternatives on cost reimbursement can be quickly and economically determined.

- A user can quickly determine the effect of audit adjustments proposed by the Medicare intermediary. This information can assist the hospital in devising a strategy for discussing the adjustments with an intermediary.

- The model simplifies the preparation of cost reports by greatly reducing manual calculations and by automatically preparing worksheets for the cost report.

- Cost reimbursement and related contractual allowances can be estimated for interim periods.

- The model assists in developing realistic budgets and forecasts by providing the capability to determine cost reimbursement and related contractual allowances using budgeted and forecasted data.

- The model allows analysis of reimbursement and preparation of special reports that assist in developing an appropriate reimbursement strategy.

Additionally, a few models have been designed with the user in mind. These provide for the following:

- Data can be entered directly from the Medicare worksheets. This feature eliminates the need for information being entered on special input worksheets prior to entry to the system. The only requirement of the individual preparing the data for input is familiarity with the Medicare worksheets.

- Internal data can be exchanged; this enables the user to enter data once even though the data are used on several of the worksheets. These models automatically transfer the data to the appropriate worksheets.

- Preset standard cost centers and descriptions appear on Form SSA-2552. Additionally, the user has the ability to modify the arrangement of cost centers and their descriptions as desired.

This provides almost complete freedom in choosing the appropriate number and composition of cost centers.

THE CUSTOM MODEL

The custom model is required when the simulation or analysis desired is so complicated or detailed that it cannot be performed by a model within the general or industry category. This category is best illustrated by a model used by a major midwest medical center.

The analysis to be undertaken was directed at assessing the cost impact of consolidating clinical services among the member institutions within the medical center. Figure 1 gives a conceptual illustration of the interactions required to implement the medical service transfers contemplated by the medical center.

The model was designed to aid the planning process specifically in the area of projecting the cost changes resulting from a planned shared clinical service program, not only for the total medical center consortium, but at each institution within the consortium.

The model provides the planners with the capability to:

- project the cost impact of a specific shared clinical service program under consideration,

- project the cost impact of alternative programs, and

- update the financial projections related to an acceptable program with each year's current cost data and patient information.

The model is based on the concept that the patient utilization of an institution's ancillary services (laboratory, radiology, physical therapy, etc.) and therefore the ancillary service cost depend on the type of clinical service provided by the institution (pediatrics, oncology, renal medicine, etc.).

Accordingly, two types of data are used by the model: (1) data representing patient usage (patient profile) of ancillary services for each clinical service provided at each institution in the consortium, and (2) cost data for each institution segregated into fixed and variable elements.

The model integrates the patient profile data and cost data for each hospital to generate a cost matrix reflecting the operating costs of each ancillary service attributable to each clinical service "before" patient transfers and consolidations at each institution. Then each institution's "before" patient transfer cost matrix is operated on by the computer by relating the costs of each ancillary service used by each clinical service to the number of patients admitted to each respective clinical service.

After all changes are made to the cost matrix of each hospital, the computer prepares a report reflecting the costs, by ancillary service, for each clinical service within each institution and for the total medical center consortium, "after" the patient transfers associated with the proposed planned shared clinical service program. By comparing the change in costs between the "before" and "after" conditions, the planners are able to test the financial impact of the numerous clinical service transfer alternatives to identify those programs that will not only provide improved health care, but will provide that care at a lower cost.

As developed, the model does not address every potential financial evalua-

Figure 1   Clinical Service Transfers Between Institutions Within the Consortium: 1,000-Bed General Acute Care Hospital Specializing in Oncology

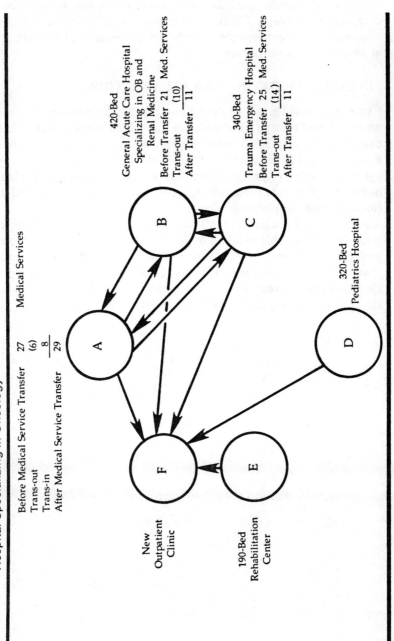

tion problem associated with clinical service consolidation; however, it illustrates how the development of a custom computer model can assist health care planners or hospital financial executives to analyze some of the financial considerations encountered during the development of a hospital's or group of hospitals' long-range plan.

FINANCIAL MODELING—A VALUABLE TOOL

Experience gained in industry and more recently within the health care field at major for-profit hospital corporations and large nonprofit institutions indicates that financial modeling techniques can be a valuable tool in a hospital's management. The satisfaction of these users indicates that almost any management problem or process in which there is repetitiveness, some logic, and numerous changes in the assumptions or decisions criteria is a candidate for financial model application.

As hospital managers face this new era of financial and operational planning, they will be able to take a more aggressive position if they can quickly predict the outcome of their decisions or the impact of actions outside their span of control. Certainly financial modeling provides one of the answers to the increasing demand for more detailed and thorough planning and provides the ability to rapidly respond to the question, What happens if. . .?

24. Cost Control Challenge for Hospitals

ROBERT A. VRACIU and JOHN R. GRIFFITH

Vraciu, Robert A., and Griffith, John R. "Cost Control Challenge for Hospitals." *Health Care Management Review*, Spring 1979.

American health care is emerging from an era in which it held a highly favored position in the American economy. The old era was characterized by a rapid increase in health insurance, first private and later federal programs, that have stimulated the use of health services; subsidies for capital growth (Hill-Burton Program and tax-exempt bonds) that allowed for rapid growth in health facilities; and government-funded research that led to new technologies whose dissemination was rapid and rarely based upon careful analysis of the costs and the benefits. The result has been a 15 percent or greater increase in health care expenditures in most of the last decade.

In an environment as rapidly changing as ours, no sector of the economy will keep such a favored position indefinitely. Sectors of the economy such as the space industry and education are recent examples of favored industries that are losing their generous fiscal support. It is being made increasingly clear to the health industry that its "fat" years are over.

If the guidelines for the 1950s, 1960s, and early 1970s were for virtually unlimited and subsidized expansion, the guidelines for the 1980s will be clearly more restrictive. We have already witnessed actions by the federal and state governments and business to restrain the rate of cost increases in those facets of the health industry that are under their control. These actions reflect a change in attitude toward health spending; there is every indication that this attitude will continue and intensify.

Proposals abound for ways to contain costs in the health services industry. Debate will continue not only on the form of future regulations but also on the amount of reduction desired. Nevertheless, there is a strong indication that the underlying goal of the final program will be to restrict the growth of expenses on a long-term basis to some level related to either the consumer price index (CPI) or growth in the economy.

369

For example, reference to these targets can be found in President Carter's legislative proposal,[1] in the National Health Planning Goals,[2] the Joint Steering Committee of the American Hospital Association (AHA), the American Medical Association (AMA) and the Federation of American Hospitals (FAH),[3] and in public statements by corporate leaders such as Zink of General Motors. In assuming such a goal, it is noteworthy that neither a current-dollar nor a real-dollar reduction in health care expenditures has been suggested. Rather the consensus is that it is sufficient to reduce the rate of increases until it equals a "national economy-wide average," even though there are obvious disagreements over what this average is as well as how to reach it.

The cost-containment proposals currently under consideration share this goal of reducing the rate of increase of national expenditures for hospital care. Although the proposals differ in how the maximum allowable increase (MAI) will be translated into individual hospital expenditures, it is likely that, at some point, each hospital will have a target expenditure level that is derived from the national target. In fact, one has been accepted by the Voluntary Effort of AHA, AMA, and FAH. The existence of such a hospital-specific target level, referred to as MAI, and its recognition by the hospital industry represent a significant change from the current modus operandi in most states.

To operate successfully under this new scenario, hospital managers must change their attitudes. The chief executive and chief financial officers of hospitals and at least the finance committee of the board must understand the form of the constraint and the ultimate level of severity as it affects the hospital's budgeting and planning decisions.

CHARACTERIZING THE TARGET

The ultimate form of the national ceiling will have a major impact on management autonomy, the possible reactions, and the ultimate success of any cost-containment program. Four definitional concerns are associated with specifying that "form:" total costs versus total charges, total versus unit costs, GNP versus CPI indices, and general versus hospital-industry-specific CPI.

Total Costs versus Total Charges

A cost-containment constraint based on restricting total costs would be different from one based on total charges (net of allowances). In absolute amounts, the difference between the two is the hospital's surplus or genera-tion of capital from operations. If the target is defined in terms of total costs, then no constraint is applied to the generation of capital per se. A hospital could theoretically raise charges at a greater rate than the MAI and increase its planned surplus, that is, its generation of capital. If, however, the target were defined in terms of total charges, capital generation would be available only if the hospital could successfully contain total costs at a level less than the increase in revenues. Under cost-based reimbursement, of course, the difference between the two bases disappears.

Total versus Unit Costs

Approaches to control such as unit cost, for example, per diem cost or per admission cost, are not necessarily consistent with the assumed goal of constraining total hospital costs. In the absence of effective utilization controls, a hospital could, for example, increase services to a fixed population, shift patient mix to lower intensity of services, and so on, and lower the unit costs. The evidence shows that the total costs of providing health care to the service population will rise, even though the unit costs are controlled.[4] The individual hospital will, in effect, translate its increased volumes into a larger percentage increase in total costs than the one imposed on the unit cost.

GNP versus CPI Indices

While increases in both GNP and CPI have been suggested as targets for allowable increases, they will have different impacts on the "tightness" of cost constraints. This is because the increase in GNP is equal to the sum of an increase in expenditures attributable to inflation plus real growth in GNP. The inflation component is measured by the GNP implicit price deflator, a number that is analogous to the CPI. Allowing total hospital costs to increase only at a rate equal to the CPI excludes "real growth" of GNP. The differences for 1976 and 1977 were 6.0 and 4.9 percent, respectively.[5]

The hospital industry's percentage of total GNP would decrease over time under a MAI set equal to the CPI. It would remain constant if the MAI were equal to the total growth in GNP.

General versus Hospital-Industry-Specific CPI

A price index is constructed by weighting the price increases of some set of commodities. The specific component rates (price increases) and weighting vector will influence the final weighted amount, and thus the MAI faced by hospitals. Two alternatives for defining the component rates are (1) the actual rates of increase for the inputs of hospital services, and (2) the component and subcomponent rates of surrogate commodities in the CPI and WPI.

The first method is susceptible to charges that hospitals will not aggressively try to minimize the price of purchased goods. To the extent that prices paid by hospitals for labor, supplies, utilities, and so forth, exceed economy-wide averages, the increases would be allowed by the first method, regardless of the appropriateness. The second approach is more normative in that it restricts allowable increases to an economy-wide average and is likely to be more restrictive.

The final index reflects a weighting of these component rates. Its accuracy depends upon the vector of weights used. Not only do hospitals use inputs in different proportions from other industries or purchasers, but regional and interhospital differences do exist, and for defensible reasons. These problems can be addressed by using weights that are region- or hospital-specific.

Variations in MAI

Individual hospitals' MAIs will not be equal, and certainly they will not be constant every year. For example:

- Year-to-year fluctuations in the general economy are likely; and correspondingly, economic indicators such as growth in GNP or CPI are likely to vary.

- There are likely to be both regional and temporal variations in inflation rates for input factors.

- There are likely to be differences between institutions to reflect shifts in service populations.

- There may be ranges established that reflect different levels of hospital performance.

COST CONTAINMENT STRATEGIES

Faced with an MAI in total operating costs, many hospital administrators will be challenged to reduce the rate of increase without reducing the quality of care. The exact amount of required reduction, if any, will depend upon the level of the target ceiling and the budget decisions of each hospital. Some hospitals will find that their "natural" rate of increase is below the ceiling and will not require additional reductions. The target ceilings associated with current proposals—for example, 13 percent with the Voluntary Effort and 9 percent plus significant pass-through amounts from the Carter administration's cost-containment proposal—are well above the current national inflation rate for hospital input prices (approximately 8 to 9 percent). (These estimates are based on actual price increases for the hospital industry. Aggregate inflation estimates derived from component price increases in more generic industries can be 2 to 3 percentage points lower.) The GNP increased 11 percent (current dollars) from 1976 to 1977; and, because of such factors as decreasing lengths of stay, regional differences in wage rates and increased access to ambulatory care in nonhospital settings, this would be a comfortable ceiling for many hospitals.

However, many hospitals will be faced with a need to develop strategies for reducing their "normal" rate of increase. This will be particularly true if the target ceiling is set at a rate lower than currently contemplated, as hospitals are forced to live under an MAI for several successful years, and if a hospital experiences significant increases in demand without adequate volume adjustments built into the ceiling.

Four general categories of cost-containment strategies are available to hospital administrators. Since administrators need a framework for examining cost-containment options with a three- to five-year planning horizon, this article focuses on likely effectiveness and time lags rather than providing a laundry list of options. Although some strategies appear to have adequate potential to meet even a CPI-level MAI for many years, time lags of several years can delay the realization of savings. Thus advance planning will be a vital administrative response.

Short-Term Amenities' Reductions and Purchase Delays

There are a number of short-term strategies to pursue for an immediate expense reduction: minor benefits to employees might be reduced, educational programs cut back, planning activities curtailed, community relations reduced, plant and equipment replacement deferred, and implementation of new services and equipment purchases delayed. These short-term strategies reduce existing operating expenses, defer capital costs, and may defer increases in operating expenses associated with new programs.

Potential savings from these strategies clearly would vary substantially among hospitals. Expenditures for such items are not likely to disappear either completely or permanently, since they make a long-term contribution to patient satisfaction, recruitment, and community support. Moreover, these types of activities do not represent a major part of a typical hospital's budget, and it is unlikely that for any group of hospitals the savings are likely to exceed two to five percent.

Regardless of the amount, the savings will accrue immediately. The savings will, however, benefit the hospital only once, since in subsequent years they reduce the costs used as the "base" in the percentage increase calculation.

Input Price Reductions

At some point where goods and services are purchased, management has some ability to affect the negotiated price. This is illustrated in the negotiation of wages and salaries where the administrator can bargain harder and perhaps hold down the total settlement. Ironically, this particular strategy is denied by many administrators, but the 1977 Carter proposal specifically forestalled it by making nonsupervisory labor costs a "pass through." It appears that some administrators feel they cannot, and others feel they should not, bargain hard to control wage increases. Since the so-called gap between health care workers' earnings and earnings in other industries has been closing,[6] it is reasonable to expect future increases in hospital labor rates to be close to the general level of wage increases if hospitals bargain as hard as other employers. If the number of employees per unit of output remains constant, changes in the rate of increase in labor costs will be reflected in the total. Similar savings might be expected through group purchasing (both of supplies and capital equipment) and substitution of less expensive inputs, for example, revision of insurance programs. Substitution of less expensive capital for labor, as in the case of computerizing labor-based activities, is a more complex way to reduce expenditures. Projects of this kind may be very attractive because they can fix the costs of some inputs, for example, through long-term leases; however they can cause adverse labor and reimbursement consequences.

In general, this second strategy has only limited opportunities. Better management, harder bargaining, and good luck might yield a savings of one or two percentage points per year compared to present practices. While the savings associated with more effective negotiations may be incurred more than once, possible hidden costs include the likelihood that the other side will respond in turn. The savings associated with group purchasing and substitution of less expensive inputs will generally benefit the hospital only in the year of implementation.

Savings may be realized from these strategies in a reasonably short period of time or may lag one to two years. Negotiations with employee groups and unions generally occur once a year. The hospital's "toughened" negotiating position might require prior work and delaying activities, for example, developing a good system to resolve grievances and implementation of a system to measure productivity. Shared purchasing arrangements and implementation of computerized systems often take one to three years before savings are realized.

Improved Production Efficiency

The typical hospital faces a wide range of opportunities to improve its internal efficiency (output divided by input) given a constant volume of services.

These opportunities range from the simple—employee suggestion programs for improved methods, optimum inventory purchasing policies, and so on—to more complicated changes in the technology—setting capacity to correspond to demand via admissions scheduling, variable staffing, operating room scheduling, and contracting with outside organizations to provide services that take advantage of economies of scale. The simple methods still have potential, since few hospitals have done everything that can be done. The payouts, however, are equally modest—often in the tens of thousands of dollars per year, sometimes less. A one percent savings in a medium-sized hospital corresponds to more than $100,000.

The more complex approaches are rapidly becoming more popular. Their payment is quite promising in many settings, but installation cost time lags are correspondingly high.

These strategies are likely to require advance expenditures for increased management capabilities, such as the use of industrial engineers and well-trained assistant administrators. Some require new capital, and most require time to plan and negotiate. A prerequisite to implementing the more fruitful of these strategies is a strong commitment on the part of department supervisors and sometimes physicians to improve efficiency by undertaking changes in procedures. Relatively serious retraining is sometimes involved.[7] Even with well-intentioned, well-trained supervisory staff, effectively designed manpower budgeting and reporting systems must be in place in order to recover a real savings. As a result, strategies in this category are often implemented piecemeal and time lags of one to ten years might be expected before savings are realized.

How much these general efficiency strategies will save, net of investment, is unclear. Although engineers are fond of citing figures in the 10 to 15 percent range for potential improvements,[8] it is not clear that all of this potential is real, and it is even less clear whether the savings could be realized in the near term. While the cost savings associated with each improvement is by itself a one-time savings, the process of searching for more efficient technologies is likely to yield additional ideas and subsequent savings. Thus, important savings from this area are likely over a continuing period, but immediate returns are limited.

Improved Market Efficiency (Volume Reduction)

Evidence abounds to show a wide variation in physicians' approaches to the basic hospitalization decisions, for example, when to admit, when to operate, and when to discharge. [9,10] These decisions are reflected in population measures of the admissions rate, the discharge rate, and the rate of various types of surgery. When carefully compiled data are assembled, it appears that these statistics vary by as much as 100 percent in populations where there is no recognizable difference in terms of risk of illness or where the differences in risk explain a small part of the observed variations in utilization. Further evidence is found in the performance of HMOs where the rates of admission are slightly lower, length of stay much lower, and rates of surgery generally lower than those of comparable U.S. populations under conventional delivery systems. [11,12] Communities have been identified that have maintained low levels of use for many years without apparent ill health or dissatisfaction.[13]

Taken as a whole, this evidence suggests strongly that a potential exists for reducing the use rate of hospital services without adversely affecting the quality of care. Further, the responsibility for achieving these lower use rates lies jointly with the physician, hospital representative, and community. Analysis of the HMO and the low-use communities suggests that important decisions about organization of services that influence utilization are made by all parties but that the hospital's commitment to making available adequate ambulatory care services and creating a milieu that encourages cost-effective clinical decisions is not only a prerequisite but an important catalyst.

This fourth category of cost controls includes programs that reduce the volume of inpatient services. Such programs either shift services to a lower-cost setting or reduce the total number by eliminating unnecessary services. Such programs include preadmission testing and ambulatory surgery (substitute outpatient for inpatient services), utilization review (reduce number of admissions and length of stay), and discharge planning (substitute lower-cost chronic care services). The net effect of many of these programs will be to decrease the volume of patient days. Others will eliminate unnecessary ancillary services

However, evidence suggests that hospital administrators turn first to other cost-control strategies,[14] since the complexities of involving the medical staff slow progress.[15] Consequently, significant changes in volume are likely to occur only after several years in a cost-control environment, reflecting long lead times before strategies are implemented and further lags before they become effective. The magnitude of the dollar savings will vary according to the hospital's willingness to curtail services and the hospital's operating conditions. An approximation can be obtained by using a simple linear cost function: Total Costs = Fixed Costs + (Unit Variable Costs x Number of Patient Days). Using this definition, it can be shown that the percentage change in patient days (X) necessary to change total costs by (a) percentage points is: $X = b/a$, where (b) is the percent of total costs that are variable with patient days. Thus, if 50 percent of a hospital's costs are considered variable over a three- to five-year period, then a two percent decrease in patient days is necessary to decrease total costs by one percent.

HOSPITAL RESPONSES

The estimates of the potential savings associated with these four strategies are tenuous at best. There is such variance in hospital operations and capabilities that speaking in general terms has little meaning; individual hospitals might be able to pursue a single strategy for years, achieving any amount of required reduction in costs.

However, as the MAI becomes more binding for hospitals, administrators will be forced to think in terms of three- to five-year planning horizons for implementing cost containment strategies. Such a time frame is necessary because of the lead times associated with different categories of cost-containment strategies. An individual hospital should recognize these lead times and develop a package of strategies that matches the cost savings with the expected MAI.

For the purpose of discussing hospital behavior, hospitals can generally be judged by two criteria. The first is the hospital's production efficiency, that is, the relation between inputs and outputs. Common measures include cost per patient day (stratified by size, location, and type of institution) or position in hospital administrative services (HAS) distribution. The second criterion is that of market efficiency, that is, the relative amount of care used by the hospital's service population. Data on these use rates are only crudely estimated, but an increasing number of regions are attempting measurement.[16] Methodological problems interfere with measuring and interpreting a specific hospital's position on either criterion, but it is generally possible to identify gross differences.

An administrator facing a specific MAI has a number of areas in which cost-containment activities can be directed. For planning purposes, a useful way of displaying the possible trade-offs is to view the MAI as the sum of three-percentage increases or decreases (see Figure 1). Thus a hospital facing an input price inflation rate of 9 percent and an MAI of 13 percent can increase total cost up to 4 percent for reasons other than increased input prices. On the other hand, if the MAI is 7 percent and the input inflation rate is 9 percent, a 2 percent decrease in total costs due to improvements in efficiency and/or a decrease in volume must occur.

Since the input inflation rate was approximately 9.0 percent in 1977,[17] if the MAI is linked to increases in GNP—10.8 percent in 1977—the hospital could increase amenities, decrease efficiency, and/or increase volume to the point of increasing costs by approximately 2.0 percent. The figure used for the Voluntary Effort, 13.0 percent, is not particularly demanding. On the other hand, if the MIA were linked to CPI—6.8 percent in 1977—then hospitals would have to decrease amenities, improve efficiency, and/or decrease volume to generate approximately 2.0 percent in savings.

Figure 1 Percentage Increases Associated with Cost-Containment Strategies Relative to MAI

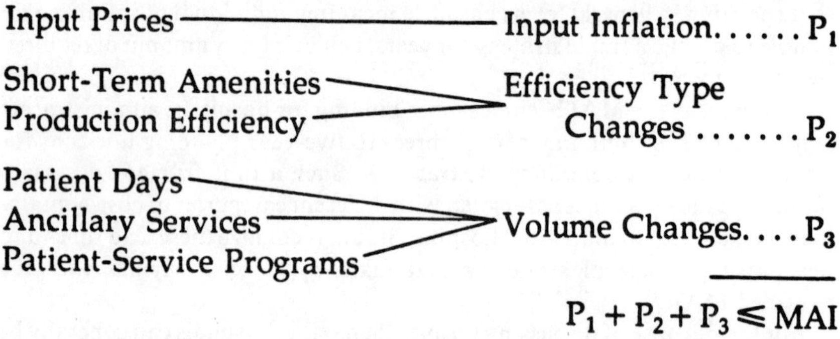

Input Prices ———————————— Input Inflation . . . . . . P_1

Short-Term Amenities ⟍
Production Efficiency ⟋ Efficiency Type Changes . . . . P_2

Patient Days ⟍
Ancillary Services ——————⟍⟋ Volume Changes . . . . P_3
Patient-Service Programs ⟋

$$P_1 + P_2 + P_3 \leqslant MAI$$

While individual hospitals will react differently to a binding MAI, a set of general responses can be speculated (not necessarily proposed) for the industry as a whole:

- Hospitals will tend to view the MAI as a target.

- Hospitals will tend to implement strategies for cost containment in the order listed above. Decreases in volume will be the last resort.

- There will be an incentive for hospitals to delay cutback until necessary and in some sense to "save" potential cutbacks.

- Some hospitals will fail to initiate the latter strategies (volume reductions and production efficiency) until the associated lag times exceed the time in which savings can be realized from other opportunities. These hospitals will deplete capital and be forced into austerity budgets, mergers, and/or bankruptcy.

- The required decrease in volume that corresponds to a required reduction in expenses is a function of the variable costs of operation. Over a three- to five-year planning horizon, hospitals can expect the proportion of variable costs to be reasonably high; for example, if 70.0 percent of total costs are variable, a 1.0 percent increase or decrease in total costs corresponds to a 1.4 percent increase or decrease in volume. This high percentage of variable costs will be achieved in well-run hospitals by coordinating capital purchases/replacements and staffing decisions with volume reductions.

In their comparative behavior, hospitals may respond in various ways:

- Less efficient hospitals are in a better position to delay reductions in volume in order to live within a specific MAI. Stated in another way, the more efficient hospitals will be relatively harder hit by any MAI. The benefits of retaining large amounts of slack within the hospital are somewhat of an illusion, however. Less efficient hospitals typically lack systems for strategic planning or cost control and are unable to manage the liquidation of the slack as needed.

- Hospitals in a high-use-rate area will have a greater ability to reduce volume. Hospitals in a low-use-rate area will have more difficulty reducing volume, and any highly efficient hospital in such an area will have more difficulty living within the MAI. This is because these hospitals have "used up" potential cost-saving activities.

- The successful hospitals under the new environment will be characterized by good information, decision, and control systems, that is, they will be able to develop specific applications of all four strategies, integrate them smoothly into a long-range plan, and operate according to the plan. Given the number of cost containment opportunities, the quality of management will determine success or failure far more than the current financial position.

REFERENCES

1. "Hospital Cost Containment Act of 1977." H.R. 6575, introduced in the U.S. House of Representatives, April 25, 1977.
2. "National Health Planning Goals." HEW National Health Planning Council, January 6, 1978.
3. See announcement in *Health Care Week* 1:26 (January 9, 1978) p. 1.
4. Dowling, W. L., et al. "The Impact of the Blue Cross and Medicaid Prospective Reimbursement Systems in Downstate New York." Report submitted to HEW Office of Research and Statistics, Social Security Administration, June 1976.
5. *Economic Report of the President, 1978*. Washington, D.C.: Government Printing Office, 1978. Table B-2, p. 259.
6. Yett, D.E. *An Economic Analysis of the Nurse Shortage.* Lexington, Mass.: Lexington Books, 1975.
7. Munson, F., and Hancock, W. "Implementation of Hospital Control Systems." *Cost Control in Hospitals,* edited by J.R. Griffith. Ann Arbor: Health Administration Press, 1976, pp. 297-316.
8. Bartscht, K., and Coffey, R. "Management Engineering—A Method to Improve Productivity." *Topics in Health Care Financing* 3 (Spring 1977): 39-62.
9. Wennberg, J., et al. "Health Care Delivery in Maine: I—Patterns of Use of Common Surgical Procedures, II—Conditions Explaining Hospital Admissions." *Journal of Maine Medical Association* 66 (1975): 123-130, 255-261.

10. Lewis, C.E. "Variation in the Incidence of Surgery." *New England Journal of Medicine* 281 (October 16, 1969): 880-884.

11. Roemer, M., and Schonick, W. "HMO Performance: The Recent Evidence." *Health and Society* (Milbank Memorial Fund Quarterly) (Summer 1973) pp. 271-318.

12. Gaus, C.R.; Cooper, B.S.; and Hirschman, C.G. "Contrast in HMO and Fee-For-Service Performance." *Social Security Bulletin* (May 1976) pp. 3-14.

13. Griffith, J.R., and Chernow, R. "Cost-Effective Acute Care Facilities Planning in Michigan." *Inquiry* 14 (September 1977).

14. Allison, R.F. "Administrative Responses to Prospective Reimbursement." *Topics in Health Care Financing* 3 (Winter 1976): 97-111.

15. Munson and Hancock. "Implementation of Hospital Control Systems."

16. Griffith, J.R. "A Proposal for New Hospital Performance Measures." *Hospital and Health Services Administration* (Spring 1978) pp. 60-84.

17. *Rate Controls* 2 (Published by Arnold P. Silver, C.P.A., Phoenix, Arizona, May 1978) p. 8.

25. The *Really* Effective Health Service Delivery System

DUNCAN NEUHAUSER

Neuhauser, Duncan. "The *Really* Effective Health Service Delivery System. *"Health Care Management Review,* Winter 1976.

Your mission, should you choose to accept it, is to take over the management of a large, traditional health care delivery system. Your goal for the organization is to maximize the quantity and quality of life for a defined population and with a fixed budget. . . .

Of course, the idea that there could be such an organization systematically pursuing such a goal is science fiction and such a managerial task befits "Mission Impossible." So, we will have to speculate a bit on what this mission would require.

Imagine starting with a typical American delivery system—nonsystem, if you wish—with general hospitals, doctors in private practice, nursing homes, and such, serving a population of typical Americans with a budget equivalent to eight percent of the Gross National Product and obtaining its funds from various sources. First, we would have to define the population served, which might be those people who say one of your staff doctors is "my doctor," or who regularly appear at your hospital clinics and emergency departments.

QUANTITY OF LIFE

We would also have to start measuring benefit. First, consider quantity of life, which might be measured in years of life saved. Let us assume that all years of life are of equal value, so that we can avoid such philosophically interesting quandries as

- Is a year of life at age 25 to be differently evaluated than a year of life at age 65?

- Is your year of life worth more than mine because you earn more money than I do? and

- Is saving one year of life apiece for two people worth the same as saving two years of life for one person?

381

We might also become fascinated with problems of definition. Assuming the definition of life as starting at conception, then an abortion would be a death at age zero to nine months. This would wreak havoc with our benefit measure. On the other hand, if we suppose abortions and our population produce lots of children with long life expectancy, then we may show a striking rise in life expectancy if we fail to consider some adjustment for age mix in our population.

Next, one might have to estimate what are the causes of death and the magnitude of the years of life lost thereby. Here we are interested in two aspects: we gain more by saving young lives than by saving old lives, and there are some illnesses that are more devastating than others. Table 1 gives some indication of where to commit our resources: there is a greater payoff in saving young lives. Table 2 indicates the potential effect on life expectancy by the elimination of various diseases.

Next, we must consider the interventions that we can use to prolong life, and what they cost. These figures are exceedingly difficult to come by; only a few such numbers are available for our consideration. The reason why measuring benefit is such a problem is that in the traditional system there was no need to. All that had to be shown was that, for *this* type of patient, treatment A is better than treatment B.

When we know the cost effectiveness of our interventions, we can rank order them, start at the top of the list and run down it until we exhaust our budget. This is shown in Figure 1, where we could apply interventions A, B, C, D, and some of E until we exhaust our budget. We would not undertake intervention F.

But this too is an oversimplification. A treatment that is stunningly successful for severely ill patients is likely to be applied with less benefit to less ill patients having the same disease. For example, hypertension is a continuous variable from normal to very high blood pressure. The very-high-blood-pressure patient benefits very much by treatment; the moderately-high-blood-pressure patient benefits less, and so on. When does intervention stop? This problem may well have a more massive impact on the costs of health care than any other. The reason for this is that, traditionally, doctors feel obliged to do something for each patient. If an intervention worked very well on one patient, try it on another. Perhaps the great successes are remembered and the rest forgotten.

To get to specifics, let us imagine that one of our most cost-effective interventions, A in Figure 1, is for starvation. The short-run remedy is food, and the long-run remedy is a job. Will starving people appear at our emergency department or at our doctors' offices, or will we have to go find them? How do we find them?

Table 1 Mortality, Ten Leading Causes of Death, Age Group and Sex, 1971

	All Ages		Age 1-14		Age 15-34		Age 35-54		Age 55-74		75+	
	Male	Female	Male	Female	Male	Female	Male	Female	Male	Female	Male	Female
	Heart Diseases 419,585	Heart Diseases 323,553	Accidents 8,075	Accidents 4,314	Accidents 29,805	Accidents 7,794	Heart Diseases 52,722	Cancer 29,340	Heart Diseases 203,611	Heart Diseases 108,785	Heart Diseases 160,019	Heart Diseases 196,158
	Cancer 183,877	Cancer 153,521	Cancer 1,914	Cancer 1,305	Homicide 7,717	Cancer 3,316	Cancer 26,201	Heart Diseases 16,653	Cancer 101,500	Heart Diseases 74,230	Cancer 50,198	Stroke 75,635
	Stroke 94,239	Stroke 114,853	Congenital Malformations 1,182	Congenital Malformations 1,046	Suicide 5,027	Suicide 1,987	Accidents 16,638	Stroke 6,385	Stroke 36,253	Stroke 31,624	Stroke 50,077	Cancer 45,141
	Accidents 78,195	Accidents 35,244	Pneumonia, Influenza 787	Pneumonia, Influenza 733	Cancer 3,964	Heart Diseases 1,334	Cirrhosis of Liver 8,586	Accidents 5,764	Accidents 14,614	Diabetes 10,317	Pneumonia, Influenza 14,178	Arteriosclerosis 15,588
	Pneumonia Influenza 31,590	Pneumonia Influenza 25,604	Homicide 381	Homicide 302	Heart Diseases 2,523	Stroke 923	Stroke 6,693	Cirrhosis of Liver 4,866	Emphysema 10,972	Accidents 7,387	Arteriosclerosis 9,992	Pneumonia Influenza 14,686
	Diseases of Infancy 22,576	Diabetes 22,634	Heart Diseases 311	Heart Diseases 300	Pneumonia, Influenza 958	Pneumonia, Influenza 712	Suicide 5,512	Suicide 3,056	Cirrhosis of Liver 9,958	Pneumonia, Influenza 5,367	Accidents 7,667	Diabetes 9,863
	Cirrhosis of Liver 20,680	Arterio-sclerosis 18,187	Stroke 215	Stroke 196	Stroke 898	Complications of Pregnancy 512	Homicide 4,810	Diabetes 2,003	Pneumonia, Influenza 9,620	Cirrhosis of Liver 4,808	Emphysema 6,260	Accidents 9,028
	Emphysema 18,502	Diseases of Infancy 15,918	Meningitis 171	Cystic Fibrosis 156	Cirrhosis of Liver 767	Cirrhosis of Liver 491	Pneumonia, Influenza 2,910	Pneumonia, Influenza 1,822	Diabetes 7,663	Arterio-sclerosis 2,473	Diabetes 5,370	Infection of 2,214
	Suicide 16,860	Cirrhosis of Liver 11,128	Cerebral Palsy 162	Cerebral Palsy 134	Congenital Malformations 640	Congenital Malformations 449	Diabetes 2,088	Homicide 1,214	Suicide 4,874	Emphysema 2,179	Hypertension 1,849	Hypertension 2,086
	Diabetes 15,622	Congenital Malformations 7,423	Benign Neoplasms 130 Bronchitis 130	Meningitis 133	Diabetes 445	Diabetes 374	Emphysema 1,210	Nephritis 705	Arterio-sclerosis 3,116	Suicide 1,843	Infection of Kidney 1,807	Hernia & Intestinal Obstr. 2,007

Source: Vital Statistics of the United States, 1971.

Table 2 Years of Life Expectancy at Age Zero Per Person Added by the Elimination of the Disease: Men and Women 1964—USA

Disease	Years of Life Added	
	Men	**Women**
Tuberculosis	.080	.040
Other Infectious Parasitic Diseases	.121	.111
Cancer	2.265	2.358
Cardiovascular	13.299	1.068
Influenza, Pneumonia, Bronchitis	.570	.518
Diarrheal	.079	.090
Degenerative	.627	.637
Maternal	.000	.048
Disease of Infancy	1.143	.930
Motor Vehicle	.874	.366
Other Violence	1.329	.625

The effect of simultaneously eliminating two causes of death cannot be inferred from the effect of eliminating each individually. Samuel H. Preston, *et al. Causes of Death.* New York: Seminar Press, 1972, pp. 769, 771. Reprinted with permission.

Dr. Jack Gieger, who started the Mound Bayou Health Center in Mississippi, found them, as *Fortune* magazine reported in its January 1970 issue:

> Dr. Geiger wrote prescriptions for food to deal with widespread hunger and nutritional deficiencies. Since the Center was established, he estimates infant mortality in the target area has been reduced by almost two-thirds, but Dr. Geiger gives most of the credit to environmental improvements. "If I could do just one thing to improve the health of the people," he says, "I would double their per capita income." [1]

In lectures he gleefully tells of the Washington bureaucrats who descended on his clinic protesting that he could not prescribe food. He replied that the diagnosis was hunger—what else could the remedy be?

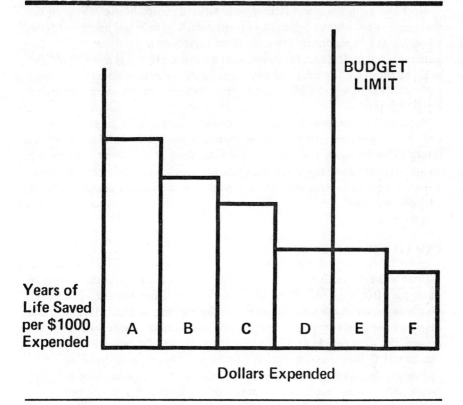

Figure 1 Resource Allocation: Years of Life Saved Per $1000 Expended, Dollars Expended, Budget Limit, and Interventions A—F

In similar but more ambitious fashion, the Grenfell Mission in northern Newfoundland and Labrador found a population with serious malnutrition at the turn of the century. So, in addition to their hospitals and doctors, they started dairy farms, handicraft industries, and shipyards to provide jobs. They broke the high prices of monopolistic store owners by setting up cooperative grocery stores, which, when financially stable, were spun off into separate independent corporations.

THE $20,000 DEATH

One of the least cost effective interventions, I am told, is the treatment of long-term alcoholics with bleeding esophageal varices. This may require innumerable transfusions and two operations on the esophagus, plus a porta caval shunt. This allows the patient to die of kidney failure rather than by bleeding from the esophagus. At worst, it means a socially acceptable form of death. At best, it allows the alcoholic to return to the bottle for a few more months before death. The cost per case may approach $20,000, and the cost per year of life saved may approach a million dollars.

Here the problem is a different one. Once a junior house officer in the emergency department decides to accept such a patient, he precipitates the whole $20,000 expenditure. Ethically, local doctors do not feel they can let such patients bleed to death on the street; after admission they feel morally obliged to do all they can. If we are to pursue our goals, we must discreetly hide such patients where they can bleed to death at low cost and without creating a public scandal.

Perhaps the outrageousness of our organizational goal begins to be apparent. The traditional health system manager need lose no sleep over the thought that someone may die of hunger—as long as he doesn't drag himself to his hospital's doorstep. But turning the old drunk away from the emergency department door is more than we can, with clear conscience, deal with. Traditionally, we cope with those who appear and ignore those who don't. That will have to stop.

QUALITY OF LIFE

If there was ever a subjective, personally defined variable, it is the quality of one's life. But we can not let everyone define it for himself. Otherwise, everyone would have a vested interest in exaggerating his present anguish and his desperate need to receive our ministrations—the same way, as Titmus has pointed out, that people who wish to sell their blood have every reason to hide the fact that they have hepatitis. [2] Our only choice is to have objective standards that can be dispassionately applied to everyone. One way out would be to implant electrodes in everybody's skull to measure current levels of happiness. In informal conversation with a neurologist or two, I was told that this may be feasible, but it is not being done in part because of the public uproar that would occur as a result of tampering with our God-given brains. Since this is not available to us, we must rely on a clearly suboptimal alternative scale such as this one. The idea is based on the payment schedule posted on a machine at an airport. For 25 cents it sells you flight insurance.

Value of 1 Year of Life Saved	1.0
Year of Life Missing One Leg	.8
Year of Life Missing One Arm	.7
Year of Life Missing Arm and a Leg	.4
Year of Life Missing Both Arms	.2

This list could be expanded indefinitely, and some interesting decision-analytic tools can be used to scale these numbers. However, they all depend on whom you ask and how they feel.

One way to finesse the problem of life-quality evaluation is to provide health services in a purely competitive market where all people have an equal amount of money, no insurance coverage, and perfect public information. There must be multiple sellers and the elimination of all licensure and of nearly all government regulation. This is the approach that Milton Friedman would argue for.[3] However, there is one feature that makes health services a unique commodity—the placebo effect, which implies that the more ignorant you are about your treatment the more you will benefit by it. In no other market is this true. If you want the most out of health care, you must remain uninformed and, therefore, the free market is inappropriate.

Another fascinating intellectual exercise is to design a health service delivery system for the United States today that maximizes the placebo effect. It would probably include doctors who had very high status—high income, upper class, gray hair, high education, male and WASP. Doctors would wear distinctive uniforms, be surrounded by lots of impressive technology, use an arcane scientific language, and have large numbers of ancillary personnel to do their bidding, all in a large institution where scientific breakthroughs are occurring daily. In short, it would look just about as health services are today. If one accepts the estimate that prior to 1890 the major benefit of health services was the placebo effect, then this is not a surprising conclusion.

SUM OF THE BENEFITS

For our mission, however, the point of considering the placebo effect is that it makes the competitive market a nonoptional solution, and therefore we must consider a system with an objective, universally applicable benefit scale with which to measure performance.

Under the old system, there was no need for health benefits to "add up." Consider the following patients.

In the old system, health care did not have to produce more total health for the population served. The elderly herniorrhaphy patient could probabilistically shorten his life but improve the quality of it by not having to wear a truss. That patient, if he so chose, would be happy to have a shorter but more comfortable life. The kidney-dialysis patient will prolong his life but the quality of his life will be miserable. However, he too may be happy with the exchange. But what does it all add up to in "objective" terms? Nothing. Because we use our "objective," uniform quality index to measure benefits and their relative values, there may be no *total* increase in life expectancy and

	Length of Life	Quality of Life
Hernia repair in a 65-year old man	—	+
Kidney Dialysis	+	—
Sum Benefit	0	0

no *total* increase in quality of life, but a lot of money spent. Although this could happen in the old system, under your new goals neither should get care because it is the sum of the benefits that you will be concerned with.

Just as we have listed interventions that *prolong* life in a cost-effective manner, we must do the same for interventions affecting the *quality* of life. Imagine sending this problem off to your staff analysts and the report comes back that the most cost-effective way to obtain quality of life is to keep everyone over the age of 50 high by smoking opium. Although working out the health system implications of this is fascinating, it is important to be realistic, and so answering that question will be left for another time. However, it does give us a hint of the cultural constraints that limit what types of quality of life we are allowed to obtain. For example, we are still heirs to the puritanical idea that a lifetime of hard work is essential to the achievement of happiness.

ORGANIZATIONAL DESIGN

Now that we have considered some of the issues related to the achievement of our goal, let's turn to the organizational implications.

First, management must now become heavily involved in clinical decision making so that treatments are directed to patients who will benefit most. For example, thyrotoxicosis can be treated medically, surgically, or with radiation therapy, and the treatment may well depend on which specialist the patient sees. There are short- and long-run cost differences, different risks, probabilities of benefit, and substantial debate as to which is better. This would seem a clear place where central management would have to step in, choose the cost-effective alternative, develop a set of decision rules, and require adherence to them. At first glance, medical treatment seems cheaper. However, in the traditional system, this rule could not be readily imposed because clinical decisions are rarely, if ever, based on costs, professional autonomy allows reliance on decisions made on the basis of clinical experience, and there would be the retort that we know so little about this disease that we must await further research before coming to a decision.

All this would have to change. Even though benefits are often very difficult to measure, costs are often much easier to measure. If this is true, the decision rule would be to use the cheapest intervention. Therefore, management would be directly involved in a large number of clinical decisions.

Consequently, not only must management be knowledgeable about the production process, it must centralize control particularly in such areas where several different treatments are possible. This suggests that, in the short run, managers must be physicians. In the long run, it implies a new form of education based heavily on clinical decision making, but not on the laying on of hands. This education will be heavy on cost benefit analysis, decision trees, Bayesian statistics, epidemiology, and economics.[4] For example, the manager must be an expert in deciding *when* to perform coronary bypass surgery, not *how* to perform it. This implies a triage with a front-line generalist and a limited decision-making role for specialists who may function by referral only.

Second, the major differences in health care costs are not explained by how efficiently the hospital runs its kitchen or laundry but on what doctors decide to do for their patients. Take hypertension, for example. If a patient has high blood pressure and sees some rural general practitioner in Florida, the GP will measure the blood pressure and if it is high will start medication—a diagnostic workup that may cost 10 or 15 dollars. If the same patient appears before Dr. Laragh in New York, he is likely to spend 10 days in a teaching hospital with a diagnostic workup costing, at 1973 prices, over $1,800. It is not clear which patient will benefit most, particularly since only 25 percent of patients with high blood pressure take their medication regularly enough to control their problem. It is a sign of the times that Dr. Laragh gets his picture on the cover of *Time* magazine, while the rural doctor is often referred to in a derogatory way as an LMD.

Another example is surgery for hernias. Presently, the average length of stay in the U.S. for hernia patients is about seven days, for a total cost of about $1,500. There are several randomized trials showing that up to 95 percent of hernia operations can be carried out on an outpatient basis. Dr. Velez-Gil undertook to do outpatient hernia operations in Cali, Colombia, at $757 per case.[5] Using simplified equipment and performing two operations simultaneously he could reduce the cost to $188. John Bunker pointed out that, in England, half as many hernia operations are performed per capita as in the United States. Thus, we might cut the per capita cost of hernia repair by as much as 15-fold! Of course, these are rough figures, but they give some idea of the magnitude of potential savings.

Third, hospital control and hierarchy are usually function-based. Cost and responsibility centers include nursing, dietary, laboratories, and such. This would have to shift to a product organization, perhaps following the catego-

ries shown in Table 1. In part, our functional efficiency and product ineffi-
ciency are a result of the control system within hospitals and for health care in
general.

For example, one division would probably be suicide and murder control.
This would be a cost center in the budget and hierarchy. Its performance
would be measured by age-adjusted suicide and homicide within the
population.

This cost center would receive a fixed budget that would pay for prevention
and treatment. If a hospital emergency ward received a suicide attempter, it
would have to clear with the suicide division in order to receive a transfer
payment. If this patient were too far gone, the head of the suicide division
would refuse to pay, and the patient would not be treated. The division
director then would have to allocate his budget between treatment and
prevention (nets under the Golden Gate Bridge, hot lines, lobbying for
gun-control laws, etc.). He might be paid on a bonus plan, depending on the
degree that suicide mortality is reduced in the population.

SHIFTING THE POWER BASE

Another alternative organizational design would have all people sign up with
neighborhood health centers to receive their primary care. The medical
director of such a health center would have a budget to pay for all their health
care and would purchase hospital services as needed. This medical director
would have to make decisions on who gets treated and who does not, perhaps
using the protocols developed by the disease divisions described above. Such
a medical director would be the key to the whole system and perhaps would
have the highest paid position. This would radically shift the power base away
from the large urban teaching hospitals, which would now have to respond,
perhaps in a competitive market, to those powerful, knowledgeable, wholesale purchasers of hospital services.

Clearly the information system for this organization would be entirely
different, being based on the careful collection of data on population health
levels matched to responsibility centers, which would either be the neighborhood health centers, the disease divisions, or both.

Since one might expect an immediate reduction in hospital admissions by
at least 40 percent, perhaps the first thing this new organization would do
would be to sell off all its hospitals, expecting that their value would plummet,
and that competition would be so fierce for admissions that wholesale purchase would be at rock-bottom prices.

One can even forecast some of the managerial problems associated with
this form of organization, including the elaborate use of transfer payments,
defining who is a suicide victim, and cost allocation for patients with more
than one illness.

POLITICO-RELIGIOUS MEDICINE

If one speculates further on the directions this organization might take, there are two possibilities that seem most likely. It would either evolve into a political action organization, focusing on marketing political changes, such as reducing the speed and quantity of driving and promotion of air bags, fluoridation, gun control, and tobacco and alcohol limitations. Or it would become a new religion. Since the days of the decadent Roman Empire, there has never been a more fertile time for a new religion than in today's disorganized, pessimistic, cynical, hedonistic, and anomic society. The task is to create the religion that will maximize quantity and quality of life. It should draw on the aspect of Judaism that leads to low rates of alcoholism, of Catholicism that leads to low suicide rates, of the Transcendental Meditation movement that can reduce blood pressure, of Swedish culture with its concern for physical fitness and exercise, and so on. In any case, perhaps over half the budget would be spent toward behavior modification. Given the exhaustion of natural resources, starting with oil, this is clearly the beginning of massive social changes that would provide fertile ground for a new religion. We must go back to reading Max Weber on charismatic leadership as education for the new health care manager.[6]

Of course, this is an organizational paradox. To design such a religion would take a substantial amount of research and careful thought. This would require a bureaucratic authority pattern. But to expound it would require a charismatic authority pattern. Although Weber discusses the bureaucratization of charisma, he does not consider the reverse process. It may be impossible.

The empirical demonstration that traditional health services are not very successful in achieving this goal is to consider Christian Science, which, as is well known, considers doctors and hospitals unnecessary for good health. The test is this: find the nearest senior executive of an insurance company that writes life and health insurance. Preferably, it should be a for-profit company in this highly competitive industry. Ask him, in confidence, Does his company sell life insurance to Christian Scientists, and, if so, at higher rates because they die young? Does it sell health insurance to Christian Scientists, and at what rates? You will most likely find that the company is delighted to do both, and at no penalty. Christian Scientists tend to lead long, sober, virtuous, middle-class lives; and their health expenditures on Christian Science readers and nursing homes are comparatively low.

MORE FORMULAE FINAGLING

Perhaps by now we can conclude that an organization whose goal is to maximize quantity and quality of life for a defined population and with a budget constraint, is unethical, outrageous, socially reprehensible, and has never and will never materialize. If this is true, it can also be concluded that the social goal of a long, nice life is not what we want.

With relief, we can go back to our present health nonsystem, whose goals are to hustle money wherever it can be found by finagling the reimbursement formulae; where the senior doctors do as they please, and the house staff can run amok with empty order pages in the medical charts; where the goal is to do something for any patient who asks for it, and to ignore those who don't ask. The nonsystem thrives where most managers are entirely ignorant about production decisions, the placebo effect is maximized, and resource allocation is defined by organizational power politics. The measurement of benefits doesn't matter; costs have to be justified, rather than contained. Today's health care managers have invested years in learning to play these games. It is the system we all know and love and is, therefore, the best of all possible worlds.

What could be more obvious?

REFERENCES

1. FORTUNE Magazine. © 1970 Time, Inc. All rights reserved.

2. Titmus, Richard. *The Gift Relationship: From Human Blood to Social Policy.* New York: Pantheon Publications, 1971.

3. Friedman, Milton. *Capitalism and Freedom.* Chicago: University of Chicago Press, 1971.

4. (a) Raiffa, Howard. *Decision Analysis.* Reading, Massachusetts: Addison-Wesley, 1970. (b) Schelling, Thomas. "The Life You Save May Be Your Own." In *Problems in Public Expenditure Analysis,* edited by S.B. Chase, Washington, D.C.: Brookings Institution, 1968, pp. 127-167. (c) Bunker, John; Barnes, Benjamin; and Mosteller, Frederick. *Costs, Benefits and Risks of Surgery.* New York: Oxford University Press, 1977. (d) Babson, John H. *Disease Costing.* Manchester, England: University Press, 1973. (e) *New England Journal of Medicine.* July 31, 1975. Special Issue devoted to decision analysis in medicine.

5. Velez-Gil, Adolfo, *et al.* "A Simplified System for Surgical Operations: The Economics of Treating Hernia." *Surgery* 77 (March 1975): 391-394.

6. Weber, Max. *The Theory of Social and Economic Organization.* Glencoe, Ill.: The Free Press of Glencoe, 1964.

Index

ABOUT THE EDITORS

William A. Flexner, Dr.P.H., is President of Flexner & Associates, a management consulting firm providing marketing and strategic planning services to the health care industry. Prior to forming his own consulting firm, he was an assistant professor in the Center for Health Services Research, School of Public Health, University of Minnesota. Flexner is a frequent contributor of articles to *Health Care Management Review* and other health care journals and serves on the editorial review boards of the *Health Care Planning and Marketing Quarterly* and the *Journal of Health Care Marketing.*

Eric N. Berkowitz, Ph.D., is an assistant professor of marketing in the College of Business Administration and a research associate in the Center for Health Services Research, School of Public Health, at the University of Minnesota. He is a regular faculty presenter at programs sponsored by the American Hospital Association and the American Academy of Medical Directors. He has published numerous articles in both health and business journals and is a member of the editorial review boards of the *Health Care Planning and Marketing Quarterly* and the *Journal of Health Care Marketing.*

Montague Brown, D.P.H., is a consultant in corporate strategy and editor of the *Health Care Management Review.* Dr. Brown is a former professor of health administration at Duke University and associate professor and director of graduate studies in health administration at the Graduate School of Management, Northwestern University. Brown's work on corporate strategy and multihospital systems has appeared in many professional journals. He is author and editor of several books, including *Multihospital Systems: Strategies for Organization and Management,* coedited with Barbara P. McCool, Ph.D., and published in 1979 by Aspen Systems Corporation. Brown is currently completing his law degree at the University of North Carolina and extending his work on strategy to look at the impact of regulation, including antitrust laws, on organizations and emerging issues, leading to more fundamental reorganization strategies for hospitals and other elements of the health care system.

DATE DUE